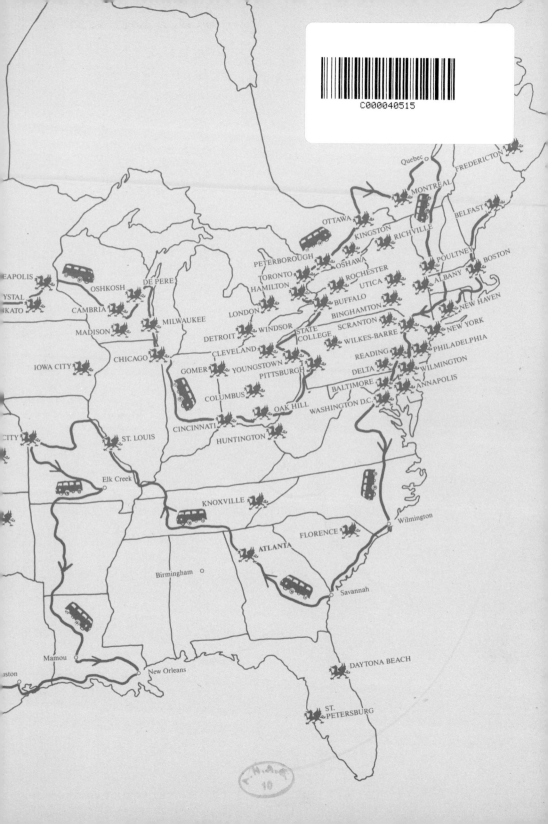

WELSH FEVER

WELSH FEVER

Welsh Activities
in the United States and Canada Today

DAVID GREENSLADE

1986
D. BROWN AND SONS
COWBRIDGE, WALES

DESIGNED AND PRINTED IN WALES BY
D. Brown and Sons Ltd., Cowbridge and Bridgend, Glamorgan

Contents

List of Illustrations

Letterheads
Letterheads
Celtic contacts

Gwynn Parri, Wisconsin,
  founder of Welsh Associated Youth of America and Canada
Richard Loomis, translator of *Dafydd Ap Gwilym: The Poems*
Ellis Jones, Founder of the Gustavus Adolphus Cymanfa Ganu, Minnesota
Cerwyn Davies, minister of Dewi Sant Welsh United Church, Toronto
Robert A. Fowkes, New York City
Islyn Thomas OBE, author of *Our Welsh Heritage*

Edythe Peterson, Lake Crystal, Minnesota
Jane Hughes (Siani Flewog), St. Catharines, Ontario
Mildred Bangert, Oak Hill, Ohio
Donna Davies, San Francisco

Hamilton Orpheus Male Choir, Ontario
St. David's Welsh Male Chorus, Edmonton, Alberta
Côr Gwalia Ohio, Cincinnati

Vancouver Welsh Men's Choir, British Columbia
Côr Dewi Sant, Utica, New York

Amy Lynn Jones and Karen Pugh singing at the Wilkes-Barre National Cymanfa,
  1983
Cynonfardd Children's Eisteddfod, Edwardsville, Pennsylvania, 1984
Children's Dance, Cwrs Cymraeg y Cymoedd, Wilkes-Barre, 1984
Elinor Hughes performing at Awr y Plant, Peterborough, Ontario, 1984

Between pages 208 and 209

Côr Meibion De Cymru at Niagara Falls, November 1983

Dic Jones, Welsh language teacher in Seattle, Washington
Old Man's Creek Welsh Church, Iowa
Hywel Thomas, organizer of the Côr Meibion De Cymru tour, 1983
Evan Gwyndaf Roberts, Organist, Utica, New York

WELSH EVENTS IN THE WYOMING VALLEY, PENNSYLVANIA
Welsh Exhibit, Osterhouse Free Library, February 1982
Flag raising at Luzerne County Courthouse, March 1, 1983
Members of the St. David's Society of Wyoming Valley Inc., November 1984
120th Anniversary, First Welsh Presbyterian Church, Wilkes-Barre, October 1985

Ladies from St. David's Welsh Society, Edmonton, Alberta
The Vancouver Cambrian Circle Singers in Cardiff, July 1983

1983 National Cymanfa Ganu Planning Committee, Wilkes-Barre, Pennsylvania
1981 National Cymanfa Ganu Planning Committee, Utica, New York

List of Illustrations

Helen F. Richards, Chicago, Illinois
Anne and David Habermehl, Marion, New York
Earl T. Williams Jr., Connecticut

Joan Phelps, Binghamton, New York
Daisy Heaton, Toronto, Ontario
Margot McKinney Bouchard, Poultney, Vermont

Suzanne and David Greenslade promoting St. David's Day in Atlanta, Georgia,
February 1984

I fy nhad a mam yng nghyfraith

SAM a BARBARA HIRSCH

.

Rhaid cychwyn yma wrth ein traed,
A hon yw'r awr, yr ore' gaed.

———

The starting point is at our feet
This is the hour, the best yet.

Myrddin ap Dafydd
©Sain

Author's Preface

Some people mentioned in this grass-roots description of Welsh activities in North America may not now be the actual officers of their group. Invariably, however, they will have been deeply involved in regional and often national Welsh American and Welsh Canadian programs. I apologize if any project or individual that should have been included has been overlooked. I have listed a diversity of Welsh meeting places and Welsh events throughout Canada and the United States and I have included as many alternative contacts as possible. I have made every effort to make titles, addresses and dates accurate, but I particularly apologize for any mis-spelling of personal names.

Many readers will be more familiar than me with their own Welsh society and would almost certainly describe its activities and their own contribution quite differently. Wherever possible, however, portions of the book were read by leaders of the local organization and revised according to their recommendations. Acknowledgement of this invaluable help can be found at the back of the book. I also thank those who very kindly sent me photographs and other material. This material has since been given to the National Library of Wales.

In response to enquiries we've had about the fate of our dog Amiga—I should say that, before moving to Wales in November 1985, feeling that British quarantine regulations would be too much for a dog of Amiga's age, we left her with Suzanne's parents in Atlanta, where she is enjoying a comfortable retirement.

It gives me great pleasure to thank the following people, without whose help completing this book would have been impossible. My principal thanks go to Dr. Robert A. Fowkes for his contribution of a Foreword and for reading every page of my original typescript. I am deeply indebted to Mrs. Patricia Powell Viets for early editorial advice and for access to *Y Drych*'s incomparable collection of photographs. I must also thank Dr. Arturo Roberts for a complete collection of *Ninnau*. I am extremely grateful to the St. David's Society of the State of New York for two very generous grants which enabled me to duplicate photographs and to have the manuscript professionally typed. Finally, I should like to thank my friends in the St. David's Welsh Society of Georgia for their moral support during the entire work.

David Greenslade
June 1986

Foreword

I am happy to write this foreword to David Greenslade's book and am flattered that he invited me, a man four decades his senior, to perform the pleasant task. He may by now regret the invitation. Our backgrounds differ somewhat, but our involvement in *Pethau Cymreig*, Welsh matters, are strikingly similar. He was born and raised in Wales in a town where the Welsh Language was not habitually spoken, but where Welsh hearts still beat in Welsh breasts. My closest connection with a Welsh-speaking forebear was with Annie Davies (pronounced Davis), my grandmother (*mamgu*). She was a native of Swansea—*Abertawe* to her, of course. Her Welsh was superior to her English and she encouraged her ten children, *pum mab a phum merch*, to use Welsh *ar yr aelwyd* "on the hearth," as she cozily put it.

In the course of time, my interest in the language has brought me into association with many individuals and organizations in many parts of the country, and in other countries who share that interest. I have also heard from people who are indifferent to the language itself but are vitally concerned with Welsh history, genealogy, art, music, politics, sports, industry, agriculture, theology, education, cooking, even smuggling and piracy. To them I say *pob bendith*, but they are overlooking the main element, the language. Some time ago, a young woman of Welsh descent attended a meeting of our St. David's Society of the State of New York, with the intent to join. When she found out that the Society had a Welsh Studies Committee, she was astonished to learn (from me) that our chief concern was with the study of the Welsh language. I pretended to be shocked that Welsh studies could mean anything else.

Individuals vary greatly in the nature and direction of their attachment to ancestral ties. From time to time we encounter Welsh Americans of the third generation who speak the language amazingly well. That bespeaks lasting parental devotion and strong family unity throughout the years. It is not a frequent phenomenon and the usual story is the loss of the Welsh language after one generation, as is characteristic of most languages and cultures transplanted to America. (Patagonia is the shining example of a notable exception). For the Welsh, that demise could easily occur almost immediately, since, in most instances, they arrived with a knowledge of English to begin with, and the temptation to slip into the use of the English exclusively was therefore doubly great. For a while I was skeptical about the existence of "third generation Welsh speakers" and had a sneaking suspicion that their numbers might approximate those of Welsh Indians. And then I met some (Welsh

Americans, not Indians) at the National Gymanfa and the Cwrs Cymraeg and elsewhere. They not only retained the ancient language with vigor and naturalness, but also exhibited regional characteristics—the folks from Sir Fôn and the rest of the North pronouncing their magnificent vowels, those from the South retaining their special intonation. All this without any particular awareness on their part (without their necessarily ever having been to Wales!), for the kind of Welsh spoken by their grandparents had been transmitted to them by their parents, with no great loss of quality in the process. Sadly, but inevitably, it does not look as if that process will continue with their children, although some of the latter have participated in Welsh courses and have joined the recent wave of enthusiasm for Welshness—a wave, hardly an ocean.

What is vividly brought home to the reader of the present volume is the significance of *Cymru ar Wasgar*, which has a special connotation for the United States and Canada. We are often separated by thousands of miles from one another and we may not even know in what communities Welsh Americans live. We may know little or nothing of many organizations, clubs, societies, classes. Sometimes we are not that far away and still suffer from the same lack of awareness.

The kind of trip taken by Suzanne and David Greenslade seems unmatched even by the famous journey of John Evans, 1795-1797, although the latter spent more time in his quest for Welsh Indians, which he never found, than the Greenslades did in visiting Welsh and other communities. He also had no van.

There was no insistence on visiting only communities in which there were Welsh connections or inhabitants of Welsh descent, for the Greenslades encountered the Sioux, Cajuns, Basques, Japanese, and all manner of interesting groups and spent time with them. The narration of their experiences among these people is fully as fascinating as their accounts of Welsh Americans, although the main emphasis is on the latter, as the title and subtitle plainly imply. The view the book provides of other ethnic groups casts a relevant light on Welsh American experiences too.

We need this book, for it not only illumines vast areas of our ignorance but corrects peculiar notions which often pass for knowledge. While the book has no didactic purpose and no special axe to grind, it does at times spread a brilliant light of realism and permits us to see both the achievements and the shortcomings of our various organizations. We can also read between the lines and observe how certain dedicated individuals, often few in number, are the secret of success of Welsh American activities; and the same invisible ink tells a story of apathy, indifference, or pretense elsewhere. For even Welsh Americans are human and God did not endow them with a monotonous monopoly of all virtue. The history of the Welsh everywhere, when definitively told without distortion, will doubtless reveal a reasonable proportion of saints and sinners, of wise men and fools, of idealists and opportunists. We like to think that in all of those pairings, the positive outweighs the negative.

And even the sinners have probably been interestingly individualistic in their misdeeds. Do not, however, expect lurid accounts of them in this volume, it is not that kind of a book.

Rather, be prepared to learn of pockets of concentration of unusual talent in out-of-the-way places (and in more accessible places too), of learned Welshmen and Welshwomen imparting their knowledge and wisdom to others, of hard-working, honest folk, decently proud of their heritage.

There is considerable misunderstanding of Welsh Americans by our kinfolk in Wales. Not only do they have weird notions of what America is all about, but they also fail to understand that Welsh Americans can be Americans first and sons and daughters of Wales second. This has to be true of most people who were born here, although a few of them have felt the urge to go to Wales and have done so.

Our organizations are American and Welsh-American. It is not always easy to hold fast to the traditions of our Welsh, or any other, ancestry. Some take such matters very lightly. Others condemn the notion of what they call "hyphenated Americans," as if treason was involved. That should cause no loss of sleep. If we know about our background, we have an identity which cannot, and should not, be dismissed. Some Welsh Americans find the term "ethnic" repulsive, as if reluctant to let themselves be grouped with "blooming foreigners." Yet we are actually all the richer, I would say, for our co-existence with the many other colorful ethnic elements in our American population, and we probably even enrich them in our mutual contact. We do more than that. We marry them. A glance at some of the names in this book will reveal that effective leaders in Welsh American activities often have mates of quite different national origin.

Nothing in this foreword is the responsibility of the author of the book. He has rashly given me free rein to indulge my own notions. Even my severest strictures, however, stem from profound respect for the Welsh tradition and from an undying love for the "old language", as well as the country itself. On my all too infrequent trips to Wales I have always met with kindness, friendship and helpfulness. You instinctively sense from the vibrations that you are on the right wave length. This book nourishes the soundest instincts by affording new insight into the vast ramifications of Welsh-American affairs as well as into Welshness itself.

Robert A. Fowkes

Glossary

ceilidh—Scottish noson lawen

côr—choir

côr meibion—male choir

cwrs—course

cwrs Cymraeg—Welsh language course

cylch—circle, group

cymanfa ganu—(pl. cymanfaoedd canu) hymn singing festival

cymdeithas—society

Cymdeithas Yr Iaith Gymraeg—Welsh Language Society

cymmrodorion—fellowship

Cymraeg—Welsh language

Cymreig—pertaining to Wales

Cymru—Wales

Cymry—Welsh people

dosbarth—class

eisteddfod—(pl. eisteddfodau) cultural festival

fest noz—Breton noson lawen

gobaith—hope

Hen Wlad Fy Nhadau—Land Of My Fathers (the Welsh national anthem)

Ninnau—'We Welsh'

noson lawen—(pl. nosweithiau llawen) an informal evening of song, recitation and other entertainment

pethau—things

te bach—light refreshments, usually tea and Welsh cakes

Y Ddraig Goch—The Red Dragon

Y Drych—The Mirror

Yr Enfys—The Rainbow

I

Setting Out. The Cape Fear Welsh Society

There never was a turnback point. We had a policy that held the trip together. We were living, not traveling. This trip was not temporary. We expected it to last fifteen months and a purposeless vacation could never hold our interest that long.

We knew we were going to take this trip before we moved from Wales to the United States. As soon as we arrived in Atlanta we bought a Volkswagen Vanagon, and in Wilmington, North Carolina, while living at the beach we spent one year fitting it out. When we were finished, the van was as well-equipped and comfortable as a small yacht or Japanese apartment. We had a kitchen, office, books, games, camera, hardware and clothes for every season on the road. We also took our dog, Amiga, Suzanne's companion since her college days in New Orleans. Amiga was small, brave and smart, and her canine sense of proportion became a barometer of our own. If she became restless or uncomfortable, invariably we felt the same. As if to justify our confidence in her, a week before we left, Amiga took third prize for "best trick" at the Atlanta Humane Society Mutt Show.

Suzanne and I met in Tokyo in 1978. Where else would an American girl meet her Welsh husband? Suzanne was studying Japanese art and language and I was living in a Zen Buddhist Temple. We were both deeply immersed in traditional Japanese culture, speaking Japanese over 90% of the time. Temple life, despite or because of its rigours, was deeply invigorating and when I transferred to a rural temple in north Japan, Suzanne moved into the Tokyo branch. We lived in the temple following its ascetic 4 a.m. to 9 p.m. schedule for two years, until we were married and returned to Wales.

The winter of 1980-1981, we spent in Wales where it rained every single day, excellent weather for incubating travel plans.

While we were in Wales, we tried to find out about Welsh people in North America. We knew that ministers went over, we'd even heard of an American Cymanfa Ganu. If we were going to tour we wanted to know more. In February, 1981, we heard the name of John Albert Evans as someone who traveled to the United States often and even taught Welsh language classes to Americans.

A graduate of Bangor Normal College and of the University of Wales at Aberystwyth, John Albert Evans is Welsh Language Adviser to Mid Glamorgan Education Authority, the largest educational board in Wales. He is also a Vice-Chairman of the Nant Gwrtheyrn Trust and Chairman of the Cardiff

Welsh Fever

Chapter of The Urdd. We spent thirty minutes with him at Duffryn House
near Cardiff.

Could he give us a lead how to contact the Welsh in North America?

John Albert told us about Cymdeithas Madog, The Welsh Studies Institute. Cymdeithas Madog, founded by Anne Cowie, holds an annual Welsh
course in various cities of Canada and the United States. John Albert has
flown out every year since 1977 to teach Cymdeithas Madog's Cwrs Cymraeg
(Welsh course). However we did not discuss *Ninnau* or *Y Drych* the North
American Welsh newspapers which we later discovered for ourselves.

Jane Pryddarch, whom we met in North Carolina, was a little more helpful
in this respect. It was she who first showed us how active and dynamic Welsh
Americans could be.

On March 1st, 1982, on the front page of the *Wilmington Morning Star*, was
a column heading, WELSH PRIDE—BEACH RESIDENT RUNS ONE
WOMAN ETHNIC CRUSADE. Curiously, we read about Jayne Pryddarch
and her search for Welsh people in the area. After some detective work, we
found Jayne and her husband, Harold living aboard a sailboat at a marina less
than an hour away. Within a week, we were sitting down to our first American
version of a Welsh high tea. Jayne had slices of ham, cheese, dressmakers'
sandwiches, some pastries, even a plate of canned salmon, and, of course, a pot
of hot, strong tea.

A robust woman with long white hair, Jayne kept files on everything from
rock groups to cemeteries as long as there was a Welsh connection she could
develop. She told us of her recent visit to Wales and of a meeting she had with
Gwynfor Evans on the Eisteddfod field.

We were not the only people who contacted Jayne. As a result of the
newspaper article she had a list of eight Welsh families in the Wilmington
area. Within a month Jayne launched the Cape Fear Welsh Society and had
copies of *Ninnau*, the Welsh American newspaper, for all of us. With five
months until our trip, this was the break we had been waiting for.

In our first *Ninnau* we read of Welsh clubs in Detroit, Toronto, Vancouver,
Minneapolis and many other North American cities. By our third issue, we
were contributing articles of our own. Onto an index file, alongside Japanese
and personal contacts, we added the locations of Welsh societies that coincided with our route.

Jayne, originally from New York, had lived in San Francisco and had been
editor of *Pethau Cymreig*, the newsletter of the Welsh American Society of
Northern California. She was the first editor of *Ninnau*, from 1978 to 1980,
and from her boat still held the post of Editor at Large.

At the first meeting of the Cape Fear Welsh Society there were two others
who were born in Wales apart from Jayne and me. Mrs. Louisa Glenn, aged
eighty, born in Porth and Huw Christopher, a young Presbyterian minister
from Mountain Ash. Mrs. Vicki Hall had documents threading her lineage
back to the Pilgrim Fathers and then to Hywel Dda! Wendell Eslick was a
pleasant man who told us Eslick was a Welsh name but could think of no

2

Welsh people in his background. Altogether we were about sixteen in a large, drafty church hall.

We held several meetings and even combined with the Burgaw Historical Society for restoration ceremonies at the Welsh Historical Tract, on Route 117 north of Burgaw. But, by the time of our Welsh Society picnic, members were not showing up. It was mainly out of loyalty to Jayne that we went ourselves. None of us had any real idea what a Welsh American society should do, and lacking inspiration, the Society fizzled out. We still visited the boat and learned from Jayne about the beginning and development of *Ninnau*.

We learned that there is a National Cymanfa Ganu held every year either in Canada or the United States. The National Cymanfa has been held every year, except 1943, 1944 and 1945, since 1929 when the first National was held at Niagara Falls. By the 1960's however, attendance at the National Cymanfa was showing a marked decline and various regional cymanfaoedd were finding it difficult to continue. By the time of the New York City National in 1975, members of the North American Welsh community realized there was an urgent need for a widely distributed newsletter and an improved communications network. From a table in the lobby of the Hilton Hotel, headquarters of the Cymanfa and the 1975 "Welsh Week in New York", Jayne Pryddarch, Arturo Roberts and Jack O. Morgans of Detroit launched *Ninnau* and took over two hundred subscriptions in two days. Ten years later, *Ninnau* had a circulation of 3,000 and between 1975 and 1985 at least 18 new Welsh American societies had been formed. A sign of the recovery in North American Welsh life was the Wilkes-Barre National Cymanfa in 1983 which attracted 3,500 people.

We began to hear about the work of Arturo Roberts from Patagonia, first manager of *Ninnau* and its editor since 1980. Arturo had formerly edited an American-Argentinian paper and brought this experience to the early days of *Ninnau*. It was not until Kansas City that we heard about the other Welsh American newspaper, *Y Drych*.

☆

As we drove on I-24 in a gusty and difficult rain towards the Mississippi River, we were passing a slow, huge truck with its soaked tarps flapping when I noticed two headlights coming at us from up ahead.

I screamed out, "Stop! Pull back! Pull back!," but the situation could not register fast enough. Suzanne yelled "Why?" I screamed again, "Pull in! Pull in!" We ducked back behind the truck just in time to avoid a head-on collision with a car on the wrong side of the freeway. It was a close escape that shook us up for the rest of the day.

We were at the Mississippi by 9 a.m. We followed the river north, driving through the apple abundant Illinois Ozarks.

Cape Girardeau was the final resting place of John Evans of Waunfawr, Caernarfon. From 1795 to 1797, Evans led an expedition up the Missouri into unknown Indian territory. He was searching for Welsh Indians. The detailed notes and maps he left eventually made their way to President Thomas Jefferson and made a vital contribution to the Lewis and Clark expedition.

In St. Louis, we had our first Welsh encounter of the trip. Lost on Euclid Avenue, we rolled down the window to ask directions. A tall, attractive blond girl whose attention we finally caught told us that she was new in St. Louis. She was sorry, but she "hadn't a clue." It was a long shot, but her accent was unmistakable. "Are you Welsh?" we asked.

We had met Angharad Garlick, from Carmarthen. Angharad was the daughter of Welsh poet and professor, Raymond Garlick, who was instrumental in founding Oriel, the Welsh Arts Council bookstore in Cardiff. Angharad had been in the States less than a week. No wonder she didn't know her way around.

Angharad was visiting the American poet John Dressel, who keeps Dressel's Pub around the corner from another Welsh pub, Llewellyn's.

In 1979, at Caernarfon, John Dressel won the National Eisteddfod Bardic Crown under the pen name Ianws (Janus). Ianws was, however, two poets, John Dressel and T. James Jones and their entry, a translation from the original English, was disallowed.

While teaching at the University of Iowa in 1975, John established an International Studies Program at Trinity College, Carmarthen. Living in Wales as Director of the program, John immersed himself in Welsh literary life. He is a member of Yr Academi Gymreig and in 1980, Gwasg Gomer brought out a book of T. James Jones's and John Dressel's Eisteddfod collaboration.

Dressel's Pub holds an annual eisteddfod and the walls are decorated with posters from Wales, the Welsh National Opera, covers of Welsh magazines and portraits of Welsh literary giants. Until 1984 Dressel's and Llewellyn's made up for the Welsh society St. Louis lacked.

During 1984 a small group of Welsh Americans in the St. Louis area discussed the formation of a Welsh society. In January 1985, 34 people elected Paul Abrams, President; Roberta Jones, Vice-President; Midge Abrams, Secretary; Ida Mae Arnold, Treasurer and Betty Horton, Historian, as their first committee. Donald Horton and Houston Jones were also important members of this formative group. During 1985 the Welsh Society in St. Louis held pot luck dinners, singing meetings and hosted their first Welsh visitors as a formal organization.

At the base of Eero Saarinen's Gateway Arch is a Pioneer Heritage Museum. In 1860, there were six Welsh settlements in Missouri and six in neighboring Illinois, yet in the lists of immigrants at the Pioneer Heritage Museum there is no mention of the Welsh. We came across this repeatedly— Welsh immigrants absorbed into English statistics.

Staying by the Mississippi we drove north to Hannibal, Missouri. The street where Mark Twain lived has been reconstructed and there's a historical map indicating material that ultimately made its way into his books.

There is a lighthouse on Cardiff Hill. Steps leading to it begin at a statue of Tom Sawyer and Huckleberry Finn. Lighthouse Hill was renamed Cardiff Hill during Hannibal's recent period of renewal during the bicentennial. The Mark Twain Foundation researched a walking tour map and discovered a Welshman's home, as referred to briefly in *The Adventures of Tom Sawyer*.

The Welshman's house which once belonged to a Mr. Davies is at the corner of North Third and North. It is an original small stone building. Near the statue, however, was something much more exciting, Toppers Choice T-Shirt Shop. Toppers Choice awards a diploma to everyone who climbs all 184 steps to the top of Cardiff Hill and even Amiga received one.

If raising ghosts of Welsh immigrants was the main purpose of our trip, all we had to do was drive through Missouri along Route 36. Bevier, New Cambria, Brookfield and Chillicothe were once all Welsh communities. But tracing every Welsh contact was not our original goal. We had seen Wales when we had lived there. Now we wanted to see America before settling down. We should have liked the Welsh aspect to remain incidental, but things didn't turn out that way. Our Welsh connections grew and grew, eventually leading to a depth of involvement in the North American Welsh scene that neither of us could have imagined.

In Siloam Chapel, in my native village Cefn Cribwr, there is a memorial to T. G. Griffiths, a Congregational Minister who died in Kansas City in 1898. We thought it would be a simple matter to drive into Kansas City, trace T. G. Griffiths and drive on again. It was a simple-minded plan and showed how ignorant of genealogy and Welsh American methods we were.

There are two Kansas Cities, one in Kansas and one in Missouri, each having its own set of records. Our lead was a suddenly inadequate piece of paper with the dates of the birth and death of T. G. Griffiths.

After studying miles of microfilm in the Missouri Valley Room of the Kansas City Library, we still couldn't find our man. The librarian suggested we go to Kansas City Library, Kansas where we would probably have to search through files of original documents. We decided to change our course and contact the local St. David's Society instead.

The St. David's Society of Greater Kansas City was founded in 1900, and like many other Welsh societies, is not listed in the telephone book. The latest record of the Society in the library was a newspaper clipping from 1964.

After using a lot of quarters, I finally traced the number of the St. David's Society's current President, Dr. E. H. Gwynne-Thomas. We spoke to Mrs. Gwynne-Thomas who told us where we could find her husband in his office at the University.

It was while talking to Dr. Gwynne-Thomas that we first heard of *Y Drych*. Dr. Gwynne-Thomas had not heard of *Ninnau* and I gave him *Ninnau*'s address. He didn't have the address of *Y Drych* and I didn't follow it up. This was a mistake which would cost us many lost contacts in the months ahead.

Y Drych, we later discovered has been serving the Welsh community for over 134 years. At the turn of the century, *Y Drych*'s office in Utica, New

York, was the largest publisher of Welsh books in America. During the 1950's and 1960's *Y Drych* was the only publication serving North American Welsh people and in 1972 its editor Horace Powell received the O.B.E. for his "outstanding contribution" to Welsh life. Horace Powell died in June, 1980, and when his daughter, Pat Viets, took over the paper in October, she received as many as 100 letters a day from loyal subscribers. By 1984, *Y Drych* was once again the foremost Welsh publication in North America.

Born in Swansea, Eric Gwynne-Thomas was the third successive Kansas City St. David's Society president born in Wales. In 1979 Eric took a small tour party to Wales and he teaches a 30 minute Welsh language class before Society meetings. The Society meets on the first Sunday of October, December, February, March and May. It hosts a Welsh picnic during the summer. Other meetings usually feature slide shows, guest speakers or entertainment by the Society's small Welsh choir. The choir, singing folk songs and hymns, participates in various festivals in the Kansas City area and rehearses at the home of pianist, Sally Jones. Soloists have been Kay Bode and Shirley Coleman. The choir also features the violin playing of Mr. David Isaac, formerly of Clydach, Wales. William Kent and Ivor Jones were also born in Wales and other active members of the small group have been Toby Giese, Rachel Davies, Jenkin David and Ramona Platt. Others who have provided enduring support are Mr. and Mrs. Stanley Keiter and Mr. and Mrs. Elmer Jones.

Ann McFerrin and Judith Brougham attended Welsh Heritage Week in July, 1983 and at the next Society picnic, new and younger members, David Watson and Dan Berkowitz, introduced harp music, folk singing and folk dancing. Dr. John Ditto, Music Director of St. Paul's Episcopal Church, also joined and added to the pool of musical talent.

By 1984 the tempo of the Society had quickened. The Reverend William Nicolas and Mrs. Catherine Beachy made a genealogical visit to Wales and harp, vocal and dulcimer renditions of Welsh music had become a regular feature of Society events. Among the new wave of younger members joining the Society through an interest in drama, folk music and dancing, were Carolyn Jones, Genelle Slagle and Jane Fopeano, Jenkin David's daughter.

The most significant, recent development for the St. David's Society in Kansas City was the launching of the Welsh Harp Society of North America at Welsh Heritage Week in 1984. Kansas City members, David Watson and Judith Brougham, became President and Secretary of the new Harp Society and contributions by harpists, folk dancers and singers have been the single greatest influence on the Kansas City St. David's Society's rejuvenation and growth.

2

Four Mid-Western States:
Welsh Work in Kansas, Oklahoma, Nebraska and Iowa

KANSAS

In June, 1979, 200 Welsh descendants in the community of Bala near Manhattan, Kansas formed the Bala Pioneer Heritage Society. In the 1870's the Welsh Land and Immigration Society of America, whose President was the respected Reverend Rhys Gwesyn Jones of Utica, New York, promoted the Welsh settlement of Bala yn Powys. There were nine other Welsh communities in the northeastern part of Kansas with a combined population of approximately 4,000. The Welsh community in Bala formed a Calvinistic Methodist Church in 1872 which merged with the Presbyterian Church of America in 1890. That the church still stands is something of a phenomenon, and it was mainly in response to the existence of the building that the present Pioneer Heritage Society was formed.

One of the Heritage Society's first acts was to restore the old church bell which had been broken since the 1930's. Laura Llewelyn prepared a book of local family histories and the Society now holds a popular yearly service on the Church's anniversary. Kevin Larson has been one of the main organizers of the group which is led by Phillip Parry, Evelyn Williams and David Lodge. When, out of 200 Welsh descendants and friends, they found no one able to read a verse in Welsh, J. Trevor Lewis of the Welsh group in Emporia, Kansas, volunteered. Mr. Ifan Payne, a Professor at Kansas State University, Manhattan, offered to translate the Society's Welsh documents.

Over 100 years since the first emigration share was sold in Wales, Welsh heritage has been restored in Bala and the new Welsh Society joins neighboring groups for traditional celebrations. The Lyon County St. David's Society, based in Emporia, was founded in 1888. The association's main event is its annual St. David's concert. For 96 years the Lyon County Society has held its annual March 1st concert, which derives from eisteddfodau once held in the Old Emporia County Courthouse.

The singing is mainly in English but includes some Welsh verses led by Maxine Mitchell with Katheryn Perkins and Anne Atherton as accompanists.

The Welsh group in Lyon County forms a Society whose once a year program is appealing to younger generations. The consistency with which people like Claudia Williams Mayes, Margaret Jones, Lucina Jones, Evan W.

Roberts, William Williams and Margaret J. Rees produce the concert and organize the te bach following, provides inspiration to the Welsh who remain in the area. Recently, with renewed interest shown by neighboring Welsh groups and individuals, attendance at the March 1st concert in 1985 drew over 200 people.

OKLAHOMA

South of Kansas, in Enid, Oklahoma, a small Welsh flame has been kept alive through the efforts of Dr. David Lloyd Edwards and his family. On October 8th, 1982, the Edwardses, Traynors, Champlins, Cromwells and Dillinghams hosted the Welsh ensemble, Parti Ceredigion. Parti Ceredigion was the highly successful tour party of Ifan Lloyd, Bethan Bryn, Delyth Evans, Margaret Rhys and Dafydd Edwards, whose 1982 itinerary was organized by Palmer Jones of Granville, Ohio. Palmer Jones and D. L. Edwards were cousins and the concert in Enid took the form of an Edwards' family reunion. Four hundred guests were present. Among those in the audience was Stafford G. Davis who, with the help of Blodwen Osborne, formed the Owain Glendower Society in Tulsa, Oklahoma.

Jenkin Lloyd Jones, syndicated columnist and senior editor of the *Tulsa Tribune*, was the Owain Glendower Society's speaker at its first banquet in 1983, which also featured the Tulsa Boy Singers. The Boy Singers' Choir, searching for Welsh material, decided upon the hymn selection from the wedding of Prince Charles and Lady Diana Spencer and the English language version of Ar Hyd Y Nos. The Choir attracted publicity and the dinner was covered by local radio, television and newspapers.

In the fall of 1983 the Owain Glendower Society sponsored a visit and parade by the Welsh Guards Regimental Band. Through its support of the Tulsa Boy Singers the Society also created a scholarship for any boy singer of Welsh descent. The most imaginative idea of the new Society was its First Annual Daffodil Show on the weekend nearest March 1, 1984. Co-sponsored by the American Daffodil Society the show was extremely successful and attracted a lot of public attention. The leaders of the Owain Glendower Society have made the Daffodil Show an annual event, with the express intention of making daffodils, Wales and St. David synonymous in the general public's mind.

NEBRASKA

In the 1870's in Nebraska, the Welsh were slowly settling in. In Welsh, Nebraska was known as "Dwfr Bas" or "Shallow Water" because of the River Platte, whose pools of quicksand made a formidable obstacle for emigrants. In 1870 there were 200 Welsh scattered across the State, and by the 1900 census there were 922. Today, the American descendants of those pioneers maintain

Welsh societies in Lincoln, Omaha and Wymore. Among the most active are the Nebraska Joneses in the Welsh community of Wymore. The Joneses mail a regular newsletter and every three years they hold a well attended Jones reunion. Family historians have also compiled a well bound series of Jones biographies, tracing immigration, lineage and dissolution into the American melting pot. For the 1982 reunion Everett Jones posted Welsh language signs all over Wymore and on all approaching highways—81 people gathered from a dozen states to honor their common ancestors and the Jones Welsh Male Chorus sang at Wymore Church.

The vast majority of people at the various Welsh societies are American, not Welsh. Welsh visitors soon realize how European they are when they arrive in the United States and try to adjust to American life. From Welsh Americans writing for *Ninnau* and *Y Drych*, we can get some very sympathetic yet objective descriptions of Wales.

In August, 1983, 24 people from the St. David's Welsh Society of Nebraska visited Cardiff, Snowdonia, St. David's Cathedral and the Llangollen International Eisteddfod. The tour was extremely well planned and everyone took advantage of open days to visit distant cousins and the birthplace of their forefathers. Olen and Helen Brake, who hosted Bethan Bryn when Parti Ceredigion gave a concert in Lincoln, made a side trip to Aberystwyth and were entertained at Bethan's home. Bethan Bryn is very popular among Welsh people in America and her visits have done a lot to promote Welsh harp music which, for a while, was being overlooked in the Celtic-American revival.

St. David's Society celebrations in Nebraska began in 1910 in Omaha. In 1959, the annual St. David's banquet moved to Lincoln and is held in April in order to enjoy less hostile weather.

The Lincoln Welsh group has an excellent music director in Mr. Tom Hughes of Norfolk who, as well as leading hymns, puts an emphasis on Welsh folk tunes. Norfolk and Lincoln are 121 miles apart, so we can appreciate the commitment of people like Tom Hughes who work so hard to preserve Welsh Heritage in America. The Nebraska St. David's Society's correspondent is Rosalind Morris, who was born in Ruthin, Wales. Other leaders of the club are Mrs. Leonard Egan, Hazel Schreiber and Marjorie Roderick. The Society was incorporated in 1980, started collecting dues in 1982 and also raises money from the sale of Welsh imports. 138 people attended the Nebraska St. David's Society Diamond (75th) Anniversary Banquet in April 1985. The 1985-1986 Society committee consisted of Helen Brake, President; Arthur Welty, Vice-President; Al Evans, Secretary; Oliver Grace, Treasurer and Morgan Bevan, Historian. Dr. Orvid Owens organized the Society's highly successful cymanfa ganu on October 6, 1985. Olwen Welk conducted and almost 200 people came to Eastridge Presbyterian Church in Lincoln.

Every June, Omaha holds an annual ethnic festival. The Nebraska Welsh have taken part since 1976. Thanks to the consistent hard work of Helen Brake, Esther Pilster, Hope Rees and Vera and Maldwyn Closs, every year 20,000 people are exposed to one Welsh booth among 36 others.

IOWA

In Pella, Iowa, Central College offers American students its excellent Foreign Studies Program at Trinity College, Carmarthen. The American Coordinator is Mrs. Barbara Butler and the Director in Wales is John Dressel. Eligible American sophomores can take a one year course in Trinity with all electives transferable to the U.S. Students can take Conversational Welsh, Language in Wales, Welsh Writers In English and Welsh Landscape. There are seven Welsh options and two Celtic in a humanities prospectus that has 63 courses to choose from. Two semesters in Trinity College gain 32 credit hours at a cost (in 1984) of $7,500. At present over 50 students from 20 U.S. colleges are taking part, a large number of whom admit to having some kind of Welsh background.

In Ames, Iowa, Professor Phillips G. Davies, for years, has been translating historic Welsh American documents. His translations from obscure originals have appeared in University and Historical Society journals throughout the United States. In November, 1983, Phillips G. Davies' translation of R. D. Thomas' *Hanes Cymry America* was published, making available to the English reading public the most detailed account of Welsh immigration and settlement during the 1860's and 1870's.

Born in El Paso in 1925, Phillips G. Davies' interest in the Welsh language started in the 1950's when he found a copy of *Hanes Cymru America* in a second hand book shop and started translating it. Professor Davies' Welsh connection was through his great-great grandfather, David Charles Davies, who emigrated from Newcastle Emlyn to New York in 1854. In America David Charles Davies became a physician, editor of *Y Drych* and a State Senator for Wisconsin.

In 1981, Des Moines Friendship Force spent two weeks in Cardiff, and in return hosted their Welsh counterparts for two weeks in Iowa. Cardiff has an active Friendship Force and in 1982 arranged an exchange with 29 people from Winston-Salem, North Carolina. In 1983 an exchange took place between Cardiff and Orlando, Florida, and in 1984, the Cardiff group visited Memphis, Tennessee and Atlanta, Georgia.

The International Friendship Force was founded in 1977 by President Jimmy Carter and Premier James Callaghan of Britain. James Callaghan's own city of Cardiff joined Friendship Force in 1980 and since then about 200 Welsh people have taken advantage of the exchange idea to see America. Today, the International Friendship Force has ambassadors in over 30 countries. The Welsh Director of International Friendship Force is Roy Guy in Cardiff while the American headquarters is at Omni International in Atlanta.

In Iowa City in 1972, a group of Welsh Americans revived the city's traditional cymanfa ganu, an event that dated back to the 1860's but in the 1960's had all but disappeared. In 1954 the Welsh Church in Iowa City was forced to close its doors for a total of eighteen years. It was only due to the tenacity and determination of the Welsh Ladies Missionary Society, which continued to meet during this depressing period, that the cymanfa was restored. Thanks to the work of Keith Tudor, Richard Pate, Agnes Jones and the Ladies Missionary Society, the First Welsh Congregational Church in Iowa City was reopened in 1972 and is now listed on the National Register of Historic Places.

The Iowa City cymanfa ganu is held on the first Sunday in July and other Welsh activities have revived all round. The church's original organ has been restored and the Society has an excellent organist and singing teacher in Margaret Hootman. Michael Evans has learned Welsh and is the Welsh reader during services and the Society's special events are fully reported by Stella Thomas.

The re-establishment of the Welsh Congregational Church in Iowa City led directly to the formation of a broader based Celtic Heritage League. Margaret Hootman is the main Welsh contributor to the Celtic Heritage League which often features Welsh programs on its agenda.

Further north, Lime Springs, Iowa, is preserving its Welsh heritage. In 1977 Lidtke's Mill, originally a Welsh flour mill owned and operated by D. W. Davies, and named after his daughter, was restored and declared a State Historical Site.

Until the mid-1960's Lime Springs had a Welsh Church with a reliable, if elderly, Welsh congregation. Founded in 1892 as part of the Welsh Presbyterian Church, it is today the Westminster Presbyterian Church. The church's minister, the Reverend R. Lewis Jones, emigrated to the U.S.A. in 1922 and after a distinguished career serving Welsh American congregations in Iowa, Illinois and Pennsylvania, he retired in 1963. During Reverend Lewis Jones's ministry in Lime Springs, Welsh language services were held every Sunday afternoon. In recognition of his work, Dr. Lewis Jones was made a member of the Welsh National Eisteddfod Gorsedd. In 1981, he retired as acting pastor of the First Presbyterian Church in Rockwell, Iowa, but maintained a schedule of Welsh and English writing as well as speaking and traveling throughout the midwestern states.

Welsh Americans in Lime Springs and Iowa City maintain contact with the Welsh in neighboring Minnesota. A Minnesota-Iowa Cymanfa Ganu is held every September and contacts between the states result in numerous Welsh events during the year.

3

The Welsh in Arkansas, Alabama, Mississippi and Florida: The Cajuns in Louisiana

From Kansas City we made a two day drive southeast to the heart of the Ozark Mountains. A plateau without peaks, the Ozarks are gentler than the Southern Oachitas and are a lot like the Welsh Prescellys. Vastly different in fauna, they are similar in topography, with the highest Ozark peak being 1,772 feet on Taum Sauk Mountain and the Prescellys at 1,760 feet on Moel Cwm Cerwyn. They are similar, too, in their shallow glades, abundance of clean, swift streams and the beauty of sudden, unexpected hamlets.

At one hamlet, Elk Creek, connected to the world by dirt packed roads, we were the guests of Christine and Mac McKinney. Christine was a school friend of my parents. She grew up in the Mid Glamorgan village of Cefn Cribwr and as a teenager went to the weekend dances in Porthcawl. During the war, she met her American husband, Mac, and became one of thousands of women brought home by the American Army. GI housing in New Orleans gave her a terrible first impression of the United States and we were amazed that after 35 years, she was ready to return to Cefn Cribwr "like a shot."

If the Ozarks, with their sinkholes, turtles, paddlefish and walnut trees were unmistakably American, the interior of Christine's home was unmistakably Welsh. Every detail might have come from a Bridgend china shop. From net curtains to an electric kettle, from a blazing paisley carpet to an immaculate china cabinet, everything was a recreation of what a modern home would be in Wales. Gleaming brasses on the wall, a wind-up Welsh lady on the mantelpiece and in the knitting basket, a novel based upon Mid Glamorgan legends. Our first night, we ate Spam sandwiches and sipped hot tea, while Mac drank Coke and ate potato chips.

Mac and Christine wake at 5 a.m. and drive 50 miles to work at Fort Leonard Wood Air Force Base. On weekends, Christine goes to church while Mac works on the tractor, cropping the relentless weeds of their untilled fields. Christine could not have been more hospitable and our happiest times were listening to recollections of her schooldays in Wales.

Louisiana, we loved, from the first shimmering fields to the last shell chenier along the Gulf of Mexico. Our first night, we spent in the yard of a high school in Arcadia. The next day, we found ourselves in Louisiane Française.

Napoleon repossessed Louisiana from the Spanish in 1800 and then negotiated its sale to the United States in 1803. There were already four or five thousand Arcadian exiles from Nova Scotia and France in Louisiana and by 1880, swollen by immigration and the numbers of French speaking slaves, the Arcadian population reached 270,000.

Cajun is a variant of Arcadian. In 1921 Cajun French was forbidden in Louisiana by the State Constitution. Cajun children were punished for speaking French by being forced to kneel with their noses in tiny chalk circles on the blackboard.

In 1968, however, a group of Louisiana French speakers created CODO-FIL, the Council for the Development of French in Louisiana. CODOFIL is an official state organization that organizes French teaching programs in the schools, French radio and television broadcasts, Cajun festivals, cooking, folklore and other projects connected with the re-establishment of Cajun identity. While the work of CODOFIL has been unevenly financed, it has made enormous progress and has built a bridge between children and their grandparents. The whole generation in between, however, has been forced to regard their language as an oddity and something to be forgotten.

Our French encounter started at Melrose in Cane River country. Descended principally from one man, the free French slave, Augustine Metoyers, the Cane River people have fine pointed features and a delicate brown complexion. We stopped at Mrs. LaCour's Doll House. In 1976, Mrs. Lair LaCour won the State bicentennial doll contest, with a Creole Ma-Man Doll that has been in her family for generations. While she and her daughter sewed, grandchildren climbed over bobbins and material like kittens.

Mrs. LaCour told us how country people, who still speak only Cajun, regarded French as a handicap. One woman's attempt to stop her daughter speaking French was foiled when she came home one day and said, "Ma, I speak French good. I know what 'bonjour' means. Bonjour means howdy."

The majority of people, however, support the work of CODOFIL and in a state referendum, 97% of those surveyed, voted for the re-introduction of French at school. Today over 50,000 Cajun children are learning French and the language can be heard in the shops and businesses of Arcadian towns.

That night we camped at St. Augustine Catholic Church in Melrose, with its portrait of Augustine Metoyers hanging above the door. We woke up to the screeching of mocking birds fighting in the magnolia trees. Sister Theresa, who lived in the small church house, invited us inside to bathe and freshen up.

Attracted by all things French, we drove to Mansura in search of cochon de lait, (roast suckling pig), but settled for tasso (smoked beef) and boudin, a spicy Cajun sausage. In Opelousas we found the best French bread at Hull's Bakery and the best boucherie at Merche's Meatmarket on Route 190 out of town. In all our inquiries about Cajun life, one name kept coming up time after time—Mamou, in Evangeline Parish. We went there, and driving down Mamou's plain Main Street, we wondered why on earth we had come. Mamou was a simple, small Louisiana town, with a drugstore, a garage and a row of taverns.

We parked the van and walked through Mamou calling "Bonjour! Ça va!" to passers by. People stopped and struck up animated conversations in French. When we spoke in English they directed us to the Police Station from where we were sent to talk to Revon Reed and Mike DesHotels.

Revon Reed is a member of the Louisiana Folklore Association and has built twin city links with Quebec and organized many Cajun music festivals. Mike DesHotels was editor of the Arcadian Press. Both men sent us to meet Paul Tate, a Mamou attorney, Secretary of the Louisiana Section of the International Association of French speaking Legislators and a member of the original CODOFIL council in 1968.

Paul Tate spoke to us at length about CODOFIL and the feelings of Cajun people as a minority in Louisiana. The campaign to save the French language in Louisiana was started in 1967 by James Domengeaux, a Louisiana Congressman. Domengeaux persuaded the Quebec government to open an office in Lafayette, obtained financial assistance from the state and federal government and organized French classes in the high schools taught by French, Belgian and Quebecois teachers. In Louisiana high schools over sixty branches of CODOJEUNE, the youth wing of CODOFIL have been started, making the language an in-thing among teenagers. Today, it is also fashionable to speak French in Arcadian civic clubs and state and county committees conduct their meetings and record their minutes in French. Paul Tate emphasized that CODOFIL encouraged the use of French at every level of society. As James Domengeaux wrote,

> You have to hear the language when you turn the radio on in your car, you have to see it spoken when you turn on the television set in your home, you have to dance to it when you put a quarter in the juke box, you have to speak it at your family table.

The ambition of CODOFIL is to achieve a bilingual Louisiana. As Paul Tate said when we were leaving, Cajun people in Louisiana are Americans and they have a culture and a language of their own. Promoting that culture does not threaten but adds to America's national life. He encouraged us to see more of Louisiana, visit festivals, even the taverns in Mamou where a Cajun band plays almost every night.

Out in the street, we didn't want to leave Mamou, but after another walk, could find no excuse to hang around. We decided to walk up and down Main Street one more time in the hope of meeting someone and making a friend. At that moment a young couple pulled up in a car and mistook us for Canadians.

We told them about our trip, about our interest in Louisiana French and after a glance at one another, they invited us home for dinner. They were Tony and Diana Sue Soileau. Tony played drums in a Cajun band and was performing that night in Mamou. While Tony played us Zachary Richard records, Diana Sue fixed a spicy meal of Cajun beef and dirty rice. Their own knowledge of French was uneven but surprisingly, Diana Sue could read it and Tony could sing and understand it perfectly. They told us story upon story of Cajun festivals, unusual food, musical parties and their own large family gatherings.

We went with Tony to the Casanova Bar and joined other couples doing the Mamou two step across the floor. People stared at us, but when they saw that we were willing to join in, they ignored our crude crunching on one another's feet.

By 1:30 one hot September afternoon, we were at Carville, Louisiana, at the gates of the National Hansen's Disease Center, the largest, most modern leprosy clinic in the world. As we waited with the security guard, all kinds of doubts surfaced inside us. Would we find ourselves staring at the patients? Would we see severely deformed people with dreadful sores? What if we caught leprosy?

Our guide was Joe, a former merchant seaman from the Virgin Islands. Joe took us to the clinic's TV studio where we saw an introductory video on leprosy today. We learned that although Hansen's Disease is one of the least contagious diseases in the world (since Carville became a hospital in 1921 not one staff member has contracted it) hundreds of new victims are reported in the United States every year. Modern treatment, while unable to cure the disease, is able to arrest its development and treatment today involves teaching victims to monitor themselves and adjust to associated injuries they may have already incurred. Treatment can take several years and the clinic has schools, a library, restaurant, supermarket, even a modern cinema and an 18 hole golf course.

Once a patient of the clinic, Joe had since made the United States his home and found work at Carville as a tour guide. The clinic is visited by thousands of visitors annually and the public is always welcome.

Joe explained that horror portraits of leprosy in movies like Ben Hur and Papillon perpetuate myths about the disease that date from biblical times. The clinic's monthly publication, *The Star*, which has a worldwide circulation of 84,000 reminds doctors, health workers and patients, especially in California, Hawaii, Florida, and New York where most American victims are found that Hansen's Disease still exists, but if diagnosed, can effectively be stopped.

It was only after repeated tests that Joe's doctors sent a skin sample to Carville and Hansen's Disease was diagnosed. Joe was able to treat the disease in time and prevent the further spread of damage to his extremities. Joe's openness about his own experience and the well managed informative services of the clinic had cast light on a deep area of darkness within us. After an invitation to relax in the cafeteria, we returned to the van and headed south to New Orleans via Baton Rouge.

There is one Welsh activist in New Orleans, Miss Barbara Martin. Non-Welsh by birth, Barbara told us she studies the Welsh language "religiously every day." It was the beauty of the language that first attracted her. Later, on a visit to Wales, the friendliness of the people and the beauty of the countryside made her a hopeless Cambrophile. In 1984 Barbara took a summer language course at Bangor and stayed. She would like to make Wales her home.

MISSISSIPPI

The Daffodil Journal, quarterly publication of the American Daffodil Society, is published in Hernando, Mississippi. Editor, Mrs. Leslie Anderson has visited Wales and was impressed by the number of daffodils there. She has written that in Wales, she saw some of the most beautiful formal arrangements of daffodils that she had ever seen. The American Daffodil Society was founded in 1954 and has over 16,000 members. The Society organizes workshops, has an annual convention, publishes a breeding and selection catalog, and every issue of *The Daffodil Journal* has a list of exhibitions nationwide and Daffodil societies around the world. Following the collaboration of the Tulsa Daffodil Society and the Oklahoma Owain Glendower Society, the National Daffodil Society is willing to connect local chapters with Welsh societies that may want to sponsor similar daffodil shows.

ALABAMA

Dr. Robert E. Morgan has maintained a strong Welsh presence from his home in Birmingham, Alabama since the early 1960's. With the cooperation of the Welsh Office and Welsh artists, John and Kusha Petts, Dr. Morgan made the Welsh contribution to the 1970 Birmingham Festival of Arts the most forceful and effective display there. He arranged a teaching position in Anglo-Welsh literature for Roland Mathias at the University of Alabama and a visit to the University by Ray Handy on his "Dylan Thomas Lived Here tour" in 1978. Robert E. Morgan also founded Wales International which later merged with, and became the English wing of, Undeb y Cymry ar Wasgar, the worldwide distribution of Welsh people who assemble every year on the National Eisteddfod stage. For "significant contributions to Welsh culture" Bob Morgan was made a member of the National Eisteddfod Gorsedd in 1970 and was awarded the St. David's Society of the State of New York Hopkins Medal in 1973.

In 1965 in reaction to the bombing of a black church in Birmingham, Alabama in which four children were killed, Welsh stained glass artist John Petts designed and built a new window for the church. Financed by contributions from the people of Wales, the window was constructed over a period of a year. The window was made in Llanstephan, displayed in London and is now mounted at 16th Street Baptist Church in Birmingham. Bob Morgan arranged the purchase of John Petts' working cartoons for the window and donated them to the University of Alabama Library.

Wales International grew out of Bob Morgan's contact with artists, editors and politicians in Wales. In 1969 Glyn Alban Roberts visited America to promote the new organization. Contacts in Wales were less enthusiastic than their counterparts in America, however, and Wales International was salvaged by its merger with Undeb y Cymry ar Wasgar which has distributed its international journal *Yr Enfys* since 1949.

The Birmingham Festival of Arts in 1970 was called "Salute to Britain" and Bob Morgan invited the Welsh Office in London to contribute regalia from the 1969 Royal Investiture. The Investiture displays attracted a lot of publicity and Ednyfed Davies of the Welsh Office flew over, adding weight to the Welsh contribution. John Petts held an exhibition of his work and spoke at the Museum of Art as a guest of the Birmingham Arts Association. Kusha Petts held several readings of her work on the college campus.

Hundreds of miles from the nearest Welsh society, Bob Morgan has refused to be isolated in Alabama. Guest speaker at southern St. David's societies and a Vice-President of the London Cymmrodorion, the potential of Wales International still inspires him and he has repeatedly expressed a willingness to make Birmingham a station on any Welsh American network that might be built.

South of Birmingham, the Mobile Chamber of Commerce and the Mobile Chapter of the Daughters of the American Revolution have erected two plaques of interest to Welsh people.

Mobile is where Prince Madoc the Welsh discoverer of America is supposed to have landed with his fleet of three ships and there is a plaque to Madoc ap Owain Gwynedd on the wall of the Fine Arts Center of the South. The plaque of the Daughters of the American Revolution is located on the public strand of Mobile Bay and reads,

"In memory of Prince Madoc, a Welsh explorer, who landed on the shores of Mobile Bay in 1170 and left behind, with the Indians, the Welsh language."

References to Prince Madoc keep cropping up in the South and with increasing frequency among fringe pre-Columbian historians. At Fort Mountain State Park near Chatsworth, Georgia, there are references to Prince Madoc in relation to a mysterious stone wall there.

FLORIDA

At St. Petersburg and Cape Canaveral, Florida has two important Welsh Societies—important because many people from the North American community retire to Florida or go there to visit relatives and friends. At St. David's Day banquets, the Florida Welsh entertain visitors from Wales, Canada and over a dozen American states. Past speakers and visitors have included Faith King, Osian Ellis, Tammy Jones, David Mandry, Islyn Thomas, Gwynfor Evans, Ellis W. Roberts and Lord Gordon Parry. The retired Welsh community has a fund of oral history and a wealth of family heirlooms. A lot of Florida Welsh Society members, now in their 70's and 80's emigrated from Wales when young. Hugh Lloyd Jones, for example, who died in 1983, left Gwynedd in 1927 and started work in the slate quarries of Granville, New York. From his home in Florida he was often heard on BBC Welsh radio reports when telephoned by the ubiquitous Alun Williams.

The Florida Welsh community responded well to the 1979 Welsh National Eisteddfod "Million Pounds Appeal." Nellie Wilson Miller of St. Petersburg wrote that, "Society members are Welsh Americans and feel that anything that prolongs Welsh heritage should have their continued support." Nellie's statement is an accurate reflection of the feelings of people of Welsh background in the state.

The St. David's Society of St. Petersburg and the Sun Coast was founded in 1924. For St. David's Day the Society holds a banquet and cymanfa on the weekend closest to March 1st. Over 100 people usually attend. Regular monthly meetings of the St. Petersburg Society are held every third Tuesday from October to May. Meetings are held at Woodlawn Presbyterian Church and between 60 and 70 people usually appear.

The St. Petersburg St. David's Society has had many active and dedicated members, among them Doris Pottenger, Helen Jones, Ann Thomas, Cyril Watkins and William Ladd Thomas. But without the work of two remarkable women, May Evans Dawe and Nellie Wilson Miller, the Society would not have the membership it has today. Through the 1960's and 1970's, since retiring, May Dawe and Nellie Miller labored tirelessly, organizing Welsh events such as the Cambrian Welsh Chorus' visit in 1979 and an annual Welsh booth at the St. Petersburg International Folk Fair. In 1984 at 93 and 96 years of age respectively both women attended every Welsh Society function. Age does not hinder the club's activities; the only difference it makes is in monthly reports to *Ninnau* and *Y Drych* which almost always include an account of the death of a Society member. The 1985-1986 leaders of the Society were Marian Mathews, President; Cyril L. Watkins, First Vice-President; Larry N. Herschelman, Second Vice-President; Elaine Johnson, Secretary; Ann Thomas, Treasurer; Florence Jose, Membership Chairman.

The Sun Coast Society is well served by Nellie Miller's sister, Annie Wilson Jayne, formerly of Charleston, West Virginia. Annie is an accomplished director who in the past has conducted the Wisconsin State Cymanfa Ganu. Annie Jayne has conducted some of the St. Petersburg cymanfoedd canu. The club has talented soloists in Robert Watkins and Roberto Sylvano. Not everyone is elderly, however, and at one banquet members were entertained with Welsh songs from 15 year old Georgianna Martin.

The Florida Welsh scene is always improving. In 1982, for the first time in 58 years, a te bach was held following the annual cymanfa. The te bach was very successful and has since become a regular event. The banquet is increasingly well organized with excellent speakers and with well designed Welsh theme decorations on the tables. The Society has staffed a booth at the

International Folk Fair which attracts 60,000 visitors and has thirty different ethnic stands. Society leader Emyr Griffiths was among the first to enroll for the first Cwrs Cymraeg held in Poultney, Vermont in 1977. Over 30 Society members attended the 1985 National Cymanfa Ganu which was held in Montreal.

In December, 1981, Glyn Williams launched the Space Coast Welsh Society, attracting people from the eastern coast of Florida. The club proved instantly successful. By May 1982 the new Society had organized its charter, dues and by-laws. Members were showing films and holding bake sales by November. In December, they participated in the Satellite Beach Arts and Crafts Fair, with sales of pillows, love spoons, dollhouses, potted plants and handmade Welsh dolls. The Space Coast Welsh Society has a first class singer in Terence Mant, formerly of the Glyndebourne Operatic Society, Edinburgh, and had a dedicated Welsh teacher in Mr. Phillip Morris. Space Coast member, Harry Jones, is a harpist and dulcimer player and has made his own Welsh harp which he plays at Society events. 1985-1986 officers of the Society were, Lorraine Colkin, President; Lillian Wynne, Vice-President; Marjorie Weare, Secretary and Glyn Williams, Treasurer.

Glyn Williams and Nancy and Lester Read work tirelessly to make the club successful and have built a strong friendship with the St. David's Society of St. Petersburg. Fifty-five people attended the 1985 Space Coast St. David's Day celebration.

Florida is also the location of the American outlet for Adlonni Recordings of Wales. Tilly Bodycombe Hughes, the famous Welsh contralto, appeared with Ethel Barrymore in the stage production of "The Corn is Green" and later in the movie version with Katherine Hepburn. In 1980 Tilly's daughter, Margaret C. Brady, learned that John Davies of Pwllheli, Wales, had vintage recordings of her mother's singing. Margaret became Adlonni's agent in America making her mother's singing and other vintage records available to Welsh Americans. For years, the St. Petersburg St. David's Society displayed Tilly Bodycombe Hughes' original Welsh costume every St. David's day. The costume is now displayed in the Drama and Folk Art collection of the Smithsonian Institute. Adlonni's catalog features cassettes of historic recordings transferred onto modern equipment. Most date before 1930 and include David Brazell, the Family Hudson and Tilly Bodycombe Hughes as well as several Welsh singers recorded in the United States.

4

Driving West:
Through Texas, New Mexico and Colorado

The main Welsh nugget in Texas is the Dylan Thomas archive at the University of Texas in Austin. The University has the largest and most important collection of Dylan Thomas papers in the world. Filed on over 600 index cards, with a large portion still kept in cardboard boxes, this material is housed in the Humanities Research Center. The papers, acquired in the years immediately following the poet's death in New York in 1953, were mined extensively by Paul Ferris, Dylan Thomas' latest and most meticulous biographer. The University of Texas at Austin also has an extensive collection of Welsh novelist Rhys Davies' manuscripts and papers.

There is one other glimmer of Welsh in the classics department. Professor Gareth Morgan, a native of Port Talbot, teaches a course on Medieval Welsh. Started in September, 1980, this is the first time Welsh has been taught at the University of Texas. Further north in Dallas, John Williams, Nathan Hughes and Thomas McCross are making progress towards the formation of a Welsh society there.

We entered Texas, a state larger than France, at Sabine Pass, a narrow channel of water where huge oil tankers from all over the world passed by our camp during the night. From Sabine Pass to El Paso we drove 1,200 miles in nine days that took us from the forests east of Houston to the arid deserts of New Mexico.

There was once a Welsh society in Houston but it dissolved in the 1960's due to the advanced age of its members combined with lack of interest. Carl R. Yochum, a resident of Houston, has been trying to organize some Welsh events but with no success. The best way to start a Welsh society is with a lot of publicity. Get a Welsh report in the newspaper or on television and calls come pouring in. Publicity can be generated in a number of ways, but interest focussed on a local event, group or individual is usually the most effective. For Texas the Dylan Thomas angle or even something like Dallas Symphony's performance of music by Welsh composer William Mathias in 1983 could form a spark to set things off.

Once out of Houston the vistas of Texas opened up and we made two particularly memorable stops, one at the Attwater Prairie Chicken Refuge and another at Palmetto State Park.

The prairie chicken was almost made extinct until the World Wildlife Fund helped establish this preserve. We sat out in the sand and sage for four long hours. We didn't see a chicken but we did see the crested cara cara and a herd of skinny cows cropping the broad leaved grass much as bison did a hundred years ago. Mainly, we were repaid by bathing in the original atmosphere and unblemished sky of the open prairie.

Semi-tropical contrast awaited us at Palmetto State Park, an isolated Texan pocket of exotic palm. We were amazed at the number of armadillos in the park, as tame and as unafraid as suburban squirrels. That evening, an armadillo ventured to the doorstop of our van, and despite Amiga's frantic barking, sat up on its hind legs to investigate. That night it rained and in the morning all the armadillos had gone. A search for water had prompted the armadillos to drop their natural timidity.

Interstate 35 delivered us to the gates of the Alamo, located in the heart of San Antonio. The Alamo museum has a flag for the state and nationality of every man that died there. There is one Welsh flag. In 1836 Lewis Johnson of Wales died at the Alamo along with 185 others. The Alamo Role of Heroes and Revolutionary Ancestors has several Welsh names, most of them migrants from Pennsylvania. Lewis Johnson was the only one born in Wales. He emigrated to Louisiana and fought at the Alamo as a private under the enlistment of Jim Bowie, then a slave owner in Opelousas, Louisiana. In 1854 and 1856, twenty years after the battle, Lewis Johnson's heirs received a total of 4,560 acres of land for his having fallen at the battle of the Alamo.

The Institute of Texas Culture in San Antonio is an ethnic heritage museum with a display for every conceivable nationality. Even though there must have been some Welsh people in the state there is not one mention of Wales. Texas is the center of the angora mohair wool business. The merino sheep, another important wool producing animal, was introduced to the United States by Welsh American James B. David in 1849 and several Welsh sheepherding families farmed in the Edwards Plateau during the latter 1800's.

At Del Rio, we drove to the Mexican border. School was letting out and the parents of hundreds of black haired children waited in cars and pickup trucks. We tuned our radio like theirs to the blaring local station and heard the deafening echoes of virile Mexican advertisements.

West of Del Rio were linear half abandoned desert towns, the once bright paint of cars and gas stations were lacerated by driving sand. We took a swim in the scummy waters of Lake Armistad. It was October and with the Rocky Mountains ahead we knew it might be our last swim for some time.

Langtry was a ghost town, a junction of deserted buildings and unpaved roads. The heat was glaring and intense, yet in the shade, cool enough for an overcoat. In Bud and Pansy's Bar we heard tall stories about the rain. We were told of an eight year old girl who had never seen the rain and when it fell, ran terrified into her mother's arms. The man who told us this shook salt into his beer every time he took a sip.

Closer to El Paso we rested on the interstate. It was Friday night and the rest area was packed with trucks racing home for the weekend. Drivers whacked their dozen wheels with baseball bats, checking them for wear after driving hundreds of miles from Dallas and Abilene at 80 miles an hour.

El Paso in the wind and sand flapped like a garish rug. We came into it by the low, long buildings and armored parking lots of Fort Bliss Military Reservation. Streets were deserted and cars were few. The sand storm seemed to have blown everyone inside.

The saving grace of El Paso is Chamizal Peace Park at the international border. We attended a folk festival here and heard Irish, Cajun, Scottish and Japanese music. This festival is one of thousands of fall events held across America that would welcome any touring Welsh band that applied in time. Every state has an index of its annual festivals and setting up a tour should not be any harder than arranging the choral tours that there are so many of.

NEW MEXICO

In the 1960's Ruth and Edwin Lewis hosted occasional St. David's Day dinners at their Albuquerque home. Informal gatherings continued over the years but nothing well advertised occurred until Ceridwen Roberts, prompted by Palmer Jones of Ohio, organized a formal society with the purpose of hosting Parti Ceredigion in mind. Ceridwen, who had been active in the Welsh community of New York, had a wide circle of personal contacts and a fuller idea of what a Welsh American society could do.

Thirty-nine people came to the Society's first organized meeting in October, 1981. They were entertained by Ceridwen's slides of her visit to the Nant Gwrtheyrn Language Center in Wales. Impromptu singing broke out and in the euphoria following, the group planned for the next St. David's Day. Publicity prior to March 1st attracted over 120 calls and the new Society's first official luncheon was an outstanding success. Emlyn Davies, Jean Pritchard Rhoades and Rhianwen Gerard were all soloists, and Gwenythy Coss led community bilingual singing. The luncheon earned a brief television spot and by the end of the day the Welsh were very much part of the Albuquerque scene.

By the time of its first anniversary the New Mexico Welsh Society had organized a first class concert and elaborate reception for Parti Ceredigion. Edwin Lewis, Ruth Lewis, Merlyn Davies and Jean Pritchard Rhoades co-ordinated the appearance with the indefatigable Palmer Jones. Three hundred and seventy-five people saw Parti Ceredigion sing at the Episcopalian Cathedral and the concert and arrangements for it had a great formative influence on the Society. In August 1984, the Society hosted Hogia'r Wyddfa on their West Coast tour. Hogia'r Wyddfa attracted a lot of attention and the Society grew even more. During the winter of 1984-1985 Dr. Alan Hudson-Edwards taught a Welsh class every Tuesday night at the University of New Mexico.

After years of wondering whether there were enough people interested, the Welsh of Albuquerque finally pulled their club together. Today the New

Mexico Welsh Society is as strong as any in the United States. The Society has quite a few members who are Welsh born and frequent visitors from Wales help keep meetings fresh and informal. Jerry Phillips has visited Wales and completed his master's thesis on sociological differences between Welsh and English speakers in Wales. The 1985-1986 committee consisted of Dick Jones, President; Emlyn Davies, Vice President; Barbara Nell Roberts, Secretary; Judy Jaeger, Treasurer; Irene Thompson, Historian and Ed Lewis, Hildur Szerlip and Franklin Thomas, Directors. Other leaders of this new and extremely active group are Wynne Wood, Sue Burgess, Ruth Davies, Ruth Lewis, Harriet Evans, Dorothea Lassiter and Maggie Lopez.

In the fall of 1983, the New Mexico Welsh Society rented its first booth at Albuquerque's International Hot Air Balloon Festival. With bright red dragon flags and dragon shaped cookies they attracted a lot of interest from the people who attended. The main focus of the club, however, remains on bimonthly luncheons hosted by Rhianwen Gerard. The club has also developed a reportoire of folk songs and has expanded into folk dancing, which adds greatly to the Society's vitality and entertainment. By 1984, the New Mexico Welsh were consolidated and confident enough to have a full March 1st program. One hundred and thirty-two people came to the banquet which featured Ann Davies Thomas as visiting conductor, and formal entertainment by a professional harpist with their own Maggie Lopez as soprano soloist.

We were in Albuquerque during a freezing rain that further north became the first snow storm of the year. News reports were predicting one of the severest winters ahead and we had to make some drastic revisions in our itinerary. We solved the problem of managing to see everything and avoid bad weather by designing a large figure eight that took us north through the Rocky Mountains to Boulder, then down through the national parks of Utah and Arizona and back into New Mexico. Meanwhile in Cuba, New Mexico, we experienced our first big freeze. Our locks, windshield, water tank, Amiga's bowl, even our pee in the chamberpot, all froze. The only way to thaw out before breakfast was to drive for an hour with the heat on and shake everything around.

The road to Durango took us through bleak Navajo uplands. Isolated hogans stood always a formidable distance from the road. Nageezi Trading Post, painted potassium green, served as a supplier of general merchandise. With its pot-bellied woodstove casting light on blankets, jewelry, canned food, blacksmith tools, bolts of cloth and a bilingual Navajo-English bulletin board, the interior was a haven from the swirling sand and snow outside.

A Rocky Mountain saying is that the snow does not melt, but just gets blown around. The first fields of snow had formed and the back country was alive with luminous hunters wearing safety jackets. News reports were filled with stories of hunters shooting one another. We kept Amiga in the van and stayed away from any unmarked trails.

The Million Dollar Highway from Durango to Silverton was named for the wealth of gold and other minerals the roadbed yielded. Today the Standard

23

Metals Company located in the Southern Rockies still mines $6,000,000 a year in precious metals.

Silverton Congregational Church built in 1881 was the first church built on the western slope. Thousands of prospectors left their unsuccessful diggings for more reliable work on the narrow gauge railroad and on the wagon road. Hundreds died of hard work and boredom, among them men of Welsh descent whose names like Lloyd, Jenkins, Hopkins and Meredith can be seen in the Silverton churchyard.

Ouray has a spa, the Wiesbaden. Below ground, along a tunnel and in a cavern protected by a heavy metal hatch, there is a pool of water with a temperature around 110 degrees Fahrenheit. It cost us $5.00 to sit and soak, visit the sauna, cool and return to soak again before returning to the snow flurries that pattered on the van.

The scale of Colorado never once diminished and at Black Canyon of the Gunnison we felt thoroughly dwarfed, almost punished by the relentless magnificence of the scenery. We began to recognize that we were in a state of shock brought on by the altitude, constant movement and Nature's vastness. We devoted the next few days to long and patient hikes in order to adjust to the environment.

The road to Marble Mountain was strewn with enormous chunks of marble that looked as though they must have broken the mule trains' backs and then remained exactly where they fell. At the beginning of the six mile track leading to the quarry were enormous marble cutting shops reminiscent of classical ruins in their immense and empty grandeur.

Monumentalism was taking its effect. While we debated whether to hike up to the quarry, another man, muffled in his parka, came along and started bellowing in an enormous voice about the overwhelming grandeur of it all. We automatically backed away from him.

Closer to the workings, we had to climb across a sheer face of marble with a river rushing forty feet below. This was the most dangerous part and we had to carry Amiga clinging on our shoulders. Once beyond this natural defense we were rewarded by an awesome view of hundreds of blocks of marble strewn as carelessly as cubes of sugar. Beyond were gaping rectangular caverns that fell dizzily into the depths of the mountainside. We ate a picnic sitting on a marble block as big as a mobile home, before starting the two hour walk back down.

We should have rested but there was a name on the map that appealed to us, Cardiff, and foolishly we pressed on. By the time we camped it was dark. We both had headaches, were utterly exhausted and climbed into sleeping bags instead of making up a real bed.

From the snow of the Rocky Mountains, unshaved and unlaundered, we descended into the urban oasis of Boulder. In Boulder we had a contact, a haven, where we could wash our hair, wash our clothes and even (maybe) wash the van.

Trudy Pomerantz's mother and Suzanne's mother had been the best of friends while growing up. We'd met Trudy only briefly for five minutes on the beach in Wilmington, North Carolina. At 10 a.m. in late October, we were knocking on her door. Her husband, Bernie, came and Suzanne tried to explain the slim connection. Bernie told us that Trudy's parents had both been killed yesterday, when their car plunged off a cliff in Yugoslavia.

We said we would go away. Please, forget it, we were sorry to disturb them. Our condolences sounded trivial and irrelevant and we started to say goodbye. Trudy appeared at the door and insisted we come inside. Swollen faced, she told us she and Bernie and their children had to fly to Philadelphia and would probably have to stay at least a week. We would be doing them a favor by housesitting while they were away.

We asked for a list of what we could do to help them out and while they were gone we painted, vacuumed, dug the garden, cleaned the windows and froze stews and curries made from their perishable food. For eight whole days we walked in their shoes, attended lectures on their calendar, even paying the fine on overdue library books. The housesitting turned into an important break and we got a lot of jobs done for ourselves.

We bathed every day, luxuriating in hot running water and the bliss of reading books and idly watching television. As well as working for our hosts, we took the van to the workshop, stocked up on supplies of food, stationery and hardware and one day made a complete assessment of what a trip like ours costs and needs. We bathed Amiga and washed every single thing we had in boiling, soapy water. At the end of three whole days, the van emerged, waxed, oiled and tuned up, its cleanest and brightest since the day we drove it from the shop.

☆

Denver has a Welsh Society with a fluctuating but currently optimistic record. A British Fair held in June, 1982, attracted 20,000 visitors, and 97 of them signed a guest list at the Welsh booth. Five ladies, Pat Max, Anne Evans, Jan Kenney, Jeanette Hunt and Margaret West, all in Welsh costume, gave the booth a strong visual impact and between them did a lot to revive Welsh interest in the state.

Anne Evans organized the exhibit and is the Society's correspondent. Born in Swansea, Anne and her husband, Keith, lived in Houston before moving to Colorado. Anne's arrival, combined with the organization and research skills of John Williams, brought the Colorado Welsh Society to a 1983 platform of expansion. At the Society's October 1982 meeting, 74 people were led by conductor Barry Roberts in what would be a successful cymanfa by anyone's standards.

On March 1st, 1983, Anne Evans and John Williams, with the assistance of Ken Jones, Peggy Brown, Robert Collins, Maryelizabeth Sefton and Barry and Jeanette Roberts, organized a St. David's dinner which was attended by 200 people.

On the foundation of the long defunct Denver Welsh Society, the present officers have built a successful Welsh organization. New member Elizabeth Corke, a folk song and folk dance enthusiast, wasted no time in making contact with the Denver folk dance community. Denver is the location of *Viltis*, an American magazine devoted to international folklore and folk dance. In 1978 Vyts Beliajus, founder and editor of *Viltis*, invited Mr. Alexander Hamilton of Baltimore to produce a March/April *"Gobaith"* issue devoted to Welsh Folk Dancing.

5

Southwest: Utah and Arizona

The National Parks of Utah and Arizona are on the world's international van route, from London, Hamburg and Copenhagen to Montreal then to Alaska and down, following fall through the Rockies to Mexico and the whole of South America.

Utah has more national parks than any other state. The parks are huge. Forty mile drives to a picnic table were not unusual. We soon discovered that most visitors refused to leave their cars and we were constantly amazed by the number of people who did not take the hikes. We usually had the whole trail to ourselves.

Arches lives up to its name with more giant femurs and gelatine sandstone webs stretched across the sky than any other place on earth. The final approach to Delicate Arch along an unearthly ledge is especially awesome in the dawn or moonlit hours.

At Arches we celebrated Halloween with a plastic pumpkin, hot apple cider, popcorn and candy bars. We made masks from supermarket bags and ducked for apples in our aluminum basin.

At Canyonlands after having driven thousands of miles to the heart of the continent we had to get out and experience the park in detail. We hiked to The Joint, a 200 yard suture between two folds of rock. To get there we wound the van along a rocky trail, loaded ourselves with a weighty gallon of water, sandwiches, a map, and set off.

We were the only ones out in the backcountry and had Chesler Park all to ourselves. Nearer The Joint were two men with overnight backpacks, but having worked so hard to get away from "it all", they also walked away from us. Once through the long cool gully of The Joint, we met another couple. They were Swiss and calmly spent three or four minutes exchanging trivial information about the time, the scenery, the trail ahead and so on. The walk took all day long; it wasn't the destination that remained the memorable part, but the accumulated visual, atmospheric data of the desert.

From Canyonlands, we continued our tour of the purple planet. So far we'd met few Americans and even fewer Utah natives. Rangers were usually from other states and our companions at the parks were Swiss, German, English and Australian, all in outfitted vans with their equipment spilling in profusion over every picnic table in sight.

The towns between Blandings and Hanksville were native, genuine and overlooked. They had the hermit's hospitality, at first gregarious but then relieved when we didn't stay too long. At the west end of Hanksville on the north side of the road is a rock shop packed with pottery, dinosaur bones, artifacts, Anasazi shards, semi-precious stones and turquoise at inexpensive prices.

Bryce Canyon has a concentration of what Canyonlands spreads over 5,000 square miles. Once again we walked our legs to jelly. One trail fueled us with energy for another and every night we returned to the international camp too tired to talk and barely able to cook rice and miso soup and then to boil a cocoa nightcap before climbing into bed.

Our last day at Bryce it snowed and the canyon filled with sleet and mist. The Swiss and Germans strapped firewood and kayaks to their vans. We buckled on our bike and picnic chairs and drove to Zion. The weather was deteriorating badly. At Zion we were, however, able to harvest a gallon of pecans from the grass around the trees. Roasted pecans and a hot drink gave the cold damp days a little cheer.

We thought that if we continued driving south the weather would improve. But northern Arizona and New Mexico can be as wintry and bleak as Wales, and this portion of our tour was a challenge to our determination.

The promise of color was always an attraction and we visited Coral Pink Sand Dunes. Long and as languid as heavy folds of silk, the dunes were a vivid salmon pink beneath the silver nitrate of a wintry sky.

Vermilion Cliffs towered over us and in our microscopic van we felt like an ivory waterbug darting beneath the reef of a dehydrated ocean. The scale was geological and vast, a hundred miles of the Colorado Plateau crumbling inch by inch while we, with our heartbeats and four cylinder van, zipped busily along. We were soon in Arizona and drove 20 miles to camp in the yard of a Navajo gas station.

The Navajo reservation is larger than Wales, larger than El Salvador, Belgium or Israel. The dust storms and droughts of Navajoland are as suited to the Navajo people as mists and drizzles are to the Welsh. Even today, apart from tourist shops and enclaves of uranium miners, few non-Navajos live in Navajoland.

The largest settlement is at Grand Canyon where provisions for over half a million tourists are as awesome as the gaping chasm viewed from the safety of an enormous concave window. The banks, lodges, churches, motels, post office, dentists, drugstores, barber shops, pizza parlors, pet kennels, service stations, beauty parlors, fast food stands, magistrates' chambers and stables for over a thousand horses and mules, add up to one of the largest cities in Arizona.

This was the last chance for visitors to see the Canyon and winter was doggedly at our heels. Another blizzard warning came and we retreated fifty-six miles down to Moenkopi. From Moenkopi we heard that all Grand Canyon approaches had been closed and that visitors would be trapped until the storm had cleared.

By tuning our radio to Navajo programs we intensified the sensation of being in another land. Listening to Navajo hymns on the Christian radio station increased the feeling that we were foreigners trying to adjust to an alien environment. Tuba City is a large Navajo town and the modern supermarket here supplies everything the community needs. No one spoke to us unless we spoke first. But no one was unfriendly and when they spoke, people were concise and to the point.

We followed Route 264 through the Navajo-Hopi joint use area and left the reservation at the "Navajo Capital" of Window Rock. The longer we stayed the more we saw how impoverished the people were. Bulletin boards gave warnings of the plague and villages were already inaccessible because of mud. In Jedito our drinking water froze and we were only able to leave our camp because the mud was frozen firm enough to give our wheels a grip. Finally, we were glad to pick up Interstate 40 and drive to Albuquerque.

After washing the van from a pump at a roadside halt we returned to Albuquerque where we treated ourselves to a feast at Pancake House. The sweet and sickly combination of eggs, pancakes, syrup and coffee was exactly what we needed and we ordered double of the special breakfast each. Our "vacation" at Trudy and Bernie's seemed like years ago and we felt as though our bodies were as cracked and fossilized as the primitive landscape where we'd recently spent so much of our time.

North of Albuquerque on Route 4, we knew of a natural outdoor hot spring. Well known to cross country skiers, wild, open air, hot springs punctuate the Rocky Mountains, with temperatures varying from as cool as 80 degrees to the pressurized steams of Yellowstone.

When Zen master Jōshū Sasaki Roshi was building his rural Zen retreat, he located it at Jemez Springs on property abundantly supplied with healing springs and pools. The hot pool we were looking for was north of Jemez Springs. Our directions were to find a pile of winter gravel, scramble down the river bank, cross a fallen tree trunk and climb up the other side. Three hundred yards up the muddy mountain slope, with an impressive view of snowy peaks, we found an oval pool of hot, dark water fed by an algae decorated spring, bubbling out of the ground at 100 degrees Fahrenheit.

It snowed while we bathed. We bathed, cooled in the chilly air, relaxed and bathed again, before driving via the Zen Center to our campsite at Coronado State Monument.

Many of the roads we had just traveled on were already blocked by snow. Thanksgiving was coming up and we had an appointment in Phoenix, Arizona.

Phoenix has maintained a continuous, if slender, Welsh presence since architect Frank Lloyd Wright established Taliesin West in nearby Scottsdale in 1937. Unmistakably proud of his Welsh roots, Frank Lloyd Wright combined the Welsh love of hearth and home with an American respect for environmental freedom and space. Frank Lloyd Wright's mother, Anna, was born in Llandysul and his strong Welsh childhood in Wisconsin is described by his sister, Maginel Wright Barney, in her book *The Valley of the God Almighty Joneses*.

The Welsh community of Arizona, located in the Sun City and Phoenix area, consists mainly of retirees from northern and eastern states. Thomas L. Thomas, the Welsh baritone from Maesteg, made Scottsdale his final home and died there in 1983. Thomas L. Thomas's father was a professional flautist and his brother David, was a Broadway actor who appeared in many New York musicals.

During the late 1970's, Irene Johnson formed the Welsh Club of Sun City, Arizona. Thanks to John Davies, Marion Ehrhardt and Dan and Joan Griffiths, the Welsh Club of Sun City has become a stable, competent organization. In 1982, members hosted twenty-four visitors from the Welsh Lawn Bowlers Association. Today, the Sun City Welsh Club has over forty members and can rely on over one hundred people of Welsh background to attend Welsh events. John Davies has taught Welsh and Tom and Emily Williams have been reliable soloists.

Meetings are held the second Thursday of each month from January through April and October through December at the Sun City room of Menke Funeral Parlor, always featuring a planned program, community singing or a guest speaker. The Club, led by Eileen Williams, President; Edie Steving, Vice-President and other officers, Lloyd Rogers, Haydn Jones, John Davies and Gilbert Evans, manages an excellent calendar. At the 1985 St. David's Day banquet in Sun City, over one hundred people were present. Elinore Hurd led choral singing with Mary Smith accompanist. Under the direction of Elinore Hurd, the Club has formed a choir which entertains at meetings. The Welsh Club of Sun City burns a bright Welsh flame and is as anxious as any Welsh American group to be part of a network of touring Welsh resources.

☆

Phoenix is the home of The Annwn Temple of Gwynfyd, a circle of "hereditary Welsh pagans." In America and Britain, during the 1960's there was a revival of interest in the various forms of witchcraft. By the 1970's, students of the occult had divided into witches, pagans, neo-pagans and many other subdivisions. Two members of the "Parent Kindred of the Old Religion" in Wales brought Hereditary Welsh Paganism to the United States in the early 1960's. Today, Welsh Pagans can be found in Georgia, Wisconsin, Minnesota, Michigan, California and West Virginia. Welsh pagans form circles with names like The Cauldron, Forever Forests and Y Tylwyth Teg. Members take symbolic "Welsh" names like Lord Myrddin Pendevig, Lady Gleannon or Gwyddion, Tirion and Siani. Welsh pagans in America also use the Welsh language in their rituals since they associate modern Welsh with the pre-Roman language of the Druids.

Welsh Pagans like other practitioners of witchcraft and paganism are basically followers of an "earth" religion. Their festivals and rituals follow traditional harvests and equinoxes and their emphasis is on peaceful ecological harmony and worship of the Earth Mother. Pagans form small, intimate groups, willing to explain their position but naturally fearful of ridicule and prejudice.

There is not a lot of material available on Welsh or Celtic paganism in America, but Ruddlwm Gawr in Georgia has written some guides and the Annwn Temple of Gwynfyd in Phoenix publishes *The Bard*. Chapter headings in *The Bard*—Swyn (magic), Trioedd (triads), Dewiniaeth (divination), Blas ar Gymru (a taste of Wales) and Gofyniadau/Atebion (questions and answers). With its Welsh language triplets, lessons and dragon decorations, *The Bard* and the works of Ruddlwm Gawr are probably the most unusual Welsh publications in North America.

☆

We crossed into California and Pacific Time at Quartzite, where in the 1880's, the U.S. Army abandoned its attempt to work with camels in the North American desert. The camels adapted well to their new environment but caused such alarm that their deployment was abandoned. The camels were eventually liberated and until the 1940's could be seen wandering in the Kofa Wildlife Refuge.

These were our last desert days and we spent them in the company of ecstatic Joshua trees.

Anza Borrego State Park was our final camping ground before reaching the Pacific. After 106 days traveling, our well-planned timetable was only four days out and we shared them with the peaceful scorpions, coyotes and tarantulas until we drove to San Diego.

Anza Borrego was our final interlude of privacy before the course of our trip was permanently changed in California. We even retreated here, when the apocalyptic madness of Los Angeles became too much for us.

From our camp, we could see the blue and darkened peaks of the Vallecito Mountains. We left Anza Borrego wearing summer shorts and T-shirts. Very soon, climbing the steep approach to Julian, we had to put on almost everything we owned. With the sun still shining on the Laguda Salada basin, at six and a half thousand feet, we were caught in driving snow. At sea level, we were in the sunshine once again. From a bend in the road, between the whitewashed walls of Southern California homes, we caught a first, faint glimpse of the Pacific and knew that we'd arrived.

6

Southern California

West coast Welsh societies, from San Diego to Vancouver, have large numbers of first generation Welsh people. It wasn't unusual for us to find ourselves at parties where Suzanne was the only American there. Among enthusiastic West Coast Welsh learners in San Francisco and Seattle, we felt like foreigners and had to adjust quickly to the keen Welsh atmosphere. As distant as they are from traditional Welsh settlements of the east, West Coast Welsh societies work hard to maintain a Welsh identity. They do this through Welsh courses, frequent visits by Welsh choirs, well attended nosweithiau llawen, some of the finest Welsh American newsletters and through the work of committed individuals.

The San Diego Cambrian Society was founded in 1892 by Mr. George Holmes. Mr. Holmes was later made a bard at the San Francisco Eisteddfod, not for the usual reason of having submitted an outstanding poem, prose piece or song, but solely in consideration of years of devotion to the Welsh. In 1984 over one hundred guests attended the Society's 92nd St. David's Day Banquet.

In 1912, Ben Haddock, the son of a Welsh Baptist minister, moved to San Diego from Maryland. In 1916, when Ben married George Holmes' daughter Edith, the San Diego Cambrian Society was given the solid rock that has held it together for over seventy-five years. Ben Haddock has worked for the Welsh American community all his life, serving for many years as a trustee and once as honorary president of the Welsh National Cymanfa Ganu Association. Ben and Edith Haddock were among the first to write for and distribute *Ninnau*. Having written articles for *The Druid* and *Y Drych* they realized the importance of this reliable new paper. Increased sales of *Ninnau* to the Welsh of San Diego became one of the factors in holding the loose-knit Cambrian Society together.

One of the most generous patrons of the San Diego Cambrian Society was Mr. Edgar H. Davies, a wealthy and prominent local businessman. Because of Edgar Davies' gifts to the Society, membership dues were never required. No dues are taken today and the Society still relies on members' voluntary contributions. Edgar Davies sponsored repeated visits to the United States by The Mountain Ash Male Choir, and when the oldest surviving Welsh church in America, the First Baptist Church in Swansea, Massachusetts celebrated its 300th birthday in 1963, Edgar Davies paid for the engraved commemorative tablet. When Mr. Davies died in 1978, the Welsh American community lost one of its most modest and genuine philanthropists.

The San Diego Cambrian Society holds four annual events with informal "get togethers" in between. For St. David's Day, the Society hosts a luncheon on the Saturday closest to March 1st and on March 1st, the Society holds a service at St. David's Episcopalian Church. St. David's Church in San Diego has a cornerstone from St. David's Cathedral in Wales, and like all Episcopal churches in Canada and the United States, holds commemorative services on St. David's Day. On March 1, 1984, a prayer written by the Bishops of Wales was read at Anglican and Episcopal churches throughout the world. The prayer was for an increase in bilingual clergy in Wales.

From 1950 to 1970 the Cambrian Society held its annual picnic on the avocado ranch of Daniel and Virginia Reese. Beginning in 1970, Mrs. Mary Happe occasionally hosted the picnic until attendance reached over a hundred and it became unmanageable. Since 1979, the picnic has been held at the recreation area of Coronado Shores.

The San Diego Cambrian Society does not hold a cymanfa of its own. Some members belong to the Welsh Church in Los Angeles and drive there twice a year to attend spring and fall cymanfaoedd canu. The Society's only other organized meeting is a Christmas Party which features refreshments, community singing led by Jeff Watkins, and entertainment such as a fund-raising auction or even conjuring and magic tricks by President, Tom Owens.

While Cambrian Society meetings have been informal and unadvertised, support for Welsh events remains strong. In 1979, a large contingent traveled from San Diego to the National Cymanfa in Vancouver. In 1984, the Cambrian Society sent another large group to the National Cymanfa in Portland, Oregon.

One other point of interest among the Welsh in San Diego is the Bardic Chair of the Reverend Watkin Joseph. The chair was won at the 1878 Conway National Eisteddfod and the Reverend Watkin Joseph subsequently became minister of the Congregational Church in Scranton, Pennsylvania. The chair passed to Watkin Joseph's son, Howell, and from him to his daughter, Mrs. Robert Whiting, who now lives in San Diego.

Since 1979, the San Diego Cambrian Society has been going through a period of change. The 1984 committee, made up of Tom Owens, President; Jeff Watkins, Vice-President; Dilys Hall, Secretary; Marian Spahn, Treasurer and Virginia Reese, Historian, has done a lot to publicize the Society and make the annual agenda appealing to a curious public. The main sense of a new direction is being provided by Glyn Long and the new Welsh Choral Society of San Diego. Glyn Long moved to San Diego from Cincinnati, Ohio in 1982. In cooperation with the successful, if elderly Cambrian Society, he advertised the new Choral Society and it was formally launched at the House of England Club in April 1984. The Welsh Choral Society immediately attracted a strong male section, including an enthusiastic corps of tenors. In March 1985, Glyn Long and the Welsh Choral Society of San Diego, directed by Claire Murphy, launched the House of Wales in Balboa Park. The inaugural concert was attended by over 100 people. Today, the Cambrian Society and the House of Wales work side by side, between them offering weekly and monthly Welsh singing rehearsals and an annual agenda of San Diego Welsh events.

☆

We spent Christmas on a Christmas tree ranch with Bob and Jean Small, just east of Los Angeles. We knew Bob and Jean through the community of Ittoen in Kyoto, Japan. Founded by Tenko Nishida in 1920, Ittoen is a member of the World Conference of Religions and has a network of friends throughout the world. Jean Small, through her work with Japanese Americans, had also visited Ittoen and she was the first of several "Friends of Light" we were to meet while traveling.

The Christmas tree season was almost over, but there were still many ways that we could help. Bob and Jean grew every kind of fruit. In spring, the Sunkist crews come to take the crop of their citrus orchard. We pickled bushels of olives, dark and bitter straight off the trees, and every morning we gathered fresh grapefruit sitting ripely on the ground. It was hard for us to leave the Smalls, but we planned to spend our winter in Los Angeles with Japanese friends and we wanted to arrive there in time for New Year's Day.

The people with whom we stayed in Little Tokyo spoke very little English, and with Japanese television, magazines and visitors, we found ourselves in an almost totally Japanese environment.

One Family, Inc. was founded by philosophy professor, Mr. Kozo Itabashi, a former student at Ittoen. At the age of eighty-nine, Mr. Itabashi opened his home to other elderly people and is head of a small group of unrelated individuals.

The program at One Family was anarchic, but sincere. Every morning we sang the Hannyashingyo, a well-known Buddhist chant as familiar as the twenty-third psalm would be to Christians. At every meal we tried to say a simple grace together. Food lay at the heart of everything. Mrs. Itabashi treated everyone as a guest and for her guests, her husband included, she cooked mountains of rice, pans of fish, gallons of soup and fried dozens of eggs. Meanwhile, Mr. Itabashi, a supremely tolerant nonagenarian, who could not have weighed a hundred pounds, held informal seminars and tutorials with students who were interested in his work.

This Dickensian environment was our base of operations for one of the most amazing cities in America. Between our chores of gardening, driving, window cleaning and street cleaning, we did find time to explore Los Angeles and to discover a little about Welsh life there.

☆

There are several agencies in Los Angeles that have kept Wales and Welsh

34

people in the public eye. In September 1980, Welsh boxing made tragic headlines when Johnny Owen, British Bantamweight Champion from Merthyr Tydfil, fought Guadalupe Pintar of Mexico. Pintar knocked Owen out in the 12th round and the Welsh fighter entered a forty-five day coma until his death on November 2nd. This put the spotlight on South Wales boxing, a valleys tradition that has in the past produced such greats as Tommy Farr, Jimmy Wilde, Freddy Welsh, Jim Driscoll, Freddy Landeg and Howard Winstone. The latest great Welsh boxer, Colin Jones of Gorseinon, knocked out his American opponent Allan Braswell in March of 1984. Critics of the Owen-Pintar fight argue that the outclassed Owen should never have been allowed to step inside the ring. During the seven weeks that Johnny Owen lay in the Los Angeles hospital, over $125,000 was raised in Wales, money that on the boxer's death was donated to the Prince of Wales Hospital in Merthyr Tydfil.

Santa Monica is the American headquarters for the sport of darts. The Southern California Darting Association (SCDA) is the largest darts organization in the United States. Every August, west coast tournaments generate over $50,000 in total prize money. Darts is a big international game and several Welsh players are on the professional international circuit. John E. Smith, one of the directors of the SCDA is Welsh, and two top Welsh players, Alun Evans and Ceri Morgan, play regularly in the regional American championships. One of the greatest dart players is Leighton Rees of Pontypridd, whose impressive record includes the unbeaten scores of 3001 with 81 darts and 501 with 10 darts. At the peak of his career in the late 1970's, Leighton Rees held over 20 championship titles, including the Cleveland Open and San Francisco Fours. Every year Leighton Rees tours on the American circuit, participating in exhibition challenge matches.

Another Pontypridd man who is a life member of the Southern California Darting Association is Thomas Woodward, better known professionally as Tom Jones.

Of all the Welsh celebrities today, Tom Jones, with his regular concert tours and television appearances, keeps the name of Wales in the American public eye. There are over eighty Tom Jones fan clubs in the United States collecting memorabilia, attending concerts and buying records. In many Tom Jones fan clubs enthusiasm for the singer has led some fans to Wales to visit the country that their idol grew up in.

In 1983 Tom Jones went home to a full scale family reunion. Tom Jones' return to the Rhondda Valley was marked by his recording of the song "Come Home Rhondda Boy", and is reminiscent of Sir Stanley Baker's periodic

35

returns to Maerdy, where he would spend whole afternoons in the Working Men's Club with former friends.

Important as the public image is, there are many who argue that Tom Jones is not a "Welsh singer" and that Dylan Thomas is not a "Welsh Poet". For them, Dafydd Iwan and Meredydd Evans are true Welsh singers. Welsh poets are Gwenallt, Euros Bowen and Bobi Jones, writers and singers whose undying loyalty is to a Welshness inseparable from the language.

☆

The first Welsh congregation in Los Angeles was formed in 1888. Today the Welsh Presbyterian Church is located in a predominantly Mexican neighborhood, at the corner of 12th and Valencia Streets. The building which the Welsh took over in 1926 was formerly a synagogue, and the Star of David can be seen in the building's stained glass windows. Every Sunday two hymns are sung in Welsh. The last Sunday of each month is Welsh Emphasis Day, and all hymns and some readings are in Welsh. Two cymanfaoedd canu are held a year, one in May and one in December. The Los Angeles cymanfaoedd canu inspire such loyalty that people come from as far away as Arizona and New Mexico. An important part of weekly services is the te bach and social hour that follows. With many driving over fifty miles to attend, meetings and discussions during the social hour take on an added importance. In the 1950's and 1960's, while cymanfa attendance was high, weekly figures were low. In 1966 Haydn Stephens launched a membership campaign from which the church has never looked back. In 1969, *Mosaics*, the Welsh newsletter, was launched. In 1973 the late Dr. Thomas Megahey was appointed minister, and in 1977 the church was guaranteed a future when it was declared a Historical-Cultural Monument by the Los Angeles City Council.

In the 1940's, the Los Angeles Welsh Church Choir recorded background music for the movie, "How Green Was My Valley", and several church members had parts in the film. In the 1970's, a Welsh-costumed choir, under the direction of E. Gwyn Thomas, sang at numerous engagements, among them a performance before the Prince of Wales during an American visit.

In Los Angeles, the Ladies Aid Society consistently promotes activities that give the Welsh community its solid base. Led principally by Gwen Jones, Melba Bill, Ada Rigby, Evelyn Hughes, Myra Simon, Barbara Davies, Nancy Thomas, Helen Thomas, Peggy Williams, Helen Graham and Harriette Warnick, the Ladies Aid Society organizes the 200 plus annual St. David's dinner. They have also produced and marketed a cassette recording of the 1983 Los Angeles Cymanfa Ganu with proceeds going to the Church.

In addition to the Ladies Aid Society, there is a Welsh American Society led by Don Davies. The Welsh American Society meets the second Saturday of each month at 7:30 p.m. at the Alamitos Bay Sports Club, 1933 Temple Avenue, Signal Hill. Time is spent playing whist and bingo, with singing and some refreshments.

The present Welsh Church congregation has no shortage of participants for a noson lawen or willing helpers for choral visits and cymanfaoedd canu. Parti Ceredigion were hosted in 1982. E. Gwyn Thomas is their regular *Y Drych* and *Yr Enfys* correspondent. E. Trevor Thomas is the official accompanist with Stanley Hughes playing also. George Powell is an impressive Welsh singing soloist. Other soloists are Gwyneth Bealer and Laurel Lee James, a St. David's Society of the State of New York scholarship winner, who has also sung for the San Diego and Los Angeles opera companies. Gwladys Wynne Jones, Hugh Howells and Mari Jones Hudson are musical directors. Terry James, director of the mammoth "A Nation Sings" festival at the Royal Albert Hall, while working in Hollywood, was often a guest conductor at the Church.

The Los Angeles Welsh congregation includes several authors, among them Frank Manley from Cefn Mawr, who has written the adventure-filled "A Veterinary Odyssey". Myra Lawrence writes the monthly *Y Drych* cross-word, a contribution that sends learners and speakers alike thumbing through their dictionaries. Samuel Jones, editor of *Mosaics*, produces one of the most readable and comprehensive newsletters of any Welsh American organization. Clerk of sessions, entertainer and master of ceremonies Haydn Stephens' second novel, *Dafydd*, is a fine contribution to Welsh American literature.

Another writer is Dora Polk, formerly of Pontnewydd, Gwent, currently a professor of English at California State University, Long Beach. Dora's book, an anthology of Welsh literature, titled *A Book Called Hiraeth*, provides a good introduction to Welsh language writing in translation. The selection of material is unified by the peculiar Welsh sentiment of "hiraeth" or "longing", which is emotional and intangible, but at the same time spiritually sharp and often agonizing.

In 1981 Neil Sandburg, professor of Sociology at Loyola-Marymount University in Los Angeles, published "*Identity and Assimilation, The Welsh-English Dichotomy—A Case Study*". Professor Sandburg was in England in 1972 doing research on English New Towns. On the radio he heard that Welsh language protestors were "sitting-in" at the BBC. Until then he knew very little about Wales, least of all that there was a Welsh language movement. News of that particular protest led eventually to Neil Sandburg's residence in Wales and his authorship of a 140-page book on the Welsh national condition. Professor Sandburg's data and analysis are an attempt at a sociological evaluation of the values, conflicts and loyalties of Welsh people today.

In Hollywood, California, Marjorie Tayloe has for over twenty-five years been a proud representative of Welsh musical traditions. She plays the Welsh triple harp. Marjorie Tayloe's love of the Welsh harp began during a visit to Wales in 1960. After days of traveling in the pouring rain with a backpack and a small harp, she finally arrived at the Llangollen International Eisteddfod. Having no ticket she couldn't get in, but she was so persistent that she managed to view the performance from the side of the stage. Later, after a long day of tramping the muddy eisteddfod field, Marjorie made contact with triple-harpist, Edith Evans, who after much persuasion, took her to see Nansi Richards. Marjorie spent several days with Nansi Richards, making tape recordings of the instructions the harpist gave her. In America, as well as playing professionally for the Hollywood Wilshire and Metropolitan Symphony orchestras, Marjorie has played at the Welsh Presbyterian church countless times.

☆

On February 17th, 1983, we left Los Angeles. Shortly before departure, Masami Hanashiro, the maid at One Family, asked for a lift to Vancouver, British Columbia. She didn't mind our leisurely place and agreed to meet us six weeks later in San Francisco where Suzanne had arranged three weeks work with nutritionist William Shurtleff at The Soyfoods Center in Lafayette.

Along the Southern California coast we were caught in a series of Pacific typhoons. It rained so hard and for so long that the fiber interior of our roof molded over in purple spots, a decoration we couldn't remove despite hours of scrubbing with soap and bleach.

In Santa Barbara we stopped over with Susie and Ron Wilde. It was late winter and their yard was filled with an orchard of ripe lemon trees. One evening we organized the kitchen for the mass production of lemon curd. This simple and delicious Welsh preserve used up the lemons as well as leaving several jars for us to take along.

Just north of Hearst Castle at Cape San Martin, the road was closed to traffic. From Malibu to Big Sur whole sections of the shoreline had been washed away, destroying millionaires' homes and toppling the giant redwood trees.

We were making a turn at Plaskett Creek, following a sandy rutted track along the edge. We had a choice of driving through the thick scrub or going through a pool of deep and muddy water. Trying to steer a middle course, we had to swerve to avoid a particularly deep and treacherous looking ditch. This sudden maneuver took us skidding to within a foot of the subsidence-liable cliff, so close, that in the passenger seat I was silenced with a gasping and breathless view of the crashing surf below. Once out of danger we walked back and saw that the cliff was hollow where we just were. With over 1000 pounds on it, that portion of the coast could have peeled away as easily as sand from a spade, dropping us and everything we owned onto the kelp-covered rocks.

Despite our shock, our relief was greater and we camped there for the night. The biggest typhoon of the season hit when we were between Big Sur and Carmel. After sitting it out for eighteen hours, we put southern California behind us and headed resolutely, if not more than a little damp and disappointed, for San Francisco.

7

San Francisco: the Turning Point

Tofu is a soybean food with one of the highest and most digestible protein contents known. High in calcium, rich in proteins, low in calories, low in fats and with zero cholesterol, tofu is inexpensive and is easily used in traditional American recipes. For us, living in the van, tofu was the perfect food. It kept well, we could find it in most towns, and it required very little time to cook in the simple but nourishing meals we prepared on our two burner stove.

The Book of Tofu was written by William Shurtleff and Akiko Aoyagi in 1975. Since then, Bill and Akiko founded the Soyfoods Center, the main agency promoting soyfoods, encouraging the establishment of tofu shops and soy dairies, and the use of tofu and tempeh in American restaurants.

When we were planning the trip, Suzanne wrote a letter to the Soyfoods Center asking Bill and Akiko if we could visit them and help in their work. We ended up working in the Soyfoods Center ten hours a day, for three weeks. Three weeks that became the most formative and influential of the trip.

Life at the Soyfoods Center maintained a devout, almost monastic calm. Bill worked for two and a half years at the Tassajara Zen Monastery and he and Akiko have the rare ability to complete an incredible amount of work with minimal fluster and zero stress. The Soyfoods Center day began an hour before dawn with meditation and exercise. Following breakfast, we each worked through a program of assignments. Increasingly, Bill finds that he is in demand as a lecturer and soyfood business consultant. It was in his capacity as a small business advisor that he started asking us what we planned to do when the trip was over. A legitimate question that we'd started asking ourselves. To answer it we began telling Bill and Akiko more and more about Wales.

It was through answering Bill's questions and describing Wales to him that the direction of the trip formed more clearly in our minds. We could feel our sense of purpose coincide with the exciting discoveries we were making about Welsh American life.

I was able to tell Bill a little about Plaid Cymru, The Urdd, Merched Y Wawr, The National Eisteddfod, Mudiad Ysgolion Meithrin and Cymdeithas yr Iaith Gymraeg. I also described the work of the Welsh Arts Council, The Welsh Academy of Writers, Oriel Bookstore in Cardiff, The Welsh Film Board, The Welsh Contemporary Music Center and the recent florescence of hundreds of Welsh craft and gift shops. In 1984 in Canada and the United States, there were over thirty Welsh import businesses. Since 1975, *Ninnau*, *Y Drych*, Cymdeithas Madog, Welsh Heritage Week, The Welsh Harp Society and the Welsh American Foundation have all increased their contacts with Wales. We began to feel as though Welsh American involvement held a great deal of promise for us. Our contact with the Welsh in San Francisco reinforced that feeling and set the pattern for our remaining nine months on the road.

☆

In San Francisco in 1984, seven separate St. David's Day celebrations were held. Each group of friends, as well as being members of the Welsh American Society of Northern California (WASNC) belongs to a more informal local circle. For St. David's Day, Cylch San Jose held a potluck dinner. In Danville, two invitation brunches marked the day, while in San Francisco, a more formal, sit-down dinner with entertainment was organized. Other festivities were held by Marin County Cylch and Cylch Cymraeg Sacramento.

In May 1982, shortly before our trip, I wrote an article for *Ninnau* about a visit Suzanne and I had made to Wales. The article prompted a reply from Stan and Margaret Williams in Concord, California. Stan turned out to be my maternal grandfather's cousin with whom we had a great, great aunt in common. We started a friendly correspondence which led to our meeting many times during our stay in the San Francisco area.

Stan and Margaret were members of the WASNC and when Côr y Brythoniaid visited San Francisco in 1980, Stan, Margaret, Stan's sister Margaret and her husband Edwin hosted the choir to a party at their home.

Our first meeting was cancelled. Stan and Margaret had been invited, along with many other Welsh people, to a public reception for Queen Elizabeth and Prince Philip. A week later, we drove with them to a Welsh American Society of Northern California recording session in a back street studio of San Francisco. The Williams' and Rowlands' had received postcards from John Nichols, treasurer of the Welsh Heritage Fund of Northern California, inviting them to a "taping session". We were to meet at 300 Brennan Street at 10:30. That was all we knew. What the "taping session" was was as much a mystery to them as it was to us.

Three hundred Brennan Street was an old brick tenement and we were the first to arrive. There was no sign on any of the doors and no sign of a recording studio. Around 11 a.m., Bob Davies, from San Jose, arrived and we were a group of about ten, shivering and wondering how much longer we would have to wait. Connie Thomson, President of the WASNC, arrived at 11:30 and we learned that the taping session was to be a recording made of the famous Welsh hymns. Only when Idris Evans arrived did a concerted search for the recording studio begin. We found the studio and John Nichols after taking a freight elevator to the sixth floor, where we'd been told a studio might be located.

By now it was noon; we were a group of about twenty-four, the largest meeting of Welsh people in America that we had encountered. We were taken up in their spontaneous sense of humor and willingness. It was the group's patience and cooperation that saved a day which became, in truth, a total fiasco and waste of money. The intention to produce an educational Welsh language singing tape had been discussed as early as 1975, and was publicized again in December of 1982. The original idea was to make individual tapes for bass, alto, tenor and soprano; each tape featuring an announcement and reading of the hymn, then the first verse and chorus by each part, finally repeated by the whole choir.

It was a good idea, but no hymns had been chosen ahead of time and it took another thirty minutes to agree on a selection. The studio which specialized in punk rock bands wasn't ready and no one knew that the piano track had to be recorded first. It was another hour before we divided into parts and the first words were actually sung. While the unrehearsed piano line was being played, the bemused and hungry choir ate tacos and hamburgers beneath posters of punk rock groups.

The recording attempt, financed by the Welsh American Foundation and the Welsh Heritage Fund of Northern California, ended up costing over $1,000. There had been no rehearsals and no attempt to round up the best singers of the Welsh community. The tape turned out disastrously, the furthest thing from an educational performance imaginable.

That Saturday turned out to be an expensive day of fun. John Ward and some of his language class turned up to swell our numbers but they couldn't read the words. For us the best part of the day was when Bob Davies burst into a spontaneous rendition of Ton y Botel, while waiting on the cold concrete warehouse stairs.

Contact, however, had been made, and during our visits to Stan and Margaret we began reading *Y Drych*. The first class features and photographs of this excellent publication were a revelation to us. We wondered how many other Welsh American publications and organizations were unknown to members of Welsh societies and to interested people in Wales. From that day on, having *Y Drych* as a resource more than doubled our connections with the Welsh American world.

While in San Francisco, we also discovered *Yr Enfys* (The Rainbow), the international periodical that has been serving Welsh people overseas since 1949. *Yr Enfys*, which appears four times a year, is the publication of "Undeb Y Cymry Ar Wasgar", or Wales International. As the only international Welsh periodical, we were surprised that *Yr Enfys* wasn't better known.

☆

Up until the second World War, San Francisco was a scene of consistent Welsh activity. Eisteddfodau were held regularly, one of the largest being at the San Francisco World's Fair in 1939. In those days there was a Welsh Presbyterian Church at the corner of Eighteenth and Castro Streets in Oakland, while in San Francisco, the Welsh church was on Fourteenth Street.

Both closed because of dwindling congregations. Today the main link with those Welsh churches of the past is through the congregation of Calvary Presbyterian at Jackson and Fillmore. The 1982 San Francisco regional cymanfa ganu was held at Calvary, as were several before it.

In February 1969, the Welsh American Society of Northern California had dwindled to a membership of three with a sum of only $15.00 in its treasury. It is largely due to the administrative talents of Donna Davies and the writing ability of Jayne Pryddarch (who became editor of the newsletter), that the WASNC has recovered to the extent it has today. Donna continues to play an active role in Welsh affairs and is still the *Y Drych* newspaper correspondent. She also contributes a monthly article on Wales and the Welsh for the 28 page *British Observer* published in San Francisco. Today the Welsh American Society of Northern California has a large membership and is the focal point of Welsh activities in the region. The Society has a healthy four-figure bank balance and a subscription list of several hundred to its newsletters. WASNC members also finance The Welsh Heritage Fund of Northern California, which more specifically sponsors Welsh American cultural events. The Welsh Heritage Fund has a selection of Welsh logo stationery and other Welsh theme souvenirs available on request.

The San Francisco Welsh community is led by individuals who comprehend Welsh American activity on a national scale. One of these is John Nichols. John has been a supporter of *Ninnau* since the beginning, and through his column, "Lean Trimmings", contributes some of the paper's most lively and readable articles. With the assistance of Professor Edward Hartmann in Boston, John Nichols has compiled a map of every Welsh church that ever stood in the United States. This compilation took over four years and could only have been attempted in the present climate of Welsh American recovery. John was working on the map when we were in San Francisco. By the National Cymanfa of 1983 the map was ready and Arturo Roberts, of *Ninnau*, started looking for a publisher.

Thanks mainly to the efforts of John Ward of Sacramento, WASNC members can attend Welsh classes on a regular basis. We attended two of a series of Welsh classes that John was teaching at the Embarcadero Pier office of Rees Williams. These excellent Saturday morning classes have now been attended by several dozen people, and are one of the main factors keeping the San Francisco Welsh scene young, informed and enthusiastic.

JoAnne Lohse is the leader of The Welsh Folk Dance Circle. JoAnne is an indispensable organizer, whether it's arranging the annual Christmas Party and Mari Lwyd or getting the Gweithdy Dawns Gwerin to and from rehearsals and performances.

Noson lawen style parties are a regular feature of the large and fluid San Francisco Welsh scene, and visitors to the city should expand their repertoire of jokes, songs and recitations. There is a range of enthusiastic talent from the soprano of Barbara Daley Harris (who as well as editing *Pethau Cymreig* with her husband, Phillip, is also a soloist for the San Jose Opera Company) to the close harmonies of Cantorion Bro Sacramento and the folk group Côr y Ddraig Goch. Other stalwarts are Gwladys Jones, Idris Evans and Bob Davies, a resonant bass with a magical talent for penillion singing.

1983 was a very good year for the Welsh in the San Francisco area. The Cwmbran Male Choir visited in September and the Society took part in the ethnic heritage festival, Black Diamond Days. Mt. Diablo was an area of coal and fine sand mining, and the Society co-sponsored a Black Diamond coal exhibit at the Oakland Museum in 1978. Black Diamond Preserve includes Rose Hill Cemetery, where several Welsh language headstones can be seen.

The Cwmbran Choir visit was the latest of several Welsh choral visits to San Francisco in recent years. The Cwmbran concerts generated over $3,000, eighty-percent of which was remitted to the choir in Wales. In 1980, Côr Meibion y Brythoniaid made a highly successful visit to northern California. This tour was sponsored in part by Kaiser Aluminum of Oakland, which has a branch in Anglesey. Côr Brythoniaid presented President Rees Williams with a commemorative slate medal which has since become the WASNC President's symbol of office.

In 1984 the WASNC hosted a group which included Hogia'r Wyddfa, Trebor Edwards, Myrddin & Rosalind and Marian Roberts. A taped recording made for this tour was released by Sain, entitled Cyfarchion Ar Gân— Musical Greetings from Wales. In late summer of 1985 the Society sponsored a series of concerts for the folk group "Plethyn".

☆

The Welsh American Society of Northern California has sponsored Cwrs Cymraeg twice, one in 1980 coordinated by Donna Lloyd-Kolkin, and before that, coordinated by Connie Thomson in 1979. In 1983, at the University of the Pacific, visiting professor Dr. G. W. Jones ran a summer Welsh course with the theme, "Experience in the Welsh Language and Culture". Another university connection was at Stanford, which mounted an exhibition of Gwen John's drawings in 1982.

The rare books library of the University of California-Berkeley has a complete collection of *Second Aeon*. *Second Aeon* was an important British poetry magazine from 1968 to 1974. *Second Aeon* was published in Cardiff by Peter Finch, who closed the magazine when invited to become the Welsh Arts Council bookshop manager. Alongside the work of Harry Guest, Danny Abse and Cyril Hodges, Peter Finch also published new work by Gary Snyder and Alan Ginsberg. At Peter Finch's repeated invitation, Alan Ginsberg visited Wales in July 1967. While in Wales Ginsberg wrote "Wales Visitation", a poem included in his "City Lights" collection of 1968.

Second Aeon was not the only fringe cultural link with San Francisco. In those days West Coast music was popular all over Wales and John Cippolina, of Quicksilver Messenger Service, spent several months playing and touring with the Welsh rock band, Man.

Bill and Akiko's interest in our trip forced us to clarify our sense of purpose. Bill's insistence on specific descriptions of Wales and Welsh American activities helped us see our tour from a greater perspective. We began to realize we were gaining an idea of the Welsh American scene as a whole, having encountered it personally in St. Louis, Kansas City, Phoenix and now in San Francisco. Our curiosity was fully aroused and we were to find that in the months ahead, nothing would deter us from making contact with at least one Welsh name wherever we believed a Welsh society to be.

8

The Celtic Connection

SACRAMENTO

Replete with a solid vegetarian breakfast, we left Bill and Akiko's and headed for Sacramento. We collected Masami Hanashiro at the railway station and made a detour to John Ward's house before continuing our journey north. We wanted John to meet Masami because as well as having learned Welsh, his latest most specific goal was learning Japanese.

After lying dormant for many years, Welsh life in Sacramento was rekindled when Alan Pritchard, an editor for the *Sacramento Bee*, attended the San Rafael Cwrs Cymraeg in 1978. Following a newspaper article on his encounter with the Welsh language, Alan received several phone calls which, by the spring of 1979, led to the formation of the Sacramento Welsh Circle. Sacramento's first St. David's Dinner was held that March. Within a year, Society members had organized language classes, singing groups, and were planning a tour of Wales. With the participation of John Ward, by July 1982, the group had organized its first Welsh American Heritage Festival.

In 1984, John Ward led a second group to Wales on one of the best Welsh tours available to American tourists. The fifteen day trip spent six days in Nant Gwrtheyrn and Snowdonia, before going south to the Eisteddfod in Lampeter. Side trips and eisteddfod events were the main focus and the group also attended services in St. David's Cathedral. A tour of the South Wales valleys followed and the tour concluded with a medieval banquet in Cardiff Castle.

Twenty-five miles northwest of Sacramento at Penryn, in Placer County, is a small museum of interest to Welsh visitors. Penryn Quarry was founded in 1864 by Griffith Griffiths and provided granite for numerous public buildings, including the California State Capitol. Deeded to the county by Griffith Griffiths' granddaughter, the small museum depicts the Welsh quarryman's story. Supported by The Friends of Griffiths Quarry, the museum also has records of the Penrhyn Male Choir brought back by Donna Davies on one of her many visits to Wales.

With access to Yosemite and Lake Tahoe blocked by one of the highest snowfalls on record, we changed plans and headed north via the Napa Valley. With three people in the van, and a dog, arrangements were snug. Adding to our stock of blankets and daily groceries, Masami had a bulging ex-army backpack and an additional basket of "best clothes". With four warm sets of lungs breathing against the chilly window panes, the van resembled a Mongolian yurt on wheels as we sped along the backroads to Guerneville.

THE HARP

Guerneville is the home of Caswell Harps, one of the busiest folk harp makers in America, and the only harp-making business which advertises regularly in *Ninnau* or *Y Drych*. California, along with parts of New England, is a center of contemporary American interest in harp and Celtic music.

Chris Caswell started playing the harp in Scotland in 1971. When he returned to California, he worked as a harp maker for Witcher Harps in Santa Rosa. Robin James Jones, the Welsh triple harpist, has been teaching Witcher folk harp workshops since 1965. Caswell Harps was established in 1977 and in 1979, Chris Caswell and his wife spent a summer in Wales studying construction techniques of the Welsh triple harp.

Celtic harp records are being made with increasing frequency. Chris Caswell records on his own label, and Patrick Ball also records and works in California. In Seattle, Pam and Chris Boulding recorded the Welsh medley, "Merch Megan" on their 1982 *Spring Tide* album. Robin Williamson, formerly of the Incredible String Band, who now lives in California, released his musical tribute to Wales with an interpretation of the *Mabinogion* in 1984. An American style of pan-Celtic music has developed, borrowing freely from all the Celtic traditions. Representatives of the new Celtic style are as diverse as Anne Heyman in Minnesota, Sylvia Woods in California and Grey Larson and Malcolm Daglish in Indiana.

The American Folk Harp Society was founded in 1962. The Harp Renaissance Society was founded in 1973. The Folk Harp Society, founded by Sylvia Woods in 1973, and the *Folk Harp Journal*, edited by Phyllis Robinson in Mt. Laguna, California, are the main agencies promoting the folk harp and giving unity to the American folk harp scene.

The September 1976 issue of the *Folk Harp Journal* was devoted exclusively to the Welsh harp. The Folk Harp Society also publishes an annual directory of harp teachers, makers and book and record sources.

The Welsh harp in America has not experienced the same tremendous revival of interest as the harp music of Ireland, Scotland and Brittany. One result has been that in Canada and the United States, the harp is associated with the other Celtic countries. Despite the level of interest, Welsh harp players remain slow to respond to the demand for folk harp music. Along with the other Celtic countries, Wales has maintained its own unbroken harp tradition. Thanks to regional and national eisteddfodau, harp standards have been maintained in Wales, and harpists have been able to transmit their knowledge from one generation to the next.

In America, the triple harp finds its champion in Anne Habermehl, who has promoted Welsh harp music at Welsh Heritage Week since 1981. Bethan Bryn and Robin James Jones have both taught harp workshops every year at Welsh

46

Heritage Week. Anne lugs her own harp to Celtic festivals and Welsh concerts all over the east coast of the United States.

Started with thirty-six members, The Welsh Harp Society of North America was launched at Welsh Heritage Week in July 1984. The Society's first officers were David Watson, President; Anne Reaves, Vice-President and Judith Brougham, Secretary/Treasurer. David and Judith, who both live in Kansas City, also edit the Society's newsletter. One of the first acts of the Society was to make a list of Welsh harp records, music and books available in Canada and America.

Among Welsh harpists who have visited the United States in recent years, apart from Bethan Bryn and Robin James Jones, are Caryl Thomas, who played at Carnegie Hall in November 1982, and Osian Ellis, who is a permanent member of the Lincoln Center's Chamber Music Society. In 1981, Osian Ellis published *"The Story of the Harp in Wales"*, an excellent introduction to the Welsh harp tradition. Among American harpists, Bron Journey, who played at the Portland National in 1984 and who plays regularly at Seattle Welsh events, is one of many Welsh society members whose knowledge of Wales has grown through an interest in the harp.

Music, not of the harp but of the fiddle and bagpipe, has given most Celtic groups their strongest public image. In the United States, Irish, Scottish and Celtic are practically synonymous. There are, however, several organizations promoting a broader interest in the traditions of all the Celtic countries. Contemporary Celtic studies concentrate on Cornish, Breton and Welsh; Manx, Irish and Gaelic. Important discoveries in ancient branches of Celtic, notably Gaulish, Galatian and Celt-Iberian have led to studies of the Celtic languages from the 3rd century B.C. to the present day.

The Society of Inter-Celtic Arts and Culture was founded in Boston in 1978. Under the direction of Kevin Gilligan, the Society of Inter-Celtic Arts and Culture publishes *Keltica*, a lavish annual journal with a circulation of 1500. Volume two of *Keltica*, published in 1983, featured a photograph of Nant Gwrtheyrn on the cover. Inside were articles on Cymdeithas Madog, Yr Academi Gymreig and an interview with Dafydd Iwan.

Inter-Celtic is a concept the majority of Welsh Americans are slow to appreciate. They have been put off by the Irish-Scottish overemphasis of the past and the pre-Christian preoccupation of some Celticists today. The largest Welsh assembly in North America is an all-day hymn singing festival. Cymanfaoedd canu are still the most common and best attended Welsh Canadian and Welsh American events. Older Welsh Americans see little relationship between their solemn hymns and wild Irish jigs, or the fringe connections established by writers like John Sharkey and Barry Fell.

In the past, it was the preservation of Welshness, especially the language, that kept superficial Celticists away from Wales. Serious Celtic students are learning the language, however. Many of them are visiting Wales as a country that has kept its tongue despite centuries of English language pressure. Inter-Celtic cooperation offers Welsh Americans an opportunity to expand during a period of sustained and growing intellectual interest.

Anne Cowie, founder of Cymdeithas Madog, was among the first to recognize the potential of a Celtic-Welsh identity. A two week study tour of Wales she designed with Johns Hopkins University in 1982 was called "Celtic Myth and Literature". The course treated the poetry of Wales, Welsh history, archeology and contemporary art as a live tradition in terms of a Celtic European whole.

In California, The Celtic Colloquium, the Celtic Educational Society and Institute of Celtic Studies attempt to strengthen the links between the independent Celtic groups. The Institute of Celtic Studies offers non-credit courses in Celtic history and society. The Celtic Educational Society is an informal group of members from other Celtic organizations, which collects information, teaches and occasionally publishes whatever it can about the Celts. It is particularly interested in collecting information on Celtic immigrant communities in the United States.

Middle Welsh has been taught at the University of California-Berkeley since 1974. The first course in Modern Welsh was offered in 1978. The Celtic Colloquium, a student organization, grew out of increased Welsh and Irish language studies at the University. In 1978, Sarah Higley, who in 1984 was a Fullbright Scholar studying in Wales, started the Celtic Colloquium. In 1979, she and Roslyn Raney launched their newsletter and a program of weekly meetings featuring speakers on predominantly Welsh and Irish language topics. In 1979, the Celtic Colloquium mounted the first annual California Celtic Studies Conference, which by 1984 had grown from a one-day to a three-day meeting. In 1983, R. Geraint Gruffydd of the National Library of Wales was the Welsh contributor to the conference.

The Celtic Colloquium maintains one of the best regular Celtic forums in the country. Led by Vincent Dunn, Eve Sweetser, Jim Duran, Theresa McCann, David Williams, Scott Engler and Bruce Webb, enrolment in Welsh Studies in California has increased and interest in the Celtic Studies Program continues to improve.

☆

The International Celtic Festival at Hunter, New York, is the largest Celtic Music Festival in America. The Welsh have taken part since the festival started in 1980. Although the festival is dominated by Scottish and Irish societies, participation by Ar Log and Anne Habermehl help Welsh Americans realize that this is their occasion too. Earl Williams of Connecticut contributes to the Welsh contingent and Joan Phelps of Binghamton, New York, makes sure that the Welsh Society in Binghamton takes advantage of this Celtic opportunity on its doorstep.

Other Celtic conferences in New York, such as The Celtic Summer Institute in 1980, and the Celtic Cultural Weekend at Cornell University in 1983, are more scholarly. Both meetings were supported by the Welsh American

Foundation and by Emlyn Griffith of Rome, who is a Cornell graduate. Welsh American Foundation support has been an important step in redressing the almost automatic Irish-Scottish-Celtic identification of the past.

The Celtic Studies Association of North America is an association of East Coast faculty members who meet once a year at an annual symposium and distribute a newsletter in between. The Celtic Studies Association's main interest is in medieval Celtic themes, and grew out of meetings of the Modern Languages Association in New York City.

The Eastern States Celtic Association concentrates on modern Celtic languages and literature, and was founded by Welshman John M. Jones in 1982. Mr. Jones judged the WAY Essay Contest of 1976, and at the 1983 ESCA Conference, read a paper on "The Welsh Language Underground Press" of the 1960's and 1970's. The Canadian Celtic Congress founded at Expo '67 was revived in 1975 by Ronald Stewart, a member of the Montreal St. David's Society, and the Montreal Welsh Male Choir. The Canadian Celtic Congress, although reactivated by the Welsh, gave attention to each Celtic group and did not over-identify with one nationality. It became inactive again in 1983.

University courses, such as the Celtic Studies course at the University of Minnesota, Minneapolis, and the Celtic Folklore Workshop at Hartford, Connecticut, offer introductions to Celticism. These courses at least attempt a balanced study of the Celtic world. In 1982, St. Thomas O'Shaughnessy College Library in St. Paul, Minnesota opened its valuable Celtic collection to the public. The Celtic collection has about five hundred Welsh items. Over a dozen American colleges offer Celtic Study courses that include Welsh options. This figure does not include colleges that offer Welsh studies through their linguistic, rhetoric or even Germanic departments. Nor does it include The University of the Pacific or Wilkes College, where a visiting Welsh professor or Cymdeithas Madog have offered special programs on the University campus.

9

Welsh Societies in Portland and Seattle

Driving north, we were three in a van that had been adapted for two. In the West Coast winter rains our van became an introverted tent. Like the Tlingit of the damp northwest, we filled our evenings with endless stories, elaborating the past into hilarious myths for each other's entertainment.

The rain was so persistent and intense it reminded Suzanne fearfully of the rain in Wales. Beneath an indigo sky, the redwood forest floor remained in inky twilight, a perpetual gloom illuminated faintly by the childsize glow of our hooded windbreakers. Gold Bluffs Beach is where giant trees come down to the Pacific shore. The beach was heaped with driftwood for miles along its length. To reach the ocean we had to climb over splinters, knots, stumps, trunks and branches for a hundred yards until we reached the sand. The wood was smoothly polished by the tides and the whole length of Gold Bluffs Beach lay wrapped in acres of slippery wood bones, bleached by the sun and swollen by the waves.

At Gold Bluffs we managed yet again to get soaked to the skin. It took a heavy dumpling stew, as well as showers and a change of clothes, to get us back in shape. Wet clothes need to dry and the van shrunk and grew according to the adventures that we had.

With Japanese compliance and composure, we developed a routine that gave us privacy in such a narrow space. Masami usually sat in the front seats, perched there, while Suzanne or I would be cooking at the stove. One by one we made two beds, ours in the back and Masami's on a thick pile of blankets next to Amiga on the floor. At night the van became a compact eiderdown of backpacks, grocery bags and baskets, with our faces peeping out.

With spiky gorse in yellow bloom, in many ways the cliffs of Oregon strongly resembled the coast of southern Wales. But while South Wales beaches strand an occasional dead whale, a porpoise or a seal, there are no eagles and we were beginning to spot the great bald eagle with increasing frequency.

In Portland we had an appointment with Idwal Parri, originally from Anglesey in Wales. When I telephoned Idwal, I told him there were now three of us but we only wanted an hour of his time. It was typical of the hospitality we received that we stayed from noon until 8 p.m. Idwal totally ignored our muddy boots and crumpled clothes and, while playing Welsh records, told us about Welsh American life in Portland.

PORTLAND

A past president of the Cambrian Society of Portland and a nationally known director of cymanfaoedd canu, Idwal was born in Denbigh, Wales and went to school in Llangefni, Anglesey. After graduating from the Manchester School of Technology, he played professional soccer for Manchester City until emigrating to Milwaukee in 1927. His brother, Gwynn, was already in America and both men have been active in Welsh American affairs.

In 1977, at the Welsh National Eisteddfod in Wrexham, Idwal was the speaker for Undeb y Cymry ar Wasgar, the *Yr Enfys* group, when the overseas Welsh assembled on the National Eisteddfod stage. His theme was "The Purity of the Welsh Language", a theme to which Welsh American language groups consistently return. The Eastern States Celtic Association, in May 1984, deplored the use of words like "prins" (prince), "yncl" (uncle), "cwin" (queen), and so on in Welsh language texts where perfectly good Welsh words already exist.

Idwal told us that the 1984 National Cymanfa Ganu would be held in Portland. 1984 was the 100th anniversary of the dedication of Bryn Seion Welsh church at Beavercreek, Oregon, located five miles south of Oregon City on Route 99 and the only Welsh church still standing along the west coast. Founded in 1884, Bryn Seion Welsh Church continues to hold services on the second and fourth Sunday every month. People come from miles away and a pot luck dinner is held afterwards. Since 1935, on the fourth Sunday of June, Bryn Seion has held an annual cymanfa ganu. The small wooden church only seats one hundred and sixty people, and latecomers gather on benches and lawn chairs on the grounds outside.

In 1984, during preparations for the Portland National Cymanfa Ganu, Bryn Seion was extensively renovated and redecorated. Preparations for a dedication service were led by Doreen Purdy, formerly of Maesteg, and Earl Purdy, president of the Portland Cambrian Society. Isola Welsh and other church members played an important role in preparing the relatively small church membership for a sudden surge in renewed outside interest. Patricia McKinney prepared a detailed commemorative booklet about the church.

Memberships of Bryn Seion Church and the Portland Cambrian Society overlap. Easter, the June cymanfa and Thanksgiving are held at the Church. Monthly meetings, a summer picnic and the St. David's banquet are organized by the Cambrian Society. Monthly meetings are held on the first Saturday every month at Waverly Heights Church, and usually feature a slide show, guest speaker or community singing. For an hour before the meeting, Richard Davies, formerly of Treorchy, occasionally teaches an informal Welsh language class.

About eleven-hundred people attended the 1984 Portland National Cymanfa Ganu held at the Marriott Hotel. Co-chairpersons Betty Pierce of Abertillery and Emmaline Davies traveled extensively the whole year before, promoting the Portland National. Their work paid off, especially in the young people's section, with particularly good attendance at the WAY luncheon and at Awr y Plant. Bron Journey of Seattle, played harp at the Saturday night concert, and the Cambrian Circle of Vancouver gave a Historic Welsh Costume show on Thursday night. Guest speaker at the Friday night banquet was Jonathan Nicholas of Merthyr Tydfil, who now writes for the *Portland Oregonian*. Other coordinators during cymanfa preparations were Gwen Lucas, Mike Charles, Roger Neale, Tom and Sharon Owens and Dale and Kevin Bowers. Hosting the National always induces a new wave of local interest in Welsh life, and many volunteers baked cakes, acted as stewards and staffed the registration and information booths. Kevin Bowers enlisted the participation of local storytellers Janet Mikesell and Rachel Foxman, which extended the appeal of the cymanfa to Celticists and other folklore societies in the city.

Our six hours with Idwal Parri flew by on the wings of song. A passionate lover of choral music, he played record after record while he kept time, conducting. With great reluctance we left Idwal just as night began to fall. Masami had decided to take the ferry to Vancouver from Port Angeles. Before seeing her off, we had the whole Olympic Peninsula to drive around.

At Sol Duc, we heard about hot spring pools along the Elwha River Road. At the end of a six mile trail, we found a bridge over the creek, and on the other side a series of black sulphureous pools with water emerging at around eighty to one-hundred-fifty degrees Fahrenheit. With spectacular views of the Olympic Mountains and with light snow falling, we bathed and steamed for three whole hours. We picnicked, soaked and healed our cramped van-life bodies. It was a glorious physical sensation, bathing in an outdoor bathtub with the natural hot spring water bubbling less than a yard away. After weeks confined in a narrow space together, our muscles relaxed and our skins reclaimed a healthy glow. We awoke next morning at the Port Angeles ferry, feeling clean, supple and rejuvenated.

With her army backpack and basket of "best clothes", Masami waved goodbye from among commuters taking the morning boat to Victoria Island. It would take her eight hours to eventually reach Vancouver. Meanwhile we took the ferry from Winslow and arrived in Seattle from its most spectacular approach with Seattle's downtown city blocks reflected in the black and icy water of Puget Sound and framed by the frigid summits of the North Cascades.

SEATTLE

Puget Sound Welsh Association (PSWA)

David Morgan's mail order store, Pethau Cymreig, was located less than a hundred yards from Carter's Volkswagen, where we took the van for its 30,000 mile check up. While our home on wheels had its belly held aloft, we visited the store. The sign above the door still said "Austral Imports", and we didn't know that Pethau Cymreig had once been primarily an Australian import operation. Australian products still occupy a dozen pages of Pethau Cymreig's catalog. As contacts in Wales improved, the Welsh lines grew and the Pethau Cymreig showroom has many more books and records than the catalog lists. We were shown around by Nerys Jones of Llanberis, Wales. Nerys had moved to Seattle to join her father, Dic Jones, who emigrated to America in 1976, but who returns to Llanberis often.

Although the Welsh Ladies Society of Seattle started celebrating St. David's Day in 1918, Welsh classes began in 1978. David Morgan and Benton Gomer Williams held the first lessons in private homes using the text "*Living Welsh*", by T. J. Rhys Jones. Dic Jones became the teacher and the group was later joined by Sadie Grove of St. David's, Wales. By 1983 Dosbarth Cymraeg Seattle had thirty students divided into beginners, intermediate and advanced study groups. Classes are held at 7:30 p.m. every Friday at Northminster Presbyterian Church. Every third Friday is devoted to choir and folk singing practice.

Côr Cymraeg Seattle varying from 16 to 24 members, grew out of Welsh class interest in folk and hymn tunes. Welsh folk material in the Welsh language and arranged for soprano, alto, tenor, bass is hard to find, and Benton Williams, the choir's first musical director, arranges the choir's hymn and folk melodies. The director in 1985 was Tim Dyck. Bob Mathews acts as the Welsh Society's publicity officer and arranges the choir's increasingly numerous public appearances. Mari Wingate holds special singing and pronunciation sessions. Jackie Cedarholm specializes in genealogy research.

Black Diamond is a coal mining town, founded by Welsh, Irish and Finnish people, fifteen miles southeast of Seattle. At Black Diamond's 1983 centennial, Côr Cymraeg Seattle concluded thirty minutes of Welsh hymn singing with a flag waving rendition of "Hen Wlad Fy Nhadau". The choir also participates in the Seattle Opera House annual Ethnic Song Festival. The choir and Puget Sound Welsh Association members participated extensively in the 1984 Portland National Cymanfa. Tim Dyck led the choir, Mari Wingate coordinated Awr y Plant and Nansi Hughes sang several solos. Bron Journey, classical harpist and reliable supporter of Seattle Welsh life, was the featured artist of the Saturday night concert.

The formation of Dosbarth Cymraeg transformed the Seattle Welsh scene. In addition to the long established Welsh Ladies Society under the leadership of Olwen Hathaway and Margaret Kroshus and the two Welsh groups, meeting at Northminster Presbyterian Church, Welsh gatherings are planned in Tacoma, and in Bellevue. They all form the Puget Sound Welsh Association whose president is Kayla Ware. In 1985, two hundred and fifty people came to the Puget Sound St. David's Day Celebration. Haydn Morgan of The St. David's Society of the Inland Empire, Spokane led community singing and gave a song recital and Bron Journey appeared with his harp.

Benton Williams circulated the first newsletter but welcomed Mark Pipes as the first editor of *Y Llais Dosbarth Cymraeg*, today known as *Y Llais*, and now edited by Jennifer Ducey. In August 1984, Puget Sound Welsh Association hosted the Hogia'r Wyddfa touring party on a home-stay basis. The Welsh American community presented the tourists at two well attended and well advertised concerts.

Before Welsh classes ever started in Seattle, two Welsh learners from the city had already earned a name for themselves in Wales. In July 1977, Peggy Lawrence and Roger Fenton from Seattle, and Craig Bowers of San Francisco were the winning team in Carreg Milltir, a Harlech Television Welsh learners competition. In the final, the three American learners beat a team of Welsh learners from Pontypridd. Roger Fenton has since settled in Wales, having married his Welsh fiancée.

In 1984, John Davies, head of the English Department at Prestatyn High School, was exchange teacher at Charles Wright Academy, Tacoma. A wood-carver and poet, John has read poems several times to the Puget Sound Welsh Association. Younger members play active roles in the Association. Cathy and Dai Davies, two other visitors from Wales, have given weekly programs, and the Society's Welsh newspaper correspondent is Jennifer Ducey. In 1985 other PGWA officers and trustees were Ed David, Jim Davies, Gary Lundell, Olwen Jackson, Joel Ware, Evelyn Thomas, Helen Watkins and Kathleen Denning.

Welsh Americans in Seattle have built a strong Society on the firm conviction that the Welsh language is interesting and compelling enough to attract and hold people's attention. Welsh language classes and folk and choral singing and occasional "pot-luck" gatherings are the Society's main activities. We left Seattle, impressed by the members' dedication and we admired the stimulating Welsh environment they had created from the most slender of possibilities.

10

The Welsh in Western Canada:
Alberta, Saskatchewan and British Columbia

VANCOUVER

We had a list of phone numbers in Vancouver, but were totally unprepared for Canadian formality and reserve. In contrast to Welsh societies in the United States, where one or two calls resulted in an invitation to the next Welsh event, in Vancouver it took at least a dozen calls to find a receptive Society officer.

We finally found the names of Alun Jones, Welsh Society President, and Dorothy Walters, leader of the Cambrian Ladies Circle. Thanks to them, we attended a rehearsal of the Vancouver Male Voice Choir and a rehearsal of the Cambrian Circle's Historical Welsh Costume Show. We also visited Cambrian Hall, headquarters of the Vancouver Welsh Society and the only Welsh clubhouse as such in Canada or the United States.

Located at E. 17th and Main Streets, Cambrian Hall is a modest brick building, looking much brighter since the extensive renovations that have proceeded quietly since 1975. Upstairs is a stage and seating area with a narrow gallery at the back. Downstairs, with renovated interiors, lobbies and restrooms, is a comfortable lounge. Equipped with a bar, piano, dartboards and public address system, the downstairs clubroom has been an important factor in the recent success of the Vancouver Welsh Society.

The Vancouver Welsh Society has a membership of about three hundred. Elections are held every December and since the excellent presidency of Glyndwr Abrahams in the late 1970's there have been a series of prominent officers. Foremost among them are Gwenfyl Jones and Dorothy Walters.

A native of Pentrepoeth near Llanelli, Gwenfyl Jones was chairperson of the 1980 Vancouver National Cymanfa Ganu. Having served many times as a National Cymanfa trustee, in 1984 she became president of the Welsh National Cymanfa Ganu Association. A visible supporter of numerous Welsh projects in North America, Gwenfyl is one of the collectors of material for the WNGGA folk song book. She also helped write the detailed narrative accompanying the Cambrian Circle's Welsh Costume Show.

The 1980 Vancouver National was the first West Coast National since Los Angeles in 1966, and was important for a number of reasons. It was Pat Viets' first National Cymanfa and saw her relaunching of *Y Drych* following Horace

Powell's death in June 1980. Vancouver Male Choir appeared alongside Llanelli Male Voice and the Vancouver National also saw the debut of the now famous Historical Welsh Costume Show.

Dorothy Walters, a past president of the Vancouver Ladies Auxiliary, obtained a grant from the federal government and organized the creation of twenty-one authentic, period Welsh costumes. For over a year, members of the Cambrian Circle met every Friday. They obtained the assistance of Mr. William Walker, a professional gown and theatrical costume designer. Complete in every detail, the only concession the costumes make is in the use of modern fabric, when original silks and homespun proved impossible to obtain. The costume show has been an outstanding success and has toured extensively. In 1983, the Cambrian Circle gave three shows during the Festival of Castles in Wales. Twelve boxes of clothes were transported to Cardiff and Swansea and then to a show in Llandudno. Since the Cambrian Ladies added folk singing to their program, they have become one of the most entertaining and visually striking of all Welsh groups.

There has been a Welsh Society in Vancouver since 1908, when it was called the Cymmrodorion Society. In 1913, Margaret Williams and her family arrived from Wales. Margaret Williams organized a new Cambrian Society that met at her house for sixteen years. In 1924, the constitution of the "Cambrian Society" was formally established, with Mr. Angel Jones as its first president. In 1929, the group, now spilling onto Margaret Williams' garden, received property from Joseph Jones, and a donation of bricks and building materials from Thomas Edwards. Volunteers built Cambrian Hall, which was opened on September 1st, 1929. In 1973, the Society's name was changed to the Welsh Society of Vancouver. Since 1980, Welsh Society activity is greater than it has been for many years. But the busiest period in the Society's history was probably in 1946, when four hundred entries were adjudicated at the Vancouver Eisteddfod, and over two thousand attended the Diamond Jubilee Cymanfa Ganu held in Stanley Park.

The Vancouver Welsh Male Voice choir, directed by Dennis Whyte and accompanied by Enid Lewis, has made a significant impact on the province of British Columbia. The choir consists of seventy-four singers. When we saw them they were preparing for an appearance in Chilliwack, seventy miles inland. There have been many male and mixed Welsh choirs in Vancouver, but the present highly successful Male Voice Choir was first organized in 1980 by Gwyn Evans, formerly of the Cwmbach Male Choir, Aberdare.

Gwyn emigrated to Canada with his family in 1975. His warm and genuine welcome to Suzanne and me, and the time we spent together, made all our attempts at contacting the Welsh Society worthwhile. Gwyn Evans introduced us to the choir, which greets visitors with a hospitable round of applause.

In its first year, the Vancouver Welsh Male Choir performed with the Vancouver Symphony. In 1982 the Choir won first prize at the Kiwanis Music Festival, sang the Canadian National Anthem in 1983 at the opening of the multi-million dollar British Columbia sports arena and in 1984, was the main subject of a 30-minute television program on Welsh life in Vancouver.

Welsh activities in Vancouver maintain a metropolitan scope. July 17 1982 was declared Welsh weekend. The City Stage Theatre presented "Under Milk Wood", Ar Log played before general audiences, and the Male Choir held several receptions at a Cambrian Hall Open House Weekend. On March 1 1984, four Vancouver radio stations broadcasted Welsh poems, songs and stories. CKVU-TV presented a show on the Welsh Society, featuring an interview with Society secretary, Ann Roberts.

The Ladies Auxiliary forms an indispensable wing of the Vancouver Welsh community. Under the leadership of Grace Thomas, Emily Davis, Nancy Abrahams and the willing and helpful attitude of all members, the Ladies Auxiliary mounts teas, parties, outings, receptions and picnics with fluent ease. A consistent force since the Society's birth, the Ladies Auxiliary is the longest continuing section, and has produced some of the Society's most able officers.

In 1983, the Welsh Society's rugby section was reformed with Ken Jones, President; Dave Gilder, Secretary and John Williams, Treasurer. The Society has an over-40's team of "Old Contemptibles" which has hosted among others, "Cardiff Old Boys", Newport Rugby Football Club and The Welsh Secondary Schools side. Vancouver is one of the few Welsh societies that maintains contact with both visiting choirs and rugby teams. Lack of rugby contact is not the fault of Welsh societies, however, as touring teams rarely contact them. The Welsh Rugby Union does not subscribe to *Ninnau* or *Y Drych*, and Welsh Rugby teams tour without knowing of the potential support of a local Welsh society.

In the fall of 1982, twenty-six representatives of the Welsh Farmers Union were given a reception at Cambrian Hall. Llanelli Male Choir came for the 1980 Vancouver National and Froncysyllte Male voice toured in summer, 1983. Emyr Jenkins, secretary of the Welsh National Eisteddfod, Lord Gordon Parry, head of the Wales Tourist Board and Lord Elwyn Jones, have all visited the Vancouver Welsh community.

Cambrian Hall forms an umbrella for a wide variety of Canadian Welsh programs and special events. Spring and fall cymanfaoedd canu are held there, always with a riotous noson lawen the night before. The Ladies Auxiliary meets every third Thursday at Cambrian Hall at 1:30 p.m. The Cambrian Circle meets at the Hall every other Friday, and the Male Choir rehearses every Tuesday at 7 p.m. Since January 1984, Eirian Tzetos has led a Welsh language class, which meets at Cambrian Hall once a week.

Cambrian Hall has catering facilities and is often rented by other immigrant groups. The Welsh Society's Children's Christmas party is held there as well as adult Christmas and New Year's parties. The Society also holds a series of summer picnics with special attention to the needs of youngsters. The Social Committee of the Vancouver Welsh Society organizes entertainment in the lower level lounge every Friday night. Every third Friday features special entertainment, such as a darts competition or themes like "Captain Morgan's Pirate Night" or "A Night at the Races".

Social Committee chairman, Rob Barclay, has a talent for organizing entertainment. While senior officers of the Vancouver Welsh Society attend to the essential business of organizing cymanfaoedd canu, visits by choirs and appearances by guest speakers, the Social Committee keeps the appeal of the Society broad and lighthearted. For the St. David's Day noson lawen in 1983, Rob Barclay persuaded President Alun Jones and Secretary Neville Thomas to dress up as druids. The druids then presided over a hilarious eating of the leek ceremony.

Since the Vancouver National Cymanfa in 1980, Welsh Society activities have been at a peak. With a wealth of singing and performing talent from Ken Edwards, Enid Lewis, Ella Roberts, J. M. Williams, Gareth Prytherch and Eirian Tzetos, and committed leaders like David Mason, Maureen Gnecht, Gwyneth Brazier and Ieuan Lampshire Jones, the Vancouver Welsh Society is one of the most completely rounded expatriate Welsh groups in the world. Vancouver Welsh people maintain close contacts with Wales and have made their city a center of Welsh activity in Canada.

VICTORIA, BRITISH COLUMBIA

The Welsh Society of Victoria was organized in 1978. In 1984 the Society had around 150 members and its major annual events were a St. David's dinner and a noson lawen at Christmas.

A much larger St. David's Society was founded in Victoria in the 1920's. The St. David's Society used to meet on a weekly basis and was a lively social club. This Society collapsed in the late 1960's.

In 1984 the Victoria Welsh Society formed a Ladies Auxiliary, had the beginnings of a Welsh language class and had confirmed plans for its first cymanfa ganu to be held in 1985. During 1985 a women's branch called Merched y Ddraig Goch was formed and entertained in Welsh costume at Welsh and British meetings.

In 1984 the officers of the Victoria Welsh Society were Dr. David Lintern, President; Sally Brinkley, Secretary; Dennis Steinie, Treasurer; Celia Morgan, Entertainment; Leanne Weber, Coordinator. Other leaders have been Ken Edwards, Blanche Powell, Gwyn Jarvis, Bernie Lewis, the Reverend Gareth Evans and the Reverend Cedric Jones.

SASKATCHEWAN

The St. David's Society of Regina, Saskatchewan was founded in 1912. The Society meets five times a year and in March 1984, consisted of eighty-eight members. Mrs. Llywela Argue of Regina, the Society's musical director, came to Canada from Swansea, Wales, in 1955. She has conducted cymanfaoedd canu held in Saskatoon, and those held in Regina; she has also conducted all the Ponoka, Alberta cymanfaoedd canu since 1965. Every year The Regina St. David's Society participates in the Regina Multicultural Mosaic Festival, and in 1984 sold over 1,200 dozen Welsh cakes from the Celtic booth.

As well as the St. David's Society, Regina has a St. David's Welsh Choir, The Welsh Dancers of Regina (aged nine to fifteen), and the Celtics Soccer Club.

The annual Regina St. David's Day banquet attracts one hundred and fifty people every year. The speaker in 1984 was Emyr Jenkins, Director of the National Esiteddfod of Wales. Mr. Jenkins was in Regina visiting Llywela Argue, his sister.

Officers of the Society include Tom White, Gwyneth Baker, Lloyd Jones, Harold and Margaret Woodward, Frances Zerr, Christine Jackson, Valerie Davies, Morfydd Llewellyn, Margaret Gliddon, and President, Georgina Lazzarotto. Mrs. Anne Brown, who contacts all Welsh people in and around Regina, has been nicknamed the "mother of the Regina Welsh Society" because of the work she has done to make the Society a success.

East of Regina, at Bangor near Melville, Welsh life persists among the descendants of Patagonian colonists. Around the turn of the century, a group of disaffected Patagonian colonists migrated to western Canada, arriving in Saltcoats, Saskatchewan in 1902. Evidence of these settlers remains at Capel Bethel and Llywelyn Cemetery, Bangor, and in the names of ranches like "Y Bedol", "Pant Mawr" and "Bryn Gobaith". Members of the community still celebrate St. David's Day, but no organized St. David's societies exist.

ALBERTA

In 1984, the President of the Calgary, Alberta Welsh Society was Ken Mason. Muriel Roberts and Roland Thomas, with their occasional columns to *Ninnau* and *Y Drych*, also promote Welsh Society activities. The Calgary Welsh Society was founded in 1906. The Society's main event is its annual March 1st banquet. For a while, Welsh classes were held in 1979. In 1977, the Prince of Wales High School, Calgary was opened with the official Welsh language motto, "Yn Chwilio Gwybodaeth"—(In search of knowledge). The Calgary Boys Choir competed in the Llangollen International Eisteddfod in 1978.

Other Alberta Welsh Societies exist in Lethbridge, Ross Hughes, President; Red Deer, Mrs. Ivy Carney, President; and Medicine Hat, Mrs. Celia Griffiths, President.

The Ponoka Dewi Sant Society has held an annual cymanfa ganu since 1942. The Society was incorporated as a non-profit organization in 1975, and in 1984 had about forty members. The Society meets on the first Sunday of every month at the Ponoka Senior Citizens Center, and organizes a program of films, slides, a visiting speaker or community singing.

Over a hundred people attend the St. David's Day banquet, and over two hundred attend the annual Ponoka cymanfa held on the second Sunday in August. The Society holds a noson lawen the night before the cymanfa, and a lively Christmas party on the second Sunday in December. Under the leadership of Glyn Owen, Hugh Roberts, Griff and Patricia Jones and the present committee of Elinor Davies, Ethel Gardner and Glynes Jorgenssen, the Ponoka Dewi Sant Society is flourishing.

In 1980, the *Ponoka Herald* published *From Wales to Wood River*, a seventy-five page booklet compiled by Kelt Hughes and Griff Jones. Telling the story of Welsh immigration to the Ponoka area, the dissolution of their churches and eisteddfodau, and their integration into the Canadian mosaic, *From Wales to Wood River* is one of the few printed histories of the Welsh in Western Canada.

There are four Welsh associations in Edmonton, Alberta. They are: The Sons of Wales, President, Dennis Gleed; The Dylan Thomas Society, President, Dr. Norman Thomas; The St. David's Welsh Society, President, Gerry Stone and the St. David's Male Voice Choir, President, Mr. Pat James. Edmonton also has a Druids Rugby Club, some of whose players are members of the Welsh societies.

The Dylan Thomas Society and The Sons of Wales are dormant groups, reviving only for special occasions. Today The Sons of Wales is managed by many of the same people as the St. George's English Society and is nominally a British organization. The St. David's Welsh Society of Edmonton was founded in 1908. Under the leadership of Jean Thomas, Colin Clarke, Frieda Jones, Blodwen Thomas, Dilys Griffiths and Helen Rantanen, a calendar of banquets, cymanfaoedd canu and visiting choirs is organized every year. The St. David's banquet in Edmonton usually attracts between one hundred and one hundred and fifty people. The banquet features the Edmonton St. David's Welsh Male Choir, and concludes with community singing.

The St. David's Welsh Society of Edmonton holds an annual cymanfa on the first Sunday in May. Mr. Pat James is the conductor and Frank Johnson is the organist. The St. David's Male Choir always participates in the cymanfa which draws people from as far away as Ponoka and Calgary.

The St. David's Welsh Male Choir is the oldest choir in Alberta, and consists of between forty and fifty singers. In 1983, the choir gave a command performance at Government House for the Prince and Princess of Wales on their Canadian Tour. Led by officers Pryce Ashton and Ian Dunlap, conductor Richard Williams and accompanist Joy Nicol, in 1984 the Welsh Male Choir organized its first Invitational Concert for Male Choirs. Future plans include a tour of Wales, and participating in the Llangollen International Eisteddfod.

The St. David's Society of Edmonton is one of many Welsh Societies that regularly hosts touring Welsh choirs. Pendyrus Male Choir has visited Edmonton twice, Godre Aran visited in the late 1970's and Llanelli Male Voice Choir toured in 1980. The last Welsh choir to visit was Froncysyllte, which toured Alberta and British Columbia in August 1983. Also in August 1983, the Mid-Wales Development Board held a promotional conference in Edmonton with entertainment provided by Welsh musicians Bethan Bryn and Sharon Leslie Lloyd.

I I

The Almira Great Run: Meeting the Welsh in Eastern Washington and the Basques in Idaho and Oregon

At the American border, we were welcomed by armed guards, and told to walk into the State Border security rooms. Here we were asked to prove we were who we said we were. There had been a robbery in Washington and the thieves escaped into Canada. Our van fitted the description and two officers spent fifteen minutes looking in every cupboard that we had. Anxious that our careful packing wouldn't come apart, we emptied out soups, games, sheets, kettles, cameras and tennis balls so that the policemen could probe to their hearts content. We were cleared and welcomed back to the United States.

We were glad to be back in America though. North of the border we were definitely visitors. Over and over again we had been reminded of Canadian separation and independence.

We drove into Almira, Washington, a hamlet of 349 people, marvelling at the sudden lushness of brown plowed fields and acres of waving emerald grass. Almira was the childhood home of John Nichols in San Francisco, and John had given us the number of his cousin, Lanny Evans, who was the Mayor there. "Now tell me," were Lanny's opening words, "just how are we related?"

Lanny took us to see the old Welsh cemetery, protected by a rusty fence and isolated in the middle of a thousand-acre wheatfield. The field was just starting to be broken by the plow, which only served to highlight the tangle of weeds and brambles that climbed over the fencing and the graves. Most of the memorial stones were in the Welsh language. Descendants of those buried there, Lanny said, still lived on farms around Almira.

Almira was a Welsh agricultural town named after Almira Davis, wife of Charles Davis, the original town surveyor in 1889. By 1900, one million bushels of wheat were being shipped to Seattle on the Northern Pacific Railroad. As in Oregon, where the Lewelling brothers had started hugely productive orchards, Almira proved fruitful for pears, apples, apricots, as well as oats, rye, wheat, flax and barley. The Welsh pioneers built a church which today is a shed on one of Almira's farms. The cemetery though, remains intact, and is one of the most atmospheric and isolated monuments to Welsh pioneers in the far west.

Lanny introduced us to Emrys and Bertha Hughes. Emrys was born in Almira in 1899. He grew up speaking Welsh and as we spoke, odd phrases of the language he hadn't spoken since his parents died came back to him in snatches.

Lanny and his wife, Marge, adopted us as closely as long lost members of their family. Their daughter and son-in-law, Judy and Dave, had just returned from Wales with slates and iron fixtures from the now dilapidated original family home. Dave's first words on meeting us were "welcome to America."

The next day, Sunday, April 24th, our 242nd day of traveling, was the Almira Great Run, a Lions Club charity race. The whole town took part. Those who didn't run were gathered in the tennis courts, where an open air lunch of beans, bread, hot dogs, potato salad, coffee and lemonade lay waiting for 325 runners to cross the finishing line.

It wasn't the next day that we ached, but the day following that. Our legs trembled and our arms creaked. Only long soaks in the hot pools of Idaho could cure us. Following a brief visit in Spokane, we headed south for the scalding and medicinal waters of Zim's Outdoor Plunge.

SPOKANE

"Welsh St. David's Society of the Inland Empire, Inc.," is the full title of the Welsh Society in Spokane. This small Society attracts around 65 members to its annual St. David's banquet. The Society also holds an October cymanfa ganu. The Spokane cymanfa has, in all recent years, been directed by Idwal Parri of Portland and Haydn Morgan of Spokane. Haydn Morgan also conducts regularly in Seattle and the Spokane Society has received a lot of encouragement from increased Welsh activity in the Seattle area.

The annual business meeting of the St. David's Society of The Inland Empire is held the last week in March. As with many Welsh American societies it remains the Ladies' Welsh St. David's Auxiliary which hosts regular monthly programs and so holds the group together. The Ladies' Auxiliary meets for lunch and a brief meeting the second Tuesday of every month except during July and August.

Spokane's Welsh Society has persisted since 1889 when the first Welsh Sunday school was formed. The Welsh "roots phenomenon" has not seized the club nor has the "Welsh fever" of language classes, visits to Wales and ordering from the catalogs of the import shops. Even so, the Spokane Society continues to wave the Red Dragon in the spring and fall of every year.

A Welsh church was built in Spokane in 1912 and for a while mission stations were maintained at Kellog and Warner in Idaho. By the 1950's, however, the first generation of pioneers had passed away and the Welsh church closed. Since its reorganization in 1957, the Welsh St. David's Society of the Inland Empire, Inc. has donated books, records and paintings to the public library in Spokane. In the 1970's the Society sponsored two American students through a summer semester at the University of Wales, Bangor.

The morning we pulled up at Zim's Plunge, Idaho, the meadows were gripped in thick and icy frost. Streams of hot water running through the fields sent columns of steam into the cold and foggy air. Eager to bathe, yet again outdoors, in naturally thermal water, we were at Zim's thirty minutes before it opened. Soon we were swimming in a pool, fed by water steaming from the ground at 149 degrees Fahrenheit. We stayed four hours, soaking in the water, then chilling quickly in the wintry open air.

From Zim's we crossed back into Oregon, where we had more difficulty with the time zones than with the pronunciation of Basque surnames like Exteberria, Ytrionbieta, and Zugazagoitia.

THE BASQUES

If Welsh is the language of heaven, Basque is the language of Eden. Basque people are of distinct and ancient ethnic stock and some ethnologists believe that the Basques are direct descendants of cro-magnon man. Their language, one of the oldest and most singular in Europe, is still widely spoken in the Basque provinces of Spain and France. During the late 1800's large numbers of Basque families emigrated to California. From California they dispersed, forming communities in Oregon, Nevada, Idaho and Wyoming.

Isolated by their decision to settle in remote areas, it is only in relatively recent years that the Basques have integrated into the American melting pot. Integration, although late, has been swift and irreversible. Today in the small Oregon towns of Basque, French Glen and Jordan Valley, only the oldest people speak the language among themselves.

In 1972, in response to growing ethnic awareness among second and third generation Basque Americans, the North American Basque Organizations, Inc. was formed (NABO). NABO has been the main agency, coordinating and encouraging Basque events. In contrast to their former obscurity, because of Basque festivals and colorful dancers, the Basques today are one of America's most highly visible ethnic groups.

Here in eastern Oregon, driving by irrigated acres of lettuce and strawberries, we were heading for Jordan Valley. Jordan Valley was once a Basque center for the traditional occupations of mining, ranching, sheepherding, and hotelkeeping, with which they had become associated. Sheepherding was never an occupation Basque young men sought with any enthusiasm. This unwanted and lonely job merely provided immigration opportunities that rural people in the Basque provinces took full advantage of.

Jordan Valley is a town of one hundred and fifty homes. Jose Navarro and Antonio Azcuega were the first to arrive from Vizcaya in 1889. The pelota court, built by Ambrosio Elorriaga in 1915, still stands. Today the Basque national game of pelota is flourishing among the large Basque American population in Miami, Florida.

We started making our enquiries at the stores and gas stations of Jordan Valley. At the Texaco station, we met Joe Zatica and a group of younger men who taught us "egun on" (bore da) and "eskerik asko" (diolch yn fawr). At Phillips Gas we met Joe Corda and Pete Larinaga, both in their eighties; Pete, who never stopped laughing and Joe, who never cracked a smile. The younger men were embarrassed by their lack of knowledge of their grandparents' language. They told us that the only Basque they knew were swearing words.

Joe Tellaria was sorting out bills at the back of his grocery store. Responding to our curiosity, he admitted that as a youth aged eighteen, being a shepherd was lonely and frustrating. Now, in later life, he could imagine being with his wife, enjoying the tranquility of a shepherd's camp on the open range. Joe recommended we go and find Joe Eiguren. Joe Eiguren was a Basque writer and teacher. We could ask for him at the Basque Center in Boise.

At the Basque Center in Boise, we drank several cups of coffee among elderly Basque-speaking immigrants. One or two spoke neither Spanish nor English, but from those who did we learned about what the Basque Center does. The Boise Basque Center restricts itself mainly to leisure activities. The hall is used for dance practices and festivals, while the main business of the membership is playing muz, a complicated card game, and organizing card game tournaments. The people we were talking to made it clear that teaching the language in America made little sense to them. They left all that to people like Joe Eiguren.

Because of the work of Joe Eiguren and the demands of third generation Basque Americans, the University of Idaho at Boise has, in recent years, offered starter courses in Basque studies. The University bookstore did not have any Basque books, however, and this was our first indication that Basque material might be hard to find. Our next problem was to camp overnight and keep our appointment with Joe Eiguren in the morning. A customer at the checkout counter invited us to park on the street in front of his house. He introduced himself as Dan Griep, drew us a map, and asked us to wake him in the morning before we drove away.

Dan's prompt and unsuspicious kindness relieved us of our usual anxiety of trying to make camp in a large city. Our stay with Dan was one of the finest pit-stops that we made. As well as taking a shower each, while eating breakfast we did two loads of laundry, and washed all our pots and crockery. Later we even found time to fill our water tank and wash the van. Dan understood our needs perfectly and provided the greatest assistance by giving us the means to complete important jobs. As if this weren't enough, when we were leaving he presented us with two loaves of fresh, home-baked bread.

Thanks to Dan we arrived at Joe Eiguren's wearing clean, pressed clothes, polished shoes, and in a clean and gleaming van. Not bad when you consider all the miles we'd put behind us.

A tall, angular man with a shock of grey wavy hair, Joe Eiguren practically pulled us through the door. The first thing he asked was why we were so interested in the Basques. We replied that we felt there were similarities between Basque and Welsh conditions in Europe. We were particularly interested in Basque heritage among Americans. In Wales today, we pointed out, more and more organizations are working for the recovery of Welsh language culture and political life. As a result of our travels, Suzanne and I were beginning to feel that increased activity in Wales was being reflected in Canada and the United States. Developments in North America, we felt, were of importance to the cultural and political revival occurring in Wales. Anything we could learn from the success of the Basques and Basque Americans should be very informative.

Wales has an area of eight thousand square miles with a population of two and three-quarter million. The area of the Basque country is twelve thousand, six hundred and fifty-five square miles with a population of two and a half million. About 27% of the Basque speak their native language, compared with 21% in Wales. In the Basque country today some 30,000 adults are enrolled in language classes, while higher education in Basque is available to more students than at any other time in the country's history. The same is true in Wales, with more Welsh schools and adult language classes available than at any other time.

Basque activists have gone much further, however, achieving semi-autonomous status with legislative chambers, conducting business in their native tongue. Fluency in Basque is an asset at all job opportunities and is the mark of an ambitious and cultivated person.

Joe pointed out that these developments are new, occurring since the end of the Franco era of suppression, and in America coinciding with the "roots phenomenon" from 1970 on. Since the formation of the North American Basque Organizations, Inc., regional festivals, university programs and language classes have become more generally available.

Born in 1915 in Jordan Valley, Joe Eiguren became a shepherd until serving in the army during World War II. In 1964, in response to requests from younger people, Joe started holding Basque language classes in his home. In 1969, he published two text books with cassettes called "How To Learn to Speak Basque". Since then Joe founded and became director of the Institute of Basque Studies and established the Basque Studies program at the University of Idaho.

In 1970 the first American students arrived at the University in the Basque city of Ustaritz. Among them was Lynne Fereday, a twenty-one year old who died in a tragic accident at her host family's home. Lynne's college papers and organizational work, however, became a model of the Basque American study relationship. The Lynne Fereday Scholarship Memorial has become one more agency between American and European Basques. The largest Basque studies program is at the University of Nevada at Reno. Other institutions with an active Basque connection are the University of Idaho at Moscow and Boise, and social clubs in Fresno, Redwood City and San Francisco, California. Social clubs also exist in Ely, Reno and Elko, Nevada, as well as in Miami, New York City and Salt Lake City.

Joe confessed that the majority of people at the Boise Social Club had little interest in university programs. Social Club members did not feel there were any threatening pressures on their culture. Most outside enquiries to the Boise Basque Center are referred to Joe, while the members are content to go on playing muz and attending festivals.

In general, while they share Basque American indifference to homeland politics, Welsh Americans are more actively supportive of their leadership. Welsh societies are served by several national newspapers and newsletters, while Basque newsletters have had to close through lack of news and contributions. Joe was intrigued by *Ninnau* and *Y Drych*, and was impressed by the letters and unsolicited articles they received. Welsh societies, while lacking the visual impact of Basque dancers with their scarlet berets and tunics, nevertheless support a wide variety of import stores, college courses, monthly programs and singing festivals. Welsh societies are dispersed however, which dilutes their regional impact. The Basques, concentrated between Boise and Reno, maintain solid university programs which consistently encourage Basque American research and student involvement.

Our next Welsh encounter was dinner with a druid in Salt Lake City, before plunging once more into the Rocky Mountains and then Wyoming.

12

Genealogists, Druids and Hot Springs;
Utah and Wyoming

The druid we were waiting for in the parking lot of Sizzler restaurant was Gwenolwen of California, better known as Ann Davies Thomas. One of the best known personalities on the Welsh American cymanfa circuit, Ann had conducted more cymanfaoedd canu than Suzanne or I had eaten T-bone steaks.

Born in Abergynolwen, Wales, Ann emigrated with her parents to the Welsh town of Emporia, Kansas in 1922. A talented musician, she studied at the Royal Academy in London and at the American Conservatory in Chicago. For thirty years she was a faculty member of Kansas State Teachers College. When the Welsh National Cymanfa Ganu Association published its new hymnal in 1979, Ann Davies Thomas was the editor.

One of the first choirs Ann ever organized was a Welsh Children's Choir in Emporia. Since then she has formed choirs wherever she's lived, taking four of them on Welsh and European tours. She has directed four North American nationals and dozens of regional and local cymanfaoedd canu. In 1983 alone, she conducted festivals as far apart as Oregon, Pennsylvania and Wales. Ann Davies Thomas is still one of the most able directors available to North American cymanfa sponsoring committees.

The Cambrian Society in Salt Lake City was founded in 1852. Dr. J. Preston Hughes, President of the Society and Dr. Thomas Llewelyn Jones arranged the 1985 March St. David's program. There is also a Welsh Ladies Club in the city.

On February 29, 1984, Ronald Dennis, a professor in the College of Humanities at Brigham Young University, organized an eisteddfod at the Wilkinson Center. There were fifteen competitions. Prizes were attractive and the eisteddfod, the first in the University's history, was a considerable success.

Ronald Dennis is a great-great grandson of Captain Dan Jones, the famous Mormon missionary in Merthyr Tydfil. While studying the Welsh language pamphlets and articles of his ancestor, Ronald Dennis started learning Welsh himself. In 1976 he spent six months at the University of Wales, Aberystwyth. Since then he has returned to Wales several times, appearing on Welsh television and Radio Cymru.

Ronald Dennis has taught a Welsh class at Brigham Young University since 1977. Some students from these classes have continued their studies at the

University of Wales, one student taking her M.A. in Celtic Studies at Bangor.

The Prayer of the Gorsedd opening the 1984 eisteddfod was led by Leslie Norris, the Anglo-Welsh poet who joined the Brigham Young English faculty in 1983. Earlier, in 1973 and 1978, Leslie Norris occupied the Visiting Poet's Chair at the University of Washington, Seattle. The Brigham Young University Eisteddfod Committee consisted of Leslie and Kitty Norris, Ronald Dennis, Norma Davis and Arthur Bassett. University choirs, quartets and deans of the faculty all participated, making the eisteddfod a broad-based, officially recognized University competition. With its attention to the Welsh language, descriptions of eisteddfodau and the Gorsedd tradition in Wales, the Brigham Young University Eisteddfod, scheduled to be an annual event, is one of the most encouraging Welsh American developments.

Welsh Americans are among tens of thousands who come to the vast International Genealogical Index located in Salt Lake City. The Index, which contains over forty-five million entries with original documents housed in nuclear bomb-proof vaults, is being compiled by the Mormon Church.

Having established a well-documented family tree, approved by church examiners, Mormons can take the tree through Temple rites and convert their ancestors. Mormon collectors have spent millions of dollars, copying registers and population indices all over the world. In some Welsh dioceses, however, Mormon collectors met with religious objections. Welsh record keepers, bishops and clergy, objected to the ultimate use of the information, and as a result, Index collectors copied less than half of the pre-1837 Welsh records available. Even so, the International Genealogical Index in Utah and microfilm files at Mormon libraries in America and around the world (there is one in Merthyr Tydfil) are among the most accessible sources of genealogical information. Mormon bookstores at the larger Temples also have some of the best method books and reference guides for genealogists.

The Welsh Heritage Research Foundation based in Midvale, Utah, is an accredited genealogical agency and is one of many genealogical agencies found in the Salt Lake City area. Bert Rawlins, owner of the firm, studied for a while at the University of Wales, Aberystwyth, which gave him some knowledge of Welsh record keeping in the field.

The search for roots prompts letters of enquiry to every issue of *Ninnau* and *Y Drych*. In November 1978, genealogist Marylou Wilkinson joined the *Ninnau* volunteer staff. Certified by the Board of Genealogists in Washington, Marylou Wilkinson has completed the Brigham Young University Course in Welsh Genealogical Research and the National Archive Course at the National Institute for Genealogical Research. The great-grand-daughter of Welsh immigrants, Marylou Wilkinson is uniquely qualified to advise Welsh American ancestor hunters. She has written a monthly column for *Ninnau* since November 1978, and for *Y Drych* since November 1981.

Genealogical curiosity is often the first reason for Americans joining a Welsh society. When the St. David's Welsh Society of Georgia was founded in January 1984, over 75% of those who joined it said their main concern was tracing their ancestors whom they knew to be Welsh or of Welsh stock.

Responding to genealogical enthusiasm, increasing amounts of material are becoming available. The Association of Family History Societies of Wales was founded in 1981. In 1983 alone, seven new Welsh genealogical agents advertised in *Ninnau* and *Y Drych*. In 1984 the Wales Tourist Board published a revised catalog of genealogical resources. This free booklet lists many possible record sources, archives and private businesses willing to undertake research for a fee. One of the latest Welsh genealogical agencies is called Welsh Heritage, based in Llandrindod Wells. In addition to the usual ancestor links and copying archive documents, Welsh Heritage arranges travel schedules, hotel accommodations, and even buys small plots of land at original ancestral locations.

☆

We approached the National Parks of Grand Teton and Yellowstone along Star Valley from Geneva to Alpine. Bear Lake was a cloudy, arctic blue. Further north, Jackson Lake was frozen into level silence. We made camp near Moran, where moose and elk peered at us from snowy pastures among the leafless aspens. At Grand Teton all trails were closed because of snow, open only to cross-country skiers or those with snow shoes. Bison hadn't yet migrated to the higher meadows; bears, on the other hand, hadn't yet ventured down to the tourists' breakfast table.

On our second day in Yellowstone, on the 6th of May, a light snowfall came as no surprise to us. Its assured grip on the environment, however, seemed outrageously inconsiderate. The snow fell in a growing blanket over all the roads we'd driven on the day before. Following a casual breakfast, our van joined Winnebagos, 4-wheel-drive pick-ups and hired cars, confident of leaving the park on whatever road we chose.

Our first indication of the seriousness of the storm was an overturned Toyota and a family standing unhurt, but grim-faced in the snow. The second sign was another car that had skidded off the road and down the river bank. Our road to Cody had been closed. In less than two hours, we, with hundreds of other early visitors, had become hostages of the weather.

It was here we made the most serious error of judgment of the trip. Our inability to recognize a critical weather pattern put our lives in danger as we climbed above 10,000 feet through increasingly difficult conditions.

Soon we could neither turn around nor drive ahead without skidding wildly from side to side. Every sharp bend in the steep and narrow road brought new dangers; an inability for our wheels to grip, an avalanche, or worst of all, an approaching car steering as unpredictably as ourselves. We were forced to keep going. At least each half mile forward took us closer to the eastern slope which we hoped would provide an easier descent.

A ranger's headlights appeared behind us, adding to the tension, but also bringing relief. When we pulled over, the ranger said he ought to send us back, which would have been the cruellest and most senseless thing to do. Instead he told us that from here the road ahead should be clearer and easier to negotiate. He was right. At Pahaska, we were east of the continental divide and free of the Rocky Mountains. There was no snow and the temperature rose from about zero to five degrees.

The call of the world's largest mineral hot spring at Thermopolis, eighty-five miles south of Cody, was impossible for us to resist. As we drove there, for one and a half hours the brown and olive features of the Wyoming landscape seemed determined to lull us into a drugged and uninspired sleep. Even the radio with its lonesome calls of the country and western steel guitar could not break the utter monotony of the land around us. The desert with its life potential, perpetually at the edge of action and survival, had kept us endlessly fascinated and alert. Only in Wyoming did we endure the "sickness of vision" described by Robert Louis Stevenson in his "Across the Plains" in 1879.

We soon tired of peering down gullies or waiting till we passed the slightest hill with a hope of discovering a tree, a rock or ruin that might stimulate an observation or insight into the local country. We learned how important it was to find what we wanted in the towns or to search until we found it. We saw nothing in between except marmots, porcupines and the lifeless wire fence separating acres of alkaline sand and sage from the road on which we sped along.

In Thermopolis we cleaned the van and ourselves free of all the grime and snow-brought grit of the mountains. The State Bath House at Hot Springs State Park was a small, clean, indoor pool. Use of this pool was free, complying to conditions by which the pools were ceded to the state by the Shoshones in 1897. There were two other hot spring pools, public, inexpensive, and swimming pool size, with lockers, drink machines, sunchairs and all the other trimmings. The only difference between these and ordinary pools was the odor of sulphureous rotten eggs and slimy algae that grew daily on the floor and walls.

Leaving Thermopolis we climbed the Big Horn Mountains into Buffalo. In Gillette, our visit coincided with a junior rodeo. Nothing demonstrated the traditional skills of the ranching community better than seeing hundreds of teenagers compete at calf roping, bull riding, bronco busting and steer wrestling. The rodeo, an essentially local affair, was a confirmation of the rugged abilities still required of ranchers today. Cowboy boots, clean jeans and crisp white shirts set competitors apart. As onlookers we were excluded from the relationship of human strength and skill against the provoked stubborness of the animals.

13

*The Sioux: Wakantanka Kici Yaon Nin**

Our introduction to the contemporary world of the Sioux started with a casual visit to the Northern Lights Gallery in Deadwood, South Dakota. On the walls were porcupine quill belts and leggings, moccasins, eagle whistles, breastplates and Plains Indian shirts. All the artifacts were new, but all conformed to traditional Sioux standards of design. Contemporary art portrayed the modern Indian condition in bronze and acrylic with titles like, "Urban Indian", and "Children at the Pow Wow".

The owner, Mark St. Pierre, was a mixture of Sioux and French-Canadian. His wife, Colleen, was a full-blood whose parents still lived on Pine Ridge Reservation. They were as interested in "Celtic mysteries" as I was in understanding the world of Native Americans.

We were invited to stay for dinner and sat down with Mark, Colleen, and their daughter, Starshine. Dinner was spaghetti and French bread. While eating there was little conversation. Eating appeared to be a serious business, and there was a straightforward concentration on eating as quickly as possible. Afterwards, Mark wanted to hear samples of the Welsh language, stories, and songs, which he repaid in kind by singing some Dakota Indian songs. Mark played some Buddy Red Bow albums, Sioux-rock with highly evocative rhythms and lyrics, depicting Sioux life today.

Present generations of Sioux, scattered over the Rosebud, Pine Ridge, Sisseton, Cheyenne River and Standing Rock Reservations grow up with an uneven knowledge of their own language and traditions. Some speak no Sioux, while others speak poor English. There is a great inconsistency of support for and commitment to Sioux lifestyle and values in the face of aggressive Anglo civilization. School boards and tribal councils are sometimes bitterly divided between traditionalists with long plaited hair and profiteers who urge the sale and commercialization of Indian lands. On the reservations today, with independent language and cultural groups, artists' co-ops, political activists and patriots, we inevitably had to think of Wales where committed individuals and societies still have to struggle in the face of hostility from fellow countrymen. The inherent value of a distinct cultural identity is recognized, but there can be no compensation for the wasted years of a people deliberately separated from their language and traditions.

Sioux dancers have recently organized themselves into well managed

---

* Sioux for 'God be with you till we meet again'.

groups that tour the U.S.A. Native Americans have never appeared at the Llangollen International Eisteddfod, and when we returned to Atlanta, one of the first things we did was send Mark St. Pierre the International Eisteddfod application forms.

One morning in Custer State Park, we were taking an early morning swim when snowflakes started to fall. Taking the weather very seriously now, we drove to the eastern lowlands near Hermosa. Over the radio we heard about the sudden storm that had already stranded hundreds of tourists' cars.

We perched by the roadside on an uncomfortable shoulder that in all likelihood would become our campsight for the night. We didn't like the idea of parking here, but the thought of spending hours searching for a better place depressed us even more. Every twenty minutes or so a passing car went speeding by, shaking the van, making our camp less and less appealing. Abruptly, a good half mile further down the road, a beat-up old Lincoln Thunderbird came skidding to a halt, then reversed back to us at top speed, lurching from the roadway to the verge. A young man with long hair got out.

"My name is Lauren Two Bulls, do you want to buy some paintings?" He'd been trying to sell them in the galleries in Rapid City. We couldn't really use a painting in the van, but that didn't seem to bother him. Lauren promptly offered to lead us to a campsite overlooking the Badlands. "I know the Badlands like the back of my hand," he said, and we were off, coaxing our van to 70 miles an hour as we chased him into the reservation. Our bedroom for the night was a rampart of pavement above the sodium chasms of the world below. We had an incomparable view of the desert and of the plains. The Black Hills were hidden by the storm that prompted us to drive this far.

Lights out, deep silence, longer between each late night passing car and we both fell sound asleep. Around 2 a.m. we were awakened by the ferocity of the wind, rocking the whole van as easily as a storm-tossed crib. When we got up the sun was glaring with a wintry intensity. We'd had a fall of snow and Suzanne rolled down the window to take a look at it. Double glazing! There was another windowpane! The entire northern side, the front, back, and roof of the van were coated in half an inch of ice. Only the southern leeward side was free. Suzanne punched a hole in the ice and we had to hack ice away to open any doors. It was still below freezing. In the clear sunshine the distant Black Hills were like rolling cakes of frost where the storm had dumped almost a foot of snow on them.

Despite chipping away all day, we never completely cleared the van of ice. More freezing rain or intense cold would interrupt the job and at the long day's end pelts of ice still clung to the lower body work and across the roof. That night we camped inside the Badlands National Monument at Cedar Pass, where we had another fall of snow.

Next morning it was cold but dry and I took Amiga with me when I walked to the public restrooms. Suddenly I heard an anguished grunt and saw the front half of Amiga's body disappear into a hole in the ground. Her hind legs clung bravely until one of them collapsed and she twisted and fell with head and shoulders deeper in the hole. When I pulled Amiga out, her snout, mouth, eyes and ears were filled with a mulch of slush and icy grime. The rut was two feet deep and the filth covered her neck and underside in a sticky, hyperthermal dough. Picking Amiga up, I ran back to the van where we wiped her, boiled water and washed her coat as best we could. Then we dried and brushed her. Her mouth and eyes had filled and she was stunned by her misadventure. Amiga spent the whole day coddled in sleeping bags—a convalescence she didn't seem to mind.

Mark St. Pierre had given us the name of Ethel Black Crow, a porcupine quill-worker. In Kyle, we found Ethel's house, standing as all Indian houses do, at least a mile back from the road. Should we drive up? She didn't know us and we didn't know her. To say we wanted to buy some quill-work would have been a lie, since the fine Sioux crafts were priced beyond our range. Also, it was becoming clear that the Indian reservations were another country. Perhaps walking up to the door of a perfect stranger was not okay. Finally we reasoned that the responsibility of fulfilling this opportunity was ours. If we didn't knock on the door, contact with Ethel Black Crow of any kind would not be made.

"Come around the other side!" a voice called out, and I walked around the back. Ethel was in Rapid City with her daughter, Rachel Red Bear, and only her husband, Francis Richard, was at home. Francis didn't seem at all surprised to see us and after a short talk about the scenery and weather, he asked us to come inside.

In every Sioux home we visited, the aroma of percolated coffee beans preceded several cups of coffee served with cookies or home-baked bread. From Francis our coffee came strong and black and we returned to the stove, taking several mugs during an hour of calm, unhurried conversation.

The living room was a sparsely furnished linoleum space with minimal decoration. There was a deep, broken couch and an easy chair with split plastic upholstery. Near the large wood stove stood a thin formica table and four hard chairs. There was a television with a vase of plastic flowers on it and behind that, a heap of firewood piled on a floor, already patched and tracked with the mud and gravel of the outside world. Francis took a chair and sat opposite us by the corridor to the rest of his small home.

He told us that he didn't have any quill-work at the moment. In a few weeks though, before the tourist season, he would hunt some porcupines and his wife and daughter would have the home "filled with quills". Would any porcupine do? Apparently not. The porcupine had to be of a certain maturity and then only a certain portion of the quills could be used. Francis also told us how the Native American religion and Indian languages were being more widely used. Today, at least, children could receive an education in their native tongue. We spent an hour by the warmth of this stove and he brought out some fossils for us to see. He often found them in a gravel pit behind the house. When he had the time, he went in his pick-up to sell them to the manager of Wall Drug on Interstate 90.

Our next stop was at Wounded Knee, the sight of the massacre in 1865 and of the high school occupation by members of the American Indian Movement (AIM) in 1973. Wounded Knee was typical of almost every Indian town we saw—a cluster of prefabricated homes set back from the road. Our contact here was Tom Casey. We drove straight over the junk of Tom's cluttered yard and parked on a naked patch of mud between his backdoor and the clothesline.

Tom Casey had plaited ginger hair hanging below his shoulderblades. He was sitting down to coffee with Mike Her Many Horses, a tribal councillor, whose black braids reached the waistband of his clean pressed jeans. As a photographer, Tom's work is found in posters, tribal bulletins and magazines. One of his latest and biggest projects was providing hundreds of photos for the Oglala Sioux Community College Report. The second tribal institution of its kind anywhere in the USA, the Oglala Sioux Community College emphasizes support for all aspects of Sioux culture with its purpose clearly stated, "to provide the Oglala Sioux, as a sovereign people, with trained human resources and personnel."

Mike Her Many Horses said that very slowly, despite many obstacles, a qualified professional Sioux workforce was beginning to graduate into the general Indian population. Since the 1970's, greater numbers of Sioux teachers have been teaching Sioux children. Since 1980, Catholic and Bureau of Indian Affairs schools were being taken over by qualified tribal members. These developments, despite an enormous and contradictory federal government bureaucracy, and despite desperate economic conditions, give some Indian leaders a basis for optimism. We were to find that the schools, with their classes of confident Sioux-speaking children, were the most vibrant and visible representatives of tribal hope.

Pine Ridge was a third world, poverty-stricken mess; to us incomprehensible and foreign. The stores were boarded up and the whole mercantile area seemed besieged by poverty and want. While in Pine Ridge we found more specific political literature on Sioux problems. Also in Pine Ridge we saw posters declaring "Free Leonard Peltier" and "Solidarity with Dennis Banks", Sioux leaders generally believed to have been victimized.

Mike Her Many Horses had a cousin, Emil, at St. Francis Mission on the Rosebud Reservation. We found Emil working in a busy office, but when he found a key he quickly volunteered to take us on a tour of the Mission's small museum. In contrast to the Jesuit priests, Emil spoke no Sioux. He had spent time in Paris, London and Rome, and he loved Europe. He was well dressed, had short hair, and here at the Mission school he worked in the administration. When our tour was over, we gave Emil a ride back to his home in Rosebud. Around the compact town, the rolling hills and gardens were particularly beautiful. Emil pointed out that in 1982, Rosebud was the reservation's Blue Ribbon Community of the Year.

We had taken seven days to drive 250 miles from Deadwood to Wagner. In Wagner we had the vaguest of directions to find Clarence Rockboy and a "Give-Away" he was holding in memory of his father.

To find the Give-Away, first we had to find Clarence Rockboy's home in Wagner. Indian housing was grouped at the edge of a bourgeois farming town. After asking in several places we were told to go to Lake Andes. Quentin Burgier, a minister in The Native American Church, lived there and he would be directing the Give-Away ceremony. When we came to a rise, we ought to see a tepee, that would be Quentin Burgier's. Down a dusty track we came to a rectangular home surrounded by cars, pick-ups, and motor bikes spread randomly across two fields. Behind the cars and by the house stood a twenty-eight foot tepee that served as a church in the Native American Religion.

Joe Rockboy, Clarence Rockboy's father, had been a prominent elder in the Native American Church. Joe Rockboy had died one year ago and the Give-Away was to mark the end of the family's period of mourning. Friends and family had traveled from as far away as Oklahoma, Montana, Florida and New Mexico.

Women had just finished setting out plates, bowls and tureens of food when we arrived. Several large tables had been put together in the center of an open space. On it were salads, vegetables, preserves, fried bread, mutton stew, quarters of chicken, cake, kool-aid, iced tea, urns of coffee and cartons of cigarettes. A lot of people were still arriving but almost all the men had been up all night at a peyote ceremony in the Church. When we found Mark St. Pierre he was hollow-eyed and very tired. Mark introduced us to Clarence Rockboy who told us to help ourselves to some food and find a spot among the parked cars and picnic chairs.

There were over two hundred people present, some Navajo and Cherokee, but mainly relatives of the Rockboy family. Behind the picnic, on mats spread out on the grass, Clarence and his wife had made an enormous mound of the things they planned to give away. People came forward and gave him money or presents that he could use. One of the presents he received, and later gave away, was a feather war bonnet, an item of contemporary craftwork worth several thousand dollars.

When people had stopped returning to fill their plates, Clarence stood by the pile of gifts and made a speech. Turning to every person there, he thanked them for the gifts they'd given him that day. He thanked Quentin Burgier, he thanked the Church and he thanked God for the especially beautiful day we all enjoyed.

Then, calling people's names, individuals came forward and Clarence gave each one of them a gift. Some received splendid gifts such as the war bonnet, while others were more modest like belts and western shirts. Mark received a scarlet prayer shawl, hand embroidered with a long decorative fringe. Some people, when they received their gift, held it above them and made a high pitched tremolo. When the pile of presents was low and Clarence had started giving away the rugs on which the gifts had stood, we were surprised to hear our names called out. We were given two beautiful cushions and were touched and surprised at being included in a ceremony where we were little more than curious intruders.

When all the presents were given away, relatives walked from group to group, urging people to take another piece of cake or to have another cup of coffee. Others came by with tools, sewing kits, bolts of cloth and handfuls of cigarettes. They came by again, putting more cigarettes into people's pockets, giving away pens, thread and stationery.

An atmosphere of plenty, trust and generosity found tangible expression in the gifts that people carried. The peaceful murmur of friends in conversation filled the air with a calm and festive happiness. Before leaving we found Clarence and thanked him. He towered above us and gently shook our hands.

Mark had a long drive ahead of him back to Deadwood, and we arranged to have supper together at Fort Randall Dam on the Missouri. The picnic area here had showers, which we made use of with great relief. After a hearty meal of soup and bread, we said goodbye. Mark's unselfish sharing of information had given us the keys to a series of unique and privileged experiences that had enabled us to penetrate the contemporary and enduring world of the Sioux.

Our detailed progress across South Dakota however, had been at the expense of days planned for Minnesota. In an effort to make up time, we indulged in a rare night drive along the Interstate. With the radio on and with a thermos of coffee, we pressed ahead into the cultivated farmland of southern Minnesota.

14

Welsh Hospitality in Minnesota

Swamped by a predominantly Swedish population, Welsh migrants into Minnesota settled in south central Blue Earth and Le Sueur counties, where a concentration of their descendants continues to live today. In 1865, when some two thousand Welsh people were living in Minnesota, the frontier was tense enough to provoke the devastating and violent Sioux uprising against all settlers in the Minnesota Valley. Between 1855 and 1899, however, the Welsh in Blue Earth and Le Sueur counties built fifteen places of worship. Welsh American societies in these counties continue to meet for some of the finest regional cymanfaoedd canu held in the United States.

Unknown to her until the moment we knocked on her door, our contact in Lake Crystal was Edythe Peterson, *Y Drych* correspondent and former secretary of the Minnesota-Iowa Cymanfa Ganu Association. The reception Edythe gave us was typical of the wonderful welcomes we received from Welsh people throughout our trip. Bedraggled as we were, Edythe invited us in without a moment's hesitation.

A fountain of information about Welsh events, people, and places throughout the district, Edythe was a dynamo, constantly active and full of ideas. Burt, her husband, would remind her not to race ahead, but she'd be back on the phone, digging for an old St. David's Society bulletin or making another list of people she wanted us to meet.

Our first evening, at the home of Roland and Rosella Jones, surrounded by a menagerie of Welsh china dogs and horses, Edythe introduced us to the intimate Welsh American world of Lake Crystal. Roland and Rosella were Blue Earth Senior Citizens of the Year, and are both champions of their heritage. Like many people we met, Roland and Rosella subscribed to *Ninnau, Y Drych* and *Yr Enfys*, but they also subscribed to *WAY*, the newsletter of Welsh Associated Youth of America and Canada, an organization we knew very little about.

In 1980, Rosella Jones and Edythe Peterson co-chaired a Welsh Month at Mankato Public Library. Held in December, the theme was Christmas in Wales. In addition to displays and exhibitions, Rosella and Edythe organized lectures, slide shows, school concerts and choral singing. Welsh Month was the latest in a series of renewed Welsh activities. Another contribution was the enormous sign for Llanfairpwllgwyngyllgogerychwyrndrobwllllantysiliogogogoch Gardens, which stands in Lake Crystal Park.

Edythe had visited Wales in 1979. Her first taste of "Welsh" food was a meal in an Indian restaurant. The next day she had an impossible task asking for a "coke" in a North Wales "drugstore".

In 1981, Edythe became a writer for *Y Drych* and deepened her involvement in Welsh American events. I asked her about WAY. What was it? What did it do? She told us that WAY stood for Welsh Associated Youth and was an attempt to involve the younger generation in the WNGGA. WAY was run entirely by younger people. She couldn't tell us any more than that as she'd never met anyone who worked for WAY.

Every year on the last Sunday in September, Welsh people from the Mankato area combine with those from northern Iowa for the Minnesota-Iowa Cymanfa Ganu, held at Gustavus Adolphus College in St. Peter. Led by individuals like Grace Hewitt, Viva Bowen, Janet Zehnder, and with accompanists Karen Jones and Eleanor Cole, this cymanfa regularly attracts up to 600 people. The Minnesota-Iowa Cymanfa Ganu Association has a talented director in Dr. Jane Roberts. Dr. Roberts was born on the Jones-Roberts farm where Cwrdd Mawr (Big Meetings) were held from 1892 to 1916. In 1976 Jane Roberts formed a Welsh senior citizens choir in Mankato. The two sessions of the Minnesota-Iowa cymanfa are always followed by a lively supper of tea, sandwiches and Welsh cakes.

Ellis Jones, distinguished Professor of Business at Gustavus Adolphus College, introduced the predominantly Swedish American staff and students to Welsh hymn singing in 1973. Inspired by the continued success of the Minnesota-Iowa regional cymanfa, Professor Jones organizes a spring St. David's service on the Sunday nearest March 1st at Gustavus Adolphus Chapel. The service features hymns in the Welsh language and attracts Welsh Americans from the surrounding towns of Cambria, Le Sueur, Butternut and Jerusalem, where the original pioneer chapels stood. As officer of the Minnesota-Iowa Cymanfa Ganu Association, with David Williams and David Thomas, Ellis Jones helped arrange Welsh soprano Nansi Richards' recital at the college and her appearance at the 1983 regional cymanfa. Over 700 people attended the March 1st service at Gustavus Adolphus Chapel in 1985.

The Blue Earth County Museum in Mankato has a collection of Minnesota Welsh items, books and pamphlets. The museum library has an excellent local archive which we studied one afternoon on one of Edythe's whirlwind tours. Upstairs we saw the "Welsh room" which contains artifacts from various Welsh immigrant homesteads and the original rough-hewn prairie pulpit used at the Cwrdd Mawr on the Jones-Roberts farm.

Edythe took us to the home of Elma and Vernon Jones. Elma is regular accompanist at Lake Crystal Welsh meetings and she already had Myfanwy Pugh from Utica, New York and Elaine Hood visiting for morning tea. When we were joined by Alice Ann Jones and Margaret and Irwin Williams, Elma's home became a conference of local Welsh personalities.

Margaret and Irwin told us about their home on the Jones-Roberts farm, which in 1980 was declared a National Historic Site. Their farm is a rare surviving complex of buildings associated with the most concentrated settlement of Welsh people in Minnesota. A plaque at the beginning of the drive shows the location of eleven chapels which once stood in Blue Earth County. The Jones-Roberts farm from 1892 to 1916 was the site of the largest "Big Meetings" held in Minnesota. In October 1982, Margaret and Irwin hosted the first revived Cwrdd Mawr on their property. With Elma Jones playing piano and Jane Roberts directing from the farmhouse balcony, a congregation of enthusiasts sang from benches and lawn chairs on the grounds below.

We were only the latest in a stream of visitors hosted by the Welsh of Lake Crystal and Mankato. Marion Carr's annual tours of Wales generate increased visits by personal friends and relations. Parti Ceredigion performed in Mankato in 1980, and Nansi Richards has appeared there several times.

In 1981 a party of thirty representatives visited Blue Earth County from the Young Farmers Club of Wales. The Young Farmers were amazed to hear Welsh hymns sung so fervently in Minnesota. The Americans, on the other hand, were surprised how few of their visitors spoke Welsh, and how unfamiliar they were with the famous hymns. The encounter underlined a significant generation gap between Welsh American societies and people in Wales today. In Wales, less than two percent of the population go to chapel, and cymanfaoedd canu do not attract large crowds.

Marion Carr of Mankato has been taking tour groups to Wales every year since 1982. In 1984 Mr. Carr's tours cost $1850 from Minneapolis or $1650 from Boston. Like the Sacramento tour, Marion Carr's is all inclusive and spends the whole time in Wales. His tour is an introduction to the Welsh world of castles, cathedrals, festivals and National Parks. The tours are increasingly popular and in 1984, Marion organized two consecutive visits from June 1st to the 16th, and from June 15th to June 30th.

Leaving our campsight among the flourishing orchards of Welsh Heritage Farms, we drove to Minneapolis. Edythe had taken us on a whirlwind tour of all the Welsh people and places she could think of. Going from her to the shop of John Dingley in White Bear Lake, however, was like going from a tornado to a hurricane. We were in for a deluge of hospitality which left us stunned from a bombardment of good will and generosity.

In Minneapolis, we visited the Swedish American Institute. Housed in the former mansion home of Swedish American publisher, Swan Turnblad, the Institute has seven thousand members. It serves as museum, library, archive, gift shop, travel and information bureau and reception center for visiting Swedish dignitaries and trade delegations. The Institute holds language classes, folk-art, dance and weaving workshops as well as a wider range of activities that explore and strengthen Swedish American heritage. Contemporary Sweden is represented in traveling exhibits and the visits of artists, musicians and lecturers.

Like Welsh Americans, during the 1970's Swedish Americans experienced a revival of interest in their ethnic origins and immigration history. Swedish pioneer homesteads were restored and language classes and ethnic study programs flourished. Established Swedish American organizations, such as

Donald Anthony, Pennsylvania

Olwen Welk, Wisconsin   Ann Davies Thomas,   Morris Wrench, Ohio
Editor of the
WNGGA Hymnal

DIRECTORS OF CYMANFAOEDD CANU IN NORTH AMERICA

Wales Investment Agency (WINvest) promotion in Pittsburgh,
March 1, 1984

Minnesota Welsh Picnic, July 1984

Governor of Pennsylvania, Richard Thornburg, signing first proclamation
of St. David's Day, 1983

1982 National Cymanfa Ganu, Toronto

Florida Space Coast
Welsh Society leaders,
October 1984

First meeting of the
St. David's Welsh Society
of Georgia, January 1984

Brethyn Cartref Folk
Dance, Boston,
Massachusetts,
March 1, 1984

Pendyrus Male Choir in
Delta, Pennsylvania,
July 1984

Minnesota Cymanfa
Ganu Committee, 1984

Portland, Oregon,
National Cymanfa
work party, May 1984

Folk dancing at Welsh Heritage Week

Edward Morus Jones leading a class at Welsh Heritage Week

Peggy Jones teaching a
Welsh class in
Remson, N.Y.

Alun Hughes
teaching at
Cwrs Cymraeg
y Cymoedd

Bethan Bryn teaching
harp at
Welsh Heritage Week

Mini Cwrs Cymraeg
St. Paul, Minnesota,
October 1984

Cwrs Cymraeg, Wilkes-
Barre, Pennsylvania,
August 1984

the Order of the Vikings, still oriented towards the values of older immigrants, found themselves unable to involve the younger Swedish American generation. This generation bypassed their parents and grandparents by enrolling directly in Swedish study courses, or going to Sweden for themselves. Since 1973, dozens of courses in Scandinavian Studies have been created in American colleges, with over 3,000 students studying the Swedish language. One notable Swedish American student is poet Robert Bly, whose contemporary Swedish translations have found a wide international audience.

The Welsh community has never had a benefactor on the scale of Swan Turnblad, nor has there ever been a Welsh American Center catering to the Welsh American community as a whole. Until the mid-1970's the Welsh National Cymanfa Ganu Association, the principal Welsh organization, was growing more and more out of touch with the younger generation. While they were aware of declining interest, WNGGA officers and trustees were unable to make Welsh language hymn singing appealing to a wider group.

Only since the foundation of WAY, Awr y Plant, Cymdeithas Madog and Welsh Heritage Week, have young Americans been offered contemporary and traditional Welsh culture in a form that might appeal to them. It is still true, however, that the exciting Welsh folk music, folk dance, and folk craft movements find little consistent support among the majority of Welsh American societies. The societies have been unable to design outreach programs offering classes and workshops to a curious American public. Some organizations, notably The St. David's Society of Utica, N.Y., The Welsh-American Society of Washington, D.C. and the Ontario Cymanfa Ganu Association, have successfully campaigned to include new members, but their work, although effective, is essentially local and independent.

A Welsh American Center located either in New York or Pennsylvania could play the same role as the Swedish American Institute. Such a center could provide the Welsh American community with the guidance and centralized information source it presently lacks. The Center, as well as developing a contemporary relationship with Wales, could be an advisor to the large number of Welsh societies who are aware they could be doing more, but lack direction. If such an ambition is unrealistic, the role at least is being fulfilled by *Ninnau*. *Ninnau's* office is probably the largest active Welsh information center in North America. The paper has a council of executives that reads like a who's who of the Welsh American network. *Y Drych* too, since Pat Viets took over in 1980, has created a community of interconnected groups and individuals. *Y Drych* has readers in Wales who have said they get more news of Wales in *Y Drych* than they do in some of the newspapers back home.

In Minneapolis, the Minnesota Welsh Society has existed for over seventy years. The recent progress of the Society can be charted very easily.

1978   Spring—Welsh classes started by Elizabeth Edwards. Voices of the Red Dragon formed.

1978   September—National Cymanfa Ganu first held in Minnesota.

1978 April—Minnesota Welsh Society newsletter launched by Dorothy Jones and Mary Mergenthal.

1979 Summer—Welsh picnic revived.

1980 Spring—Father Ron Bauer initiates St. David's Day mini-gymanfa at St. David's Episcopal Church on St. David's Road.

1980 Spring—Mary Mergenthal forms a Welsh American Children's Choir.

1980 October—Hosted first visiting Welsh performers, Parti Ceredigion.

1982 Summer—Marion Carr leads first Minnesota tour of Wales.

1982 October—The Cwrdd Mawr (Big Meeting) revived in Lake Crystal.

1983 Spring Quarter—Professor Frederick Suppe starts a Welsh Studies Course at the University of Minnesota, Minneapolis.

1983 June—Musical Tribute to Wales held at the Hyatt Hotel, Minneapolis.

1983 August—Cwrs Cymraeg held at Hamline University, Chairman John Kudlaty.

1983 Fall—hosted second visiting choir, Llwynengrin Mixed.

1983 December—held first Plygain Christmas service.

1984 January—Welsh language classes started by Delyth James.

The St. David's Society of Minnesota has been holding a St. David's Day banquet since 1910. Other regular calendar events are a spring and fall cymanfa, participation in the International Festival of Nations and an annual Christmas tea. Since 1980, at the instigation of Father Ron Bauer, the banquet has been combined with a mini-gymanfa on the Sunday nearest March 1st, with the result that St. David celebrations now last almost a week.

Since 1956, the Welsh have mounted their display among the displays of 60 other nationalities at the International Institute's Festival of Nations. In 1982, Don and Mae Anderson and veteran Society officer Jack Davis built a plywood castle, had hostesses in Welsh costume, a battery of information telephones and featured folk singing by the Voices of the Red Dragon, directed by Robert Carr. The castle attracted some attention and 160 people signed up for more Welsh Society information. Welsh displays at the State Fair and the International Festival have also featured an import booth organized by Helen Thomas. Import sales, as well as benefiting Welsh merchants, have raised hundreds of dollars for the Society.

Mrs. Elizabeth Edwards, *Ninnau* correspondent for Minnesota, has organized language and singing classes and trips to distant cymanfoedd canu. Her Minnesota column is one of the most dependable of *Ninnau*'s "Around the Societies" page. Mrs. Edwards' son is Jonathan Edwards, the million selling pop singer who recorded the hit single "Sunshine" in 1972.

Y Drych correspondent for the Minnesota Welsh Society is Mary Mergenthal. Mary's father, Griff Morris, is an entertainer on the musical saw, on which he plays Welsh airs. Griff Morris has performed at State Fairs and on State television and National Public Radio. Mary Mergenthal has been one of the most influential Welsh Society leaders. She was chairperson of the Festival of Nations in 1981 and in 1983, with John Kudlaty, she helped organize the Cwrs Cymraeg at Hamline University. Mary Mergenthal has also been editor of the informative Cymdeithas Madog newsletter, *Cyfeillion Madog*.

The Minnesota Welsh Society has never lacked leadership. Secretary Francis Sanderson did an enormous amount of work to maintain interest during the 1960's and early 1970's. David Thomas chaired the 1978 National Cymanfa sponsoring committee. The committee held a series of seminars dealing with topics such as "Travel in Wales", "The Welsh Language Today", and "The Welsh in South America" and David Thomas subsequently became one of a panel of three setting up the new WNGGA's scholarship scheme.

Other notable officers have included Betty Kinsey, Trilby Chistensen, Richard Roberts, the Reverend Neil Lloyd and Dr. David Williams. Dorothy Jones, editor of the newsletter, also produced the first directory, distributed to the expanded membership as a whole. The 1985-1986 committee consisted of Kay Thomas, President; Trilby Chistensen, Vice-President; Robert Carr, Treasurer; Dorothy Jones, Secretary and representatives John Davies, Louise Morrison and Betty Kinsey.

Visitors to Minnesota frequently arrive from Wales. The Reverend Sidney Booth of Colwyn Bay spoke for four successive Sundays in Edina in July 1977. The Reverend Vivian Jones arrived from Wales in 1979 and immediately joined the Welsh Society. A first class public speaker, Mr. Jones soon became the Master of Ceremonies at Society banquets and other large events. In April 1984, an exchange party of Welsh secondary school teachers arrived in Minneapolis. They were given an unexpected reception by the Welsh Society.

There are no Welsh churches in Minneapolis today. The Welsh Presbyterian Church closed in 1947 and Society activites are dispersed through several Church hall locations.

For many years, Park Avenue United Methodist Church has been the venue for cymanfaoedd canu and Christmas teas. St. David's Episcopal hosts the new spring mini-gymanfa. Voices of the Red Dragon, the singing group, meets on the third Sunday every month at the Bread of Life Lutheran Church on 38th Avenue South. In December 1983, the Society held its first Plygain (Welsh Carol) service. Held in the afternoon instead of at dawn as it is in Wales, the service is very popular with everyone participating in the bilingual presentation and reception that follows. In 1984, the Society embarked on two new ventures. Having given money to Welsh causes in the past, in February a committee was established to organize a scholarship scheme. 1984 also saw Welsh language classes taught by Delyth James at St. Paul's Church Under the Hill, Minneapolis.

Minnesota has one of the most enduring Welsh Societies. For years the only monthly meetings were held by executive officers and trustees. Now the

Voices of the Red Dragon meets regularly as well as the new Welsh language class. An annual calendar of spring and fall cymanfaoedd canu, summer picnics and a Christmas tea is not enough to satisfy current interest. Today, dedicated singers think nothing of organizing bus trips to regionals in Mankato, or even a 5:00 a.m. departure to the cymanfa at the Welsh church in Old Man's Creek, Iowa, 350 miles away.

☆

The short lane to John D. Dingley's home in White Bear Lake was framed by two tight borders of close-cropped hedgerow. When he left school at the age of fourteen, John started working on his father's farm. At sixteen, between milking cows in the morning and rounding them up at night, he started an apprenticeship at Dalton Glass in Builth Wells, Powys. Since arriving in the United States in 1976, John has obtained two university degrees at the University of Minnesota. The hedgerows were just a small aspect of the Welsh world he has built around him. Roland Jones told us that when in Minneapolis we ought to visit "Ding a Ling", the eccentric nickname John's incredibly energetic manner has earned him. John Dingley squeezed more conversation, information and activity into one short evening than we could take.

John's shop, Gwenwst Glass, is located in the center of town. An intense wiry man with a farmer's reserve of strength, he gripped us in the crush of a welcoming handshake. His shop was a crystal display of panes, plates, bowls, goblets, pitchers and decanters—every kind of glass that a craftsman could engrave on. He had a small studio at the back and among patterns of traditional Welsh themes was the recurring motif that gives Gwenwst its name, a spray of opening pods named after the stream that runs through Maes Y Groes Uchaf, John's birthplace near Llanafan Fawr, Builth Wells.

Arriving from Wales with barely the fare to get him home, John is now married and has a successful business. He played us Welsh records, he sang us a song, he took us to the pub, he called his friends and he called a radio station. But we were tired. John, we pleaded, we've been traveling for days across South Dakota, please let us eat supper in the van and we'll join you later. But he had to show us a restaurant where a series of his windows were displayed. Okay, but when we arrived at the restaurant, there was a table for three already reserved and we were invited to sit down to a huge traditional British meal.

When Rhos Male Voice Choir came to White Bear Lake in 1983, John hung Welsh flags and banners in the shops. He hoisted the Red Dragon on the pole at City Hall, organized a public pig roast and gave every man in the fifty-voice choir a Minnesota Welsh Society commemorative T-shirt.

As a member of the St. David's Society, John immediately joined the Voices of the Red Dragon choir. He has served as MC and conductor at concerts, sold his crafts from the Welsh booth, giving 25% to the Society and enrolled in the 1983 Minneapolis Cwrs Cymraeg.

Over dinner we could barely keep awake, and we longed for the confined tranquility of our home on wheels. Back at the studio, with a male voice cassette playing and John singing over his engraving wheel, he carved "Cymru am Byth" on each piece of a delicate sugar and creamer set and gave it to us as a present. Following this, we went home where mercy allowed us to make camp outside his house.

The encounter had been exhausting. Next morning we woke at 6:45 a.m. and woke John to tell him we had to be moving on. Bleary eyed and generous to the last, he wouldn't let us leave without one more present, a Felinfoel "Welsh Bitter" tavern napkin that he'd been sent from Wales.

We crossed the Mississippi, east of St. Paul, and we immediately felt as though we'd left the hardships of the West behind. In the first rest area we stopped for a session of sleep, cleaning and recuperation. We realized how much we had missed the amenities of the East when we discovered with delight that every roadside park in the soft Wisconsin Dells had clean restrooms and a functioning fresh water pump.

15

Cymanfaoedd Canu in Wisconsin

The Welsh Gymanfa Ganu Association of Wisconsin is a genuinely state-wide organization. Founded at the Welsh Presbyterian Church in Racine in 1933, the first committee consisted of John R. Jones, Milton M. Jones, John R. Williams and their Secretary for twenty-one years, the noted Welsh soprano Mary King Sarah. The Association was incorporated in 1960, and a larger board of trustees was appointed to gain a fairer representation from rural groups. This enlarged the state cymanfa "circuit" considerably and a revised constitution was drawn up in 1961. In 1980, a new constitution and by-laws were established.

The Association compiled its own hymnal in 1934. In 1972, under the supervision of Florence Morris, a new hymnal was designed. In 1978 this hymnal was extensively revised with hyphenated Welsh words printed between the staves, making them easier to sing. This new two hundred and sixty-four page compilation was published as the official Welsh Gymanfa Ganu Association of Wisconsin hymnal.

In 1968, the WGGAW established the Wisconsin Welsh Singers, an occasional choir that performs at cymanfaoedd canu and concerts under the direction of Olwen Welk. A more independent group in Waupun called Ecclesiastes III, made up of Greta Aberg, Carol Welch and Ann Lemmenes, also performs at Welsh events state wide. Ann Lemmenes studied for a year at the Welsh College of Music and Drama in Cardiff. Ecclesiastes III is well known for its close harmonies and repertoire of Welsh language folk songs.

In 1978 the Wisconsin State Christmas Cymanfa Ganu was established, and ever since then Wisconsin has had a cymanfa ganu every month from May to November. The annual calendar is as follows:

> 1st Sunday in May—State Cymanfa (at a different location every year)
> 2nd Sunday in June—Wild Rose
> 3rd Sunday in July—Rock Hill (Dalton)
> 4th Sunday in August—Peniel (Pickett)
> 3rd Sunday in September—Madison
> 2nd Sunday in October—Cambria
> 2nd Sunday in November—State Christmas Cymanfa

In 1983, the Association's Jubilee year, a Saturday evening noson lawen was organized for the evening before the Sunday sessions of the State Cymanfa. In

1985-1986 the WGGAW committee consisted of Lee Morgan, President; Catherine Mays, Vice-President; Olwen Welk, Secretary and Lucille Bean, Treasurer.

Our involvement with the Wisconsin Welsh world started in Cambria, a stronghold of Welshness, approximately thirty miles north of Madison. Cambria, population six hundred, was the first town where we saw Welsh street signs and Welsh markers for historical sites. Cambria's annual October cymanfa has been held without a break since 1944, and visitors come to it from as far away as Iowa, Illinois, Michigan and Minnesota. The St. David's Day Banquet takes place on the nearest Sunday to March 1st. About seventy people usually attend for a steak dinner and a program of singing and entertainment. Cambria has supplied its share of officers to the State association, with leaders like Catherine Mays, John Lloyd, Jay Williams, Gwladys Hughes, Tom Williams, Bella Rees, Hugh Griffiths, Eleanor Davies and Margaret Willard.

Our day in Cambria started with a call on Mrs. Catherine Mays, organist, *Y Drych* and *Ninnau* correspondent and former Secretary and President of the WGGAW. From Catherine we found out how lively a small town like Cambria could be. Welsh people, but mainly the older generation she pointed out, held informal monthly meetings. For larger concerts, such as Parti Ceredigion's tour in 1982, they organized a trip to Milwaukee, one hundred and fifteen miles away. To see how deep Cambria's Welsh roots were, Catherine suggested we visit Mary Lloyd, who left Wales in 1910 when she was eighteen years old.

Originally from Llanfair-yng-Nghornwy in Anglesey, Mary Lloyd came to Wisconsin to join her brother and his wife. A calm, perceptive woman, spry and confident, she invited us to stay for lunch. She had recently celebrated her ninetieth birthday, and told us of a world tour she made when she was eighty, visiting family and friends in Wales, Hawaii, California, Madagascar and New Zealand. Over delicious ham sandwiches, fruit salad and hot tea, Mary told us of her arrival in the U.S.A.

She came over on the Britannia and disembarked at Montreal. Taking the train to Chicago, she arrived a day ahead of schedule. Timid, and speaking poor English, she waited all day long at the station platform until, late at night, a policeman suggested she find somewhere to stay. The policeman led her to Hull House, a social center for immigrant arrivals. Here Mary met Jane Addams, the Nobel Prize winner, who showed her to a room. The next day Mary was reunited with her brother, whom she couldn't recognize until he started naming people and places only they could know. It would be forty years before she went home, and she never saw her parents alive again.

In the fall quarter of 1978, Welsh classes were organized in Cambria under the auspices of Wisconsin State University, Madison, Vocational Education Department. Mrs. William Williams of Cambria and Dr. Llewelyn Williams of Randolf were the teachers. A class of twenty attended ten weekly lessons in the local high school.

Now in her eighties and living alone in a large house on Towyn Street, I asked Mrs. Williams where she was from in Wales. In a low voice she replied, "Bethesda", revealing in the awful pause that followed how dear the place still was to her. She told us she would go back to Wales tomorrow, only love for her children and grandchildren kept her in America.

Teaching the Cambria Welsh classes eventually became too much work for her. She felt that if classes were revived by a younger person, they would attract more students than before, as interest in Welsh heritage had increased considerably. Evidence of this was The Welsh Shop, a new store that had opened on Edgewater Street, run by Joan Williams.

Catering specifically to the Wisconsin Welsh societies, Joan Williams manages a growing mail order business. Her catalog features dolls, brass lamps, lovespoons, tea towels, Welsh tapestries and a range of smaller inexpensive souvenirs.

We were surprised to hear how difficult it was to get supplies from Wales. Joan showed us letters from Wales that had no return address. Many of the letters were confirmations of orders with no indication who the sender was. Other times goods would arrive improperly wrapped and consignments of mugs or dolls would be broken or crushed. The only way to get regular and reliable supplies, she realized, was to get them herself. Even then, she pointed out, she was greeted with suspicion by some Welsh dealers who suspected her of building a fortune at their expense.

Her complaints were the same as those we heard from other Welsh importers. Welsh American stores are crying out for souvenirs from Wales. The response is often lethargic, and thousands of pounds in craft and souvenir export sales have been lost.

In Door County, Wisconsin, we visited The Irish House, an import shop filled with every kind of Irish product. The proprietors, Rose and Thomas Murray, told us they once experienced the same lack of response from Irish suppliers. They credited this to merchants being unable to visualize American interest in their products. Once Irish suppliers grasped the size and dependability of the market however, dolls, china, manufactured ornaments and knitted and woven goods began arriving by the score. Some Irish craftspeople regularly visit the U.S.A. in order to keep abreast of tastes and gear their products accordingly.

The heart of Wisconsin Welsh country forms a triangle between Oshkosh, Madison and Milwaukee. We stopped in the rural heart of the Wisconsin state cymanfa circuit at Ripon, home of Olwen Welk, cymanfa director, and Ilah and Lee Morgan, her brother and sister. Our hosts were Maurice, Lois and Kay Morgan, friends of Margaret and Irwin Williams in Lake Crystal, Minnesota. Maurice greeted us with crushing hugs. Had Margaret and Irwin called ahead? No. Maurice didn't know who we were. It didn't seem to matter. Maurice Morgan gave us the most trusting and unconditional welcome we have ever experienced. Without pausing, Morris and Lois opened their home and their remarkable friendship to us. On their dairy farm, we felt at home the second we entered the door.

We had several meetings with Olwen Welk, and her brother Lee took us on a tour of the Welsh chapels and farms of Pickett and its environs. From Olwen and Lee's involvement in the WGGAW, we obtained a good picture of Welsh activities throughout the state.

RACINE

Racine, thirty miles south of Milwaukee, is where the Wisconsin State Cymanfa Ganu Association was born in 1933. Racine was the first Welsh urban settlement in Wisconsin. The Racine St. David's Society was founded in 1889, when some 10% of the city's population was Welsh. But Racine in 1905 was also one of the first to cease Welsh language religious services (Cambria stopped in 1944). Significantly, the Racine cymanfa ganu was revived in 1975 at the First Presbyterian Church when it hosted the annual Wisconsin State Cymanfa. The Racine St. David's dinner has always been a regular event. Through contacts with the Welsh Women's Club in Milwaukee, the Welsh Society in Racine maintains a small Society whose main concern is organizing the spring annual banquet. Their efforts are led by John G. Edwards, T. Glyn Roberts and the widely requested, Alyce Evans O'Neil.

MILWAUKEE

Milwaukee has one of the most vigorous and longstanding Welsh Women's Clubs in America. The club meets on the first Saturday of every month, from October through June. Under the leadership of Gwen Howell, Margaret Guerci and Arline Barsamian, the Welsh Women's Club of Milwaukee and Waukesha County is at the vanguard of Welsh life in Wisconsin.

The club was conceived in 1951 by the Reverend D. Kendrick Roberts when the Welsh Presbyterian Church in Milwaukee closed. In 1955, Mr. Roberts started the Welsh Women's Club annual music scholarship, a Welsh society scholarship of unusual fertility. Recipients have included Jan Pergole, Wendy Runnels, Loree Barsamian and Stephen Jensen, who subsequently played organ at the 1978 Minneapolis National as well as giving many performances at Wisconsin Welsh events.

Over eighty women regularly attend the bi-monthly Welsh Women's Club luncheon meetings. In 1977, the Welsh Women's Club joined Milwaukee's International Institute and embarked on a series of ventures. Their first was the creation of a Welsh kitchen, baking cakes, bara brith and brewing hot tea with hostesses in costume and Mrs. Dilys Spransey demonstrating wool carding, spinning and weaving. Since then the Club has maintained a booth at every International Institute Folk Fair. In December 1979, a "Welsh shop" was opened in the British Isles section of the European Village built on the grounds of Milwaukee Public Museum. Altogether thirty-two immigrant cultures are represented. The Welsh shop features a stone built house, Welsh books, china, cabinets, tapestries, spinning wheel and authentic tall beaver hats. At the grand opening, Olwen Welk conducted the Wisconsin Welsh Singers and Linda Schlotter played the harp.

The Welsh classes of the Reverend Lincoln Hartford are an important part of Milwaukee Welsh life. The Reverend Lincoln Hartford first visited Wales in 1980, as part of a pastoral exchange program. He spent three months sabbatical leave in Wales researching the origins of Welsh hymn tunes and hymn singing. Inspired by the Brock University Cwrs Cymraeg in Ontario, Mr. Hartford started his own Welsh classes. Students met every Saturday morning at Kenwood United Methodist Church. By 1983, there were three Welsh language classes; the Reverend Lincoln Hartford's on Friday, Emma Harder's on Saturday and Gwynn Parri teaching friends at home. In March 1984, Mr. Hartford organized a "mini-Cwrs Cymraeg" at Kenwood Church. Complete with an intense day-long program and a Saturday Noson Lawen, the cwrs-bach cost $25, with Cymdeithas Madog president Alun Hughes of Ontario, directing the whole event. In addition to teaching in Milwaukee, in 1983 Mr. Hartford drove 180 miles round trip every week for ten weeks to teach a University of Wisconsin Welsh course in Oshkosh.

Continuing the involvement of the state university in Welsh American activities, in July 1983 the University of Wisconsin-Stout in Menomonie, offered a ten day study course in Wales. Co-sponsored by the European Center for Folk Studies in Llangollen, the course was called "Village Life in Europe". Combined with lectures, festivals and field trips, the tour cost $550 per student, excluding fare from the U.S.A. to Wales.

Jan Jones Hartford formed the Milwaukee Folk Choir in September, 1980. The choir sings the folk songs of all Milwaukee immigrants with an emphasis on the British Isles, but with particular stress on the choir's personal roots in Wales.

The Wales Wool Shop, started by Mary Griswold, opened in Milwaukee in 1983. Highly fashionable, The Wales Wool Shop has direct links with suppliers in Wales and is an American outlet for Christine Lewis woolen designs of Penmachno Welsh Woolen Mills.

In 1985 leaders of the Welsh Society in Milwaukee were Richard Myers, President; Martha Griffiths, Vice-President; Nora Myers, Secretary and Greg Davies, Treasurer.

WAY

WAY (Welsh Associated Youth of Canada and the United States) was launched at the Milwaukee National Cymanfa in 1970. The brainchild of Gwynn Parri and directed by Mary Griswold, the whole cymanfa weekend was devoted to Youth themes.

Following the Milwaukee National, successive WAY committees, led by

Cynthia Jones, Rod Owen and Bruce Chris Johnson tried to promote the organization but with little success. Its few supporters were mainly grandparents taking out subscriptions for their grandchildren.

In the 1980's however, WAY began to have a slight impact. One hundred and fifty memberships were taken at the Utica National Cymanfa Ganu in 1981, 80 more were taken at Toronto in 1982 and more at Wilkes-Barre in 1983. WAY's membership in 1984 was 209 and the WAY luncheon at the Portland National, directed by Kevin Bowers, was one of the best youth contributions ever to a National Cymanfa.

In 1980 WAY was given a permanent seat on the WNGGA board of trustees. As a trustee, WAY has been able to lobby for funds and youth considerations at an otherwise adult weekend.

As the Portland WAY luncheon showed, WAY can connect its Welsh American base with a growing folk music and folk dance audience. WAY's major obstacle appears to be to convince St. David's Societies that young adults would be interested in their programs if an appropriate format were found.

WALES AND WAUKESHA

Morris Stealey, tenor, teacher and personality of Wales, Wisconsin, became in 1980 the Women's Welsh Club of Milwaukee and Waukesha County's first male recruit. Morris Stealey is a widely respected representative of his heritage. He has taught Welsh classes in Waukesha and from his home, Drws Coch, in Wales, has campaigned to give Welsh names to the streets and houses of his hometown.

Barely twelve miles from Milwaukee, Waukesha maintains an enthusiastic and independent Welsh Society. In Wisconsin no society exists in isolation, and for Waukesha St. David's Society banquets, concerts and the State Cymanfa, which was held in Waukesha in May 1984, visitors come from all over the state, as well as from Chicago. Prior to the Sunday sessions the Waukesha committee held a noson lawen attended by one hundred and fifty people.

Over three hundred people regularly attend the Waukesha St. David's Society March 1st banquet. This celebration has been held every year since 1932, reaching a record four hundred people at the 50th Jubilee in 1982. Recent officers include Ralph Jones, Charles Davies and 1985 President Eloise Morris, who was only the second woman president in the Society's history.

In the fall of 1981, Gwen and Delbert Howell started Welsh language classes every Saturday morning at their home. Twenty people attended and emphasis was placed on achieving fluency sufficient to sing the famous Welsh hymns. Morris Stealey was the teacher, armed with a one hundred year old antique Welsh primer he found in a closet at home.

When we visited Morris in Wales, he had recently remarried, and his new wife, LaVelva, was working bravely to undo the chaos that two years of widowed bachelorhood had wrought. Born in Wilkes-Barre, Morris was raised speaking Welsh. When the village of Wales celebrated its centenary in 1982, Morris arranged to have festivities begin on March 1st, which he opened with "Hen Wlad Fy Nhadau". He decorated public buildings with Welsh flags and signs including the prominent "Croeso i Gymru"—Welcome to Wales. In addition he gave Welsh names to streets and buildings—names like "Bron Derw", "Nant y Calch" and "Ochr-y-Foel". While we were there Morris received two calls from neighbors trying to think of appropriate Welsh names for their homes.

A past president of the Welsh Gymanfa Ganu Association óf Wisconsin, Morris Stealey has seen the whole development of Welsh heritage preservation in the state. He was unselfish in his praise of others, particularly Gwynn Parri, Arline Barsamian and Gwen and Delbert Howell. His greatest praise, however, went to Mary King Sarah, The Welsh Nightingale, who as first secretary of the Wisconsin Cymanfa Ganu Association, built the Wisconsin circuit into what it is today.

Born in Nantlle, North Wales in 1886, Mary King Sarah swept the board at the 1906 Caernarfon National Eisteddfod. She took first prize for soprano and mezzo-soprano solos, and tenor-soprano duet with Evan Lewis from Capel Curig. In 1908 she was the first person to sing "Unwaith Eto'n Nghymru Annwyl" which has since been sung every year at the National Eisteddfod ceremony of welcome to Welsh expatriots. In 1909, aged twenty-three, Mary King Sarah toured the U.S.A. as soloist with the Royal Moelwyn Choir. She decided to stay in America and accepted a position as soloist with the Welsh Congregational Church in Waukesha. At that time (1911) there were six active Welsh churches within a ten mile radius of Waukesha. In 1930, Mary King Sarah organized the "Cymric Choral Society" in Wisconsin. In 1933 her choir joined six hundred other voices that sang at the World's Fair and then the Welsh National Cymanfa Ganu held in Chicago. This experience prompted Mary to make the Cymric Choral Society the basis of a state-wide gymanfa association. Through the choir she also founded the Waukesha County St. David's Society. In 1959 her sterling work was recognized in Wales when she was appointed a member of the National Eisteddfod Gorsedd of Bards.

MADISON

Despite the large number of Welsh descendants in Madison, it wasn't until the summer of 1982, under the leadership of Roy and Estelle Schubert, when they retired to Wisconsin from Chicago, that the present Welsh Society was formed. A lifetime supporter of the North American cymanfa, Estelle Schubert is a highly accomplished organist and has a hymn (Llysfaen, No. 95) in the WNGGA hymnal.

In 1979 the Wisconsin State Gymanfa was held in Madison, directed by

Lyn Harry of Ontario. The impetus of this large assembly prompted a gathering in March 1980 of people trying to organize a Welsh club. Finally in 1982, seeing the increase in Wisconsin Welsh life all around them, Roy and Betty Davies, Tom Buchauser, Ann and Myron Davies and Roy and Estelle Schubert sent out a newsletter announcing the formation of a Cambrian Heritage Society. The first meeting in September attracted fifty people and featured a display of Welsh heirlooms and brochures, and community singing led by Olwen Welk. By November 1982 the Society hosted over one hundred members at an inauguration slide program and a concert of Welsh music.

Bob Gwynne organized a formal ten-week Welsh language class every Monday at Madison Technical College. By January 1983 the new Society had a St. David's Day banquet and a fall cymanfa ganu securely on the slate. The committee that pulled all this together included Roy Schubert, President; Wynn Davies, Vice-President; Megan Nelson, Secretary; Thomas Buchhauser, Treasurer and Ann Davies, Historian. The 1986 leadership consisted of Eunice Evans, Megan Nelson, Kay Newton, Ray Williams and Ann Davies.

The new Society was encouraged by members of the Welsh Women's Club of Milwaukee who came to Madison in December 1982 to decorate a Welsh Christmas tree, among seven other ethnic trees in the Governor's Mansion. Five thousand people visited the display and saw the Welsh contribution.

Barbara Hughes, the Cambrian Heritage Society's correspondent, has kept the Welsh American newspapers, *Ninnau* and *Y Drych*, reliably informed of the club's consistent growth and development. In 1983 and 1984 David Harris, a Fulbright Exchange teacher from Pencoed, South Wales, became an immensely popular visiting member. He taught Welsh courses, was guest speaker at the Society's first St. David's banquet, hosted several of their meetings and he promoted Welsh American activities at numerous speaking engagements. After returning to Wales following the exchange period, David Harris then emigrated to the United States, making his home in Oshkosh, Wisconsin in 1985.

Meetings of the Cambrian Heritage Society are held every other month at Covenant Presbyterian Church in Madison. For the Society's first anniversary on September 18, 1983, Ann Davies Thomas conducted a cymanfa ganu attended by over three hundred people. In June 1983, the Cambrian Heritage Society held its first picnic and general meeting, where a vote of confidence was given to the Society's original committee.

In October 1983, Thomas Buchhauser received the Wisconsin Music Educators Distinguished Service Award. As co-chairman of the Cambrian Society's first cymanfa and of their second St. David's Day banquet in 1984, Tom Buchhauser has been responsible for the good quality musical presentations this Society enjoys.

☆

RIPON AND PICKETT

Moses Morgan, the father of Lee Morgan, Ilah Morgan and Olwen Welk, was a well known director of Wisconsin cymanfaoedd canu and deacon of Wisconsin Welsh religious life. Lee Morgan was a fount of local Welsh knowledge, and the third generation of the Morgan family to farm the same property.

Secretary of the Wisconsin Cymanfa Ganu Association, Olwen Welk, has conducted regional and local cymanfaoedd canu for over thirty years. A striking, attractive woman, she welcomed us with hot tea, Welsh cakes and bara ceirch. Olwen and her sister Ilah live together. An old fashioned reed organ is prominent in their living room. Here, fueled by countless midnight cups of tea, Olwen and Ann Davies Thomas hammered out and edited the new 150-page WNGGA hymnal in 1979.

Olwen had volumes of Welsh American material, including a WNGGA phonetic hymnal. This is the phonetic version of the Welsh National Anthem from the hymnal:

My hāne lahd vun had-eye un an-oo-il ee mee
Glahd Bīre*th* ah *ch*an-torr-yon en-wog-yon oh vree;

But the booklets of eighty phonetic Welsh hymns were never widely introduced. This was a rather desperate attempt to improve Welsh hymn singing before the more spontaneous development of Welsh language classes and local choirs.

Olwen and Ilah urged us to attend the 1983 National Cymanfa Ganu being held in Wilkes-Barre. Held in September, the Gymanfa weekend would fall right on our route through Pennsylvania. In the back of our minds we began to try and fit it in.

Lee and Nora Morgan's farm in Pickett was only a short drive away. Lee had mentioned a pile of old Welsh books his neighbor, David Miller, was planning to burn, since no one wanted them. When I arrived at the farm Lee and Nora had four boxes of books sitting on their kitchen floor. Musty, broken, twisted and mildewed, they appeared to me like precious jewels. We set them out in the sun and examined them carefully. All but two were in the Welsh language, and close to a third had been published in the United States, either in Efrog Newydd (New York) or through the offices of *Y Drych* in Utica. The oldest was published in 1842 in Caernarfon, while the majority dated from the 1860's and 1870's. The books were mainly Bibles or collections of sermons with an occasional local history. The hoard did include, however, a biography of Ann Griffiths by H. Elvet Lewis, an illustrated Welsh language *Pilgrim's Progress*, and an illustrated first edition of *Hunangofiant Tomi* by E. Tegla Davies. Unwisely I grew a little too enthusiastic over some of the books and Lee promptly took them back. After airing the books thoroughly, I eventually gave most of them to Dic Thomas and Alun Hughes, both serious book collectors in Ontario.

94

Lee told me there were "loads" of old books stored at Peniel Welsh church. Other neighbors had boxes of books, stored away in their attics and cellars. I asked to be taken to Peniel. On the way we stopped at the farm of Walter and Lois Davies. We were telling Walter and Lois of our errand when Walter put down his tea and started digging under boxes and shoes in the kitchen closet. He emerged with a bent and wrinkled program from the 1939 San Francisco Eisteddfod.

A cymanfa ganu circuit was started among the churches in the Oshkosh Welsh Settlement by R. S. Parry, in 1904. The others discontinued but Peniel Welsh Church kept on and has held its cymanfa ganu every year since 1923. The small wooden church is adjacent to the farm of Ivor Owens, former President of the Oshkosh St. David's Society and a cigar-chewing draft-horse champion who loudly informed me he hadn't missed a Chicago cymanfa in twenty five years. Ivor appeared at the church to supervise our tour of the vestry and kitchen area. In boxes, among the plumbing, crushed beneath crates of china behind the piano, absorbing more damp and mildew every year, were hundreds of Welsh language books, records, photographs, pamphlets and souvenirs. When I expressed an interest in the welfare of this trove of Welsh Americana, I raised the hackles of my hosts, who informed me brusquely they had their plans for it.

Later, at Lee's farm, Lee brought out old sepia photographs of past Wisconsin Welsh events. The photographs tore just a little more every time we handled them. Lee was so amazed when I suggested that the W.G.G.A.W. laminate them, I felt like an interfering meddler. Lee also had a 1890 copy of *Y Drych* which we unfolded on the kitchen table. Out in the barn, Nora said, at the bottom of an old wardrobe, were "dozens" of *Y Cyfaill*, an important magazine published in New York from 1838 to 1926, and in Wales, Wisconsin from 1926 until 1933. No, said Lee, it would not be convenient to go look for them.

☆

Maurice and Lois Morgan had provided us with a base during our deepest immersion yet into Welsh American life. The phone had been ringing four or five times a day; usually it was Olwen calling with more information or the names of Welsh people she felt we ought to meet. Among them was Mildred Bangert at Oak Hill in Ohio, and Olwen left us with a last reminder that we ought to attend the National Cymanfa in Wilkes-Barre. With a last bone crushing hug from Maurice Morgan and a gallon of fresh milk from the dairy, we left the Pickett area and headed for Oshkosh.

OSHKOSH AND WILD ROSE

Dorothy Kutz has been a supporter of the W.G.G.A.W. and an officer in the Oshkosh St. David's Society. Her daughter, Margaret Dewey, organized cymanfaoedd canu in Fort Wayne, Indiana in 1981 and 1983. We told Dorothy about the box of Welsh books now filling up our van, and she told us that she'd given away dozens of Welsh language books to local rummage sales!

The St. David's Society in Oshkosh was founded in 1919, and is the second largest Welsh Society in the state. Oshkosh was the site of the Wisconsin Jubilee (50th) gymanfa in 1983. Betty Wilcox, Mr. Louis Kinyon, Lucille Bean and Mr. C. Sidney Jones are prominent officers. The Society also has a men's chorus that sings at occasional events. We learned that the old Welsh church at Rock Hill is on the private property of a woman unsympathetic to Welsh traditions, and that the Cymanfa Association has to pay a fairly stiff rent to use it once a year. The owner is not willing to part with the property and there have been rumors that this historic church will eventually be destroyed.

The St. David's banquet in Oshkosh is held on the nearest Sunday to March 1st. In 1983, the Society conducted a ten-week Welsh language course through the University of Wisconsin, taught by the Reverend Lincoln Hartford of Milwaukee. Dorothy pointed out that since 1980, the number of people attending Welsh events, especially cymanfaoedd canu, had doubled. Directors often asked newcomers to stand, and for a while over half the people there were attending for the first time in their lives. Dorothy said that we shouldn't leave Oshkosh without trying to meet Mr. Cadwallader Sidney Jones, former trustee of the W.G.G.A.W., and the man who added the Wild Rose June Cymanfa to the Wisconsin circuit.

Mr. Jones recollected exactly how and why the Wild Rose Cymanfa was established in 1968. He felt that Welsh people in the area, were a little short-sighted when it came to actively preserving their heritage. He regretted the absence of language classes, but reminded us that in the 1960's the demand wasn't there.

In 1900 there were six Welsh churches around Wild Rose, which today is a village of six hundred people. Horeb, the original Welsh Calvinist Methodist Church, still stands and is now a member of the United Presbyterian Church of America. Unable to see Horeb Welsh Church in Wild Rose fail to maintain a song festival, Mr. Jones organized support committees. On the 23rd of June, 1968 Mr. Morris Wrench of Youngstown added one more cymanfa to his impressive record.

Y DRYCH

When we left Atlanta in August of 1982, we had never heard of *Y Drych*. In May 1983, we pulled up at the home of its latest owner and editor, Patricia Powell Viets and her husband, John.

There were two Welsh periodicals in America before *Y Drych*: *Cymro America*, founded in 1832, and *Haul Gomer*, founded in 1848. Both of these however failed within a year of opening. *Y Drych* first appeared in New York

City in November 1850 (dated January 2, 1851). In 1854, John Morgan Jones, the paper's second owner, moved it to Utica where it passed through many ownerships until Horace Breese Powell became owner and editor in July 1960. Horace Powell moved the paper to Milwaukee, where he was a professional journalist for the *Milwaukee Journal*.

For over fifteen years, from 1960 to 1975, *Y Drych* was the only national Welsh American publication. With its combination of news from Wales, items on American and Canadian societies, *Y Drych* maintained the traditions of the Welsh American and Canadian communities.

Horace Powell died aged 83, on June 12, 1980. He was awarded the O.B.E. in 1972 for services to the British community abroad.

Pat Viets told us about her immersion into Welsh America, an immersion much deeper and more sudden than our own. Prior to her father's death, her interest in *Y Drych*, she admitted, had been marginal. Horace Powell's idiosyncratic personality excluded outsiders and Pat rarely gave the Welsh world a second thought. But, as a journalism graduate of the University of Wisconsin and a free-lance writer, when she suddenly found herself able to realize every journalist's dream—to run a paper of her own, she jumped at the opportunity. She held conferences with Gwynn Parri and started attending Wisconsin cymanfaoedd canu. At the 1980 Vancouver National she saw the Welsh American and Welsh Canadian communties at their best and she became convinced that she could make the paper work. Her first issue appeared in October 1980. By 1984, *Y Drych* had grown to a solid twenty pages, and was a welcome and re-established cornerstone of the Welsh American world.

Pat took us to *Y Drych*'s office, where with a part-time assistant, files and correspondence are kept up to date. The June 1983 paper lay in its paste-up stages on a large desk in the center of the room. In another room, boxes of material spilled, being cut and mined for graphics and references. The three room headquarters was small and busy. Correspondence arrived daily and a bulletin board of deadlines and appointments revealed the amount of work that goes into every issue. Pat was particularly proud of her extensive contacts in Wales, her growing list of feature writers and of *Y Drych*'s library of photographs.

In *Y Drych*, Pat Viets provides Welsh readers with a professional, well-designed newspaper. In 1984 she visited Wales for the first time and her own descriptions of Wales were sympathetic and clear. As a result of its editor's professional background, *Y Drych* is unmaudlin, combining reports of Wales today with good coverage of North American Welsh activities. *Y Drych* is an interesting monthly paper. It is prepared with the attitude that its material should be readable to all subscribers whether they are Welsh or not.

Pat shattered our preconceptions of a Welsh lady searching for Cambrian tid-bits. There was no shortage of material sent by correspondents every month. With a high impact format, greatly assisted by excellent front page photographs, *Y Drych* packs a punch that shows no signs of tiring. In Pat

Viets' capable hands circulation has tripled, feature articles match news items in column space and the paper has a professional ambience complementing the integrity of its readership, while keeping them informed and entertained.

16

Welsh Variety and a Breton Connection; Through Illinois, Indiana and Michigan

Chicago remains a city of Eastern European immigrants. Over seventy-four ethnic publications have their headquarters there, including seven Czech, five Polish, seven Ukranian and fifteen Lithuanian. Many ethnic newsletters and bulletins, however, collapse through lack of interesting material. Compared with some other immigrant groups, the Welsh are served by several well-managed journals of consistent good quality and subject matter.

From 1845 on, nine Welsh churches were established in Chicago. The last to close was Southside Welsh Congregational which merged with Hebron Welsh Presbyterian in 1958. The Hebron congregation still exists, having merged with the Presbyterian Church of America in 1920, and worshipping today at Hebron Welsh Westminster United Presbyterian Church in Des Plaines, directly adjacent to O'Hare International Airport.

The Reverend Aeron Davies supervised the closing of the Hebron Welsh Church premises on Francisco Street, Chicago, and the move to Des Plaines. This complicated task was completed on March 21, 1976 with a dedication and mini-cymanfa led by Idwal Parri of Oregon. Hebron's present minister is the Reverend Henry Warkentin, who still leads a bilingual service for the dwindling Welsh congregation. Hebron produces *Yr Utgorn* (The Clarion), a monthly newsletter that always contains one or two prayers and a bible reading in the Welsh language. There are no Welsh classes, meetings or other Welsh events held at the church, however, which has yet to become a venue for Welsh American programs.

Welsh activities in Chicago are maintained by the Cambrian Benevolent Society and the Women's Welsh Club of Illinois. There is also a Chicago Cymanfa Ganu Association and a Friends of the Chicago Cymanfa.

The Cambrian Benevolent Society was founded in 1854 as an immigrant support group. The Society's main function today is sponsoring the annual St. David's banquet which is held on the Saturday evening closest to March 1st. In recent years, the banquets have featured a dinner/dance with attendance being around two hundred people. The Cambrian Benevolent Society has an annual general meeting in April. Its only other regular event is a picnic in July which about fifty usually attend. The Society's most active leaders in recent years have been Evelyn Finnegan and David W. Davies, assisted by Janice Batty, Mrs. Howard Jones and John and Gwynedd Moriarty.

The Women's Welsh Club of Illinois meets on the third Saturday of every month at the Wesleyan Methodist Church in Broadview. Apart from raising money for the Welsh Retirement Home in Cleveland, which is the primary function of all the Women's Welsh Clubs, the WWC of Illinois also doubles as the cymanfa committee and provides refreshments for the supper between cymanfa sessions. Faithful and persistent leaders of the WWC of Illinois include Margaret Evans, Muriel Watchel, Ceinwen Thomas, Blodwen Owen, Beulah Saxton and two ladies with whom we spent an afternoon, Rae Jones and Margaret Davies.

The annual Chicago Cymanfa Ganu is held the third Sunday every May at Park View Presbyterian Church in Oak Park, with sessions at 3 p.m. and 6 p.m. In 1981, the Reverend R. Gordon Collier, a member of the Chicago Cymanfa Ganu Association, started a new Christmas Cymanfa at his church, Eden United Church of Christ. Combined with a Women's Welsh Club Christmas tea, this Advent Cymanfa, held on the last Sunday in November, is the best and most encouraging Chicago Welsh innovation in recent years.

In Chicago, we had several Welsh encounters. One interesting meeting was with two Welsh girls working as au pair in Highland Park. *Lady Magazine* in Britain advertises for au pair and there exits an informal au pair network in Merthyr Tydfil and Newport. Being unofficial however, this work is untaxed and illegal, but girls hear from one another who the good employers are.

One young woman, Donna Marie Staple, set up a Welsh booth at Deerfield's Ethno-Center in 1979. Surrounded by flags, banners and records, Donna also gave away buttons saying 'Rhowch gusan i mi' (Give me a kiss) to anyone who would attempt to read them. Donna's effort was inspired by the Lewisburg Cwrs Cymraeg, which she attended in 1978. Unfortunately, it was never repeated. Donna designed the highly effective Cymdeithas Madog logo, one of the most recognizable motifs of any Welsh association.

Our most rewarding visit in Chicago was an afternoon in the company of Helen F. Richards. With her slim figure and lively manner, Helen could have passed for sixty. When she told us she was ninety, we were openly amazed. A past president of the Women's Welsh Club of Illinois and a former WNGGA trustee, Helen was born in Lampeter and emigrated to America with her parents. Deeply involved with the Welsh community in Chicago for over twenty years, she used to broadcast Welsh music every St. David's Day.

Helen Richards' determination to promote Welsh awareness has earned her the nickname of "the Barbara Walters of the Welsh world". She regularly sends contributions to *Ninnau*, *Y Drych* and *Yr Enfys*, and was overseas speaker from the stage at the Lampeter National Eisteddfod in 1984. She is a staunch supporter of *WAY*, and sends the editor new subscriptions taken out by her youngest friends. In 1984, she organized a St. David's dinner for older people in Evanston for whom, the dinner/dance would have been too much. Helen runs the only Welsh language class in Chicago, teaching two friends, Cora Winston and Margaret Williams, who both attended Brock University Cwrs Cymraeg in 1979.

In 1981 Margaret Williams published *And They Came To America*, a novel based on her grandparents' immigration from Wales. In 1984, a bardic chair carved by John B. Reese, the subject of the novel, was exhibited at the Chicago Historical Society. The chair was subsequently shown as part of a "Unique Furniture Exhibition" in New York and Washington D.C. Another novel about Chicago, *I Chicago'n Bymtheg Oed*, (To Chicago at Fifteen), was written by Mrs. Ellen G. Evans when she was ninety years old.

Outside Chicago, there is another Welsh touchstone, in Macomb, at Western Illinois University. In 1984, Fred Jones, professor at the University and a graduate of Cardiff College of Art, finalized a touring portfolio/exhibit of Welsh poets and painters. Supported by the Welsh Arts Council, the Illinois Arts Council and the Welsh American Foundation, the portfolio featured the work of seven painters and seven poets, with calligraphy by Jonah Jones. This major project was the first Welsh fine art touring exhibit of its type in the U.S.A. All of the organization was done by Fred Jones through State and University gallery networks.

INDIANA

In Door County, Wisconsin on the last weekend in May, we were shivering in the snow. We thought winter would never end. The heat finally caught up with us, reaching 94° when we were on a tour of the Frank Lloyd Wright Home and Studio in Oak Park, Illinois. As we drove into the cornbelt of northern Indiana, the full heat of summer came upon us and we paused to rearrange the van and put our winter clothes away.

The strongest Welsh presence established in Indiana was by Robert Owen, a Welsh industrialist and father of the British cooperative movement. Robert Owen was born in 1771, in Newtown, Montgomeryshire (now Powys). A Utopian philosopher and social philanthropist, he bought the property of a religious community that had existed at New Harmony, on the banks of the Illinois River. Robert Owen's writing, made an impact in the U.S.A. and earned him an introduction to President John Quincy Adams. The experimental community at New Harmony did not succeed and Robert Owen returned to Wales. His son, Robert Dale Owen, remained in the States and became a congressman for Indiana. Robert Dale Owen was a strong representative for women's rights in the pre-suffragette years, and played an important role in the establishment of the Smithsonian Institute.

In 1965 Joyce Varney of Indianapolis published her autobiographical novel, *A Welsh Story*, which describes the emotions and experiences of growing up in a Welsh American home, only hearing about Wales through the stories of her parents and their friends. The only Welsh church built in Indiana was at Gas City, about fifty miles south of Fort Wayne. The church stood for about ten years around 1900. Today it is the custom for Welsh Americans in Indiana drive to Gomer or Cincinnati in Ohio to participate in Welsh programs there.

There was a St. David's Society in Fort Wayne, but it disbanded in the early 1960's. Margaret Dewey, daughter of Dorothy and Orin Kutz in Oshkosh, Wisconsin, was given custody of the Society's old WNGGA hymnbooks. Margaret Dewey organized two cymanfaoedd canu in Fort Wayne in 1981 and 1983. Both were held at Forest Park United Methodist church and over one hundred people attended. The future of the cymanfa is in doubt though, since no Welsh society or congregation exists to maintain it. Rhys Price Jones, who conducted the 1983 cymanfa, is from Bangor, Wales, and teaches mathematics at Purdue University. For a while in 1979-1980, Rhys Jones taught Welsh classes at the University, but they closed through lack of interest.

☆

The Welsh Black Cattle Association of The United States has its headquarters in Shelburn, Indiana. Welsh Black Cattle were first imported into the U.S.A. in 1963 by Frank Welsh of Reno, Nevada. In June 1974, with the help of the Welsh and Canadian Black Cattle Associations, the U.S. Welsh Black Cattle Association was born. In 1984, there were 275 purebred Welsh Black females, 104 pure-bred males and 525 percentage Welsh Black Cattle recorded in America. Through their annual conference and periodical *Welsh Black Cattle World*, breeders are developing a profitable agricultural connection with Wales. Welsh Young Farmers and American 4-H Clubs have increased contacts considerably in recent years, and the Welsh Black, commemorated on a 1984 British postage stamp, is one of the most visible signs of their cooperation.

Other American breeding groups include the Welsh Pony and Cob Society, the Welsh Terrier Club and the Cardigan and the Pembroke Welsh Corgi Clubs.

☆

The Welsh Pony and Cob Society of American was founded in 1906, and has its headquarters in East Troy, Wisconsin. With membership approaching one thousand, the Society publishes *Welsh Roundabout*. The magazine advertizes Welsh ponies for sale throughout the U.S.A., many of which have Welsh-sounding names like Parc Angharad, Tylwyth Tuppence, Penrhyn Puccini and Coed Coch Meilyr. *Welsh Roundabout* encourages visits to Wales and promotes an appreciation of "the equine aspect of Welsh history and culture". As well as the Welsh Pony Society of America, there are Welsh Pony societies in over thirty foreign countries.

☆

The Welsh Terrier Club of America was founded in 1900, fifteen years after the first pair were imported from Caernarfon. The quarterly publication of the Welsh Terrier Club is the *Welsh Wag*, and an annual convention is held every October at Montgomery City, Pennsylvania. The Montgomery County Kennel Club Dog Show is limited to Welsh Terriers only, and usually draws about seventy-five competitors. The Club has about 350 members nation-wide. Its newsletter, decorated with red dragons, includes Welsh recipes, and dogs are frequently given Welsh names. The Welsh terrier is a black and tan (red) dog of about twenty pounds, not unlike a miniature Airedale, but with folded ears and a cropped tail. A major campaign of the Welsh Terrier Club is to restore the quality of an original "tan" red color instead of the "yellow" that tan is mistakenly assumed to be.

☆

There are two Welsh Corgi Clubs in the United States, the Cardigan and the Pembroke. The main difference between the two is that the Cardigan Corgi keeps its bushy tail, while the tail of the Pembroke is cropped. Both clubs were founded in 1936.

The Cardigan Welsh Corgi Club has 246 members. The first pair were imported in 1931. The Pembroke Welsh Corgi Club has a larger membership and Pembrokes are the official dog of Queen Elizabeth II. Welsh American writer Esther Elias also bred Pembrokes and her dogs are the subject of two enchanting canine biographies, *Profile of Glindy* and *The Queening of Cerid-wen*. As the smallest working dog in American Kennel Club competitions, at first corgis appeared comical alongside noble golden retrievers and great German shepherds. Since winning many firsts in the working category, how-ever, this intelligent herding breed is winning the admiration of a growing circle of American owners. American corgis also receive Welsh names and their owners are among the most regular visitors to breeders' homes in Wales.

BRETON

Bloomington, Indiana is where Lois Kuter established the American Branch of the International Committee for the Defense of the Breton Lan-guage in 1981.

Along with Welsh and Cornish, Breton makes up the Brythonic branch of the Celtic languages. Breton today is the closest living cousin of Welsh and Bretons have to struggle for the survival of their national tongue and their identity as a people.

In the 1980's Breton activists have made some improvements for the status of their language. But the situation for Breton under French centralist rule is grim compared with the relative tolerance of the British government in Lon-don. Bretons have been looking to Welsh language campaigns as an example. The National Eisteddfod of Wales has helped re-establish Breton eisteddfo-dau, and some Breton language militants have adopted the painting out roadsigns technique originated by Cymdeithas yr Iaith Gymraeg. In 1978, Bangor, North Wales, twinned with the Breton town Lannion, and since the creation of S4C in 1982, Breton television programs have appeared on Welsh TV.

The International Committee for the Defense of the Breton Language was established in Brussels in 1975 to generate extra-Breton support for the language campaign in their country. The ICDBL has fourteen international branches involving non-Bretons in struggles against the mono-lingual policies of Paris. This non-Breton aspect allows Welsh societies to observe Breton techniques in restoring their threatened language. The ICDBL U.S. branch has approximately 150 members nationwide, including the editor of *WAY* and the director of Welsh Heritage Week.

The relentless campaigns of Cymdeithas yr Iaith Gymraeg, the American success of Cymdeithas Madog and the establishment of the Nant Gwrtheyrn Trust (saved from early oblivion through generous support by the Prince of Wales Trust) reflect different aspects of the new chance Welsh is being given. The conditions for Breton are savage by comparison. There is no school certificate at any level for Breton, and in the whole country there is no official Breton classroom time. One of the main campaigns of the ICDBL is to create a Breton teaching certificate and Breton medium schools at least at the elementary level.

The U.S. Branch of the ICDBL, through the tireless pen of Lois Kuter, has an impressive shelf of publications for sale. ICDBL textbooks, histories, directories and bibliographies demonstrate a whole aspect of language promotion that Welsh Americans could explore. The ICDBL U.S. Branch's highly effective work for the recognition and preservation of the Breton language has many lessons for Welsh American organizations. Welsh American societies could only benefit from an improved understanding of this dynamic group so closely related, yet significantly different from themselves.

MICHIGAN

It was in Detroit, Michigan that *Ninnau* was first conceived by retired journalist, Jack O. Morgans, originally from Newcastle Emlyn, Dyfed.

As voluntary P.R. Officer for the WNGGA, Jack was already submitting articles to *Y Drych, Yr Enfys, The Hymn* and many other outlets. He also writes for the *Western Mail* and is part of Alun Williams' "Alun yn Galw" (Alun Calling) worldwide telephone network. In 1975 Jack discussed the feasibility of *Ninnau* with Arturo Roberts, then living in Grosse Pointe Woods, Michigan, and the editor of an American Argentinian newsletter. Both men felt the decline of interest in the National Cymanfa was avoidable and could be reversed. Jack Morgans in particular believed the fall in National Cymanfa attendance was the result of a lack of communication between Welsh people, and that a newsletter would bring them back.

At the New York City National Cymanfa in 1975, Jack Morgans and Arturo

Roberts discussed the idea with Donna Davies and Jayne Pryddarch, both former editors of *Pethau Cymreig* in San Francisco. Talk about the new paper spread among supporters of the National as they gathered in the Hilton Hotel, where the New York National was being held. Feelings were expressed that a good Cymanfa Ganu presence was essential for the bi-centennial National in Philadelphia in 1976. This deadline motivated *Ninnau* supporters. In two days they raised over two hundred new subscriptions.

The first *Ninnau* appeared in November 1975. The editorial council consisted of Arturo Roberts, Jayne Pryddarch and Jack O. Morgans; Anne Cowie, Baltimore; Gwynn Parri, Milwaukee; Ben Haddock, San Diego; Donna Davies, San Francisco; Richard Loomis, Rochester; Owen C. Roberts, Montreal and the Reverend Bill Lewis, Scranton—all well connected supporters of Welsh life in North America. Editorial correspondents doubled in the first month and the paper was joined by John Nichols, Gwenfyl Jones, Esther Elias, Daisy Heaton, Elizabeth Edwards, John R. Owen and Llinos Owen Boys.

Within six months, *Ninnau* grew from four duplicated sheets to a folded twelve-page magazine. By the time *Ninnau* graduated to its present newspaper format in November 1978, Arturo Roberts had created a network of over seventy correspondents in Canada and the United States. By November 1979, three thousand copies of *Ninnau* were being printed. By November 1984, the paper had a press run of six thousand, and by 1985 on its 10th anniversary celebration the paper could boast an Editorial Council of 159 contributors from America, Canada, Wales and Patagonia

The appearance of *Ninnau* has, possibly, been the single most important development in recent Canadian and American Welsh life. *Ninnau*'s search for outlets and its front page support for every Welsh American project, has transformed the level of Welsh activities in North America. At least eighteen Welsh societies have been started since 1975, and if we include subdivisions, language groups and musical societies, the figure is nearer fifty.

☆

When Gwynfor Evans visited Detroit in 1958, he spoke to a packed audience at the Welsh Presbyterian Church. The Reverend John R. Owen was the minister and Menna Williams and ladies in Welsh costume provided a sumptuous reception. But in the summer of 1975, Welsh life in Detroit was dormant, to say the least. Depressed by the violent closure of their church on Monerrey Avenue during the race riots of the 1970's, the Welsh congregation had not reorganized.

A Welsh church in Detroit was founded in 1853, reorganized in 1919, and its own building was dedicated in 1935. Detroit has held an annual St. David's Day banquet since 1908. During the 1970's, however, most Detroit members attended the Windsor, Ontario celebrations. Slowly, Bill and Joan Ley, Mary Aubrey and Florence Rutherford have re-established the Detroit St. David's banquet. One hundred and twenty attended in 1984, including a large contingent from Windsor. In Windsor, Ontario, The Welsh Ladies Society, led by Mrs. Melba Dick, Gillian Price and Gwen Meyrick holds the annual St. David's banquet. Started in 1939, the banquet is the only regular Welsh event that Windsor has. Ivor Chandler, who died in 1979, born in Abersychan, Wales, was a prominent personality in Windsor Welsh life.

Flora Jones is a Welsh graduate of the University of Wales, Cardiff. Flora has tried to revive Windsor Welsh enthusiasm, acting as guest speaker at the Windsor banquet three years in a row. Her ideas, however, fell on more fertile soil in Detroit. As a result of her and her husband's contributions, the Detroit banquet has become a mini-festival in its own right.

Mary Aubrey, a competitive elocutionist and winner at the Urdd National Eisteddfod in Wales, recites and sings. Rhys Lewis conducts, Ruth Lewis is accompanist and Flora Jones and Gwen Davies sing folk songs. In 1983, Flora and Joseph Jones initiated a "Chairing of the Bard" for the best Welsh and English language poem. These dedicated people, sharing jobs and providing refreshments and entertainment, have brought Detroit Welsh life back to the fore of ethnic activities in Michigan.

In 1969, the Reverend Meurwyn Williams from Wales became pastor of the Outward Drive Church in Detroit. While in Detroit, Mr. Williams invited forty Welsh teenagers over for two weeks home-stay with members of his congregation. Arrangements in Wales were made by R. Emrys Jones of Towyn, Gwynedd. The closure of their church in 1975 seriously affected Welsh people in Detroit. The minister of the Church during this very difficult period was the Reverend Emrys Jones, now living in Carmarthen, Wales.

During the 1940's, the Reverend Daniel Hughes, was the vicar of the Detroit Welsh Church. Under his ministry, church singing flourished, there were several choirs, and a church Welsh Male Quartet performed regularly on Detroit radio. The Reverend Hughes was also known as "The Sledgehammer Parson": while minister of a chapel in Wales, wealthier patrons had locked the gates, keeping other members of the congregation out. Daniel Hughes sent for a miner's hammer and smashed the locks. He was prosecuted for this but was given ministry of another chapel, taking the majority of the former congregation with him.

While living in Wales, Daniel Hughes won four National Eisteddfod Bardic chairs and served as an eisteddfod adjudicator. He was also the author of several books and plays. He served on the Court of Governors of the University of Wales and on the governing body of the National Library of Wales. In America he founded the Welsh American Library and made extensive translations of hymns into Welsh and English. In Detroit, this powerful man compiled a bilingual hymnal still used by many churches today, among them, Dewi Sant Welsh United Church in Toronto.

On September 27, 1981, and again in April 1983, cymanfaoedd canu were held in Grand Rapids, Michigan, led by Morris Wrench. Both were organized by resident minister, the Reverend Joseph Howell. At the 1981 Grand Rapids cymanfa, out of 125 people present, only eight had ever been to a cymanfa before. In April 1984, a new cymanfa organized by the Reverend Arvel Steece was held at the First Congregational Church Detroit attracting 150 people.

In 1978 the Detroit Welsh congregation began to reassemble at Redford Presbyterian Church on W. McNichols Street. Here, the annual cymanfa ganu, a tradition since 1937, had been revived under the baton of John R. Jones of Lansing and the organ accompaniment of Bill Jones.

At Redford Presbyterian Church, Welsh people gather after services every week in what has become a "Welsh corner" for coffee and cookies. These weekly meetings hatch other plans, including an informal Christmas tea that has now become a regular Welsh Society celebration, with singing and refreshments provided by the Dorcas Circle.

The Detroit Welsh Society can also rely on Huw Lewis from Abertillery, Wales, former organ scholar at Emmanuel College, Cambridge and a graduate of the Royal Academy, London. A winner of the American National Organ Competition in Fort Wayne, Huw is currently musical director at St. John's Episcopal Church, Detroit, and is on the organ faculty of Wayne State University. In 1982, Huw led the Detroit St. John's Choir on a tour of the British Isles.

Outside Detroit on the University of Michigan's Ann Arbor golf course, a refreshingly different Welsh American meeting has been held every year since 1979, The Bobby Jones Golf Tournament. Bobby Jones, still considered one of the greatest golfers of all time, achieved the "grand slam" in 1930, when he won the British Amateur, British Open, American Amateur and the American Open. Following his retirement to practice law in Atlanta, Ga., Bobby Jones built the Augusta National Golfcourse and founded the Masters Tournament, the most prestigious tournament in American golf.

In 1978, Robert A. "Computer" Jones of Michigan organized the Bobby Jones Golf Tournament, with the only rule of entry being that participants must be known by some form of Robert or Roberta Jones. Seven golfers entered in 1979, eighteen in 1980 and sixty in 1983. All entrants were given nicknames like "Hubcap" Jones, "Rolaids" Jones, or "Too Tall" Jones, to distinguish one player from another. Funds raised from the tournament are donated to syringomyelia research, the spinal disease of which Bobby Jones died. "Computer" Jones estimates there must be ten thousand Bobby Joneses in the United States, and through *Ninnau* and *Y Drych* he reaches a growing number of them every year.

Ann Arbor, where The Bobby Jones Open is played, is also the twin city of Brecon, Wales. The Brecon Cathedral Choir toured here in 1976.

Detroit Choirs led by Harry Lansford have won more competitions at the Llangollen International Musical Eisteddfod than any other choirs from Canada or the United States. In the male category, The University of Michigan's Men's Glee Club has taken more firsts than any other choir in the world, from over fifty competing countries. Many Canadian and American choirs make the trip to Wales, but the record from Detroit is most impressive.

American and Canadian Winners
at Llangollen International Eisteddfod

Male Choirs

1959 1st Prize, University of Michigan Men's Glee Club, Detroit.
1968 1st Prize, University of Michigan Men's Glee Club, Detroit.
1971 1st Prize, University of Michigan Men's Glee Club, Detroit.
1978 1st Prize, University of Michigan Men's Glee Club, Detroit.
1981 1st Prize, University of Michigan Men's Glee Club, Detroit.
1982 2nd Prize, Second Apollo Club of Minneapolis.

Mixed Choirs

1965 1st Prize, Bakersfield College Choir, California.
1968 1st Prize, Brigham Young University A Cappella Choir, Provo, Utah.
1973 3rd Prize, Wayne State University Chamber Singers, Detroit.
1979 3rd Prize, Wayne State University Chamber Singers, Detroit.
1982 3rd Prize, Wayne State University Chamber Singers, Detroit.
1983 3rd Prize, Wayne State University Chamber Singers, Detroit.

Female Choirs

1958 1st Prize, Smith College Singers, Northampton, Mass.
1968 1st Prize, Anne Campbell Singers, Lethbridge, Canada.
1971 1st Prize, Denby High School Glee Club, Detroit.

Folk Song Parties

1951 1st Prize, St. Joseph's University Choir, Canada.
1961 1st Prize, Bob Mantzke Choralaires, United States.
1965 1st Prize, St. John's University Men's Chorus, U.S.A.
1967 1st Prize, Bob Mantzke Choralaires, United States.

Children's Choirs

1982 1st Prize, Toronto Children's Choir, Canada.

Youth Choirs

1973 1st Prize, Denby High School Glee Club, Detroit.
1979 2nd Prize, University Concert Choir of California.

In 1983, Harry Langford took Margaret Rees to Llangollen with the Wayne State Chamber Singers. Margaret, aged 23, won first prize in the soprano solo competition against fifty-three other contestants. A soloist at Detroit cyman-faoedd canu and St. David's banquets, Margaret won a St. David's Society of the State of New York competition in 1980, and attended the Lewisburg, Pa. Cwrs Cymraeg in 1981. Winning at Llangollen brought her a series of Welsh Arts Council sponsored appearances. Through courses offered by Cymdeith-as Madog and the support of her parents, Mr. and Mrs. Carlyle Rees, Margaret Rees has a good command of Welsh. At a December 1983 concert at Redford Church, following her victory in Wales, she sang several hymns in Welsh. While studying in London she competed in Welsh National Eisteddfod soprano competitions, which require twenty minutes of singing in the Welsh language.

The Llangollen International Music Eisteddfod was founded in 1947. By 1977, close to three thousand competitors were arriving in Llangollen every year. Public attendance is now at 125,000 annually, and over fifty countries send representatives to Wales. Competitions are held in twenty-one musical categories, ranging from choral to solo, solo instrumental, folk and folk dance.

The whole event is a volunteer effort, requiring an amateur staff of three hundred and fifty townspeople. Contestants are billeted in private homes for a twenty mile radius around the town. The international nature of the eisteddfod makes the Llangollen Festival one of the most enjoyable and special gatherings in Wales. Music and dance performances are likely to spring up at any time in pubs, on street corners and in people's homes and gardens. Throughout the week competitors mingle with the spectators and Llangollen truly becomes a center of international communication and understanding.

17

Welsh Leaders in Ohio

CINCINNATI

From 1818 to 1849, during the first period of strong Welsh immigration, Ohio was a familiar word on the lips of farmers in North Wales. For a while "Ohio Fever" seized several districts and immigration increased, particularly to settlements like Paddy's Run (Shandon), Venedocia and the "Welsh Hills" district of Jackson County. By 1900, Ohio followed Pennsylvania with the second largest Welsh population in America, 50% more than New York, and three times as many as Wisconsin.

Michael D. Jones was ordained a minister in Cincinnati in 1849. While living in Cincinnati, as pastor of the Lawrence Street Welsh Congregational Church, Michael D. Jones first conceived of the Patagonia Welsh Colony. Seeing the effects of American assimiliation on the Welsh language, he attempted to purchase large tracts of isolated land in Oregon and Nebraska. When this project failed, through lack of support, he returned to Wales, where he recruited colonists for the settlement in Patagonia, which he would never visit. Today, Michael D. Jones' original home in Bala, Wales is owned by his great grandson, Arturo L. Roberts, the editor of *Ninnau*.

The St. David's Society of Cincinnati was founded in 1889. In 1973 the Society closed through lack of interest and the advanced age of its leaders. In 1979, however, under the initiative of Glyn Long, a new Welsh Society of Greater Cincinnati was launched.

Provoked by the repeated absence of a Welsh booth at the annual Cincinnati International Folk Festival, Glyn Long, helped by Gert Holaday, Peter Griffiths and David Llewelyn Dodds, dug out the old St. David's Society records and organized a Welsh booth in time for the 1979 folk fair. Jane Hughes and Jane Thomas drove down from Ontario and set up a Siani Flewog sales booth. Glyn Long designed a diorama depicting the story of Prince Madog, and over one hundred and fifty potential members signed the Society's register.

For the 1980 Cincinnati International Folk Festival, the Welsh Society organized a full scale representation of the National Eisteddfod opening ceremony. Parti Ceredigion sang at the fair on their first American tour and Society members staffed food, cultural and merchandise booths. Alice Hood supervised the baking of over four hundred dozen Welsh cakes, and Peggy Sulfsted sold consignment souvenirs. Ralph Knopf, Gert Holaday, Leon

Jones, Gwen Owens, Lois Brimelow, Clyde and Lucy Campbell, Robert Rodgers, Vera Lindemann and Nancy Meredith all helped create the National Eisteddfod display.

Leon Jones and Marcia Baker both joined the Society as a result of seeing the folk fair booths. Marcia became one of the club's most enthusiastic supporters, and Leon became director of Côr Gwalia Ohio the Cincinnati Welsh Choir. Having graduated from the Cincinnati Conservatory where he studied under Welsh tenor Dan Beddoe, Leon Jones with Glyn Long as manager, organized the Cincinnati Welsh Choir into one of the foremost Welsh choirs in North America. Marilyn Hyde, Gwendolyn Owens and Sian Stow were soloists. In 1982 the choir made twenty-three public performances.

Côr Gwalia Ohio first performed at the revived Cincinnati St. David's banquet in 1981, a time-honored tradition that had not been kept since 1972. Over one hundred people came and the choir featured Gwendolyn Owens, soprano, and harpist Diane Schneider. Within a year, Côr Gwalia Ohio was registered as an ethnic musical choir, which required that over 80% of the repertoire be in Welsh. Registration entitled the choir to funding from the Ohio Arts Council, and it also received a grant from the recently formed National Welsh American Foundation. In 1984, the choir consisted of thirty singers who made a striking appearance on stage. Gert Holaday, Lucy Campbell and Vera Lindeman designed and made traditional Welsh costumes for the ladies, and the men wore black knee britches, white shirts, white stockings and scarlet waistcoats. Côr Gwalia Ohio has become the main force behind Cincinnati Welsh activities. By 1982, Welsh Society participation in the Cincinnati Folk Festival had come full circle when Côr Gwalia Ohio was invited to perform a series of city-wide concerts to generate pre-festival publicity.

The Welsh Society of Greater Cincinnati, led in 1983 by Jack Griffith, Cliff Jones, Bill Hines, Lois King, Mary Lewis and Sayde Myfanwy Davis, manages a wide range of events. Members frequently hold Welsh evenings in their homes. The 1984 fifth annual St. David's dinner attracted over one hundred diners, including Judge Chase Davies, John and Hannah Pugh and Eleanor Lortz, all past members of the previous St. David's Society.

In 1983, Glyn Long moved to San Diego, where he promptly started organizing a new San Diego Welsh Choral Society. For his remarkable success in Ohio, *Ninnau* awarded him its 1980 citation. Fluent in several European languages, while living in Arizona and New Mexico, Glyn wrote the Berlitz book of Navajo. In Welsh, however, like many Welsh people today, he is a *dysgwr*, a learner. In 1978 he was a student at Cwrs Cymraeg at Bucknell University, Pennsylvania. Glyn Long readily admits that his establishment of the Cincinnati Welsh Society is one more aspect of his rediscovery of Wales and being Welsh. His work is not an isolated case; Cymdeithas Madog, the Vancouver Welsh Male Choir and the St. David's Society of Delaware were all founded by Welsh expatriates in North America.

OAK HILL

The Cincinnati Welsh are near some of the most active Welsh societies in America; Gomer and Columbus to the north, and Oak Hill, a hamlet of a thousand people, one hundred miles to the east. Côr Gwalia Ohio, has sung several times at Oak Hill Welsh celebrations. Oak Hill was Amiga's favorite place of the trip. She was spoiled and petted, but most of all she loved the cool, wooden boards beneath the pews of the Oak Hill Welsh Heritage Museum.

Curator and founder of the Welsh Heritage Museum, Mildred Bangert let us inside the building and told us to look around. Within twenty minutes Mildred had the museum bustling with local Welsh personalities shaking our hands and telling us about their visits to Wales. While we were chatting and drinking lemonade with our new friends, we were joined by a large man in a grubby sweat-soaked T-shirt and black, baggy pants. He was the Reverend James Hanna, minister of the Presbyterian Church, and co-founder with Mildred of the Welsh Heritage Museum. He was grimy and speckled with dust because he'd been making plaster of Paris Bible figures.

Late one evening in 1971, Mildred Bangert learned that the Welsh Congregational Church, across the road from where she lived, was to be sold. At midnight she called Mr. Hanna and within a week they formed a committee to buy the church. A Museum Society was founded, and before the year was out the property was theirs.

The museum quickly received donations of books, costumes, records, china, magazines, heirlooms, furniture, pioneer relics and industrial pieces. The interior of the long red building still has most of its pews intact and the books and artifacts are displayed around the walls. On an initial browse we found back issues of *Yr Enfys*, *Y Drych* and *Ninnau*, a five volume Cambrian Minstrelsie, Edinburgh editions of Joseph Parry's music, as well as many Welsh language books dating to the early 1800's. The back issues of *Yr Enfys* and *Y Drych*, and the almost complete collection of *Ninnau* were what fascinated us. Late at night, given a key to the museum by Mildred, we sat up reading them.

Today Canadians and Americans can subscribe to three papers, four including *WAY*, each with its unique role and qualities.

Yr Enfys is a quarterly journal with articles by well known personalities and reports from Welsh societies around the world. Its layout is attractive and pleasing, and it is supported by the Wales Tourist Board. *Yr Enfys* does have an international scope, and is not afraid to publish original work. Eurgain Fowler is one of the best writers for *Yr Enfys* and the paper is worth buying for her articles alone.

Y Drych's strongest quality is its excellent use of photographs. *Y Drych*'s clear and direct format is maintained throughout its pages. Society reports are carefully shaped and arranged. Feature stories and serials, *Y Drych*'s speciality, add depth to the paper, while correspondents in Wales send precise and relevant news. *Y Drych* is confident, unambiguous and informative.

Y Drych's coverage and presentation of Welsh material make it a superior and thoughtful production.

Ninnau's principal goal was, and still is, to reach as many people as possible and encourage them to promote and preserve their Welsh heritage. The main strength of *Ninnau* is its front page support of all Welsh developments. Every new Welsh society gets front page headlines. *Ninnau* calls itself "Papur Bro Cymru Gogledd America", the regional or district paper of North America. The breadth of *Ninnau*'s regional news makes an impressive survey of Welsh activities in Canada and the United States, which the paper itself helped cultivate.

WAY, which appears three times a year, is the only publication targeted at the young—specifically under thirty, under twenty, and under ten year olds. With its quizzes, graphics features, and games, *WAY* encourages the participation of younger people in Welsh American work.

The Reverend James Hanna and Mildred Bangert were the leaders of a group that was to remain intact for our three day visit in Oak Hill. Our group included Florence Bochert and her dog, Ci Du, Eleanor Weaver, Ethel Smittle and Lucille Smith. At Mr. Hanna's suggestion, we all dined at Oak Hill's Hi-Way restaurant, on some of the finest "home cooking" we've experienced.

Welsh activities in southeastern Ohio have never been slow, but since the formation of the Museum in 1971 there has been a definite quickening of tempo. The Southeastern Circuit Cymanfa, founded in 1872, gained one more venue and is now held the last weekend in September at Nebo, Ty'n Rhos or the Welsh Heritage Museum. A fifth church, Bryn Hyfryd, was sold in 1978. The Southeastern Circuit Cymanfa is still a preaching cymanfa (cymanfa pregethu) with three sessions, one on Saturday and two on Sunday, and a total of six sermons being heard. The 113th annual gymanfa in September 1985 was recorded as one of "the best ever" in living memory, with record numbers attending. A memorial concert to the Reverend John R. Owen of Lisbon, Ohio, who was influential in starting the museum, was held on Saturday night. Soloist at the concert was Timothy Evans of Lampeter, Wales.

Betty Jones, National President of the Women's Welsh Clubs of America, was unaware of any Welsh life in the Oak Hill area until she read about it in *Yr Enfys*, mailed to her from Wales. Betty Jones spoke at the 1974 Oak Hill fall cymanfa, and on the spot organized the sixty member Cardiff Club, a Women's Welsh Club of America branch. The Cardiff Club, led by Bess Grace, Lucille Rees, Ruth Evans, Vickie Powell, Josene Moses, Mildred Bangert, Sylvia Myers, Marie Sheward and Noretta Gillespie, has since held bake sales, arts and crafts fairs, costume shows and many a noson lawen.

In 1978 the Cardiff Club held its first October cymanfa ganu at Bob Evans Farms near Rio Grande, Ohio. About four hundred people attended the cymanfa, which was directed by Roger Williams of Thurman with accompaniment by his sister, Peggy Thomas. Afterwards a Welsh tea was served to everyone there. This first outdoor cymanfa evolved into Welsh

Heritage Days, a two day event now held every June, with a noson lawen at the museum on the Saturday night and hymn singing and a picnic at Bob Evans Farms on Sunday afternoon. In 1982 at the Bob Evans Farms Festival, the ladies of the Cardiff Club baked and sold 18,000 Welsh cakes (1,500 dozen) from their booth.

The annual St. David's banquet in Oak Hill is a big event for the Welsh of Gallia and Jackson Counties. The banquet attracted over three hundred people in March 1984. Roger Williams and D. Merril Davies led group singing with Peggy Thomas at the piano. The St. David's Chorus provided special music.

In 1979 Roger Williams formed the "The Cardi's", a Welsh folk song quartet, comprising Roy Moses, Roger Rees, Lynne Rees and Roger Williams. In 1982, a new St. David's Society of S.E. Ohio was organized to reach people outside the main areas of activity. In 1983 D. Merril Davies formed the forty-five member male voice, St. David's Chorus. William McCormick has since formed a group called the New Harlech Singers.

We were invited by Reverend Hanna to speak to the parents and children of his Mt. Horeb Bible class. We told Amiga to sit at the door and wait. But no! Amiga could come too, and proudly wagging her tail, she walked to the front of the room. This was her big chance to show off her prizewinning tricks, which included sitting up, lying down, playing dead, tossing a biscuit in the air and "talking". She definitely enjoyed being the center of attraction. Mt. Horeb had some old Welsh language gravestones, and Ethel Smittle and Lucille Smith gave us a tour. Later we visited Jefferson Furnace, an old Welsh ironworks which closed in 1916, but which has been declared a State Historic Site.

Mildred had already given us tickets to the Oak Hill swimming pool. At Mt. Horeb, I was giving the children a tour of the van while Suzanne said goodbye to Reverend Hanna. As she was leaving, he thrust his hand into his baggy pockets and pressed a handful of loose change and crumpled bills into her hand. "Go buy some hot dogs or something," he said. This gesture of impulsive generosity and the kindness shown us by everyone in Oak Hill made a deep impression on us. Our last evening in Oak Hill, we were treated to a Cardiff Club potluck going away party. This was Amiga's feast, as sausage after sausage fell under the table, until she waddled into the Museum and collapsed. Our visit concluded in traditional fashion, with photographs, singing, and assurances that all Welsh visitors were always welcome.

WEST VIRGINIA

The Welsh Heritage Museum in Oak Hill has had an impact throughout the Welsh societies of Ohio—as far as Gomer, Columbus, Cincinnati, and the Canton/Youngstown area. Visits to the museum by W. Vincent Lewis of Huntington, West Virginia prompted him, in August 1982, to organize the Welsh Society of West Virginia. The Society is small but enthusiastic and gets a lot of support from the Cardiff Club and from Dr. David Lloyd Mandry, a former WNGGA trustee and president, living in Ravenswood. The Welsh Society of West Virginia meets at 7 p.m. on the first Tuesday of every month at Johnson Memorial Methodist Church, Huntington. One hundred and twenty eight people attended the Society's St. David's Day banquet in 1984, a number that surprised even the Society's founder. The Huntington Society has several Welsh singing soloists, Rebecca Lewis and Emily and Patricia Ignatiadis; and instrumentalists, Nancy Thomas, Kimberly Cremens and Avis Haeger, harpist. As a new Welsh Society, leaders are still concerned with reinforcing membership and telling people what and where Wales is. Society officers in 1984 were Nelle Davies, Paula Owen, June Ashworth, Darlene Parry and W. Vincent Lewis.

JACKSON

North of Oak Hill, Jackson continues to hold an annual Schools Eisteddfod for grades one through twelve, every April. Organized by Raymond Lynn Boothe, music director at Jackson High School, the Jackson Schools Eisteddfod was started in 1923 by descendants of Welsh settlers. Competitions today use no Welsh, but maintain the form of traditional eisteddfodau with graded competitions and adjudications. The schools re-adopted the word "eisteddfod" when the tradition was continued following World War II. Approximately two thousand children take part in the Jackson Schools Eisteddfod every year. The printed program describes what a Welsh eisteddfod is and how it arrived in the hills of southern Ohio. St. David's Society of Southeast Ohio members, Dr. Kent White and D. Merril Davies, have given the Jackson Schools Eisteddfod a lot of support, and since the eisteddfod was re-established thousands of children have taken part.

CHILLICOTHE

Near Jackson, Chillicothe, was the birthplace of Lady Diana Spencer's (The Princess of Wales') great-great grandmother. Ellen Wood, born in 1831, married millionaire Frank Work; their daughter married James Roche, the English grandfather of Princess Diana's mother. The Princess of Wales, since her marriage, has received numerous invitations to visit her "ancestral home" in Chillicothe, which still stands at 86 South Paint Street.

COLUMBUS

The Welsh Singing Society of Columbus has been the main sponsor of Welsh events in the Ohio capital since its first cymanfa in 1948. What distinguishes this society from other Welsh American societies, is the closeness of its link with Wales, a relationship reinforced through the tours of David E. Morgan.

The name of the Welsh Singing Society of Columbus was changed to The Welsh Society of Central Ohio in 1985. Leaders of the Society have been George Richards, Thomas Brownfield, Carl Burnside, Lewis Lloyd, Weldon Abels, William Miller, Mrs. Madlyn Davies, Ivan L. Davies and writers Marian Davis and Lillian Brownfield. Membership in 1978 was five hundred and fifty, but following a vigorous television, radio and newspaper campaign led by Marian Davis, almost two hundred new members were enlisted by 1981. Mrs. E. Gomer Jones, the Society's secretary for over twenty-six years, has been a particularly strong advocate of the Society's continued growth. The Society holds an annual St. David's banquet in March and a fall cymanfa ganu, usually the third or fourth Sunday in October. For its annual cymanfa the Society has, in recent years, flown over a soloist from Wales. This consistent annual sponsorship has been of immense benefit to the Society and to the invited artist.

In 1977 the Welsh Singing Society of Columbus sponsored Dafydd Edwards' first visit to America, a visit that brought the singer standing ovations in packed church halls. In 1980, the Society sponsored a visit by Angela Davies, an award-winning contralto and graduate of the Cardiff College of Music. The 1983 performance of Janice Rees, soprano, was so popular, the club sponsored her return appearance at the St. David's banquet in 1984. The Columbus Singing Society distinguishes itself by making its events part of a live Welsh tradition. Over one hundred and twenty people attended the Columbus Welsh potluck picnic in 1985, when children and adults were led in folk dancing by Mary Lee Bailey of Delaware, Ohio and in singing by Roger Williams, and D. Merril Davies.

Attorney David E. Morgan, the founder of The Columbus Singing Society, has been leading tours to Wales since 1965. David Morgan's great-great grandfather left Aberaeron, Wales in 1834 and Aberaeron is a stop on all David Morgan tours. The tour group, which numbered forty-one people in 1983, is welcomed with a cymanfa ganu and is later treated to a children's concert in the local school. David Morgan, in turn, invites friends, family and civic leaders to a dinner of his own. In 1972, tree planting ceremonies were held in Oak Hill and Aberaeron, and a bronze plaque in Aberaeron tells the story of the close Welsh-Jackson County relationship. The most fruitful product of the friendship, however, has been the Parti Ceredigion tours arranged by Palmer Jones of Ohio and Dafydd Edwards of Aberaeron.

PARTI CEREDIGION

Among those from Granville, Ohio who attended the Columbus concerts of Dafydd Edwards in 1977 and 1979 was Palmer Jones. When Palmer Jones and Dafydd Edwards discovered they were relatives, their friendship led to the highly successful Parti Ceredigion tours of 1980 and 1982. Parti Ceredigion consisted of five musicians—Ifan Lloyd, bass; Bethan Bryn, harp; Delyth Evans, soprano; Dafydd Edwards, tenor and in 1982, Margaret Rees, accompanist.

The Granville Cambrian Society of which Palmer Jones has been a president was founded in 1935. About 75 people attended the Society's 50th anniversary banquet on April 19, 1985. Officers for 1985-86 were Thomas Philips, President; Eric Jones, Vice-President; Mary M. Nash, Secretary and Jane Jones, Treasurer.

Palmer Jones' single-handed success at establishing a twice traveled circuit for Parti Ceredigion is all the more remarkable when one considers the absence of central information and that it was built on a system of personal friendships and telephone connections. Altogether, more than 20,000 people attended the ensemble's performances. The effect, says Palmer Jones, was to achieve "a cymanfa ganu on tour".

The first Parti Ceredigion tour from October 3 to October 19, 1980, consisted of thirteen concerts and visited Ohio, Minnesota and Ipswich, South Dakota. The tour ran on a home-stay plan and netted an income of approximately $600, a reimbursement of $150 per artist for three weeks touring and unpaid absence from their jobs in Wales. The second tour, in October 1982, consisted of twelve concerts in twenty-one days and visited Columbus, Granville, Lisbon, Ohio; Los Angeles, California; Albuquerque, New Mexico; Enid, Oklahoma; Minneapolis, Minnesota; Milwaukee, Wisconsin; Lincoln, Nebraska and Pittsburgh, Pennsylvania. This tour cost $10,000 to run and raised $10,000. The five artists received no fee and again received no gain. The plan was discontinued for lack of financial support.

On some occasions the musicians split into duets and soloists and gave concerts at different venues. Their versatility and willingness to perform at a folk festival stall or in an auditorium increased their scope enormously. The impact of the tours was unmistakable. In Ipswich, South Dakota in 1980, it was the first time for the town to host a party of Welsh visitors since immigration stopped three generations ago. The whole town of 1600 turned out, halting the harvest for two days. Parti Ceredigion's appearance at the 1980 Cincinnati Folk Festival played an important part in establishing the new Welsh Society there which, in turn, led to the formation of Côr Gwalia Ohio.

The 1982 Parti Ceredigion tour prompted the organization of two new Welsh American societies. Their performance in Enid, Oklahoma was attended by Stafford Davis. Soon after, Stafford organized the Tulsa Owain Glendower Society which held its first St. David's banquet in 1983. When Palmer Jones called Jean Rhoades in Albuquerque, a name he'd been given by a friend in Wales, she replied, sure, she'd organize a Parti Ceredigion concert, but how would she do it? Palmer suggested she start a Welsh society, which she did. That was in April. When Parti Ceredigion arrived in October 1982, the Welsh Society of New Mexico sold 375 tickets and some of the audience had driven over 500 miles (from Nevada) to attend.

At St. John's Episcopal Church in Albuquerque one of the most remarkable acts of the tour occurred. Following one performance, an older man came into the dressing room, murmuring his appreciation and the eerie sensation he had of his parents being in the audience beside him. This elderly and very gentle man then handed each performer a $100 bill and walked quietly from the room. Palmer Jones said there were many expressions of gratitude and letters from wherever the artists appeared.

VENEDOCIA AND GOMER

Venedocia and Gomer, two hamlets in northwest Ohio, have been holding cymanfaoedd canu every year since 1917. Recent celebrations at Gomer attracted visitors from Chicago, Detroit, Cleveland, and Cincinnati, as well as local visitors from neighbouring Welsh societies in Lima, Columbus and Oak Hill. The Venedocia cymanfa is held every Labor Day Sunday and the Welsh descendants here also hold a St. David's Day banquet. Nearby Van Wert also holds a St. David's Day banquet and a fall cymanfa.

Other towns in the area, notably Delphos and Lima, also have strong Welsh roots. Links with Wales remain close and are reinforced by visits like that of Lisa Winegardner in 1983, who carried official greetings from Gomer to the Welsh village of Llanerfyl, from which Gomer's first immigrants came in 1833.

Gomer's sesquicentennial celebrations in 1983 started with a St. David's banquet in March. Alice Bushong led combined choirs from the surrounding Welsh towns, and a Welsh quartet, consisting of David Britt, Tim Lavimore and Arbert and Ross Thomas, gave a concert. Martha Evans, a leader of Welsh life in Gomer, played music on a folk harp she'd made herself. Celebrations reached their peak in September 1983 with the publication of two commemorative booklets and a mammoth 66th anniversary cymanfa, directed by Hywel Thomas of Buffalo.

A noson lawen the night before the cymanfa clearly demonstrated the range of Gomer's Welsh talent. Under the leadership of people like Norman Diller, Martha Evans, Ross Thomas, Verona Sandy and the Reverend John Hoffman, Gomer is likely to remain a stronghold of Welsh traditions.

☆

In Wittenberg University, Springfield, a 1984 cymanfa ganu was held as part of a week-long workshop on "The Arts in Worship". Megan Lloyd, former Welsh Associated Youth secretary and an undergraduate at Wittenberg, made a contributing Welsh presence on the campus, reminding University organizations of Ohio's Welsh American background. Wittenberg is also the home of the Arthur Machen Society, an appreciation group of the works of Welsh novelist Arthur Machen, who lived from 1863 to 1947. The American Hymn Society is also based here. The Society's publication, *The Hymn*, occasionally carries articles on Welsh hymnology and the cymanfa ganu in America.

☆

YOUNGSTOWN

Leaving central Ohio, we followed the Ohio River northward through the glass manufacturing area of West Virginia, eventually to Youngstown and the home of Morris Wrench, well known cymanfa conductor and trustee of the WNGGA. The weather was hot and humid, and the proximity of the northern industrial towns made living in the van sticky and difficult. When Elsie Wrench invited us into the comfort of her home, we accepted readily.

Sipping ice cream sodas on the shady back porth, I asked Morris how he started conducting in the first place. It was something he drifted into, he said. Having been asked once he was asked again, then offers came more frequently. A well known baritone and still possessing a rich and vibrant voice, he directed his first cymanfa at the relatively late age of fifty-nine. Morris pointed out that his knowledge of music was self-taught, with some advice from D. West Richards, who taught him directing "in half an hour!"

Morris L. Wrench has conducted over 100 cymanfaoedd canu since 1963, including festivals in Ohio, Minnesota, Chicago, New York and Washington, D.C. When he attended the Investiture of Prince Charles in Caernarfon in 1969, he led a cymanfa at his birthplace of Talysarn, an occasion that gave him immeasurable joy.

Attending the Investiture of the Prince of Wales in 1969 was a source of considerable pride for many Welsh Americans. Morris showed us his Investiture invitation and recounted in great detail how the American seats were so close that he could have reached out and "touched the Prince's head."

Despite having nationally known leaders, St. David's societies in the Niles, Warren, and Youngstown area hold no regular programs, apart from the usual March banquet and fall cymanfa ganu.

The St. David's Society of Youngstown is of an old school. In 1980 its committee consisted of President, Jack Meadows (also secretary of the WNGGA); Secretary, Nelson Llewellyn (then assistant secretary of the WNGGA); and Vice-President, Paul Stevens (endowment officer of the WNGGA). The positions of Druid, Sentinel and Bard were held by Llewelyn Jones, Morris Wrench and the Reverend G. D. Walters. This committee controlled the Society for many years, Jack Meadows serving as president from 1954 until August 1984. About one hundred people continue to attend the Youngstown St. David's banquet, which has been held every year since 1891.

As is often the case among older Welsh American societies, the local Women's Welsh Clubs mount the most regular monthly meetings. The Glyn Dur Club (sic) of Youngstown was founded in 1932, and today has sixty-three members. The Glyn Dur Club meets for lunch the second Friday of every month. The Calon Lân Club in Youngstown also meets regularly and holds an annual cymanfa ganu every May.

After dinner, Morris called Dorothy Feeley, President of the Women's Welsh Clubs of America. Dorothy impressed us immediately as an articulate woman who got straight to the point. A highly effective officer, she made an excellent speech at the WNGGA annual general meeting in Wilkes-Barre in 1983, with a realistic analysis of Welsh American societies today.

WOMEN'S WELSH CLUBS OF AMERICA

There are twenty Women's Welsh Clubs in the United States. During the 1930's and 1940's, there were forty-five branches, in 1978 there were twenty-five. The last to close was the Pittsburgh Women's Welsh Club in 1981, because of insufficient attendance to form a committee. The Women's Welsh clubs suffer from a generation gap. Older members often have personal memories of Wales or of their parents' and grandparents' Welsh homes in America. Younger working women with children have no time for society luncheons and have difficulty relating to fund raising for a Welsh Retirement Home in Cleveland. Getting younger women to join is a real problem for the national committee.

Through their monthly luncheons and meetings, however, the Women's Welsh Clubs raise in excess of $20,000 annually for the Rocky River Welsh Retirement Home. The Federation of Women's Welsh Clubs is the oldest Welsh American organization still functioning and the only one, apart from the WNGGA, that holds an annual convention. The Federation has an efficient communications network with dedicated officers and local groups who respond quickly to the requirements of their leadership. If it were not for the Women's Welsh Clubs some cities would have no Welsh programs at all. Local women's groups with their singing and invited speakers form an important arm of the Welsh American community.

The annual convention of the Women's Welsh Clubs of America is always held the last week in June. The convention is hosted by a local club, and thus moves from city to city—Philadelphia in 1980, Baltimore in 1981, Warren, Ohio in 1983 and Washington D.C. in 1985. The Convention consists of a meeting of the whole executive board and board of trustees, reports from each branch and from the various committees. The Convention is well-run, and is also especially warm and friendly. Reception and registration in 1983 preceded an impromptu noson lawen with solos by Dorothy Feeley and many other women there. Since 1932 the Convention has held a mid-week cymanfa ganu, which often attracts over two hundred people.

The Federation of The Women's Welsh Clubs of America was founded in 1911 by Mrs. Mary Jane (Jones) Hasenpflug. Nineteen women gathered at Mary Jane's home to form a Ladies' Auxiliary to the Cleveland Welsh Men's Society. In 1914 the Cleveland Ladies' Auxiliary organized the Women's Welsh Clubs of America with the purpose of building a Welsh retirement home. The first home was opened in 1919 at a cost of $24,000. In 1922 the Women's Welsh Clubs of America bought property in Rocky River, where the present Welsh Home now stands. In 1948 the old building was demolished and the present structure was dedicated in 1954. The 1985-86 President of the Women's Welsh Clubs of America was Mrs. Phyllis Keutgen. Today assets of the home in the form of stocks and bonds are in excess of $3,000,000, the interest from which, supplemented by annual donations, bequests and fees, pays for everything from a maxi-van to first-class kitchens, medical care, clinic, exercise room, grounds and more than two staff for every resident. The home combines modern medical and retirement care with a genuinely relaxed family atmosphere.

THE WOMEN'S WELSH CLUBS OF AMERICA

Location	Name	Meeting Place
Cleveland, Oh.	Cleveland Club	1st Tuesday, Old Stone Church, Cleveland
	East Cleveland Club	1st and 3rd Wednesday, Hope Congregational Church, Cleveland
	West Cleveland Club	2nd and 4th Tuesday, Cymry Hall, Welsh Retirement Home, Rocky River.
Niles, Oh.	Cambria Club	1st Monday, meets for lunch.
Warren, Oh.	Mentra Gwen Club	1st Thursday, members' homes, Warren.
Youngstown, Oh.	Calon Lân Club	2nd Wednesday, members' homes, Youngstown.
	Glyn Dur Club	2nd Friday, 12:30 p.m. different locations.
Akron, Oh.	Bryn Mawr Club	3rd Tuesday, First Federal Bank Building, Akron.
Oak Hill & Jackson, Oh.	Cardiff Club	1st Wednesday, alternating Oak Hill and Jackson.
Girard, Oh.	Girard Club	2st Tuesday, 1 p.m. Methodist Church, Girard.
Masillon, Oh.	Gwynette Club	4th Monday, 7:30 p.m. members' homes
Newton Falls, Oh.	Newton Falls Club	1st Monday 7:30 p.m., members' homes.
Delaware, Oh.	Radnor Club	Once a year.
Philadelphia, Pa.	Philadelphia Club	1st Tuesday, Arch St. Presbyterian Church, Philadelphia.
Baltimore, Md.	Baltimore Club	2nd Saturday, 1:30 p.m., Enoch Pratt Library, Baltimore.
Chicago, Ill.	Illinois Club	3rd Monday, Boy Scout H.Q., Chicago.
New York, N.Y.	New York Club	1st Saturday, Rutgers Presbyterian Church, New York.
Washington, D.C.	Washington Senior Club	2nd Saturday, members' homes.
	Gwalia Club	1st Wednesday, members' homes.
Morgantown, W.V.	Morgantown Club	4th Thursday, 2 p.m., members' homes.

THE WELSH NATIONAL
GYMANFA GANU ASSOCIATION (WNGGA)

The annual Labor Day Weekend festival of the Welsh National Gymanfa Ganu Association of the United States and Canada is the largest, most important Welsh event held in North America. The annual appearance of the National is a reflection of the enduring vitality of the North American Welsh community. Three thousand four hundred people attended the National in Wilkes-Barre in 1983. One thousand one hundred attended the Portland, Oregon National in 1984. The Montreal National in 1985, attended by almost 2000 people, proved that the great Cymanfa is still of central importance to the North American Welsh community.

The National Cymanfa Ganu is a three-day concentration of what the North American Welsh community does throughout the year. All of the principal organizations are represented, and leaders from almost every Welsh society attend, as well as hundreds of others for whom the National is an annual event they feel they cannot miss.

The National Cymanfa program has been fairly consistent since 1975. On Friday night there is a banquet with light entertainment. On Saturday the WAY luncheon, Awr y Plant, the WNGGA annual general meeting and the Grand Concert. A bilingual worship service is held on Sunday morning and in the afternoon and evening, the two sessions of the cymanfa. It is only in fairly recent years, with the introduction of Awr y Plant and the regular establishment of a lively and competitive Welsh market place, that alternative events have become available. The National Cymanfa program is still very linear and has little of the diversity one normally expects of cultural festivals.

In 1979, two thousand one hundred people were at the 50th anniversary of the founding of the WNGGA on Goat Island, Niagara Falls. The occasion was marked by the unveiling of a memorial plaque made of Welsh slate, mounted on Canadian marble, by former Speaker of the British House of Commons, Viscount Tonypandy, George Thomas.

In September 1929, a picnic was held on Goat Island, attended by train-loads of people from Ohio, New York, Pennsylvania and Ontario. Estimates of the number of people there vary from as low as six hundred to as high as two thousand—but in the absence of an official register, no one knows for sure. The meeting was a day of informal fun, a picnic in the grand style of the pre-depression years, ending as all Welsh gatherings still do, with singing. The picnic and spontaneous cymanfa that followed was so successful that it was held for four consecutive years on Goat Island, until moving to Chicago for the International Exposition in 1933.

The WNGGA was incorporated as an Ohio non-profit organization in 1951. Its constitution was extensively revised in 1978. It has assets in excess of $80,000, comprising $50,000 in savings, checking and certificates, and a separate WNGGA supervised Endowment Fund with a balance in excess of $30,000. Average annual revenues in the form of donations and bequests exceed $10,000, while expenses are in the $4,000 to $5,000 range. Expenses for 1982/1983 were $4,320.43, over 50% of which was incurred by the secretary.

The WNGGA is managed by an executive board of nine. It is supervised by a Board of Trustees comprising of three residents west of the Mississippi; nine east of the Mississippi, and five residents of Canada. In 1984, the Executive consisted of Gwenfyl Jones (Vancouver), President; David Thomas (Minnesota), Vice-President; Nelson Llewellyn (Ohio), Secretary; Catherine Dodd (Ohio), Treasurer; Emmaline Davies (Oregon), Recording Secretary; Norman Williams (New York), immediate Past President; Paul Stevens (Ohio), Endowment Chairman; Berenice Van Orman (Ohio), President Women's Welsh Clubs of America; Nancy Miller (Massachusetts); Dr. David Mandry (West Virginia); Lewis Edwards (Ontario); Eluned Thomas, (Ontario); Thomas Field (Ontario); Hugh Rowe (Alberta); Owen Roberts (Quebec). Since 1978, the President of WAY has been able to vote at WNGGA Board of Trustees meetings.

Since 1978 annual membership in the WNGGA has cost $5.00, life membership costs $20.00 and life membership for an organization costs $25.00. In 1984 there were about 500 life members of the WNGGA. The main advantage of life membership is entrance to and voting rights at the WNGGA annual general meeting. One need not be a member to attend the National Cymanfa, which requires a $5.00 local registration fee from everyone. In 1984 the cost of going to every event at the National, excluding the cost of meals, the hotel room and transportation, was about $50.00.

As an Ohio non-profit corporation, the WNGGA has no legal authority outside Ohio and therefore relies on local Sponsoring Committees to be its agent where the National is being held. The local Sponsoring Committee is required by the WNGGA constitution to give half of any surplus to the parent Association. Sponsoring Committees are not legally bound, however, and this division has technically to be made in the form of a donation. Terminology at the National is also misleading and could challenge its non-profit status. Instead of fees, charges, ticket costs, etc., terms like gift, suggested donation, and so on should be used, as they are by most American and Canadian non-profit organizations.

As one of the largest and most experienced North American Welsh organizations, critics feel that the WNGGA has not remained abreast of developments either in Wales, Canada or the United States. Innovations at the National are the work of local organizers. Any artist, speaker, musician or importer wishing to participate in the National Cymanfa bypasses the WNGGA board and applies to the local Sponsoring Committee. The WNGGA acts in a financial and supervisory role, and is required only to mail one annual announcement of the forthcoming National and annual general meeting to its members.

The WNGGA is seen by many as the main Welsh organization in North America. It is the only Welsh association consistently listed in indices of ethnic and international clubs. Despite criticisms, the endurance of the

WNGGA has maintained Welsh awareness in North America. Without the WNGGA there would have been no feeling of continuity with a more vigorous Welsh immigrant past. None of the new Welsh organizations have the historical authority of the National Cymanfa Ganu, which pulls every thread of the Welsh community together. The National, with its deep spiritual base, is likely to remain the premiere Welsh event and its solid position is largely due to the work of one man, George Bundy.

George Bundy was born in Abercarn, Gwent, where he worked in the Prince of Wales Colliery until emigrating to Warren, Ohio in 1906 at the age of twenty-nine. In Warren he worked as a blacksmith and he joined the Youngstown St. David's Society. In 1925 he became President of the Cymric Association of America. When this dissolved in 1930, he formed the Trumbull County (Ohio) Eisteddfod Association, serving as its president and secretary until it too disolved in 1944. George Bundy became one of the leaders of the National Eisteddfod Association of America, which existed from 1923 to 1940, and was a member of the American Gorsedd. He was secretary of the WNGGA from 1934 until he retired in 1968 at the age of ninety. For a twelve year period during the 1930's and 1940's, George Bundy was treasurer and secretary of the WNGGA, effectively acting as its only controlling officer. He traveled widely, urging local Welsh societies to host the National. He devoted the rest of his life to strengthening support for the annual cymanfa in Canada and the United States.

Numerous Welsh American organizations and publications collapsed during the 1930's; *Y Cyfaill* folded in 1933, *The Welsh American Magazine* in 1936 and *The Druid* in 1937. Because of diminishing numbers and lack of support, Welsh American churches and societies continued to close in the 1950's and 1960's. The National Cymanfa was their one remaining institution. In 1963 the WNGGA executive consisted of devoted, but elderly, men— Ben Haddock, Harry Jones, Judge David Jenkins and George Bundy. In 1982 the National Cymanfa Ganu program included a necrology of over four hundred names. It took over fifteen years for Welsh American organizations to emerge with a younger, more contemporary form of leadership.

NILES, WARREN AND CANTON

Members of the eight Women's Welsh Clubs in northeastern Ohio are the main sponsors of Welsh events in the Niles/Canton area. Additional leadership is provided by the Niles Cymanfa Ganu Association. We spent an hour with Niles Cymanfa Ganu Association President, Nelson Llewellyn and his wife Betty, former National President of the Women's Welsh Clubs of America. Former Assistant Secretary of the WNGGA, Nelson became full Secretary following Jack Meadows' retirement in 1983.

Nelson and Betty Llewellyn, assisted by Gordon Brooks and the Reverend John and Mrs. Joan Owen in Lisbon, Ohio have been the leaders of Welsh life in this corner of the state. Other prominent supporters include Donald Locke, Marie Watkins, Goldie Davies, Margaret Newey and Ann L. Jenkins.

John and Joan Owen have been two important personalities in the North American Welsh community. The Reverend John Owen was a graduate of the University of Wales, Bangor and was interim pastor of the Welsh Church in Detroit during the 1950's. When *Ninnau* was launched, he became Welsh language editor and contributed a regular *Ninnau* column, as well as broadcasting an occasional "Letter from America" for BBC Wales. Joan Owen, a first prize National Eisteddfod winner in elocution and a prominent member of the Urdd, was Undeb y Cymry ar Wasgar leader in 1976. She is a regular soloist and speaker at Welsh American meetings, and she and her husband have both taught at the annual Welsh Heritage Week in New York. The Reverend John Owen's death on December 18, 1984 was felt as a severe blow by his many friends in Wales and in America.

The eight Women's Welsh Clubs of northeast Ohio annual luncheon is a well attended meeting, as is the St. David's Day banquet, which attracts over one hundred people. Entertainment is provided by Nelson Llewellyn who has a distinguished baritone voice and was soloist at the Philadelphia bicentennial National Cymanfa in 1976. Accompanists in the Society are Gordon Brooks and Donald Locke. The main event in Niles is the annual cymanfa held every year since 1926 on the first Sunday in October. In recent years, attendance at the cymanfa has consistently been around five hundred people.

The Niles Cymanfa Ganu Association was formerly the Niles Druid Club. In 1971 the men's only Druid Club was dissolved and the new association was formed. On June 4, 1982, the Niles Cymanfa Ganu Association sponsored a free concert by the Dowlais Male Choir at the First Presbyterian Church, Warren. The Dowlais Choir was hosted by the Canton Chorale, which toured Wales in 1980.

Niles also has an occasional Cymanfa Quartet, directed by Gordon Brooks and consisting of James Antell, Maxine Hughes, Wanda Griffin and Nelson Llewellyn. The quartet sings at Welsh meetings and has carried several programs for Gwynnette Women's Welsh Club at the annual International Festival of Stark County.

Another sign of Welsh American interest, beyond what the Welsh societies do, is the Welsh library display mounted by Sally Crossen in Canfield, Ohio in 1983. Kent State University also has a large library archive of old Welsh books and magazines. In 1981, Salem Community Theater staged the musical "The Red Dragon", produced and directed by Catherine Verhoff. "The Red Dragon" portrayed the life of Owain Glyndwr, the great Welsh warrior prince.

Cymanfaoedd canu and St. David's dinners in Ohio continue to be well attended, but with the exception of Columbus, Cincinnati and Oak Hill, the older Welsh societies rarely sponsor other Welsh events. Nowhere is this more evident than in Cleveland, where Welsh American life has hibernated since the National Cymanfa was last held there in 1974.

CLEVELAND

Mrs. D. Griffiths and Mrs. K. Anderson have made attempts to revive Cleveland Welsh activities. In 1980 a Welsh "Bazooka Group" revived the Welsh picnic in July. The picnic was held again in 1982, but not since. The East Cleveland Women's Welsh Club holds an annual cymanfa in May, which is the city's best attended Welsh meeting.

Before the Second World War, Cleveland had a vigorous Welsh community. There was a large Men's Society and the Cleveland Orpheus Male Chorus toured Wales twice. Cleveland has hosted the National Cymanfa four times, and the Welsh form one of the city's oldest ethnic populations.

Cleveland is a mosaic of active ethnic groups. Beachwood Park has gardens maintained by immigrant societies. The city council actively encourages Saturday morning schools teaching over 24 languages from Arabic to Eskimo. Welsh people are uninvolved in any of these activities.

ROCKY RIVER

West of Cleveland, in Rocky River, set in ten and a half acres of grounds is the Welsh Retirement Home for the Elderly. Matron Winifred Redfern made us feel immediately welcome, as though we were visiting a real home and not an institution. Residents vary in age from being young at sixty-five to the very old and those requiring care. While at the home, we spent time with Mr. Obediah Cobley, who emigrated from Mountain Ash in 1924, and twice served as a trustee of the WNGGA. Mr. Cobley was extremely ill but alert and coherent. He died less than a month later at the age of ninety-one. The atmosphere at the Welsh Home was cheerful and relaxed. Both the paid and the volunteer staff enjoy a good friendship with the residents, and the Home is compact enough that we could be shown around to meet everyone in turn. Amiga was once again invited in and she made a terrific hit with everyone wanting to fuss and hold her. Our guides, Marian Biggs and Dora Morgan, introduced us to other residents like David Scott, who played soccer for Merthyr as a young man, before emigrating to America at the age of twenty-three. We also met Maude Watkins from Brynaman, and Olwen Huws, who gave us several Welsh theme place mats and napkins she'd made in the Home's Activities Room.

Catherine Dodd, an officer with the Women's Welsh Clubs of America, is a devoted volunteer at the Home and organizes a wide range of events. In 1982 she persuaded the touring Côr Alawon Menai to visit Cleveland and give a concert at the Home. The three women's clubs in Cleveland, led by Maxine Thomas and Catherine Dodd, planned the afternoon and provided refreshments afterwards. In October 1983, Anne Habermehl visited the Home demonstrating harp music and the next day giving a travelog on Wales.

The Welsh Retirement Home accommodates up to thirty-four residents. Following expansion plans considered during 1985 and 1986 the home will take up to 60 residents. The renovation and extension program cost in the region of $800,000 and the Home is also planning a $1,000,000 extended care facility. It is regulated by state and federal laws and provides first class retirement facilities in an informal environment. A small parlor adjacent to the dining room, Cymry Hall is decorated with Welsh antiques, paintings and furniture. In 1983 the average age of residents was eighty-nine, and for the first time in the Home's history, as a result of wider publicity, there was a waiting list of those applying to live there.

We were given permission to park on the grounds and the next morning joined residents for breakfast. The longer we stayed at the Home, the better we understood the loyalty it wins from its supporters. The Women's Welsh Clubs have a clear sense of purpose that other Welsh American organizations often lack. Raising funds for the Welsh Retirement Home is the main purpose of the Women's Welsh Club network. Their financial contributions, regional promotion, and the character of the Home itself, combine in making it one of the best known and most respected targets of Welsh American affections.

18

Pennsylvania: Welsh-Americaland

Pennsylvania's Welsh background goes back to the promises of William Penn in 1681 and the Welsh colonies of Cambria and Beulah in 1796. In the 19th century immigration reached its highest level. At one point there were over 190 churches supported by Pennsylvania Welsh communities. T. D. Edwards, composer of Rhydygroes, was born in Pittston, Pennsylvania in 1875. He later moved to Wales, making his career in the great chapels of the Rhondda Valley, until his death in 1930.

Joseph Parry, first Professor of Music at the University of Wales, worked in the foundries of Danville, until the financial assistance of his workmates and the Welsh churches enabled him to complete his musical education at the Royal Academy in London. Joseph Parry's fictionalized biography by Jack Jones *Off to Philadelphia in the Morning*, gives a detailed account of the life of coal mining Welsh immigrants in the mid-1800's.

Starting on February 23, 1983 and repeated in 1984 & 1985 Governor of Pennsylvania, Dick Thornburgh, in a ceremony at the State Capital of Harrisburg, signed a proclamation, "In recognition of the contributions of all citizens of Welsh descent proclaiming March 1st as St. David's Day throughout the Commonwealth of Pennsylvania." Berks County Welsh Society was the main sponsor of the proclamation which was attended by Welsh leaders from all over the state. Information was provided to the Governor's office by State Representative John Davies and William Williams, and witnessed by Nancy Stoudt, Craig Peters, Jack Pritchard, David Williams, Griff Griffiths, Herbert Schaeffer, William Griffiths and Merlyn Jenkins.

PHILADELPHIA

Founded in 1729 the Welsh Society of Philadelphia is the oldest Welsh Society in the world, predating the Cymmrodorion of London by 22 years. In 1900 there were 100,000 Welsh people in Pennsylvania, only a small percentage of whom lived in Philadelphia. The majority were engaged in the mining and related metal industries located in industrial clusters in the northeast corner of the state.

Bangor, Radnor, Berwyn, Narberth, Bryn Mawr, St. David's, Haverford, and Tednyffrin are Welsh place names that pepper Philadelphia. Among Philadelphia's famous sons are many of Welsh birth and descent including George Clymer, first president of the Philadelphia Academy of Fine Arts;

John Morgan, founder of the University of Pennsylvania Medical School; Thomas Cadwallader, co-founder of the Philadelphia Public Library and Robert Wharton, Mayor of Philadelphia in the late 1700's.

On March 1, 1968 the Welsh Society of Philadelphia erected a bronze commemorative plaque on the East Façade of Philadelphia City Hall. The plaque reads:

> Perpetuating the Welsh heritage, and commemorating the vision and virtue of the following Welsh patriots in the founding of the City, Commonwealth and Nation: William Penn, 1644-1718, proclaimed freedom of religion and planned New Wales, later named Pennsylvania: Thomas Jefferson, 1743-1826, third President of the United States, composed the Declaration of Independence; Robert Morris, 1734-1806, foremost financer of the American Revolution and signer of the Declaration of Independence; Gouverneur Morris, 1755-1835, wrote the final draft of the Constitution of the United States; John Marshall, 1755-1835, Chief Justice of the United States and father of American Constitutional law.

There are four organizations in Philadelphia that promote Welsh heritage. They are: The Welsh Society of Philadelphia; The Cambrian Society of Delaware Valley; The Welsh Guild of Arch Street Presbyterian Church and The Women's Welsh Club of Philadelphia.

The Welsh Society of Philadelphia which is for men only and which has been led in recent years by R. Charles Davies, Richard H. Davis, David J. Jones, Dr. David A. Bevan, Dr. Francis K. Davis, Owen G. Williams, Jack Livzey, F. Reeve Williams and Frank H. Guinn, is the largest Welsh organization in the city. Society officer Thomas M. Rowlands (who died in January, 1984) organized a wreath laying ceremony every year at the Welsh Plaque. This St. David's Day tribute includes, readings, singing, the Philadelphia Police and Firemen's Band playing Welsh melodies and ladies in Welsh costume distributing information on Wales.

The Welsh Guild in Philadelphia dates from the merger of Girard Street Welsh Presbyterian Church with Arch Street Presbyterian in 1970. The Guild led by Sarah Jones, Irene Pritchard, Daniel Williams, Elizabeth Griffith, Larry Souder, Gladys Vale, Morfydd Livezey and Phyllis Jones, hosts speakers, maintains a small Welsh library, holds occasional series of language classes and organizes the spring and fall Arch Street Welsh Worship services. One of the latest projects has been the re-establishment of the Philadelphia Welsh Picnic. The first for many years was held in July 1984 at Longwood Gardens, and 50 people came. Since 1982 the Welsh Guild has also participated in the annual Philadelphia William Penn British Fair. Speakers at Welsh Guild luncheons have included Elfed Lewis of the National Trust in Wales and Anne Habermehl, founder of Welsh Heritage Week and of the Welsh Harp Society in North America.

The Women's Welsh Club of Philadelphia was formed in 1923 and meets the second Tuesday of every month from September to June at the Arch St. Presbyterian Church. Led by Ann Hoiden, Lillian Canaan, Beatrice Kelly, Mrs. Charles Wilson, Dorothy Hughes and Sara Jane Jones, the WWC of Philadelphia invites monthly speakers and manages the receptions at Philadelphia Welsh meetings. In 1978 WWC officer Mrs. Lillian Canaan organized *Ninnau's* first pen-pal scheme. Starting with 28 Welsh correspondents this first attempt proved very successful. Today *Ninnau's* pen-friend program, *Ninnau Dragon Friends,* is managed by Earl Williams of Connecticut.

A Chairman of the Philadelphia bicentennial National in 1976, Elisabeth Griffith has done more than anyone to re-establish the cymanfa ganu in Philadelphia. The 1976 National had a definite atmosphere of renewal, and the following year in Toronto, Elisabeth presented the WNGGA with a record $5,434.00. Since 1976 the Arch Street Welsh fall service has developed into an annual cymanfa ganu, which in 1982, was declared an official event of Philadelphia's 300th birthday celebrations. Two hundred and fifty attended the 1982 cymanfa. Records were shattered on May 29, 1982, however, with the opening concert of the Dowlais Male Voice Choir, on their 14-day tour of Pennsylvania, Ohio and New York. The Dowlais appearance was phenomenally successful, filling the huge church and attracting new interest in Philadelphia Welsh programs.

The Cambrian Society of Delaware Valley, is based in Richboro. The Cambrian Society's biggest celebration is a St. David's Day dinner which has been held every year since 1961 at Addisville Reformed Church Hall, Richboro. Arrangements are made by Mr. and Mrs. Stokley C. Ramsey and the dinner usually attracts between 75 and 100 people. Correspondent for the Cambrian Society of Delaware Valley is President Nelson Howells and the Society has a prominent soloist in Mr. Bill Lewis. Welsh meetings are held at the church every fall and spring and the church also has an informal Welsh singing group. For concerts and cymanfaoedd canu, however, members of the Cambrian Society drive to the meetings in Philadelphia.

St. David's Day celebrations in Philadelphia feature a service the Sunday before St. David's Day, a ceremony at the Welsh Plaque on March 1st and a banquet on the Saturday evening nearest March 1st. About 200 people usually attend the banquet, which is sponsored by the Philadelphia Welsh Society. The gala banquet features all the Welsh talent of Philadelphia. Soloists have included Mary Jones, Eirlys Evans and Bronwen Eastwood, with accompanists Mary Jones and Elisabeth Griffiths.

The most prominent musician of the Society is Dr. Carlton Jones Lake, Director of the Philadelphia Academy of Music Boys Choir. A choir of sixty singers between 8 and 14 years old, the Boys Choir competed at the Llangollen International Eisteddfod in 1978 and frequently sings at the Philadelphia St. David's banquet.

At the banquet the Philadelphia Welsh Society presents its annual Robert Morris award. In 1984 the award went to Gwynfor Evans who stirred the audience to an unanimous standing ovation. Past recipients have included Islyn Thomas in 1981 and labor leader John Llewellyn Lewis in 1958.

SCRANTON

The greatest concentration of people of Welsh background in the United States is still found in the Scranton/Wilkes-Barre conurbation. The majority of Welsh people in Scranton actually settled in Hyde Park, which is now part of Scranton City, and it was in Hyde Park that *Baner America* was published from 1868-1877. *The Druid* was launched in Scranton in 1907 until moving to Pittsburgh in 1912. Daniel Protheroe, the famous Welsh composer, made Scranton his home until moving to Milwaukee in 1894. In 1923 the Lackawanna and Scranton Welsh Societies, led primarily by the Scranton Women's Welsh Club, opened the Scranton Home for Aged Welsh Women. The Scranton Home closed in the early 1970's.

The only association of Welsh churches in America, The Welsh Baptists Association of Northeast Pennsylvania, is based in Scranton. The Welsh Baptist Association has churches in Taylor, Parsons, Plymouth, Nanticoke, Olyphant, Edwardsville, Warrior Run and Wilkes-Barre. Few of these churches have Welsh ministers or lead Welsh language services, but their Welsh societies and cymanfaoedd canu maintain Welsh American traditions.

Scranton has an area known as Patagonia, a section between Hampton and Eynon Streets, where Welsh immigrants lived and from where a party of 30 left for Patagonia during coal disputes of the 1870's.

Cymanfaoedd canu in the Scranton area are by far the most common kind of local Welsh American event. The Reverend William Lewis of Waverly, the genial and eloquent pastor of Jackson Street Baptist Church in Scranton, was for over 30 years one of the foremost personalities behind Scranton Welsh life. Vice-Chairman of the Wilkes-Barre National Cymanfa in 1983, and of the bicentennial National in Philadelphia in 1976 and a regular speaker and preacher at meetings throughout northeastern Pennsylvania, his death in April 1984 was a tragic blow to the Welsh community.

There is a confluence of Welsh societies along the Lackawanna River with overlapping responsiblities, memberships and calendar dates, offering Welsh Americans their choice of Welsh events throughout the year. The annual Scranton St. David's Banquet has been sponsored by the St. David's Society of Lackawanna County since 1910. In recent years attendance at the banquet has reached over 300 people, with entertainment provided by the St. David's Male Chorus. Soloists at Scranton banquets have been Anne Jones, Clem Metz, Mary Stuckhart, Karen Williams and Clarence Decker, with accompanists Harold Thorpe and Elda Hardmann. The banquet also features a "Man of the Year" award. In 1985 the award went to Edgar A. Collins, a conductor, singer and teacher in the Scranton Welsh community. Other leaders of the Lackawanna County Welsh Society include George Pugh, George Smith, Emrys Jones, Donald Hughes, David Morgan, Edgar Collins, Philip Stevens,

Lowell Stevens, Gwilym J. Morgan and in 1984 Alan F. Hughes, Arthur Brown and William Jones.

St. David's celebrations in Scranton include cymanfaoedd canu held at First Welsh Baptist Church and the North Main Baptist Church. Attendance at North Main is between two and three hundred people with congregational singing led by Donald Davis. The cymanfa ganu at First Welsh Baptist Church attracted over 600 in 1984 when the aisles and entranceways were packed and people stood outside. Other cymanfaoedd are held at Simpson Street United Methodist Church, West Scranton and Hyde Park Presbyterian.

The Lackawanna County St. David's Society meets every other month at the First Welsh Baptist Church for informal programs of community singing and talks by visiting guests. The Women's Welsh Society also meets at the First Welsh Baptist Church. Members of the Women's Society bake Welsh cakes which they distribute and sell through pastry shops, raising funds for the maintenance of the church. The First Welsh Baptist also has a "Cymdeithas Sunday School Class" maintaining a knowledge of congregational singing in the traditional style.

The St. David's Male Chorus of Scranton rehearses every Monday night at Hyde Park Presbyterian Church. The choir was founded in 1960 by William R. Hughes (1893-1976) and led by him until 1974. Today the choir has eighteen voices and is led by Evelyn Butler assisted by Mrs. Elda Hardman, accompanist. The choir's President is David Harris; Secretary, Warren Gill; Treasurer, George Davis; Business Manager, Wyndham Davies; P.R. Correspondent and Vice-President, Lionel Satterthwaite.

The St. David's Chorus sings a wide selection of Welsh language material, including the standards Myfanwy, Llanfair, Gwahoddiad and Tydi a Rhoddaist. When the Hyde Park Presbyterian Church was destroyed by fire in 1981, the St. David's Male Chorus gave a series of well attended concerts and contributed substantially to its reconstruction. The St. David's Male Chorus of Scranton is one of the few remaining Welsh male choruses in the United States performing Welsh material on a regular basis.

Since 1981 the Lackawanna County Welsh Society has participated in a December Ethnic Christmas Tree Display at Everhart Museum in Scranton. Ladies in Welsh costume staff the display and hold a Welsh Day festival. The Welsh Day has attracted over 200 people. Singing is led by Sally Stevens and Milton Hughes, with tea and Welsh cakes to follow.

Through their contacts with adjacent societies and through bus trips as far as Slatington, Pennsylvania or Binghamton, New York, Welsh Americans in Scranton are able to participate in a regular calendar of Welsh events. The emphasis on cymanfaoedd canu and hymn singing is regarded as an over-emphasis by some who would like to see these numerically strong societies diversify into programs of more general appeal. Following the Wilkes-Barre National in 1983, however, and the Wilkes College Cwrs Cymraeg in 1984 there is a slight modernization and change of emphasis taking place. In the spring and fall of 1985 the University of Scranton offered a course 'The Land & People of Wales', which was taught by Professor Susan Trussler.

WEST CLIFFORD

North of Scranton, near the hamlet of West Clifford, cymanfaoedd canu are held the last Sunday in July and the last Sunday in September at Bethel Welsh Congregational Church, Welsh Hill. Reverend Garford Williams is pastor of the Church. Miss Maude Thomas drives from New Jersey to serve as accompanist and the cymanfaoedd are directed by Donald Davis of Scranton. A large contingent drives up from Wilkes-Barre bringing attendance to above 300 people in recent years and filling the small wooden church to capacity. This is a charming rural cymanfa with good singing and soloists have been Thomas Fallon, William Morgan, Mrs. William Evans and Mrs. Martin Salamida. Bethel Church also has a very interesting Welsh cemetery nearby.

WILKES-BARRE

In and around Wilkes-Barre we find a concentration of Welsh American societies. Leaders and memberships overlap, the chairman of one committee serving as secretary of another. Wilkes-Barre hosted the National Cymanfa Ganu in 1983, Cwrs Cymraeg in 1984 and the new Luzerne County Celtic Festival in August 1984.

The Wilkes-Barre Heights St. David's Society

This Society's two main events are a men's only St. David's Banquet on the nearest Friday to March 1st and a fall cymanfa on the second Sunday in October. Both celebrations are held at the First Welsh Presbyterian Church.

The all male St. David's dinner in Wilkes-Barre has been a tradition since 1935. In recent years, over 120 men attend the dinner which is served by the Ladies' Friendship Group, led by Ellen Griffiths, Elsie Deobold and Mrs. William Davis. The dinner features invited speakers and choral singing by The Welsh Warblers led by Donald S. Anthony. A popular part of the program is impromptu singing and recitations by members of the audience. The Society is led by John Strobel, Robert Anthony, and W. Craig Peters who has been president since 1958. John Mainwaring is the accompanist and Donald Anthony directs community singing.

The Reverend George B. Johnson is pastor of the First Welsh Presbyterian Church. Under his ministry the annual October cymanfa continues to attract visitors from as far away as New York, New Jersey, Philadelphia and Maryland. Conductors have included Lyn Harry, Peter Williams, Carlton Jones Lake, Robert A. Jones and the Reverend Gwyn Walters who was pastor of the church before moving to Massachusetts.

In 1981 the First Welsh Presbyterian cymanfa featured sessions at 3 p.m. and 7 p.m. as well as a bilingual morning service. Since then, however, it has returned to a single afternoon session which packs the building to capacity with an attendance of over 700 people. The cymanfa features a choir made of members from surrounding Welsh churches and in 1983 featured the harp playing of Patricia Anderson. A Welsh tea is provided later by the ladies of the church.

In October 1983, the Second Welsh Congregational Church in Wilkes-Barre celebrated its 100th anniversary with a cymanfa ganu. Dr. Ellis W. Roberts, educator and author was the invited speaker. Chairperson of the anniversary weekend was Mrs. Blodwen Parry. Pastor of the Second Welsh Congregational is Reverend Gerald Williams and the church today has 109 adult members.

In 1985 the Heights St. David Society celebrated its 50th annual banquet with a dinner at the Regency Ballroom, Wilkes-Barre, attended by over 300 people.

St. David's Society of Wyoming Valley Inc.

The Wyoming Valley St. David's Society adds its annual banquet and Welsh Night to the pool of banquets and cymanfaoedd canu of its neighbours. The Society has held a St. David's banquet since 1879. Every year St. David's celebrations start with a well attended Welsh flag-raising ceremony over Luzerne County Courthouse. In all recent years, the banquet has been held on the Saturday closest to March 1st at the Irem Shriners Temple in Wilkes-Barre or at the American Legion Hall. In 1985 it was held at the Sheraton Crossgates Hotel, headquarters of the 1983 National Cymanfa. Over 300 people attend the St. David's dinner and the usual form of entertainment is singing by groups such as "The Welsh Cookies," three ladies from Dallas, Pennsylvania or the Youth Choir of the Welsh Baptist Church, Plymouth. Speakers have included, Islyn Thomas, Edward Hartmann and Emlyn Griffith of Rome, New York. The banquet ends with community singing led by Donald S. Anthony or Thomas H. Griffiths; regular accompanists are Carl C. Coates and John Mainwaring. Since 1979 the St. David's Society of Wyoming Valley has held a "Welsh Night" at Irem Temple Country Club in Dallas. Welsh Night is part of the Country Club's summer concert series and is a combination concert and cymanfa, with prizes for the oldest man and the oldest woman there. The prize for who has traveled furthest almost always goes to a visitor from Wales. Welsh Night is now a regular event and has attracted over 1,000 people.

All Wyoming Valley St. David's Society events tend to be variations of the banquet or the cymanfa ganu theme. For the Society's 100th anniversary in 1979 members combined their banquet with a cymanfa in Edwardsville. In June 1982, a dinner was held for all the Society's living past presidents and has been held every year since. In 1985 Elsie Deobold and *Welsh American Women* held a reunion at the Sheraton Crossgates for the women who'd worked on the National Cymanfa Ganu preparations the year before. Eighty-four attended and applauded the leadership of Jeanne Jones, Anne Roberts, Blodwen Price, Helen Miller, Shirley Owens, Elizabeth Thomas and Anne Mae Hixson. Women, however have never been members or officers of the St. David's Society of Wyoming Valley Inc. The Wyoming Valley Welsh Society also participates in the Luzerne County Courthouse festival every December which features Christmas trees from Wales, Poland, Ukraine, Lithuania and Czechoslovakia.

Since the Wilkes-Barre 1983 National a younger group under the leadership of Jack Pritchard and Stephen Killiam greatly assisted by Donna Morgan and John Simmons has started branching out. The Wyoming Valley Society was co-sponsor of an August 1984 Celtic Festival, the first of its type in the region. Anne Habermehl and her son, David, provided the main Welsh contribution, singing and playing Welsh music on the harp and violin.

John Simmons and Donna Morgan brought the 1984 Cwrs Cymraeg to Wilkes College, the fourth time for the course to be held in Pennsylvania. Following so closely on enthusiasm generated by the Wilkes-Barre National, Cwrs Cymraeg attracted over 70 students and made a very high local impact. The local rather intense circuit of cymanfaoedd canu in the Wyoming Valley townships is slowly being supplemented by choirs, folk singing groups, language classes, and an interest in more contemporary aspects of Welsh culture. The 1985-1986 committee of the St. David's Society of Wyoming Valley Inc. consisted of Reverend Edmund L. John, President; Ben J. Davis, President-Elect; Robert Anthony and Cromwell E. Thomas, Vice-Presidents; George T. Jones, Recording Secretary; Richard E. Pierce, Financial Secretary; W. Craig Peters, Treasurer and Oscar W. Jones, Historian.

EDWARDSVILLE

The Edwardsville Cynonfardd Eisteddfod has been held every year since 1889.

In 1913 Archdruid Dyfed, Evan Rees of Wales, presided over the First International Eisteddfod held in Pittsburgh. The American Gorsedd was founded here with the Reverend T. C. Edwards as the first American Archdruid, taking Cynonfardd (Bard of Cynon) as his bardic name.

In 1919 Pittsburgh became the headquarters of the American Gorsedd and 200 members were initiated. The American Gorsedd folded in 1945 due mainly to the decline in the use of Welsh language among Welsh Americans and the vast distances that separated members. During its existence there were only three Archdruids, Cynonfardd, followed by the Reverend William Survidal of Middlepoint, Ohio and Senator James Davies of Pennsylvania. The Archdruid's regalia of Chain, Crown and Charter are missing and have not been seen since Senator Davies last wore them. Cynonfardd's own Bardic Chair, which he won in Wales, is today the property of his grandson, Cromwell Thomas, who lives in Dallas, Pa.

Before becoming minister of the Welsh Church in Edwardsville the

Reverend T. C. Edwards served at Mineral Ridge, Ohio from 1871 to 1872 and Wilkes-Barre from 1872 to 1878. When he died in 1927 the eisteddfod he established was named after him and the church was renamed the Dr. Edwards Memorial Congregational Church.

In the 1880's the Edwardsville Eisteddfod was held on St. Patrick's Day. Irish coal miners would take the day off so the Welsh followed suit and held a festival of their own. At that time a church society existed with the purpose of teaching Welsh children English. The society later became the Cynonfardd Literary Society which, through the church, succeeded in keeping the Edwardsville Eisteddfod going. Today, under the direction of the Reverend Louis Falcone, minister of the Edwards Memorial Church and Robert and Jan Whittaker, the Cynonfardd Eisteddfod continues to be a popular spring event. Held the last week in April or the first week in May, a children's eisteddfod (under 16) takes place in the afternoon. Before the evening adults' Eisteddfod, there is a short cymanfa. About 300 people usually attend the afternoon Eisteddfod and 500 attend the evening. In 1984 and 1985 attendance topped 1,000; Edwardsville itself only has a population of 6,000.

The Eisteddfod features a wide variety of vocal and instrumental competitions. Set pieces are in English; the only Welsh language used is for some verses during the mid-afternoon cymanfa. Hen Wlad Fy Nhadau is usually led by a child proficient in the Welsh language—Rhonda Whittaker in 1981, and 11 year old Amy Lynn Jones in 1982. In 1982, the Cynonfardd Eisteddfod was visited by a BBC crew who filmed the event for British television.

The Welsh of Wilkes-Barre, Edwardsville and Plymouth have participated in the annual Luzerne County Folk Festival since its inception in 1975. The Welsh contribution is organized by the Ethnic Committee of the First Welsh Presbyterian Church with Elizabeth Mates chairperson, assisted by Jeanne Jones, Mona Jones, Ellen Griffiths and Elsie Deobold with the help of many other volunteers. The Welsh booth consists mainly of displaying Welsh heirlooms and the sale of Welsh cakes and handmade Welsh dolls.

PLYMOUTH

The First Welsh Baptist Church in Plymouth has senior and junior choirs that sing in Welsh. The Plymouth cymanfa ganu is held every March with two sessions and with refreshments provided by the Ladies' Aid Society. Mrs. Harold Thomas and Mrs. Carl Futchel are the main organizers of the cymanfa, assisted by members of both choirs.

WEATHERLY

Eckley Miners' Village in Weatherly, Pennsylvania is one of several eastern Pennsylvania museums demonstrating the historic importance of coal in the state's development. Eckley Miners' Village, Ashland Anthracite Museum and Scranton Iron Furnaces all tell the story of coal and the people who mined it. Very little research has been done on Welsh contributions to the Pennsylvania anthracite industry, and the Welsh are under-represented in museum displays. Dr. Ellis Roberts of Wilkes-Barre has done some research into Pennsylvania Welsh mining history and has spoken at Eckley seminars. But no serious effort has been made to document Welsh American coal mining nor trace the connections between immigration from the South Wales coalfield and the growth of coal mining in Pennsylvania.

HAZELTON

The St. David's Society of Hazelton has observed St. David's Day since 1933. Today the March 1st program consists of a luncheon held at Hazle Village Welsh Congregational Church with a 25c nominal charge. John King continues to be the main organizer of the lunch and regular guest speaker is the humorous and popular Daniel Lewis of Mahanoy City. The "Grace Notes" of Mahanoy City sing and Esther Davis of Hazle Village Welsh Church plays Welsh preludes on the organ. About 200 people usually come to the luncheon and Welsh singing is led with great enthusiasm by the Reverend Richard E. Owens.

MAHANOY CITY

Grace Welsh Congregational Church of Mahanoy City has been holding a St. David's Day dinner every March since 1900. The Reverend Donald L. Wise is pastor there today and banquet entertainment is provided by the "Grace Notes"—Jean Reidler, William Ziegler, Frank Osenbach, Gail Osenbach, Arlene Davidson and Mary Nell Starner. Dinner is followed by congregational singing of well known hymns which are read in Welsh and English by Glynnis Schaar.

LANSFORD

Annual cymanfaoedd canu have been held in Lansford since 1975. One cymanfa is held in the First Baptist Church every September. The Reverend Haydn Gillmore is the minister and Jay Hall is cymanfa organist. A March cymanfa is held on the nearest Sunday to March 1st at the English Congregational Church. Pianist here is Professor John Sharpe with Regine De Puy at the organ. Mr. Gillmore directs the singing with readings of the Welsh hymns by William T. Richards. Under the leadership of Marian Urban and George B. Richards, well publicized Lansford cymanfaoedd canu attract around 200 people every year.

Services were held at the Welsh Congregational Church in Lansford until 1935. Recently a renovation project for the church was started by Colonel Alfred J. Reece Jr. also coordinated by Linda Murphy and Alfred Baldwin.

Over 300 people attended a Welsh fund-raising songfest in Lansford on March 24, 1985.

POTTSVILLE

The St. David's Society of Schuylkill and Carbon Counties has held an annual banquet in Pottsville since 1945. Attended by over 300 people in 1983 the banquet is usually held the first or second Saturday in April. The Society, under the leadership of Fred Hatter, Isabelle West, Merlyn Jenkins, John R. Jones and Joseph H. Jones is very active and makes an annual Welsh citizen of the year award. In 1983 the award went to Fred Hatter, leader of the Society for over 30 years and a man who has done a lot to keep the Society abreast of the times. Banquets in the past have featured speakers, singers and dramatists, among them Maldwyn Pate who spent several years in New York City and is now Modern Dance officer for the Welsh Arts Council. The Society also hosted Ray Handy during the Pryderi and His Pigs tour of 1976.

SLATINGTON

The United Presbyterian Church in Slatington, 7 miles north of Allentown, has held a November cymanfa every year since 1959. Under the leadership of Orlo Williams and the Reverend David H. Johnson, the cymanfa continues to be well attended, attracting over 400 people to the afternoon and evening sessions. The cymanfa committee always invites prominent American or Canadian conductors. Lyn Harry has directed here, and for the 25th anniversary meeting in 1983 Dr. Gwyn Walters conducted in the afternoon and Morris Wrench at night. Mary Pierce, committee leader, Lillian Jones, reader, and Sara Miller, pianist, have been with the Slatington cymanfa since its beginnings and have contributed enormously to its success. All the great Welsh hymns are sung and a regular and reliable soloist is Ethel Stillman from Palmerston. Andrea Witchen of Bethlehem, Pennsylvania plays the harp and a sit-down tea with several sittings to accommodate the large congregation is served between cymanfa sessions.

ALLENTOWN

The Welsh American Society of Lehigh County, based in Allentown, meets on the first Tuesday of every month at St. Michael's Lutheran Church at Ninth and Turner Streets. The Society holds an annual March 1st banquet at St. Michael's which is attended usually by about 50 people. In 1984 Orlo Williams was the President and in all recent years Mrs. Owen Jones and Judge William Griffiths have been the chairpersons in charge of organizing the annual St. David's Dinner. 1985 officers of the Welsh Society in Allentown were Jane Stephens, Mair Wharton, Jane Thorogood, Mary Schneck, Owen Jones and Elizabeth O'Brien.

BANGOR

The Welsh Day Association of Bangor was originally established by Mr. Albert Foulkes. For this and other work preserving Welsh traditions, Mr. Foulkes was awarded the Hopkins Medal of the St. David's Society of the State of New York in 1951. From 1964 until his death in 1976 at the age of 72, the Bangor Welsh Day Association was led by Mr. Evan Jones. Mr. Jones assisted the Pryderi Players on their American tour and organized many trips to distant Pennsylvania and New Jersey Welsh meetings. Mr. Jones taught a Welsh language class in Bangor through the state adult education program. Since his death, the Bangor Welsh Day Association has collapsed.

EAST STROUDSBURG

East Stroudsburg holds "Welsh Music Festival" on or near March 1st. The two sessions of the festival are conducted by K. Bernard Schade, Professor of Music at East Stroudsburg State College.

LAHASKA

Lahaska is the home of The Celtic Pavilion run by Ruth and John Brown, regular participants in the National Cymanfa Ganu marketplace. This store carries goods from all the Celtic countries and has a superior selection of china and lace from Brittany and a better than average selection of Welsh goods including clothing and jewelry. The Celtic Pavilion is also a source of cassette recordings of National Cymanfaoedd Canu.

POTTSTOWN

In 1974 the Pottstown branch of Rotary International sponsored a visit to South Wales by six Pottstown businessmen. Since then an active Pottstown exchange program with Wales has continued. In 1975, six Welsh businessmen stayed in Pottstown; also in 1975, 160 students from Southeastern Pennsylvania spent three weeks on homestay visits in South Wales. In 1978, again through Rotary International, 160 Welsh students visited Pennsylvania, and 13 of them spent three weeks with families in Pottstown. In 1978 the Hopkins Medal of the St. David's Society of the State of New York was given to W. Jack Davis, a Welsh American and President of Rotary International for 1977-1978.

READING

The Welsh Society of Berks County, based in Reading and Shillington, is one of the most active in southeast Pennsylvania. Dr. Peter Williams, founder of the Welsh Society in Wilmington, Delaware, is a regular speaker and conductor at Berks County Welsh meetings and cymanfaoedd canu.

The Welsh Society of Berks County was founded in the early 1960's and had about forty members in 1984. About twenty-five people usually attend the regular meetings, held every other month at Trinity Lutheran Church in Reading. Recent leaders have included Mary Stoudt, Mrs. Pat Wyn, William Griffiths and Joyce Anderson. Committee officers, in 1984, were Mr. Rush Gwyn, President; Elizabeth Evans, Vice-President: Gwen Ludawski, Secretary and Herbert Schaffer, Treasurer. In 1985, new member, Barry Tracy added to Society events by teaching a weekly Welsh language class.

Under the chairmanship of Olwen Evans and William Griffiths, the Society has been very active in Welsh Historic preservation in Berks County. The Society organizes tours of Welsh American historic churches and collaborates with the Morgantown-Caernarvon Historical Society. In 1984 the Society presented Caernarvon (Pennsylvania) township with a Welsh flag to fly above its courthouse on St. David's Day. In 1979 the Morgan Log House in Towamencin, the oldest, unchanged Welsh colonial dwelling in the U.S.A., was named best restoration of the year. The 300-year old log house demonstrates how the early Welsh pioneers lived. The house was built by Edward and Elizabeth Morgan, the grandparents of Daniel Boone.

From 1978 to 1983 Mrs. Olwen Evans organized the restoration of the Welsh Baptist Meeting House and Adams Cemetery. Founded in 1744, the building and graveyard had fallen into disrepair—but, with helpers from the Welsh societies, Mrs. Evans restored the site and managed to get it listed on the Pennsylvania Register of Historical Places.

The Berks County St. David's banquet is usually held in Shillington towards the end of March. About sixty people usually attend with Evan Lewis leading community singing and Faith King at the piano. Other soloists have been Joyce Anderson, Dr. Peter Williams, and Jane Byre and Andrea Witchen playing the harp. The society also holds an annual Welsh picnic in July. The Welsh Heritage Cymanfa Ganu of Berks County is held at Trinity Lutheran Church in Reading. This cymanfa, which attracts between 100 and 150 people, is held the fourth Sunday of every September.

STATE COLLEGE

State College, Pennsylvania has a small but dedicated Welsh Society whose main meeting is an annual St. David's Day banquet held every year since 1959. The banquet has been held in all recent years at the Autoport Restaurant and attracted over 80 people in 1985. J.C. and Nancy Griffiths lead the State College Welsh Society assisted by Dick Rowlands, Ron Williams and Darrell Griffiths. The recent arrival of Welsh-speaking Margaret Knott from North Wales has added to the Society immensely. The banquet always features musicians from Penn State University, notably Nan Gullo Man, harpist and Louise Van Kuren, from Glasgow, who sings in Welsh and English.

JOHNSTOWN

An annual cymanfa ganu is held in Johnstown about fifty miles east of Pittsburgh. The Johstown cymanfa was started in 1942 and is held the first week in May at Memorial Baptist Church. Mr. Thomas R. Barber, who emigrated from Treharris, South Wales in 1926, continues to organize and direct the cymanfa which is the only remaining Welsh event since the demise of the Johnstown Welsh Society in the 1960's. In 1984 the Johnstown cymanfa drew between 350 and 400 people. Two brothers, Dan and Ernest Ellis, play an important role in the organization of this annual event.

EBENSBURG

North of Johnstown in Ebensburg, the Welsh Calvinistic Methodist Church celebrated its 145th anniversary in August 1984. Eighty-one year old Thomas R. Barber of Johnstown organized the cymanfa and he and Dan and Ernest Ellis sang during the service. The cymanfa was attended by over 100 people. East of Ebensburg on the Beulah Road towards Nantyglo is Beulah cemetery. Beulah was a Welsh community founded in 1797 by Morgan John Rhys; in its heyday there were over 300 Welsh inhabitants. During the early 19th century, however, the community declined and was eventually abandoned altogether. Today on a hill behind a car wreck junk yard is a small untended Welsh cemetery—all that remains of the Beulah Welsh experiment. The full story of Beulah is described in detail by Gwyn A. Williams in his book, *The Search for Beulah Land*.

DELTA

Of all the Welsh societies in Pennsylvania the group at Delta on the Pennsylvania/Maryland border is the most energetic at promoting its Welsh American heritage.

Rehoboth Capel Cymraeg in Delta is the center of Welsh life. Since bicentennial celebrations in 1976, Rehoboth has experienced a tremendous revival in memberships and activities. Today Rehoboth holds bilingual Welsh-English services, cymanfaoedd canu and has a minister who leads the congregation in Welsh hymns and Welsh language lessons.

Gwen Kilburn and Betty Williams maintained interest in Rehoboth during the lean years of the 1960's and 1970's. Between them they organized the May Homecoming services year after year. Despite being the only Welsh church located at a traditional Welsh American site, interest in the church fell annually. Then, during Delta's 1980 bicentennial celebrations, renewed interest in local history seized the town and committees were organized to research Delta's Welsh past. Under the leadership of Glenn Grove and Bill and Pat St. Clair, Rehoboth advertised in the Welsh papers.

By 1982, Delta Welsh Society members were attending Welsh concerts and banquets in Baltimore. They attempted their own English language cymanfa, using Welsh very cautiously. In September 1982 the Reverend Richard Price Baskwill of Cockeysville, Maryland volunteered to serve as Rehoboth's pastor—the church's first minister for over 20 years. Through Reverend Baskwill, a learner himself, Welsh hymns have become a regular feature and 325 attended Rehoboth's first fall cymanfa and te bach that followed.

Rehoboth Welsh events now regularly attract several hundred people, Welsh classes are held every Sunday, Welsh costumes are worn and the Society has diversified into a wide range of activities. The Society has produced Rehoboth stationery, *Cymru am Byth* T-shirts, cloth leeks and other gifts for sale. In 1983 the Society provided the only Welsh presence at the Harrisburg Ethnic Fair, concluding their contribution with the new Rehoboth Welsh Choir directed by Reverend Baskwill. In May 1984 Côr Rehoboth represented Wales for the first time ever at the National Cathedral Flower Festival in Washington, D.C.

By 1984, Côr Rehoboth could mount a 1½ hour program entirely in Welsh. Rehoboth's homecoming cymanfa in May 1984 featured an all day "Welshiana" fair on the Saturday, a noson lawen Saturday night, a bilingual service Sunday morning and a cymanfa Sunday afternoon directed by Carlton Jones Lake of Philadelphia. The cymanfa was attended by over 500 people.

The Welsh group in Delta form one of the most buoyant and active Welsh clubs in America. Delta's leadership has proved that Welsh American societies can generate programs of contemporary interest if they are managed with thought and imagination. In July 1984, Rehoboth hosted the Pendyrus Male Choir on one of the choir's most successful overseas tours. The tour made great impact in New York, Baltimore and Washington, D.C., but most of all in Delta where a group of 60 people was organized which toured Wales and stayed with Pendyrus members in November 1985.

PITTSBURGH

In the late 19th century Welsh people formed the fifth largest ethnic group in Pittsburgh. According to the 1900 census, their population was the third largest concentration of Welsh people in the United States exceeded only by Wilkes-Barre and Scranton. The American Order of True Ivorites (a masonic-type organization) was founded in Pittsburgh in 1848. *The Druid* was published in Pittsburgh from 1913 to 1931 and the American Gorsedd had its headquarters there from 1919 until it folded in 1945. At one point the city's Welsh population supported six Welsh churches and hosted the North American National Cymanfa Ganu in 1938 and 1965. Since 1965, Welsh activities have slowly gone downhill.

That Welsh activities still persist is largely due to the work of J. C. Williams, David Renshaw, Byron George and the pen of Esther Elias. The St. David's Society of Pittsburgh still sponsors Welsh events, mainly a March banquet and October cymanfa. It also arranges frequent visits for choirs, soloists and other visitors from Wales. There are many Americans of Welsh background in the city, but the Welsh Society is unable to attract them; membership is low and the average age of those who belong is high. The Society has a mailing list of around 700 with membership approaching 100. Dave Renshaw has tried to promote a more dynamic image. He is a tireless letter writer, reminding Pittsburgh newspapers of the city's Welsh heritage and appearing and speaking at numerous meetings. In 1980 he taught an eight-week Welsh language class, which attracted only five students—Jane Snyder, Paul Mathews, Gordon and Margaret Thomas and Betty Renshaw, the teacher's wife. The classes stopped and the Society soldiered on with its business meetings and the terminal luncheons of the Women's Welsh Club.

The St. David's Society of Pittsburgh March 1st banquet is held every year at the Pittsburgh Theological Seminary; about 150 attend. Since 1981 the banquets have supplemented the usual hymn community singing with Welsh folk dancing organized by Franklin Watkins.

The fall cymanfa is always held at Shadyside Presbyterian Church on the second Sunday in October. About 300 people usually attend and the cymanfa has in all recent years been conducted by Morris Wrench of Youngstown with Jack Reece accompanist. In 1982, following a period of renewed activity by the Society, the Pittsburgh cymanfa drew over 450 people.

Parti Ceredigion sang at Shadyside in 1982 and five days later on October 22nd, the 33-voice Caernarfon Women's choir sang in the city. The women in the choir were hosted by Society members. When Llanddulais Male Choir turned up rather abruptly in April 1983, the Society and its officers were shaken by the sudden appearance of the choir and the necessity to host the forty choir members. President J. C. Williams worked frantically to accommodate the men, only to discover that the Choir's timetable was totally inaccurate and they required four extra days home-stay accommodation. This was too much for the St. David's Society members. With the help of Palmer Jones, a concert was arranged in Newark, Ohio and the choir was packed off there.

One of the places we visited was the 42-story "Cathedral of Learning" at the University of Pittsburgh. When the "Cathedral of Learning" was being built in the 1930's, each ethnic group was invited to finance and furnish a Nationality Room. Eighteen rooms were completed by groups as diverse as the Polish, the Greeks and the Chinese. Irish, English and Scottish rooms were furnished and each room displays the cultural and educational achievements of these countries.

No money for a Welsh room was ever raised, despite the large numbers of prosperous Welsh people living in the city. Inflexible personality conflicts were so intense that fund-raising committees made no progress whatsoever and withdrew. In 1980, Dave Renshaw and Richard Bowers organized a committee to finance one of a series of new rooms opening on the Cathedral of Learning's second floor. Two thousand dollars have been raised, but in 1984, it cost a quarter of a million dollars to build and furnish an ethnic room.

J. C. Williams, President of the Pittsburgh St. David's Society, is an outstanding baker and a prolific poet. A leader who genuinely tries to do his best for the Society, the lack of involvement by younger people was of real concern to him. He could see Welsh American life in Pittsburgh disappearing altogether unless a solution were found. Receptive and generous, when we left to visit Esther Elias at her apartment, he gave us three dozen Welsh cakes fresh out of the oven.

Before she retired in 1961, Esther Elias was the editor of the Amco Steel Corporation's Workers Publication. She has written for *Yr Enfys* since the 1950's. In 1976 and 1982, she wrote two biographies of her corgis—*A Profile of Glindy* and *The Queening of Ceridwen*. A talented writer, she makes her canine subjects entertaining heroes and heroines. In her "Pittsburghesque" columns for the Welsh papers, she even makes low key adventures of Pittsburgh Welsh Americans readable and interesting.

When I rang her bell, the door sprang open and Esther yanked me in. A bent, wiry woman with a bob of loose grey hair, she started talking immediately. When I replied, I found that she was almost completely deaf and it was only by shouting at the top of my voice that I could make myself heard.

Esther's whole apartment was a writer's studio—new filing cabinets were already filled with articles and cuttings. Magazines lay heaped around the chairs. Every question I asked sent her burrowing through books, papers, and bundled sheafs of mail. Esther could see that the Pittsburgh Welsh Society was in decline but she felt the big picture was more optimistic. She even felt that if its officers persevered, the fortunes of the Pittsburgh Society would turn around. Her own optimism and energy were obvious and when she pressed signed volumes of her corgi books into my hands, I told her our dog, Amiga, was downstairs waiting in the van.

It was pouring with rain and she put on her coat. "I wouldn't come to see you off, or to see your wife," she said, "but I'll go anywhere to see a dog." Suzanne brought Amiga over to the porch and we were impressed by Esther's instant rapport with a new animal. Amiga let herself be critically examined and approved. Esther then turned quite abruptly and went inside. When we saw her again at the Wilkes-Barre National Gymanfa, she insisted we take her to our parking place to see Amiga.

☆

In November 1983, Côr Meibion De Cymru, the mammoth 510-voice choir from South Wales, started its American tour at the Heinz Hall, Pittsburgh. The choir appeared here to packed houses on three successive nights with the Pittsburgh Symphony Orchestra. The next day the choir sang at the civic hall. In 1984, Arthur Hefin Jones visited Pittsburgh conducting musical examinations for Trinity College, London. He expressed an interest in musicians from the Welsh Society and at short notice, Dave Renshaw organized an informal evening for him. About a dozen attended, including Jerry Veech, organist and choir director in Bethel Park; Paul Mathews, organist and choir director in

Welsh Society
Newsletters

Welsh Import Stores

The Ontario
Welsh Festival

Ohio

Western Canada

Los Angeles,
San Francisco
and Seattle

Letterheads

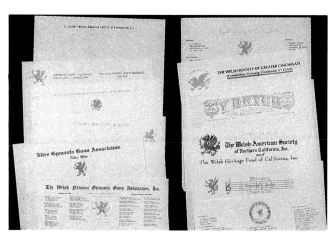

Letterheads

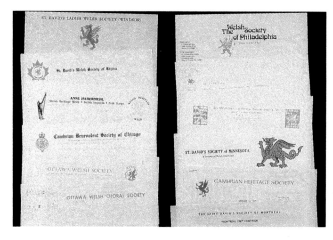

Celtic contacts

Gwynn Parri, Wisconsin, founder
of Welsh Associated Youth of
America and Canada

Richard Loomis, translator of
Dafydd Ap Gwilym: The Poems

Ellis Jones, Founder of the
Gustavus Adolphus Cymanfa G
Minnesota

Cerwyn Davies, minister of
Dewi Sant Welsh United Church,
Toronto

Robert A. Fowkes, New York City

Islyn Thomas OBE, author o
Our Welsh Heritage

Edythe Peterson, Lake Crystal, Minnesota

Jane Hughes (Siani Flewog),
St. Catharines, Ontario

Mildred Bangert, Oak Hill, Ohio

Donna Davies, San Francisco

Hamilton Orpheus Male Choir, Ontario

St. David's Welsh Male Chorus, Edmonton, Alberta

Côr Gwalia Ohio, Cincinnati

Vancouver Welsh Men's Choir, British Columbia

Côr Dewi Sant, Utica, New York

Amy Lynn Jones and Karen Pugh singing at the
Wilkes-Barre National Cymanfa, 1983

Cynonfardd Children's Eisteddfod, Edwardsville,
Pennsylvania, 1984

Children's Dance, Cwrs Cymraeg y Cymoedd,
Wilkes-Barre, 1984

Elinor Hughes performing at Awr y Plant,
Peterborough, Ontario, 1984

Jeannette; Becky Jones, music teacher and soloist; and Franklin Watkins, organist and choir director in McMurray and organizer of a small troupe of Welsh Folk Dancers.

A new form of Welsh leadership has come from an unexpected direction with the initiatives and publicity of WINvest, the Wales Investment Agency, which has its main American agent, Deckman Associates, based in Pittsburgh.

WINvest

Through WINvest (Wales Investment Agency) in America, which has offices in Chicago, Pittsburgh, New Jersey and California, a series of publicity campaigns and seminars were held in 1984 trying to draw the attention of American industry to the advantages of locating in Wales. Serious efforts to develop commercial links between America and Wales date from the opening of the Wales Trade Center in Santa Monica in 1976. Barry Smedley and George Schuler were commissioned to provide marketing services for Welsh companies trying to penetrate the American market. Meirion Lewis, Chief Executive of the Development Corporation of Wales, has visited the United States almost annually since then, refining and improving the package of information presented to potential business investors.

In 1978, the Secretary of State for Wales, John Morris, visited Midwest and West Coast locations as part of the Welsh Development Agency campaign. In September 1983, the Secretary of State for Wales, by now Nicholas Edwards, visited Chicago to open the WINvest exhibit at the International Electronics Trade Fair. In April 1984, Development Board for Rural Wales members visited Pittsburgh to speak at a series of WINvest seminars.

The Welsh Development Agency was created in 1976 as an all-Wales organization whose main objectives were to rejuvenate the larger population centers and older industrial urban areas. The Welsh Development Agency provides free advice, grants and assistance to overseas businesses considering opening in Wales. Another board, the Development Board for Rural Wales, was created in 1977. Concerned mainly with mid-Wales, DBRW strategy is to integrate industrial and rural development while preserving the natural attraction of a beautiful countryside.

Both the WDA and the DBRW sought to take advantage of growing American investment in the British Isles. With their American consultants, managers in Wales conceived of WINvest in 1982. WINvest is the semi autonomous selling arm of the economic boards of Wales. It has a dual reporting relationship to the Welsh Development Agency and to the Welsh Office of the British Government. Its main responsibility is to identify companies who may be interested in a British location and then encouraging them to locate in the industrial estates of Wales.

Today there are over 100 American companies in Welsh industrial estates. Two of the latest American companies to locate in Wales are the New York Chemical Bank and Comdial, a Washington D.C. hi-tech manufacturing company. Some American companies in Wales are sensitive to the Welsh cultural condition and Kaiser Aluminum in Anglesey was a major sponsor of Côr y Brythoniaid's tour of California in 1980.

In 1984, Deckmann Associates utilized Pittsburgh's broad Welsh American background to publicize Welsh ecomonic opportunities. WINvest launched a three-month promotional and sales campaign by giving away ten thousand daffodils on March 1st. This was followed by a series of free seminars with cultural and business displays put up in hotel lobbies. Emrys Evans and Leslie Morgan, two members of the Development Board for Rural Wales visited Pittsburgh and chaired a series of open meetings. When contacted by Richard Deckmann, members of the Pittsburgh St. David's Society were glad to help in WINvest's publicity campaign. By cooperating with WINvest, the St. David's Society could only benefit from increased exposure. Both organizations utilized Pittsburgh's Welsh American past and WINvest promotions became an opportunity for the Welsh Society to revive its folk dancing, Welsh language classes and Welsh genealogical research.

19

New York: Welsh Heritage Today

BUFFALO

Leaving the Welsh Retirement Home in Rocky River, we drove to the home of Hywel and Ruth Thomas in Buffalo, New York. Hywel Thomas, originally from Llwynhendy, Wales, visited Buffalo with the Swansea University Folk Dancers in 1970 and 1972. He met his wife, Ruth, whose mother is Welsh, while at a dance performance in Buffalo and they were married less than a year later. While living in Wales Ruth learned Welsh, and in 1975 they returned to America where Hywel started Britannia Associates. Britannia Associates is a highly successful travel agency and Hywel Thomas was the organizer of the 510 voice Côr Meibion De Cymru concert tour in 1983.

The St. David's Society in Buffalo has celebrated St. David's Day since 1943. Every year March 1st services are held at St. Paul's Episcopal Cathedral. Dean Elton Smith is very receptive to the Welsh Society, and if he doesn't conduct the service himself, the Welsh Society invites a guest preacher, usually a bilingual minister from the Welsh community in Ontario. The St. David's Society meets on the third Sunday of every month, except July and August at the Buffalo International Institute. The Society's main events are held in the spring with a banquet in March, a small eisteddfod in April, in May an outing or a concert and in June the Society picnic.

Mair Monkhouse was the leader of the Society for many years and organized many trips to distant National cymanfaoedd canu. A past trustee and officer of the WNGGA, Mair is also a firm supporter of WAY. Other leaders of the Buffalo Welsh Society have been Bess Duke, Rachel Steeley, Sarah Sterret, Ernest Williams, Jim and Terri Winston and Elizabeth Braithwaite.

St. David's Day in Buffalo is marked with a flag raising ceremony over Erie County Hall. About 120 people usually attend the annual St. David's banquet, which is followed by community singing and an informal noson lawen with soloists from the Society.

Having made contact with its leaders when he toured with Swansea University, Hywel Thomas joined the Welsh Society when he arrived in Buffalo. In 1977 Hywel initiated Welsh folk dancing at the annual Christmas party. He taught a weekly Welsh language class and he and Ruth became prominent musicians at all Welsh Society meetings. Using his resources as a travel agent, Hywel set up a tour for Dim Byd Eto, a Welsh folk/rock band in 1981. In the summer of 1981 Hywel organized a visit by Dawnswyr Tawerin, a Swansea folk dance group and first prize winners at the Machynlleth Eisteddfod. Hywel Thomas is also one of the most promising new cymanfa ganu conductors having already directed festivals in Toronto, Ontario; Gomer, Ohio and for societies in New York.

In April 1982, the ladies of the Buffalo Welsh Society, led by Debra Clark, Gwyneth Peers and Sophie Schuyler, staffed a booth at Beirs Department Store, Niagara Falls. The store holds an annual Women's Day, and in 1982 the theme was The British Isles. The ladies named their booth "The Land of Song" and attracted publicity for the St. David's Society.

Buffalo is where Welsh comedian and entertainer Ryan Davies died in April 1977. Ryan and his family were visiting Brian Jones, best man at Ryan's wedding, when Ryan was suddenly stricken with a severe asthma attack. He was rushed to the hospital but died several hours later. At the age of forty Ryan was regarded in Wales at the outstanding entertainer of his generation. With his own television show, theater appearances and recent film performance with Richard Burton (in "Under Milk Wood") he was at the peak of his career. More than any other entertainer he proved that a unique brand of Welsh comedy could be written for the television medium.

Buffalo is a regular concert venue for visiting Welsh choirs. Since Buffalo is such a traditional stop on choral tours, the majority of choirs arrive expecting Buffalo to have an active and enthusiastic Welsh Society. The truth is that the Society's membership finds it more and more difficult to accommodate visitors. Through his own experience as a tour performer in America and seeing so many choirs visit Buffalo, Hywel began to seriously examine the quality of tours arranged in Wales. Some travel agents send choirs to cities where Welsh American societies are strong, without contacting the society. Others choirs arrive expecting to be hosted by their American "cousins" when the Welsh American society consists of only a dozen people meeting for a luncheon once a month.

Hywel Thomas first thought of a massed male choral performance during conversations with Arturo Roberts in the summer of 1979. *Ninnau* has always encouraged societies interested in hosting a Welsh choir. Letters written to *Ninnau* were referred to Hywel who would connect the society with a choir and act as an advisor to both groups. The idea for a massed choir visiting the United States had been discussed by Glyn Jones and officers of the Welsh Association of Male Choirs as early as 1967. Around 1970, the Association hired a travel agent to visit America and make a feasibility study. The agent reported that the project was logistically impossible.

As a professional travel agent Hywel knew that transporting 1,000 (the original figure) male choristers would be no more difficult than transporting any other American convention group. On his next visit to Wales, Hywel met Glyn Jones and agreed to handle the American end if Welsh organizers took care of arrangements in Wales. That was in 1980 and the result in 1983 was one of the most successful collaborations ever between a Welsh choir and its American agent. Originally conceived as a tour by 1,000 voices, because of the deterioration in the pound/dollar exchange rate, the choir eventually consisted of 510 voices.

The tour opened in Pittsburgh, moved to Baltimore, then New York and concluded at the Shea Auditorium in Buffalo. This was the first time in over one hundred years of visits by choirs from Wales for a Welsh choir to appear with a professional American Symphony Orchestra and the first time that a Welsh choir's agent actively sought the general American musical audience. Critics consistently gave Côr Meibion De Cymru and conductor, Alun John, glowing reviews and the choir appeared before over twenty thousand people. Support for the tour came from the British Council and the Welsh American Foundation. Welsh Canadian singers from Hamilton joined the choir on tour. Altogether, with choir members, wives and supporters, the number of people was 640, traveling between hotels in a fleet of fourteen buses.

ROCHESTER

The St. David's Society of Rochester was started in 1972 by Dr. Richard Loomis who had recently moved there from Wilkes-Barre. An English professor at Nazareth College and with a Welsh connection on his mother's side, Dr. Loomis became interested in middle Welsh literature while studying the work of Geoffrey Chaucer. In 1971 Dr. Loomis ordered a consignment of books and a Welsh dictionary from the University of Wales which led to a series of papers on Welsh literature. Dr. Loomis next spent three summers studying Welsh at Aberystwyth, and in 1976 took a year's sabbatical to make translations of the poems of Dafydd ap Gwilym. Dr. Loomis' book, *Dafydd ap Gwilym: The Poems*, was published in 1982 by the Medieval and Renaissance Texts and Studies Department of the State University of New York and received financial assistance by the recently formed Welsh American Foundation and the St. David's Society of the State of New York. In 1985 Dr. Loomis published an edition, with translation, of the life of the 12th century St. Hugh (Bishop of Lincoln) by Gerald of Wales.

The St. David's Society in Rochester grew out of Richard Loomis's Welsh studies. The Society was reorganized in 1976 as the St. David's Society of Rochester and the Genesee Region, with meetings in October, December, March and May. The Society's first organizers were June Kern, Hugh Owen, Perry Thomas Fuller, Bill Coleman, Jean Patterson, Dotte Larsen and Anita Jones. In 1977 several Rochester members attended the first Cwrs Cymraeg held at Poultney, Vermont, which reinforced their interest enormously.

By 1981 Lee Bock could report that membership was up to seventy and the club was participating in the Rochester International Festival and the annual Celtic Picnic at Ontario Beach Park. In 1984 under the leadership of Anne Habermehl and Trudy Whitney, the Society continued to maintain a full and interesting calendar.

WELSH HERITAGE WEEK

Anne Habermehl was born and raised near Kitchener, Ontario and also lived in Drummondville, Quebec, before moving to Rochester, New York in 1969. In 1976 she made a four-week tour of the British Isles, visiting Wales only incidentally on her way to Ireland. The consistent friendliness of all Welsh people she met, especially their endearing habit of calling people "love" (milder still than the Cornish custom of calling people "my lover"), made the Welsh portion of her tour the most memorable and distinct. In 1977 Anne saw a small local ad and discovered the Rochester Welsh Society, and in 1978 she attended the Cwrs Cymraeg in Lewisburg, Pa. In 1980 she launched Welsh Heritage Week, a week long immersion in Welsh language, tradition and contemporary culture, folk dance and Welsh music, with an especially strong emphasis on the harp.

Since her first visit in 1976, Anne Habermehl has returned to Wales many times. As well as founding Welsh Heritage Week, she has established a Welsh import business, founded the Welsh Harp Society of North America, compiled a Welsh folk song book for learners, is Editorial Assistant and travel editor of *Ninnau*, and in 1981 edited *Ninnau*'s Welsh American Calendar. As a folk harp player, Anne Habermehl has appeared at numerous Celtic festivals and she is regular speaker and performer at Welsh society events. She was a member of a fact-finding committee for the ICDBL and helped write their 1983 report on the condition of the Breton language. In 1984 she introduced Breton language classes at Welsh Heritage Week.

Welsh Heritage Week is held every year in July at Keuka College in upstate New York. The week is a seven-day immersion in Welsh language and customs with a strong emphasis on studies, but with an equal emphasis on relaxation and having fun with the subject. Attendance at Welsh Heritage Week cost $255 in 1984 with special rates for families with two or more children. The attendance of young people is encouraged, Gini Jones and George Morgan who met at Welsh Heritage Week in 1983, were married there in 1984 with the rest of the students forming the congregation.

Two hours of Welsh language study are held every morning and an hour of Welsh hymn and folk singing every afternoon. The Welsh language is used constantly and students are encouraged to use as little English as possible. At the first Welsh heritage Week in 1980, the staff included Alun Hughes, who later became President of Cymdeithas Madog, Hywel Lewis and Jeanette Hudson, all native Welsh speakers living in Canada or Wales. Other members of the Welsh Heritage Week teaching staff have included John and Joan Owen from Lisbon, Ohio; Trefor Selway from Wales; Hywel Thomas from Buffalo N.Y.; Maxwell and Prydwen Roberts from London, Ontario; and Merfyn Morgan from Caernarfon. Merfyn Morgan created a learning system based on Hebrew teaching methods in Israel. His book, *Dysgu Cymraeg* is the book used at Welsh Heritage Week. In 1984 Natalie Novik taught a Breton language class and led a traditional Breton fest noz. Also in 1984, Edward Morus and Gwyneth Jones flew over from Wales bringing the staff to five from Wales and five from North America. Edward Morus Jones's language and singing classes for children during the week were very successful and Welsh Heritage Week makes a point of providing facilities for the needs of children and teenagers.

Shortly before the first Welsh Heritage Week was held in 1980, Ann Habermehl was put in touch with Robin James Jones of Llanrwst, Wales, who was about to leave for California to teach a folk harp workshop. The enrollment of Robin James Jones, who has been an official harp accompanist at the National Eisteddfod and is widely regarded as one of the foremost triple and folk harp players in Wales, made an enormous addition to Welsh Heritage Week. In 1982 Joan Seymour, a harp teacher from Dayton, Ohio, attended Welsh Heritage Week. Joan came to learn more about Welsh harping and she and Robin played at all the Week's dances and community singing. Their collaboration led to a now traditional Friday night harp concert.

Money is raised each year at Welsh Heritage Week at the Sunday morning cymanfa ganu, the Friday night harp concert and sometimes in other ways. These funds have gone to the National Eisteddfod Welsh Learner's Competition prize, the Nant Gwrtheyrn Language Center, the Nansi Richards (Telynores Maldwyn) Trust and the Welsh Harp Society of North America.

By 1984, close to 300 people had attended Welsh Heritage Week. Martha Evans of Gomer, Beverly Rodda of Boston, Earl Williams, founder of the St. David's Society of Connecticut and Peter Williams, founder of the St. David's Society of Delaware have all been students and have all been inspired to improve the programs of their Welsh society at home. After a week of such a deep immersion in Welshness, participants emerge bursting with enthusiasm. In Boston, we spent an evening with Beverly Rodda who had just returned from a double dose of Welsh Heritage Week followed by Cwrs Cymraeg. Beverly was one of the keenest Welsh learners we met, refusing to speak English when the Welsh equivalent would do.

UTICA

From 1795 for over 50 years, Oneida County, New York, had the greatest concentration of Welsh settlers in America. The Welsh settled mainly in Utica, Remsen and Steuben and established the first Welsh Church in New York State, the Welsh Baptist Church, Utica, in 1801. Eventually, thirty-six Welsh churches were established in Oneida County—a number exceeded only by Luzerne County, Pennsylvania. *Y Drych* was founded in Utica in 1851 and through the offices of *Y Drych* hundreds of Welsh language books and pamphlets were published. Until the 1930's Utica remained foremost in the publishing of Welsh books and periodicals.

While the cities and towns of upstate New York do not boast as many Welsh societies and events as neighboring Pennsylvania, there are still individuals and groups maintaining a Welsh presence. Colgate University in Hamilton has one of the finest collections of John Cowper Powys manuscripts in the world and the University has held a St. David's celebration since the 1930's. Roland Mathias spoke at the college in 1978 and there are a number of Welsh born lecturers on the staff.

The St. David's Society in Utica has a catchment area including Rome, Syracuse and Ithaca. Council Films in Syracuse is the distributor of a film, "God Has No Grandchildren" which is about the 1904-1905 revival in Wales and its after effects, especially the low level of church attendance in Wales today. Norman Williams, the personable and loquacious president of the WNGGA in 1983 and 1984, lives in Utica and is a popular master of ceremonies at Utica Welsh concerts and banquets. Emlyn Griffith of Rome, former president of the National Welsh American Foundation lives in Rome and is a reliable speaker at Welsh gatherings throughout the northeastern states. In 1984, Pamela Kneller from Syracuse left to spend a year studying at Coleg Harlech, Wales. Pamela was awarded grants by the WNGGA, the St. David's Society of Utica and the St. David's Society for the State of New York and while in Wales embarked on a series of projects promoting Welsh American research and college and schools exchanges.

Welsh heritage in the Utica area is preserved in country churches and in place names, such as the village of Camroden between Rome and Utica. Camroden is a corruption of Cymmrodorion and was founded by Welsh settlers in 1830. Rome also has a Cymrodorion Road which is the home of Edwin Evans. Mr. Evans has a large personal collection of British military insignia, including many Welsh regimental items.

Today Moriah Presbyterian is the only Welsh church still standing in Utica. Founded in 1830 Moriah still has an active Welsh congregation, although Welsh Americans also worship at Tabernacle, First Presbyterian and Plymouth-Bethesda.

The St. David's Society of Utica was founded in 1849 and is one of the most active Welsh socieities in the United States. The Society includes several nationally known Welsh American personalities, among them Evan Gwyndaf Roberts who has been organist at numerous national and regional cymanfaoedd canu. Robert A. Jones is a nationally known cymanfa director who has directed in Ohio, Illinois, California, Pennsylvania, Wisconsin and throughout New York state.

Evan Gwyndaf Roberts was born in Penrhyndeudraeth, Wales and emigrated to America at the age of eighteen. A member of the American Guild of Organists and musical director at Moriah Presbyterian Church, Evan has been acclaimed as one of the most sensitive and talented Welsh organists in America today. Miss Margaret Griffiths, long time organist at Moriah Presbytarian Church was the official accompanist for the Utica Eisteddfod while in her teens, a post she continued for almost forty years. She accompanied soloists and choirs in the area in addition to training scores of students and youth choirs.

Robert and Jeanne Jones have both been presidents of the Utica St. David's

Society. In May 1976, Mr. & Mrs. Jones formed the twenty-five voice Côr Dewi Sant. The choir has since performed every year at an increasing number of banquets, nosweithau llawen and cymanfaoedd canu throughout New York.

Mrs. Mair Lloyd is another unusually forceful and effective leader of Utica Welsh projects. Chairperson of numerous committees and a regular speaker at Society meetings, Mair has also organized Welsh language lessons at New Hartford Central School. A graduate in Welsh from the University of Wales, Aberystwyth, Mair Lloyd has been on the teaching staff of Cymdeithas Madog since 1979.

One of the most outstanding older Welsh personalities in Utica was John Mawddwy Jones, a native of Dinas Mawddwy, Merionethshire. A resident of Utica for many years, he had a remarkable memory and could vividly recall Patagonia colonists leaving for South America. His recollection of events in Wales and America led to repeated Welsh radio and TV. appearances. When he died in 1985 his passing was a great loss to the Utica Welsh community.

The Utica St. David's Society is successful because of the commitment of so many of its members. The Society's strength is in the imagination and intelligence of its leaders who conceive an idea and follow it through to its conclusion. Special tribute is paid in Utica to Irene Jones and Ellesworth (Al) Jones. Both have labored diligently for the cause of the Welsh in Mohawk Valley and both are active members of the Society, Irene as an executive board member and Ellsworth as Treasurer. These two have made an outstanding contribution for over four decades of Welsh activity. Leonard Wynne, Vaughn Evans, Eric Roberts, Owen Edwards, Lorena Reynolds, Priscilla Hepburn, David Maldwyn Ellis, William E. Richards and Jay and Hermine Williams all make important contributions to the growth and diversity of the Utica St. David's Society.

Support of Welsh music and culture is a priority with the Utica St. David's Society. In 1979, the Society donated $1,340 to the National Eisteddfod Million Pounds Appeal. The check was delivered in Wales by David Maldwyn Ellis and Jay Williams, both lecturers at Hamilton College in Clinton. In the 1970's, the Society, through *Yr Enfys*, arranged three children's exchanges between Utica and Wales. Two exchanges of three boys and three girls were arranged. A third exchange was in 1978 when three teenagers from Cardiff and three from Utica swapped families and homes for a month during the summer.

Utica St. David's Society members host Welsh relatives and friends on a regular basis. Mrs. Mair Lloyd's brother, a member of the National Eisteddfod Gorsedd and visiting professor at the University of California in Berkeley during 1978 and 1979, has spoken at Utica Welsh meetings. Other visitors in 1979 included Dafydd Iwan and Hefin Elis. In 1982, the Society hosted the thirty women of Côr Alawon Menai on the choir's successful tour of Ohio, Ontario and New York. Rhos Male Choir performed before a packed house in Utica in April 1985.

In 1983 Jay and Hermine Williams invited two Welsh music students to attend the Sobolevsky Summer School for Strings held at Hamilton College. The Williams' obtained grants from the Utica St. David's Society, the Summer School Scholarship Fund, the Education Trust Fund of Wales and donations from Society members. The two Welsh high school students chosen were Katy and Jonathan Clark of Swansea. Katy studied violin and Jonathan the cello. Jay and Hermine Williams are now examining ways of making this an annual invitation with the long-term goal of a tour by the National Youth Orchestra of Wales.

The Utica National in 1981 was attended by over 2,000 people and marked another stage in the development of Welsh American organizations. WAY enrolled more new members than ever in its eleven year history. The Welsh Marketplace was given official encouragement and each group like Cymdeithas Madog, Welsh Heritage Week and the Welsh American Foundation, was given space to publicize itself. It was at the Utica National that the Reverend John Owen suggested the important *Ninnau* column on Welsh hymns and it was here that he and Joan Owen agreed to join the staff of Welsh Heritage Week.

It was also at the National that a serious rift worsened between *Ninnau* and Cymdeithas Madog. The last advertisement for Cwrs Cymraeg appeared in *Ninnau* in October 1980, and the course has not been mentioned in the paper since. After having had so much to do with Cymdeithas Madog's early development, Arturo Roberts felt that *Ninnau* should have more control over the organization's future, a view understood but not completely shared by the Cymdeithas Madog board. Alun Hughes, President of the organization, offered concessions but Arturo refused to compromise and has effectively ignored the Society ever since.

Despite the fact that seventy people attended Cwrs Cymraeg in 1984, lack of access to *Ninnau*'s pages robs Cymdeithas Madog of considerable publicity. In the end, everyone loses out. Resources and funds are divided while people work for the same goals, promoting interests in Wales and sending contributions to the National Eisteddfod, Nant Gwrtheyrn and similar Welsh language institutions.

The main Welsh festival in Utica is Welsh American Days, which is held on the third weekend every September. Saturday night there is a well planned and highly polished noson lawen attracting performers from New York State and from places as far away as Ohio, Quebec, Ontario and Pennsylvania. A bilingual worship service and the two sessions of the cymanfa ganu are held on Sunday.

The Utica cymanfa is attended by about 300 people every year. Nansi Richards made her American directing debut here as did Glynne Jones of the Pendyrus Male Voice Choir. The Utica Cymanfa has also been directed by Lyn Harry, Alun John, Iwan Edwards of Montreal and their own Robert A. Jones. Evan Gwyndaf Roberts is always the organist and Côr Dewi Sant perform throughout the weekend. The 1985 Cymanfa was directed by Miss

Gwladys Wynne Jones of California. Gwladys is a native of Utica and was a regular yearly contestant in the Utica Eisteddfod.

The Utica St. David's Society holds a Welsh weekend near March 1st in honor of St. David. Celebrations start with a flag raising ceremony over city hall and a banquet is held on the Saturday evening, attended by upwards of one hundred people. The banquet usually features a guest speaker and entertainment by Côr Dewi Sant with soloists from the Utica musical community.

1986 officers of the Utica St. David's Society were, Janet Washburn, President; Harold O. Evans, Vice-President; Priscilla Pearl, Secretary; Ellsworth Jones, Treasurer; Edithe Evans, Historian; Jeanne Jones, Membership Secretary.

NELSON

Oneida and surrounding counties have an active circuit of cymanfaoedd canu, language classes and Welsh associations. Nelson Welsh Church on Route 20 southwest of Utica holds a cymanfa ganu every second Sunday in September. The Nelson cymanfa has been organized for years by Ellsworth Jones who was also treasurer for the 1981 Utica National. The Utica St. David's Society takes an active part in the Nelson cymanfa. Robert A. Jones conducts, Lorena Reynolds has been soloist and Côr Dewi Sant has also performed.

REMSEN

North of Utica, Remsen Welsh life has experienced a revival since the formation of the French Road Cemetery Association in 1965. The Welsh Church, Hebron, erected in the 1850's by the Welsh Methodist Society of Steuben, is known today as the French Road Church. In 1965, Edward Credle started single-handedly to restore the building. With some help from Leonard Wynne and Alex and Myron Senchyna from whom he bought the property, Edward Credle replaced all the old and rotting wood, rebuilt and repainted the walls, restored the original organ and piano and reclaimed and improved the Welsh cemetery. Today the French Road Church holds a cymanfa every July, supported by Mair Lloyd, Lorena Reynolds, Robert A. Jones and other members of the Utica St. David's Society.

In 1981, Margaret Jones of Remsen started teaching classes in conversational Welsh. Sponsored by the New York State Council for the Arts, the Welsh classes were very popular. Classes were held on Wednesdays and Fridays with a total of twenty-five students attending. Margaret Jones and her husband, Burton, are leaders of a Welsh heritage recovery in Remsen and as well as language lessons, organize St. David's celebrations and other Welsh events.

RICHVILLE

One hundred miles north of Utica in Richville, the Welsh Society which has been dormant since 1925, was re-established in September, 1974. Webster Griffiths restarted the Society and soon gathered the names of twelve interested people. Following a newspaper article, the new Welsh Society was joined by Welsh Americans from the surrounding towns of Rossie, Canton, Hammond, Potsdam and Morristown. The group re-activated the Welsh Congregational Society with the purpose of restoring and preserving the historic Welsh Meeting Hall in Richville which was built in 1859. Helen Reed, Doris Putnam and Laura Linehan organized singing lessons, Welsh language classes and established contact with *Ninnau* and *Y Drych*.

By 1976, the Society was holding its first cymanfa ganu. Members also held a small eisteddfod as part of Richville's bicentennial celebrations. A bronze commemorative plaque has been erected on the Welsh Meeting Hall and regular visitor, Dr. Islyn Thomas, whose daughter lives in Canton, has been the Society's speaker on many occasions.

In 1985, leaders of the Richville Welsh Society were Richard Moore, President; Ivan Coates, Vice-President; Helen Reed, Secretary and Doris Putnam, Treasurer. The Society enters Welsh floats at regional parades, takes part in the Canton Folk Life Festival and has introduced Welsh hymns into services at the United Methodist Church. The Society is small, but every year about twenty people meet at the home of Helen Reed to celebrate St. David's Day.

ALBANY AND SCHENECTADY

Welsh Americans in Schenectady combine with those in Albany to form the St. David's Society of the Capital District. Led by Evan Pritchard in Albany and Mair Jarvis in Schenectady, this Society maintains a varied calendar of Welsh events.

Every May, the St. David's Society of the Capital District participates in the Schenectady Festival of Nations. The Society's contribution consists of Welsh sales and display booths staffed by ladies in Welsh costume. The Schenectady Prince of Wales Pub provides the traditional Welsh fare of pasties, bara brith, Welsh cakes, sausage rolls and hot tea. A total of twenty-one national groups participate.

The President of Schenectady Union College is Dr. John Selwyn Morris, a native of the Rhondda who has lived in New York since 1954. Dr. Morris is a director of the National Welsh American Foundation and has spoken at several Albany Welsh banquets.

The St. David's Society of the Capital District was founded in 1942. Annie Pritchard, who died in 1984 at the age of 95, was one of the most remarkable Welsh Society leaders. At the age of 92 she appeared on stage with Ar Log at the Hunter Celtic Festival and at 94 she was still serving refreshments at the annual St. David's Society picnic.

The Albany and Schenectady St. David's banquet is held the first weekend in March. Speakers have included John Morris, Anne Habermehl, Emlyn Griffith and David Maldwyn Ellis. Albany has a singing group of its own, The Dewi Sant Quartet. The Quartet consists of Fred Lyons, Ralph Tooley, Margaret Blabey and Mary Milligan with Gary Hutchinson, pianist. Myfanwy Williams of Scotia, near Schenectady, sings Welsh folk and penillion material. The banquet usually concludes with community singing led by Margaret Blabey. In 1984, the Society invited Corkey Christman, a harpist, and combined harp with piano accompaniment for choral and community singing.

The St. David's Society of the Capital District holds an annual cymanfa, usually on a Sunday afternoon in October. About two hundred people attend the Albany cymanfa which attracts participants from neighboring Vermont, Connecticut and Massachusetts. The cymanfa is followed by a te bach organized by the ladies of the Society led by Gwen Koblenz, Claire Pritchard, Virginia Jehu and Elizabeth Williams. The Society also holds a bilingual Heritage Sunday every May and an annual June picnic.

In 1984, membership in the Capital District St. David's Society was more than three hundred, thanks mainly to the promotional work of Dr. John P. Jehu during his three year presidency from 1977 to 1980. Dr. Jehu is also an officer of the St. David's Society of the State of New York. Other important officers in Albany are Wayne Davis, David Reese, Dan Harris, Joyce Telisky, Henry C. Williams and Gwen and Sidney Koblenz. Ellen H. Qua and Mair Jarvis are the Society's correspondents.

BINGHAMTON

The Welsh American Society in Binghamton, New York, was started by Joan Phelps and Annette Thomas in June 1977. The two women met at a Scottish booth during the annual Two Rivers Ethnic Festival. From the Scottish booth, Joan and Annette contacted nine other Welsh people and they arranged to meet at the Scottish Society the following September. By November 1977, the group had reached twenty-three and was organizing meetings and a charter of its own.

In Binghamton, poet and publisher Gil Williams, had always maintained his own Welsh connection. Gil's friend, the poet Tony Curtis, a member of the Welsh Academy of Writers and a senior lecturer at the Polytechnic of Wales, was resident poet at the Roberson Center for the Arts in Binghamton in 1976 and 1979. In 1978, Tony Curtis taught in South Dakota on a Rotary Group traveling scholarship. In October 1984, he read at Western Illinois University as part of the Welsh Display of Poetry and Art organized by Fred Jones. Tony Curtis read at some of the early meetings of the Southern Tier Welsh Society. Another poet who visited Binghamton in 1978 was Roland Mathias.

The first elected officers of the Welsh Society of the Southern Tier were Annette Thomas, President; Dorothy Jenkins, Secretary; Sara Russell, Mem-

bership Secretary and Joan Phelps, Program Manager. From the very beginning, the Society was supported by Welsh leaders in Scranton, especially the
Reverend Bill Lewis, who drove from Pennsylvania for all the early meetings.

Singing in Welsh was given priority and a first choir practice was attempted
in 1978. Twenty-six attended. Jack Watkins led the meeting and Welsh language diction was taught by Megan Lindsay and Charlotte Williams who both
spoke Welsh as children in Utica. The Reverend Bill Lewis, Ceinwen Hughes
and Donald Davis drove up from Scranton and just over one hundred people
came to Binghamton's first cymanfa. Maisie Jones organized publicity,
Marcia Hamm played the harp and Margaret Brown and Josephine Andrews
were stewards. This cymanfa was greatly improved by Dennis Powell, baritone soloist, who had driven 150 miles from Watertown, New York.

By 1979, the Welsh Society of the Southern Tier had forty members.
Under the leadership of founding member Jack Watkins the Society found a
permanent meeting place at Eastside Congregational Church and no longer
had to move from place to place. In 1985 the Society's permanent meeting
place became Boulevard United Methodist Church which brought all the local Welsh groups together. The Society celebrated St. David's Day and held a
Welsh Christmas party complete with a Mari Lwyd procession.

At the 1979 National Cymanfa in Niagara Falls, one thousand copies of the
Western Mail were distributed to publicize the paper's "Trace Your Welsh
Roots" competition. Joan Phelps submitted an essay tracing her family tree
from New York via Saskatchewan back to Blaenau Ffestiniog. First prize was
a return flight to London and a week's paid vacation in Wales. Joan, her
husband and daughter spent several weeks in Wales visiting cousins who they
managed to discover by the score.

It wasn't until the Reverend William A. Jones of Boulevard United Methodist Church, Binghamton and Bruce McGregor, choir director at Central
United Methodist Church, Endicott decided to organize a March 1st cymanfa
in 1981, that the Southern Tier Welsh Society got the boost it needed to really
flourish. Over five hundred people attended the first Boulevard March 1st
cymanfa held in 1981. Six hundred and fifty-seven attended in 1982. The
Binghamton March cymanfa is now one of the biggest in New York State. Rehearsals for the cymanfa are held in the preceding weeks and practices at the
morning service have lasted over three hours. A lunch before the afternoon
session and te bach to follow is organized by Mr. and Mrs. Llewelyn Burge.
Mrs. Meredith Bocek (in Welsh costume) plays the harp, and soloists include
Dennis Peel, with Eloise Oliver, organist and Dilys Corino, reader in Welsh
and English.

In 1985 R. Bruce McGregor and Robert Williams organized the Triple
Cities Welsh Chorale based in Binghamton. The 40 voice choir gave a series of
concerts in Welsh throughout the upstate New York area. Dan Price and
Beverly Dunham, officers of the Southern Tier Welsh Society, were helpful in
the choir's early days. One of the first stated goals of the choir was to visit
Wales in 1988 and compete in Welsh at the Royal National Eisteddfod.

Alan Crabb, husband of the Mayor of Binghamton, Juanita Crabb, is from Maesteg, Wales. A professional opera singer, Alan Crabb took the Johnson City High School Choir to Llangollen in 1971 and in 1983 he was soloist at the Binghamton March 1st cymanfa. Juanita Crabb instituted a Welsh flag-raising ceremony over City Hall on March 1st, and throughout Broome County March 1st has been officially proclaimed St. David's Day.

NEW YORK CITY

The St. David's Society of the State of New York was established in 1841. The Society which has a permanent office at 71 West 23rd Street, succeeded the St. David's Benefit and Benevolent Society founded in 1835. In 1979, the Society gave $500 to assist Brock University's Cymdeithas Madog course. In 1981, the Society and Mrs. Gina Durand started a $1,000 matching grant to enable Mr. Edward Watkins, a Welsh speaking minister, to return to Trelew, Patagonia and re-establish a Welsh church there. In 1982, four students, two in literature, Megan Lloyd and Jeffrey Jenkins, and two in music, Lisbeth Lloyd and Laurel Lee James, received $5,000 between them. In 1983, St. David's Society of the State of New York scholarship disbursements exceeded $20,000 to eleven university students. The Society's scholarships are well monitored and fruitful. Music sholarship winners often sing at the following March 1st banquet and other recipients, notably Megan Lloyd of Ohio and Gwenfair Walters of Massachusetts, have gone on to study at the University of Wales. Other grants offered by the Society include vocal training scholarships, assistance to students going to Trinity College, Carmarthen, and specific assistance to choirs, lecturers and in publishing projects such as *Dafydd ap Gwilym: The Poems*, by Richard Loomis, and *Our Welsh Heritage*, by Islyn Thomas which had its fourth printing in 1978.

The St. David's Society of the State of New York includes among its officers and stewards some of the most capable people in Welsh American life. The Reverend Cyril Jenkins, David Allen, David Morgan, Robert Fowkes, Earl Griffiths, Wilfred Greenway, John J. Yorwerth, William G. Griffiths and the Reverend Kenneth O. Jones are the latest in a series of leaders improving the effectiveness of the Society.

In 1984, it cost $10 for a yearly membership and $75 for a life membership of the St. David's Society of the State of New York. President of the Society in 1984, Mr. William G. Griffiths, is a member of the National Eisteddfod Gorsedd. Mr. Griffiths was chairman of the 1979 Jubilee National Cymanfa Ganu and has been chairman of Cymdeithas Madog. Mr. Griffiths was the North American chairman and campaign manager of the National Eisteddfod's Million Pounds Appeal in North America.

The Reverend Kenneth O. Jones, former trustee of the WNGGA, member of the National Eisteddfod Gorsedd and former president of the St. David's Society of the State of New York, has also been chairman of the Hopkins Medal Award Committee. The Hopkins Medal was donated by Mr. William R.

Hopkins, prominent businessman and city manager of Cleveland. The medal was first awarded in 1951 and recipients have included George Bundy, Emlyn Williams, Ivor Richard and Richard Burton. In 1982, at a special Hopkins Medal presentation held at Margam Orangery in Wales, the medal was awarded to Viscount Tonypandy, George Thomas. In 1984, the Medal was awarded to Emrys Evans, National Eisteddfod President for many years and one who had done a great deal to promote the Eisteddfod in North America.

Cymanfaoedd canu are held annually in New York City. An assistant minister of the Fifth Avenue Presbyterian Church, the Reverend Kenneth O. Jones, has been responsible for the endurance of Welsh interest there. Encouraged by William G. Griffiths, Mr. Jones has organized cymanfaoedd canu, attracting over three hundred people. In 1977, David Allan and John Jerman organized a cymanfa at Lafayette Presbyterian Church in Brooklyn. Dr. David R. Allen attended the 1977 Cwrs Cymraeg in Vermont and returned feeling that the Welsh in New York could be doing more to promote their heritage. The 1977 Brooklyn cymanfa was directed by Frances Williams, the noted Welsh hymnologist. Frances Williams was born in Waunfawr, Wales, and wrote over 300 published choral works. She was the New York Society's Hopkins medalist in 1961. A graduate of Juilliard School of Music, Frances Williams was a regular conductor of New York cymanfaoedd canu in the 1960 and 1970's until her death on March 1, 1978.

By 1979, attendance at the Brooklyn cymanfa had doubled and a hot lunch was served as well as a te bach following the afternoon session. Robert A. Jones was the director, Côr Dewi Sant of Utica sang, the Reverend John Owen of Lisbon, Ohio was the minister and the Reverend Cyril Jenkins of Rutgers Presbyterian led the bilingual service. The Brooklyn cymanfa ganu lost momentum and stopped when David Allen and his wife, Janet, (from Tredegar) left the city and moved to New Jersey.

The Welsh Congregational Church in New York City became inactive in 1955 and the congregation merged with Rutgers Church and other churches in the city. The Reverend Cyril Jenkins, minister of Rutgers since 1965 and moderator of the New York City Presbytery, is from Brynaman, Wales. The Reverend Jenkins served as president of the St. David's Society of the State of New York in 1980 and he and the Reverend Kenneth O. Jones have been essential to the religious and social life of Welsh people in the city.

In 1978 Dr. Robert A. Fowkes taught a Welsh course at Manhattan Community College. Dr. Fowkes was speaker at the 1983 Wilkes-Barre National and his theme "Staying Alive" was utterly contemporary. A professor in linguistics and the Germanic languages at New York University, from 1955 to 1958 he was president of the St. David's Society of the State of New York, and in the 1960's he received a Guggenheim Fellowship to pursue Welsh studies. An important figure in Welsh American life, Robert Fowkes writes *Ninnau*'s column, "Welsh for Americans" as well as monthly feature articles for *Y Drych*.

Dr. Robert A. Fowkes' Welsh course at Manhattan Community College was organized by David Allen, a lecturer at the college. Forty-five students attended, five of whom were from Wales. In 1984 classes were still continuing and were well attended but were held at Rutgers Presbyterian Church.

For David Allen, however, weekly classes, occasional meetings and annual cymanfaoedd canu were not enough. He contacted cousins Clifford and Olwen Roderick, trustees of the funds of the dormant Welsh Congregational Church and asked the Reverend Cyril Jenkins to lead bilingual Congregational services at Rutgers Presbyterian Church. Since its founding in the 1790's, the Welsh Congregational Church in New York had moved from home to home. In the early 20th century, numbers fell sharply and for a while the group met at Harlem YWCA before moving to a rededicated library. From 1949 to 1955, the Congregationalists worshipped as part of Fort Washington Presbyterian Church and then under the wing of the Welsh Presbyterian Church on West 155th Street. They never amalgamated, however, and when the West 155th Street building was sold, the Congregationalist funds were put in trust.

In 1975 the courts ordered the funds of the Welsh Congregationalist Church to be turned over to the state unless the church was re-established. This led to some frantic activity by Clifford and Olwen Roderick who contacted William Griffith and William Rhys Howell of the St. David's Society. The church was reconstituted, with forty members, a minister (the Reverend Cyril Jenkins of Rutgers) and a board of trustees comprising David Allen, President; William. G. Griffiths, Vice-President; William Rhys Howells, Secretary; Olwen Roderick, Treasurer and Clifford Roderick, Financial Secretary. The first service of the church, attended by fifty people, was held in January, 1979. Services have been held ever since on the second Sunday every month except July and August at Rutgers Presbyterian Church. Services are held at 3 p.m. They are in Welsh and English and last an hour, with an even longer te bach to follow. The congregation quickly organized language classes and singing practices led by Maldwyn Pate, David Morgan and Robert Fowkes. Marshall Williamson has been organist for the reorganized Welsh church since its inception.

The first cymanfa of the Congregational Church was held in April 1983. Olwen Welk was the director and over $1,000 was raised for the Nant Gwrtheyrn Language Center in Wales. In 1984, the New York Welsh Congregational Church cymanfa was directed by Lyn Harry and the funds raised were donated to Mudiad Ysgolion Meithrin (The Welsh Language Nursery School Movement).

The Women's Welsh Club in New York plays an important role in New York City Welsh life. As well as maintaining monthly programs of their own, members of the club serve on other Welsh committees and the ladies always provide refreshments at New York cymanfaoedd canu, the monthly Welsh language service and other meetings and receptions. Former Women's Welsh Club presidents, Dorothy Edwards and Phyllis Keutgen, have been officers of the National Federation of Women's Welsh Clubs and Wendy Miles, president of the New York Women's Welsh Club in 1984, is one of the most reliable correspondents Welsh people in the city have. The Women's Welsh Club of New York meets once a month, except July and August, and usually invites someone involved in other New York Welsh groups to be their speaker. In 1985, leaders of the New York Women's Welsh Club were Anne Phillips, President; Marie Bove, Vice-President; Mary Anne Meconi, Secretary; Annelise Kamada, Correspondence Secretary; Audrey Roberts, Financial Secretary and Olwen Roberts, Treasurer.

New York City's Welsh associations combine for the annual St. David's Banquet organized by the St. David's Society of the State of New York. The banquet is a formal, black tie event. Entertainment is provided by music scholarship winners and the guest speaker is usually the Hopkins Medal Winner of the year.

In 1981 Bill Greenway organized a luncheon to commemorate the wedding of the Prince and Princess of Wales. The St. David's Society became responsible for a guest list of representatives from all the Commonwealth organizations in New York. The British Consulate attended and William Griffiths was general chairman. Over three hundred people saw the wedding on four giant television screens in the Plaza Grand Ballroom.

Arrangements for the royal wedding preceded the formation of the British and Commonwealth Institute of New York. Arturo Roberts and Wilfred Greenway were involved in the British Commonwealth Institute from the very beginning and are the Welsh officers on an eleven person board. The British Commonwealth Institute of New York regularly mails a calendar of British and Commonwealth events held in the Connecticut, New York and New Jersey area. Welsh announcements range from New Jersey Welsh language classes to Welsh Heritage Week and the quarterly business meetings of the St. David's Society of the State of New York.

Welsh visitors to New York City usually speak at Fifth Avenue Presbyterian Church and have included Dafydd Iwan, Terry Thomas of the Open University speaking on Dylan Thomas and Mr. Oswald Jones, a Welshman from Patagonia who now lives in Syosset, Long Island. Oswald Jones is a professional artist who has four permanent panels on display at First Presbyterian Church, Oyster Bay, Long Island.

Other Welsh visitors to New York City have been Emlyn Williams, Osian Ellis, Caryl Thomas, the harpist, and oboist John Anderson of the BBC Symphony Orchestra. Where possible, New York Welsh Americans will organize a reception for Welsh visitors who let them know they will be coming. New York, of course, is where Dylan Thomas died in 1953. In 1982, actor, Jack Raney, appeared in a one-man show, "Instant Dylan," which ran at the 13th Street Theatre. This is one of many Dylan Thomas tributes that have played in the city. Ray Handy toured America in 1979 with a production of his own called "Dylan Thomas Lived Here."

New York City has a range of talent interested in Welsh studies. Catherine McKenna, an authority on medieval Welsh literature played a role in the first services of the re-established New York City Welsh Congregational Church. Joseph Clancy, author of two volumes of translations from early Welsh literature, is a lecturer at Marymount Manhattan College. Veronica Gillian Pugh led the "Council of Two Hundred," an attempt to organize two hundred independent, active individuals into a Welsh American network, until the whole idea was politicized and collapsed around her. Maldwyn Pate was a modern dancer in Greenwich Village and a Welsh teacher in the city until returning to Wales in 1984 to become Dance Officer for the Welsh Arts Council. Michael Miranda a non-Welsh student at David Morgan's class wrote his MA thesis on Welsh Nationalism from 1800 to the present day. As in many other aspects of contemporary life, New York City is an important center of Welsh American ideas, personalities and events.

20

The Welsh Festivals of Ontario and Quebec

The WNGGA hymnal contains the national anthems of Wales, Canada and the United States. To the chagrin of Welsh Canadians, associations intended to serve Canada and the United States are often called Welsh American organizations. WAY originally stood for Welsh American Youth, while the first name suggested for the Welsh Harp Society of North America was The Welsh American Harp Society. Canadians object to being called Americans with as much justification as Welsh people refuse to be called English. Confusion is avoided but not solved by absorbing everyone into the almost neutral, "North Americans." Within this blanket term however the work of Welsh Canadians might be overlooked. Welsh societies in Canada sponsor some of the finest Welsh events outside Wales.

THE ONTARIO GYMANFA GANU ASSOCIATION

The Ontario Cymanfa Ganu Association (OGGA) was formed in 1957, its first venture being to sponsor the 28th National Cymanfa Ganu in Toronto in 1959. The first Ontario Welsh Festival (as it is now known) was held in Niagara Falls in 1961, followed by a second in London, Ontario in October of the same year. For seventeen years the Festival took place annually in Niagara Falls, but in 1978 it moved to Toronto. Since then it has been hosted by a different Ontario city each year, usually in the third or fourth week of April.

Since 1978, the OGGA Welsh Festival has been hosted by Kingston (1979), London (1980), Ottawa (1981), Hamilton (1982), Niagara Falls (1983), Peterborough (1984) and Toronto (1985). The Ontario Welsh Festival has evolved into a well attended three-day cultural event. It attracts up to 800 people every year and is probably the best showcase of Welsh cultural heritage in Canada or the United States.

The Ontario Cymanfa Ganu Association is governed by a board of five officers and six trustees. Its first president was Douglas Jones of Toronto and his successors have been Lewis Edwards of Niagara Falls, Ivor Davies of Oshawa, Lyndon Jones of London, Bill Blanch of Beamsville, the Reverend J. Humphreys Jones of Toronto, Don Mills of Ottawa and the Reverend Cerwyn Davies of Toronto. The 1986 leadership consisted of Bill Phillips, President; the Reverend Heddwyn Williams, Vice-President; Alun Hughes,

Secretary; Betty Stroud, Treasurer. Other board members in 1986 were Myfanwy Bajaj, the Reverend Cerwyn Davies, Jean Howard, Sheila Pepper, David Pugh, Christine Scott and John Watcyn Williams.

The Ontario Welsh Festival opens with a noson lawen on Friday night followed by a te bach and informal singing. Saturday morning is the OGGA annual general meeting. The Awr y Plant at which the OGGA excels is held on Saturday afternoon and the day usually concludes with a banquet, concert and dance. The two sessions of the cymanfa ganu—the climax of the festival—are held on Sunday.

The Ontario Welsh Festival is distinguished by the high quality of its programs. There is an excellent baby-sitting service and the attendance of families is encouraged. Young people are especially catered to. A young people's hymn is selected for the cymanfa, there is a special tea and dance and the Awr y Plant features everything from penillion to electric rock (in Welsh!). In 1978 there was a folk dance and the movie Dyma'r Urdd (This is the Urdd) was shown.

Performers at the Festival have ranged from choirs like Côr Dewi Sant, Utica; the Dewi Singers, Toronto; the Hamilton Orpheus Male Choir and the Ottawa Welsh Choral Society. Soloists have been, Myfanwy Jenkins (Brockville), Jeanette Hudson (Ottawa), Cheryl Clay (Toronto) and Dafydd Hughes (St. Catharines). Cymanfa conductors have included Lyn Harry (Hamilton), Robert Jones (Utica), Iwan Edwards (Montreal) and Roy Morris (Ottawa). Regular invited organists have been David Low (Toronto) and Evan Gwyndaf Roberts (Utica). Participants have also come from Wales—The Hywel Girls Choir in 1980, the folk group Dim Byd Eto in 1981 and the eleven voice Doniau'r Dderwen in 1984. Noel John of Llandeilo was cymanfa conductor in 1979, and a year later it was John Hywel Williams of Llanelli. Most recently in 1985, the conductor was T. Arwyn Walters, director of the Dunvant Male Choir, which performed in a sell-out concert on the Saturday night.

Moving the OGGA Festival from city to city has increased its scope enormously, and local Welsh societies have benefited greatly. Today, the OGGA annual Welsh Festival attracts visitors from as far away as Minnesota who join regular festivalgoers from the Canadian provinces and the eastern United States.

Mr. Lewis Edwards originally from Clynderwen, Wales, emigrated to Canada in 1955. As well as being a past president of the WNGGA and the OGGA, he once led the St. Catharines and Niagara District Welsh Society. In 1977, Lewis Edwards received the Hopkins Medal for his "service as an advocate of North American Welsh Culture."

In 1978, Lewis Edwards formed the John Matthews Foundation. John Matthews, born in Llansamlet, Wales in 1764, emigrated to Canada in 1812. In 1821, he founded Brycheiniog, the first Welsh Colony in Upper Canada near London, Ontario. John Matthews returned to Wales in 1824 recruiting more colonists for the Canadian Welsh pioneer experiment. At one point the

Welsh colony consisted of over 300 people, half of whom were born in Wales. The colony eventually dispersed, however, with settlers moving to the American states of Ohio, Wisconsin, Minnesota and Illinois. In 1978, at a ceremony attended by Nicholas Edwards, the Secretary of State for Wales, Lewis Edwards unveiled a commemorative plaque at John Matthews' renovated gravesite in St. John's Anglican Cemetery, Niagara Falls.

☆

We crossed into Canada in the middle of a sweltering heat wave on July 10, 1983. We imagined that once back on Canadian territory the temperature would somehow fall ten degrees. The temperature remained in the upper 90's, turning our van into a broiler with three wilted but persevering itinerants inside.

From a telephone booth on the Welland Canal, we called Dic and Pat Thomas in Port Colborne. Dic was the childhood friend of the Reverend R. J. Charles, the minister who had given a blessing to our marriage when we returned to Wales from Japan. We had written to the Thomases many times and this was a call we had looked forward to making.

Dic and Pat's daughter, Jane, has been a past president of WAY, editor of the *WAY* newsletter and secretary of the OGGA. Jane founded the periodical *Y Werin*, which appeared briefly during the 1970's and she has been on the board of Cymdeithas Madog almost since its inception. Jane grew up in Canada but has learned Welsh and in 1982 moved to Wales where she works for the West Wales Arts Council in Carmarthen.

Dic and Pat's visitors for the afternoon were Arthur Evans, Iris Richards and Dilys Walters. Iris and Dilys had both been active in the St. Catharines and Niagara District Welsh Society and from them we heard the Society's story from its inception in 1956 to its demise in 1976. The Society used to meet at the St. Catharines YMCA, and its last leaders were Gladys Roberts, Dilys Walters and Stan and Bess Duke. Attempts to revive the Society have not been successful and despite the large number of people in the Niagara Falls area no Welsh Canadian Society exists. The next morning we drove to St. Catharines where we visited Siani Flewog, one of the busiest Welsh import stores in North America. Jane Hughes, the owner, and Alun Hughes, her husband, are deeply involved in Welsh activities.

Alun Hughes is from Bridgend, Wales. A graduate of St. John's College, Cambridge, Alun emigrated to Canada 1969 to join the geography department at Brock University. Jane Hughes who was born in Canada and has learned Welsh, started Siani Flewog in 1978. Since then the shop has grown into an excellent source of the latest Welsh products selling mainly by mail order. Alun has been secretary of the OGGA, has taught at Welsh Heritage Week and since 1978 at most of the language courses sponsored by Cymdeithas Madog (the Welsh Studies Institute in North America). He has been

President of Cymdeithas Madog since 1982 and has taught Welsh classes at his home. He and Jane have appeared on the Canadian Broadcasting Corporation's "Identities" program, playing Welsh music taken from Siani Flewog's extensive stock. Alun and Jane's children, Dafydd and Elinor, are among many who take part in Ontario Welsh Festival children's events, Elinor playing harp and Dafydd playing electric guitar. Dafydd was boy soprano soloist in the cymanfa ganu at the 1985 Festival in Toronto.

CYMDEITHAS MADOG

While talking to Alun, we were given our best introduction to the work of Cymdeithas Madog. The first Cwrs Cymraeg or Welsh language crash course in North America was held in Vermont in 1977. It took place at Green Mountain College in Poultney and was the culmination of a whole year of Welsh events in the Vermont, "slate belt" area. Margot McKinney Bouchard of Poultney looked after local arrangements while Anne Cowie was responsible for the course program and recruiting the teaching staff.

The Poultney Welsh Year received state and federal assistance which reduced the cost of the course to less than $150 a head. John Albert Evans, Welsh language advisor to Mid-Glamorgan County Council, flew over to direct the course. Welsh language movies were screened and Welsh books, records and study materials were on sale. Other teachers were Maldwyn Pate, then living in New York City, and Ann James, former Welsh teacher at Ysgol Gymraeg Bryntaf, Cardiff, then living in Virginia. Thanks to publicity generated in the pages of *Ninnau*, the first Welsh crash course was attended by about 40 students and was a phenomenal success. Treflyn Evans attended from Seattle, Owen C. Roberts attended from Montreal, Esther Elias from Pittsburgh, as well as many more from Ontario, New York, Virginia, Maryland and Pennsylvania. By December 1977, Anne Cowie and others had organized Cymdeithas Madog and were planning for 1978.

The first Cwrs Cymraeg with its intensive teaching methods became a model for those that followed. Classes are provided for all levels of proficiency, from complete beginners to the almost fluent. Over thirty hours of classroom instruction are supplemented by private study periods and a variety of social and cultural activities involving use of the language. These include a "helfor drysor" (treasure hunt), a "twmpath dawns" (folk dance), a picnic, Welsh language films, seminars about Wales, a pub night and plenty of singing in Welsh. The teaching staff is visible at all times coaching students in the Welsh they've learned so far. One of the high spots of the week is the noson lawen. The first noson lawen in 1977 featured some impressive talent—Jane Thomas, Maldwyn Pate, Phyllis Kinney and Alex Hamilton. Subsequent courses have featured a mock eisteddfod complete with a gorsedd and a chairing of the bard. First prize at one Cwrs Cymraeg raffle was a week at the Nant Gwrtheyrn Residential Language Center in Wales.

Cymdeithas Madog has now reached several hundred people with one of the most effective language programs ever held outside Wales. Since 1977, Cwrs Cymraeg has been held at:

1977 Poultney, Vermont
1978 Lewisburg, Pennsylvania
1979 St. Catharines, Ontario
1979 San Rafael, California
1980 Haverford, Pennsylvania
1980 San Rafael, California
1981 Lewisburg, Pennsylvania
1981 Pinecrest Lake, California
1982 Toronto, Ontario
1983 St. Paul, Minnesota
1984 Wilkes-Barre, Pennsylvania (Cwrs Cymraeg y Cymoedd)
1985 Pella, Iowa (Cwrs Cymraeg y Canolbarth)
1986 Toronto, Ontario (Cwrs Cymraeg y Bedol Aur)

Apart from John Albert Evans, the staff from Wales has included Basil Davies, senior lecturer in Welsh at the Polytechnic of Wales, co-author of the Linguaphone and Catchphrase Welsh courses and author of *Y Drych*'s Golofn Gymraeg; Cennard Davies, reader in Welsh at the Polytechnic of Wales and the other author of the Linguaphone and Catchphrase courses; J. Philip Davies, senior lecturer in Welsh at the North East Wales Institute of Higher Education; Nesta Llwyd, teacher at the Gwynedd Language Center; Randall Isaac, principal of Brynaman Welsh School; Margaret Parry, senior mistress at Cardiff High School; Glyn Owen, former principal of Ysgol Yr Hendre, Gwynedd and Wil Morus Jones, director of the Eisteddfod winning choir Côr Godre'r Garth.

The visiting staff from Wales has been supplemented by teachers living permanently or temporarily in North America, among them Dulais Rhys, Mair Lloyd, Jean Howard, Jeanette Hudson, Bedwyr ap Dafydd, Hefina Philips, John and Joan Owen, Alun and Jane Hughes and Nia Llwyd.

Cwrs Cymraeg quickly gets learners speaking in Welsh. Students progress from an elementary to a well monitored advanced level. In 1984, the newly-introduced Welsh Joint Education Committee's ordinary level exam for adults was taken by six advanced learners. At a cost of $25, the exam required writing, oral and aural proficiency and good reading comprehension—five of the six passed with flying colors.

Cymdeithas Madog has more than fulfilled its promise and each year Welsh societies compete to host the course. Students at Cwrs Cymraeg have started courses of their own. For example Welsh study groups in St. Paul, Toronto, Wilkes-Barre and New York were all prompted by participation in Cwrs Cymraeg.

Cymdeithas Madog was incorporated in 1980 as a non-profit educational organization. It has received grants from the National Welsh American Foundation, the St. David's Society of the State of New York, Eglwys y Cymry—the Welsh Congregationalist Church of New York and the Multi-culturalism Directorate of the Canadian Government. Teachers attending Cwrs Cymraeg from Wales have received British Council travel grants since 1980. Cymdeithas Madog itself provides matching grants, up to $100.00 per student, to any Welsh Society that sends a member to the course. Staff and students at Cwrs Cymraeg are among the most generous supporters of Canolfan yr Iaith Nant Gwrtheyrn and several thousand dollars have been collected over the years.

In 1985, the Cymdeithas Madog board consisted of Alun Hughes (Ontario), President; Donna Lloyd-Kolkin (San Francisco), Vice-President; Eugene Owen (College Park, Maryland), Treasurer and William Clark (Rochester, New York), Secretary. Cymdeithas Madog also has a board of directors among whom have been Bob Fowkes (New York), Karen Saylor (Pennsylvania), Jane Thomas (Carmarthen, Wales) and Mary Mergenthal (Minnesota). The Cymdeithas Madog newsletter, *Cyfeillion Madog* is edited by Hank Williams in Fredericton, New Brunswick.

In 1984, it cost $285 for adults to attend Cwrs Cymraeg Y Cymoedd in Wilkes-Barre. The course was attended by seventy people and received critical acclaim from students deeply impressed by Cymdeithas Madog's commitment to high quality Welsh language teaching.

☆

Rugby competes with the language in Alun Hughes's enthusiasm for all things Welsh. He is also a bibliophile and Suzanne and I decided to share our cache of Wisconsin Welsh books with him and Dic Thomas of Port Colborne. In addition, Alun is a compulsive writer of tribannau (triplets) and has written a series of hilarious verses on the foibles of North American Welsh personalities.

I asked Alun about Welsh rugby teams visiting Canada. If we wanted to know more he suggested we drive to Brantford where George Jones, formerly of Llandeilo, had earned himself the nickname "Mr. Rugby" among Ontario's Welsh Canadians.

The Niagara peninsula separating Lake Ontario from Lake Erie is easy to travel. A grid of roads through the lush, flat farmland connects every small village and town. Although it was very hot, we were told that good weather was not unusual and that this part of Canada was called "the banana belt." In winter however, when the north wind screams across the Great Lakes, the "banana belt" is barely less cold and snowy than other parts of southern Ontario. We telephoned George Jones from Brantford City Park and within five minutes he arrived at the van wearing a pair of shorts and sandals. Bronzed and athletic, George maintained the trim physique of an accomplished and life-long athlete.

RUGBY

George and his wife Glenys left Llandeilo, Wales in 1949. George's involvement in Canadian rugby started when he and his brother, Vince Jones, founded the Brantford Harlequins. In 1950, George Jones and representatives of five other rugby clubs formed the Ontario Rugby Union. Today George is president of the Brantford Harlequins, and in 1975, was team manager of the Canadian National Squad. George has taken the Harlequins on several tours of Wales and has hosted numerous teams from Wales to the Brantford area. In 1971, he organized the building of the Brantford Harlequins Clubhouse taking out a second mortgage on his home so that the club could secure a loan. Following a tour of the clubhouse and playing fields, George showed us the files of tours he'd arranged for rugby and choral visitors from Wales.

George Jones kept some of the best and most thorough records anyone would ever need. From the first letter of inquiry to the last letter of thanks, tours were documented in their entirety. George mentioned hearing from one rugby team barely a week before it was due to arrive in Ontario. He told the team not to come to Brantford, since at that late date the tour was bound to be a disaster.

All teams leaving Wales for Canada and the United States are required to assure the Welsh Rugby Union that specific details and arrangements are confirmed. The number of visiting rugby teams from Wales to North America increases annually as contacts between clubs improve. Rugby teams, however, in Wales, Canada and the United States have yet to use *Ninnau* and *Y Drych* to publicize their games. Apart from occasional articles by George Jones, Alun Hughes and John Price, sports coverage is limited. The following list is incomplete, but gives an indication of the number of Welsh teams to visit North America since 1979.

Date	Team	Area of tour
1979	Pontypool	California
	Tredegar	East Coast
	Bridgend	Western Canada
	Newport	Ontario
	Bargoed	Canada
	Bridgend	Western Canada
	Bridgend Sports Club	Western Canada
1980	Wales B Team	West Coast
	Kenfig Hill	Massachusetts
	Newbridge	Florida
	Ebbw Vale	California
	Pontypridd	Ontario
	Gowerton Schools	Ontario
	Cwmtawe Schools	Ontario
	University College of Cardiff	Ontario
	Llandeilo	Ontario

Date	Team	Area of tour
1981	Maesteg	Ontario
	Neath	Ontario
	Caerphilly	Ontario
	Pontypool	Ontario
1982	Ebbw Vale	Ontario
	Chepstow	Ontario
	Cefn Cribwr	Ontario
	Nelson	Ontario
	Pontypridd	Ontario
	Newbridge	California and British Columbia
	Glamorgan Wanderers	Massachusetts
	Kenfig Hill	California
	Newport	Georgia
1983	Furnace RFC	Ontario
	Neath	Ontario
	London Welsh	Midwest U.S.A.
	Welsh Schoolboys	Canada
	Llanelli	Ontario
	Bridgend Sports Club	Ontario
	Gowerton Schools	Ontario
	Bishopston School	Ontario
1984	Beddau	Florida
	Bridgend	Ontario
	Monmouth Schools	Massachusetts
	Cefn Cribwr	Ontario
	Cwmtawe School	Ontario
	Barry	Florida
	Amman Valley Schools	Ontario
1985	London Welsh	Ontario
	Porthcawl	Ontario
	Pontypool	Ontario
	Olchfa	Ontario
	Gwent Schools	Ontario

The Canadian Rugby Union is the parent organization of Rugby Unions in each Canadian province. Within each province regional unions coordinate tours and visits from abroad. A Canadian national team has visited Wales and has hosted several international games.

The first American National Rugby Championship was held in 1979. The United States of America Rugby Football Union (USARFU) has found organizing a national team more difficult than their Canadian counterparts. Rugby is nevertheless an old established sport in the U.S.A. with America's having won two Olympic gold medals (in 1920 and 1924).

The four regional American rugby unions are the Eastern, Midwestern, Western and Pacific. Visitors from Wales need the approval of each regional committee to tour their district. The traffic, while mainly from Wales to America, is not all one sided. In 1984 teams from Georgia, South Carolina and New Jersey were hosted by Welsh clubs. An Eastern Rugby Union select side also toured Wales in 1984 and lost only one out of its five games, going down to Pontypridd.

In 1979 two women's rugby teams from the United States toured South Wales. The Americans faced few opposing sides and played mainly exhibition matches against each other. Women's rugby is an American phenomenon where there are over 150 teams found mainly in American colleges. The women hold their own championships and have a separate committee within the USARFU. Since the American Women's visit in 1979, some women's games have been held in Wales, but nothing has been organised on a regular basis.

Turning from his involvement with touring rugby teams, George told us about some of the choral visits he'd arranged. He put us in contact with Graham Morgan, a friend of his in Brantford. Graham Morgan has done a great deal to improve the quality of tours by the many Welsh choirs visiting Ontario.

CHORAL ASSOCIATIONS

Graham Morgan emigrated from Wales to Canada in 1971. He settled in Brantford and joined the Brant Men of Song. As secretary of the Brant Men of Song, in 1976, Graham arranged a concert tour to Wales with an appearance at his hometown, Ebbw Vale. While in Ebbw Vale in 1976, Graham met Glyn Jones, Secretary of the Welsh Association of Male Choirs and agreed to act as a liaison officer between the Welsh Association and the Associated Male Choruses of Ontario. This relationship led to a series of well managed visits by Welsh choirs to the Brantford Area.

The majority of choral tours start as an idea between friends. Other tours follow from the desire of a Welsh society to host a choir, such as Pendyrus Male Voice hosted by Delta, Pennsylvania in the fall of 1984. Some tours follow from a Welsh choir's own ambition to visit North America.

The Cardiff Polyphonic Choir is one of the few Welsh choirs that arranges its North American itineraries independently of the Welsh societies. In May 1984, the Cardiff Polyphonic made its sixth tour of North America through the Columbia Artists Community Concerts agency. The choir appeared before general audiences and stayed in motels. Welsh societies were informed through advertisements in *Ninnau* and *Y Drych*. This professional approach works beautifully for such an accomplished, relatively small and well managed choir. There are also choirs that prefer the personal contact of being hosted by another choir or by a Welsh society. If they are well organized, with the maximum advanced preparation, direct contact tours of this type generate the greatest amount of good will. However, the number of choirs that expect to tour on such a low-key basis and show a profit is unrealistic.

Viv Fisher, the President of the Welsh Association of Male Choirs, visited Ontario with Aberavon Male Voice in 1979, Port Talbot Male Voice in 1980, and with the Vale of Towy Male Voice in 1981. In 1980, Viv Fisher and Graham Morgan participated in an "international conference" between the Welsh, Canadian and American Male Choral Associations. Also present were Mel Plant of the Associated Male Choruses of America and Mervyn Downs, Secretary of the Welsh Association of Male Choirs. Minutes were taken and some successful follow-up tours arranged. However, there are still no printed guidelines available to Welsh choirs visiting North America for the first time. Each touring choir must relearn all that was achieved by preceding tour groups. This time-consuming work includes arranging venues, meals, dates, transportation and accommodations as well as learning Canadian and American etiquette and the expectations of their hosts.

Choral visits, however, remain the most popular and direct cultural link between Wales and North America. The number of mixed choirs traveling overseas is a recent development. Also, increased visits by instrumental groups and female choirs have improved the calendars of Welsh societies.

The following list gives an indication of the number of Welsh choirs and musicians who have visited North America since 1978.

Date		Choir	Area Visited
1978	July	Côr Telyn Teilo	Ontario
	July	Aber Singers, Aberdare	Ontario
	September	Pontarddulais	Ontario
	September	Port Talbot Male Voice	Ontario
	November	Trelawnyd Male Voice	Ontario
1979	March/April	Cowbridge Male Voice	Saskatchewan
	April	Richard Williams Singers	California
	May	Parti'r Ffynnon Ladies Choir	Washington DC
	September	Llanover Youth Theater	Ontario, New Jersey and Pennsylvania
	October	Aberavon Male Voice	Ontario
	November	Dafydd Iwan and Hefin Elis	Ontario, New York and Washington DC
1980	April	Côr y Brythoniaid	California
	April	Llanelli Hywel Girls Choir	Ontario
	August	Traeth Male Voice	Ontario
	August	Llanelli Male Voice	British Columbia
	October	Treorchy Male Voice	Ontario
	September	Port Talbot Male Voice	Ontario
	October	Parti Ceredigion	Ohio, Midwestern states

Date	Choir	Area Visited
1981 May	Dim Byd Eto Folk Group	Ontario, eastern U.S.A.
August	Canoldir Male Voice	British Columbia
August	Ar Log Folk Group	Eastern U.S.A.
August	Penderyn Folk Group	Eastern U.S.A.
August	Tawerin Folk Dancers	Ontario, eastern U.S.A.
September	Towy Male Voice	Ontario, New York
1982 April	Caernarfon Male Voice	Eastern U.S.A.
May	Dowlais Male Voice	Ohio, Pennsylvania
August	Traeth Male Voice	Ontario
August	Ar Log	Eastern U.S.A.
September	Aberystwyth Male Voice	Ontario
October	Burma Star Male Voice	Ontario, Quebec and New York
October	Parti Ceredigion	Midwest and western U.S.A.
October	Côr Alawon Menai	Eastern U.S.A.
October	Caernarfon Women's Choir	Eastern U.S.A.
1983 April	Llanddulais Male Voice	New York, Pennsylvania and Ohio
June	Penrhyn Male Voice	Ontario
August	Rhosllanerchrugog Male Voice	Minnesota
August	Cwmbran Operatic Society	Illinois, Minnesota
August	Froncysyllte Male Voice	Western Canada
September	Cwmbran Male Voice	California
October	Llwynengrin Mixed Choir	Wisconsin, Minnesota
October	Ceffyl Pren Rock Group	U.S.A. and Canada
November	Côr Meibion De Cymru	Eastern U.S.A.
December	BBC Welsh Symphony Orchestra	Ontario, Quebec
1984 March	Max Boyce	Ontario
May	Cardiff Welsh Choir	Southern U.S.A.
May	Doniau'r Dderwen	Ontario
June	Froncysyllte Male Voice	Ontario
July	Pendyrus Male Voice	Eastern U.S.A.
August	Amman Valley Folk Dancers	Ontario
August	Hogia'r Wyddfa	Western U.S.A.

☆

Welsh societies exist in Toronto, Ottawa, Belleville, Windsor, London, Hamilton, Kingston, Oshawa and Peterborough. These societies are not far apart and the OGGA is able to move its annual festival and still attract large numbers of people. Members of the Welsh Canadian community who live outside these main areas of activity also do not have far to drive by North American standards in order to participate in Welsh programs. As well as contributing to the success of the OGGA, Ontario Welsh societies were also involved in a $450,000 drive to establish a Celtic Chair at Ottawa University.

LONDON

The Welsh Society of London was founded by the Reverend Maxwell Roberts in 1958. Its fortunes declined until the Society was almost defunct by 1975. In the late 1970's, Mr. Ken Jones from Anglesey, a graduate of the University of Wales, Aberystwyth moved to London with his family. Ken Jones reorganized the London Welsh Society and rebuilt its membership. In March 1980, the Society's St. David's banquet attracted over 200 people. In May 1980, London hosted the OGGA Welsh festival which attracted over 500 people. Ken Jones started the London Welsh Choir which grew from eleven mixed voices in 1980 to forty-five voices in 1985.

In 1983, the Reverend Tudor Jones, also from Anglesey moved to London. Building on the enthusiasm of the strong Welsh group, the Reverend Tudor Jones organized Y Capel Cymraeg, Llundain, the London Welsh Chapel. At one point Welsh was taught every Sunday afternoon with hymn singing at night.

The London Welsh Society meets on the first Saturday of every month at All Saints Church. In 1984, the Reverend Tudor Jones was President of the Society; Christine Scott, Vice President and Janet Balfour, Treasurer. Other officers have been Fred Nowell, Lyndon Jones, Maxwell Roberts and Mrs. Morfydd Davies.

GALT AND DISTRICT WELSH SOCIETY

The Galt and District Welsh Society folded in the late 1960's. It was never a strong society but did manage a calendar that appealed to several Welsh families. As the leaders of the Society died, it faded away. In its day, the Society was led by David Ellis, John Jenkins and Mrs. W. Watkins. There is no Welsh society in the Galt area today.

HAMILTON

After a long period of inactivity, the Hamilton Welsh Society was restarted in 1982. It was revived to host the OGGA festival in May 1982, and has been an active Welsh Society since. In 1982, its officers were Graham Rees, President; Richard Morris, Secretary and Ralph Rees, Treasurer. Graham Rees is originally from Ponthenry near Llanelli, Wales and has been President of the Hamilton Welsh Society since the early 1970's. He is also fund-raising chairman of the Hamilton Orpheus Choir.

The Hamilton Orpheus Male Choir was started by Mr. Lyn Harry and eight singers in 1977. While living in London (England), Lyn Harry founded the London Welsh Male Choir which now hosts the 1,000 Male Voice Festival at the Royal Albert Hall. When he returned to Wales in the late 1960's, Lyn

Harry conducted the world famous Morriston Orpheus Male Choir. Lyn Harry first taught at the Royal Hamilton College of Music. He later opened the Hamilton Music Academy and formed the Hamilton Orpheus Male Choir soon after. In 1982 the choir had over 65 members. Today the choir gives many concerts; it has sung at the Toronto Caravan and mounts its own annual show. Sally Harry is the choir's accompanist and Gaynor Jones-Low has been the featured soloist. Lyn Harry is constantly in demand as a conductor of cymanfaoedd canu in Canada and the United States.

OSHAWA

Between Toronto and Ottawa, Welsh Canadian societies in Oshawa, Kingston and Peterborough meet regularly, enjoy growing memberships and a lively calendar of annual events.

The Oshawa and District Welsh Society grew directly out of arrangements made to host the Traeth Male Choir visiting from Anglesey in August, 1980. David Pugh organized accommodations and venues for the choir and from this initial network, the Society started. In 1984, the Society had about 100 members and was hosting visitors from Wales on a regular basis. In 1984 guests were the Amman Valley school boys rugby team and the thirty-five member Amman Valley Folk Dancers. The Oshawa and District Welsh Society meets monthly at Kedron United Church, produces an excellent newsletter and has a board of thirteen enthusiastic directors.

In the short time since it's been organized, the Society has started a Welsh books library, has shown movies from Wales, held many an entertaining noson lawen and well attended language classes.

In 1984, leaders of the Oshawa and District Welsh Society were Dave Pugh, Ruth Pugh, Phil Parry, Mary Parry, David Parry, Barbara Parry, Gwen Lundy, Jack Evans, Betty Evans, John Owen, Sheila Jones, Steve Jones and Elwyn Hughes.

KINGSTON

Kingston, at the eastern end of Lake Ontario, is the oldest city in Canada. It has a Welsh Society and hosted the Ontario Welsh Festival in 1979. Myfanwy Jenkins of Brockville, formerly from Llansadwrn, Wales, is a prominent soloist at Kingston Welsh events. Since 1982 the Society has been led by Malcolm Williams and Lynn Jones.

PETERBOROUGH

The Peterborough Welsh Society was formed in 1983 and hosted the Ontario Welsh Festival in May 1984. The Society's first president was Gwaenydd Jones. The Peterborough festival was one of the best in the OGGA's recent history.

TORONTO

As we drove into Toronto along Queen Elizabeth Way the city was sweltering in the unaccustomed grip of a heatwave. Temperatures were still in the upper nineties and by the time we found a place to park, radio announcers were telling us that the heat was threatening to reach 100 degrees. The abundance of trees and "parkettes" were our refuge as we explored the city and tried to settle in.

Toronto has a substantial Welsh population. Welsh born members of the numerous Toronto Welsh organizations sponsor the widest range of Welsh events of any city in North America. In the 1950's and 1960's, large numbers of highly qualified people emigrated from Britain during the "brain drain". In Ottawa, the colony of Welsh professionals form a Welsh Society led by a crop of lawyers, doctors, company executives and civil servants.

In Canada, Welsh events are not limited to those sponsored by Welsh societies. Welsh entertainers visit regularly, among them Max Boyce, Dafydd Iwan, Harry Secombe and the Welsh language rock group Ceffyl Pren. In October 1983, Stuart Burrows sang in Toronto with the BBC Welsh Symphony orchestra before an audience of several thousand. In 1984, Glynis Johns and Welsh baritone John Griffith appeared in "The Boyfriend". John Griffith later gave a concert at Dewi Sant Welsh Church.

Lord Gordon Parry and Viscount Tonypandy (George Thomas) are both regular visitors to Canada. Visiting Welsh celebrities and distinguished relatives of Welsh Canadians have all participated in Toronto Welsh events. Geraint Bowen, the Archdruid of Wales, was guest of honor at the annual Dewi Sant Church "Dewi's Dinner" in 1984. Speakers at the much larger Toronto St. David's Society Banquet have been, among others, Dr. Emyr Jones of the British High Commission in Ottawa; James Harding, originally from Swansea, now chief of police in Halton, Ontario; Dick Beddoes a Canadian sports writer and Lyn Harry, one of the foremost Welsh musicians living in Canada.

We knew that Toronto had several active Welsh societies, but the people on our short list of telephone numbers were out of town. The Reverend Cerwyn Davies' answering machine said that we should phone Harold Woodey in case of an emergency. Harold gave us permission to park at Dewi Sant Church which at least gave us a base for the night. Searching for shade and an evening breeze, we drove to Earl Bales Park where, despite our hopes, the northern twilight had little effect on the heat. While eating supper in the park, our neighbors were members of a dog obedience class. Observing their antics, we sat at a picnic table writing letters and sorting through scraps of paper. We noticed the name of Daisy Heaton on a note given us by Alun Hughes. Alun had said Daisy was a personality we had to meet.

Daisy Heaton made a quick witted appraisal of our situation. She immediately said, "I think you had better come over and see me." Like dozens of visitors before us, conductor Alun John, immigrants and ministers among them, Daisy's home became our haven.

Daisy's father was the Reverend Daniel Hughes of Detroit, four times winner of the bardic chair and the "Sledgehammer Parson" as he was called. Lord Parry's father and the Reverend Hughes had been friends and Gordon Parry and Daisy had played together as children. Lord and Lady Parry stayed with Daisy for two weeks before the Vancouver National in 1980.

There isn't a Welsh celebrity who visits Toronto that Daisy Heaton doesn't greet. When Harry Secombe came, she bought up three rows of seats and took her friends back to his room for a reception. When Elizabeth Taylor and Richard Burton were married in Toronto, Daisy sent them a cable and received a note from her and a signed photograph from him. Her scrapbook was filled with photographs and letters from Welsh celebrities and dignitaries. When we were there she was preparing to make one of her regular visits to Wales in time for the Llangefni Eisteddfod in August 1983. Lord and Lady Parry would meet her, and throughout Wales she had her choice of friends waiting to repay hospitality from when they were in Toronto.

Daisy has been president of the Toronto St. David's Society and was vice-president in 1984. She gladly unloaded part of her collection of menus, programs, bulletins and newsletters of Toronto Welsh events for us to study in the van. She gave us the addresses of individuals and Society officers she felt we ought to meet. Between nights spent in Dewi Sant parking lot and days spent in Daisy's drive, our time in Toronto became one of the best visits to any city that we made.

There are several Welsh associations in Toronto. As well as the St. David's Society, there is Dewi Sant Welsh United Church, the Toronto Welsh Rugby Club and Cylch Llewelyn. Under the umbrella of Dewi Sant Church are the Dewi Singers, the United Church Ladies Society, the Eisteddfod Committee, the Good Friday Cymanfa Ganu and a host of other groups contributing to a vigorous church life.

St. David's Day in Toronto is honored in many ways. The Welsh flag is raised over city halls in Toronto, Oakville and in East York where Daisy Heaton leads the flag raising ceremony in Welsh costume. Mackenzie House, an historic building in Toronto, has held receptions in honor of Wales' patron saint and Welsh music is broadcast on Toronto radio. Welsh society leaders have also appeared on Canadian television in connection with March 1st celebrations.

The St. David's Society of Toronto, founded in 1887, is the oldest and largest Welsh society in Canada. The Society meets at Dewi Sant Church and the division of duties between church-related committees and the St. David's Society is well balanced. Leaders of the St. David's Society in 1985 were Harold Woodey, President; Daisy Heaton, Vice-President; Islwyn Morris, Treasurer and Brenda Kelsall, Secretary. The 1985 committee also included John Calman, Sid Phelps, Ann Price and Glyn Roberts. Other officers have been Gwen Hodge, Clive Mason, David Morris, David Boswell, Ellis Griffiths, Dorothy Jones, Mrs. A. Gifford and Winifred Donaldson.

The St. David's Society of Toronto has now presented five goat mascots to the garrison at Old Fort Henry, Kingston, Ontario. The goats have all been called David and are given in memory of the Royal Welch Fusiliers Regiment stationed at Old Fort Henry from 1842 to 1843. Two bus loads of people made the trip from Toronto to Old Fort Henry in 1977. Daisy Heaton, in Welsh costume, presented the goat to the Regimental Colonel and the Welsh visitors were treated to tours of the Fort, displays of precision marching, cannon firing and military band music. The St. David's Society of Toronto also presented Old Fort Henry with a Welsh Flag which is flown over the Fort every St. David's Day.

The annual March 1st banquet of the St. David's Society of Toronto attracts around 300 people. The banquet is a gala occasion with messages received from around the world. An annual cable also comes from the Prince of Wales. Guests at the banquet include the Lt. Governor of Ontario, representatives from Toronto's other British societies, and leaders of all the Toronto Welsh organizations. The dinner features a guest speaker and music by members of the Society. John Calman is a baritone soloist who often leads and conducts community singing. Other distinguished soloists in a society brimming with musicians are David Low, Sheryl Clay, Bruce Shaef, Arlene McLean, Gaynor Jones-Low and David Jones who has won several Canadian prizes for singing. Glyn Roberts is the Society's regular accompanist.

THE TORONTO WELSH RUGBY CLUB

The Toronto Welsh Rugby Club is independent of the other Welsh societies but many of its members attend the annual St. David's Day banquet and larger Welsh Society and Welsh Church functions. The Toronto Welsh Rugby Club is a member of the Ontario Rugby Union and regularly hosts visiting rugby teams from Wales. The club won the Champagne Rugby Award in 1983, the Magnificent Sevens Trophy in 1983 and 1984, and was unbeaten champion of the Ontario Senior League in 1984.

The Toronto Welsh Rugby Club was led in the 1960's by Peter Hughes of Maesteg. Gerwyn Thomas, also of Maesteg, was president from 1970 to 1982, building it up into the strong club it is today. The club has about 100 members, fields two teams and plays its home games at Sunnybrook Park in Toronto. In 1984 the leaders of the Toronto Welsh Rugby Club were David George, President; Terry Robbins, Corresponding Secretary; Penny Griffin, Recording Secretary; Scott Elliot, Treasurer; Stan Miller, Fixtures; Tony and Charlie McGann, Entertainment; Blaine Grindall, Junior Development and Steve Power, Club Captain.

☆

The Toronto Caravan is one of North America's largest ethnic festivals. Every June the diverse immigrant communities of Toronto mount displays and concerts throughout the city. Each nationality staffs a pavilion in a large hall somewhere in the city. The Welsh contribution is called the Cardiff Pavilion and is decorated with a theme, such as a castle, farm, cottage or craft shop. Ladies in Welsh costume serve leek soup, Welsh cakes, bara brith and meat pies, and sell Welsh crafts and souvenirs. In 1984, the Welsh Princess and Lord Mayor of the Cardiff pavilion were Donna Morris and the Reverend Heddwyn Williams. The Cardiff pavilion also features musicians specially invited from Wales. Ar Log, Penrhyn Male Voice and the Rhondda Valley Showband have all appeared at the Toronto Caravan. Caravan is a challenging engagement for Welsh musicians who sing four times a day for the festival's whole nine days. When they appeared, both Penrhyn and Ar Log sold out their stock of promotional records and cassettes.

Daisy kept us informed what Welsh events were happening while we were there. The Dewi Singers would be rehearsing and we arranged to go along. At the rehearsal, we met Jean Iona Thompson, founder of the choir and Lowri Taylor, one of the choristers. First, however, we drove out to Brampton on the outskirts of Toronto to meet David Ware, a professional artist originally from Bridgend in Wales.

David had given up his job as an engineering draftsman to devote his time to painting. He was just making ends meet selling his work through galleries and summer shows. Soon after quitting his job, he drove from Toronto to Vancouver. The experience of the open western prairie had a profound influence on his imagination. The semi-abstract paintings he produced on that trip impressed us immediately. When we returned to Daisy's, we called David and bought a painting over the phone even though it would be months before we had anywhere to hang it.

The Dewi Singers had already started practicing when we arrived at Dewi Sant Church. A group of about thirty women and twelve men were singing in the downstairs room. The present building was built in 1960 and is spacious and modern. The upstairs sanctuary was open and this was our first chance to go inside. Welsh banners hung on the walls and *Cân a Mawl*, the hymn book compiled by Daniel Hughes and the Welsh Church in Detroit, lay stacked on the rear pews nearer the door. In the hallway were issues of *Y Gadwyn* (The Link), the informative and cheerful newsletter of Dewi Sant Welsh Church.

Dewi Sant Welsh United Church celebrated its 75th anniversary in 1982. Hosting the National Cymanfa in Toronto to coincide with the anniversary had a revitalizing effect throughout the Toronto Welsh community.

Jean Iona Thompson formed the Dewi Singers in 1979. By 1984, the choir had grown from eighteen to over forty members. Today, the choir sings hymns and Welsh folk material and, under the musical accompaniment of Jane Thomas and John Berry, has added penillion singing to its repertoire. The Dewi Singers rehearse every Thursday night and sing at all important Dewi Sant services. They have sung at Toronto City Hall, the Toronto Folk Arts Festival as well as at OGGA Welsh festivals and the Toronto Caravan. Jean Thompson is the choir's director, Cyril Evans is its coordinating officer and its accompanist, Jane Anne Thomas, is organist at Dewi Sant Church.

We were given a very warm reception by choir members. They asked where we were from. When Suzanne said Atlanta, there was silence. When I said Bridgend everyone cheered. Typically, the choir members knew more about Wales than the United States.

Lowri Taylor told us about the Dewi Sant Urdd Eisteddfod. First held in 1984, the Eisteddfod drew so many entries in over twenty categories that it lasted from 5 p.m. until after midnight. Tom Jones was chairman in 1984, Nest Holyer in 1985 and Lowri herself was chairperson for 1986.

☆

The history of the Welsh church in Toronto started in 1907 when a small group of people formed a Welsh language Bible study class in Cook's Presbyterian Church on Queen's Street East. In 1909, the Dewi Sant Welsh Presbyterian Church of Toronto was founded in affiliation with the Welsh Presbyterian Church of the United States. In 1917, with the aid of a generous grant from the parent body in America, the Toronto congregation bought a church building on Clinton Street. The decision by a majority vote to join the United Church of Canada in 1927 led to some dissent and the congregation then dispersed to various other churches until 1933 when the Clinton site was re-occupied.

From 1936 to 1946, Dewi Sant Church was without a minister. In 1946, the Reverend Heddwyn Williams was inducted and he served until 1951. The Reverend Heddwyn Williams is a graduate of the University of Wales and a member of the National Eisteddfod Gorsedd. He is highly visible in Ontario Welsh life and is one of several Welsh ministers living in Toronto. In 1951, Reverend J. Humphreys Jones from Amlwch, Anglesey, became minister of the Church until 1964. A past president of the WNGGA and the OGGA the Reverend Humphreys Jones led the drive to build a new church at Melrose Avenue on the northern city limits. Despite opposition from the Presbytery of the United Church of Canada, the congregation persisted with plans to relocate. Critics objected that a Welsh church in Toronto had no future and in 1959, the *Toronto Star* ran an article under the caption "Will Welsh Church Survive?".

In 1960, the old church on Clinton Street was sold to St. Paul's Yugoslav Congregation and the new building of the Dewi Sant Welsh Congregation was dedicated. The new location did not attract more members, however, and during the 1960's and 1970's, attendance continued to decline. Older members didn't come and younger immigrants from Wales were less committed to the chapel going tradition.

The Reverend Elwyn Hughes, minister from 1965 to 1975 and the Reverend D. J. Wynne Evans from 1975 to 1978 both worked hard to reactivate church life. The ministry of the Reverend Wynne Evans in particular, highlighted a lack of interest and even hostility to services held in the Welsh language. Increased use of the language actually drove members away. The largely English speaking congregation resented using Welsh in Canada when they had never used it in Wales. When the Reverend Wynne Evans resigned in 1978, the Reverend J. Humphreys Jones served as supply minister and a Ways and Means Committee chaired by Bryn Lloyd formerly of Rhostryfan, Caernarfonshire reviewed the church's future direction. The Ways and Means Committee resolved that the church was a place of worship above all else and should be accessible to everyone regardless of their language. It was important to bring the congregation back. Weekly services would be bilingual but mainly in English. Welsh language services would be held at 7 p.m. every other week.

The Reverend Cerwyn Davies, originally from Pembrokeshire, was appointed minister of Dewi Sant in 1979. Ordained into the Welsh Independent Church in 1951, Reverend Davies emigrated to Canada in 1963. Under his ministry, the atmosphere in the church has completely changed. Weekly attendance has increased and church related activities by members of the congregation continue to grow every year.

Cerwyn Davies is a dynamic leading minister who has harmonized the Welsh and English speaking needs of the congregation. He received his Doctorate of Divinity from Columbia University, New York in 1984. The degree ceremony actually took place in Birmingham, England and while there he was interviewed on Radio Cymru about the Welsh Church in Toronto. He is a Canadian Director of Religious Travel for Swissair and has taken Dewi Sant tours to Israel, Oberammagau and the Far East. A past president of the OGGA and speaker at Toronto banquets, Cerwyn Davies is a highly visible leader of the Canadian Welsh community.

As part of its documentation of the Canadian ethnic mosaic, the Multicultural History Society of Ontario partially funded a detailed history of Dewi Sant Church in 1977. Mr. Roger Jones of Briton Ferry and author of several local books on Gower, became the archive contributor for the Church.

Today, with a calendar of rummage sales, homecoming services, Thanksgiving, a summer picnic, St. David's Day, an Easter cymanfa, Christmas carols and New Year services, the pews of Dewi Sant are filled. Welsh language services are well attended and remind people the language is determined to survive.

Dewi Sant members hold their own Dewi Dinner close to March 1st, which like all Dewi Sant parties, is followed by a noson lawen. In 1984, Cerwyn Davies, Heddwyn Williams and J. Humphreys Jones performed as "The Three Monks". Dr. Geraint Bowen, Archdruid of Wales, and in 1984, a lecturer at the University of Montreal, was special guest and John Calman led community singing.

The flourishing life of Dewi Sant is appealing to more members of the Toronto Welsh community. Weekly services at Dewi Sant have become the inspiration behind the present richness of Toronto Welsh activities. Before leaving, we were able to attend a Sunday service at Dewi Sant where we met a lot of the people we had read about in *Ninnau*, *Y Drych* and *Y Gadwyn*. There were many other people from Wales visiting relatives who had made Canada their home.

☆

In September 1982, Welsh learners who had attended Cymdeithas Madog's Cwrs Cymraeg, Toronto started Cylch Llewelyn, a Welsh learning society. In 1983, Hefina Philips of Oakville (formerly from Ystradgynlais) was engaged to teach Welsh classes every Saturday morning and these continue to flourish, now under the auspices of The Toronto Board of Education. In 1984, Cylch Llewelyn had over thirty members and among its leaders were Laura Selleck, Dilys Williams, Marilyn Kay and Hefina Philips. Margaret Parry of Cymdeithas Madog and a teacher in Cardiff, provides Cylch Llewelyn with the latest tapes, magazines and learning materials. David Pugh has shown Welsh language movies from S4C and the Welsh Film Board. Other supplies have been donated by Clwyd Center of Educational Technology, BBC Wales and the Welsh Arts Council. As a member of the Canadian Celtic Arts Association, Cylch Llewelyn does a valuable job promoting Welsh language artists and writers of Wales. It is a society of speakers as well as learners and is one of the few study groups able to support its students with Welsh speaking immigrants.

OTTAWA

The drive from Toronto to Ottawa took us seven hours. We should have liked to have seen Ontario in more detail, but summer was coming to an end and our deadlines were only weeks away. We cut our planned visit to New Brunswick and from Montreal headed back into the United States. We arrived in Ottawa July 17, 1983; this left us six weeks to tour New England before the Wilkes-Barre National Cymanfa on September 3. We planned to arrive in Atlanta in time for Thanksgiving on the fourth Thursday of November.

The Canadian cities had all been beautiful and Ottawa was no exception. Of all our sightseeing, a day at the Canadian Film Board was the most memorable. As well as movies on Celtic immigration, we saw the Canadian Film Board's Oscar winning short movie, "If You Love This Planet", which is about the threat of nuclear war and had been banned in the U.S.A.

While in Ottawa we stayed with Idwal and Joyce Richards. Joyce is from Margam and Idwal is from Cefn Cribwr. After Idwal graduated as an architect, they emigrated to Canada in 1960. Like thousands of others, Idwal and Joyce would probably be living in Wales today if the opportunity to work were there.

We spent several evenings with leaders of the Ottawa Welsh Society. Welsh people in Ottawa play an active role in the OGGA and in the WNGGA. The Welsh Society here consists almost exclusively of Welsh people who have emigrated to Canada since World War II, including one or two members from

183

England like Bernard Kilroy, a past treasurer of the Society.

At the New York National in 1975, Ottawa bid successfully to host the National in 1977. This was the first time for Ottawa to host the festival and it made quite an impact on the local Welsh community. Pontarddulais Male Choir visited in May, and in September, the Ottawa Welsh Choral Society appeared at the National with the Royal Canadian Mounted Police Band. Ray Handy visited in October and presented his "Dylan Thomas Lived Here" one-man show.

The Ottawa Welsh Society maintains a busy calendar. Meetings take the form of picnics, car rallies, cheese and wine parties, even a sailing regatta—along with the usual slide shows and movies. December is the Society's busiest month, with children's and adult's Christmas and New Years parties and a senior citizen's tea. The noson lawen is prominent in Ottawa Welsh life. Tal Griffiths originally from Carmarthen has converted the whole downstairs of his home into a reception area that has seen many a hwyrnos (late night) by the Welsh Society.

In February 1980, the Ottawa Welsh Society led a "Celtic Noson Lawen" to raise funds for the Celtic Chair at Ottawa University. Also in 1980, a group of Welsh language teachers contacted the Society while in Ottawa studying French-Canadian language immersion techniques. Dim Byd Eto, the folk group, appeared at the OGGA festival in Ottawa in 1981 and Traeth Male Voice Choir and the Burma Star Male Choir visited in 1982.

The Ottawa Welsh Society holds its annual general meeting every May 1st. Past officers have included Don Mills, Roy Morris, Wendy Jones, Brian Powell, Evelyn Brown, Tal Griffiths and Brenda Thompson. Jeanette Hudson, past president of the OGGA and the Ottawa Welsh Choral Society who emigrated to Ottawa in 1972, has since returned to Wales to live. Jeanette was a prominent featured soloist at Ontario Welsh events. 1985-1986 officers were, Meriel Mills, President; Vic Williams and Terry Morris, Vice-Presidents; Dorothy Evans, Treasurer; Bev Clelland, Secretary; John Griffiths, Past President; Myfanwy Davies, Ticket Convener; John Davies, Social and Liquid Assets; and Convenors Ron Andrews, Tony Howard, Ken Mercer, Marie Day and Barbara Lloyd.

The Ottawa Welsh Choral Society was founded by Roy Morris in 1968. Originally from Swansea, Roy Morris is a past officer of the Ottawa Welsh Society, the OGGA and a director of the Ottawa Folk Arts Council. The Ottawa Welsh Society's accompanist since the choir's inception has been Grace Davies. The Ottawa Welsh Choir is one of the most active in North America. The choir made a tour of Wales in 1978 when it competed in the Llangollen International Eisteddfod. The Ottawa Welsh Choral Society was started with eighteen members and today has over seventy-five singers. In April 1980 the choir released its first record. The record features French, English and Welsh material in keeping with the choir's multinational but very Canadian identity. About one third of the choir's members are Welsh born and about 40 percent of its concert material is in Welsh.

While talking to Roy at his home in Kanata, I asked what he thought was the most important factor in building a successful Welsh choir. "Independence," he said. "The choir should be an organization independent from any other Welsh group." Membership can overlap, but without an independent willingness to meet and rehearse, no choir could hope to succeed. Members of the Choral Society anxious to improve their Welsh have held lessons at the High School of Commerce in Ottawa.

In 1975 seven members of the choir started Y Seithawd (The Seven). The group's music is devoted to Welsh folk songs and religious works. Y Seithawd has sung at folk festivals in Ontario and at national cymanfaoedd canu in New York and Ottawa. During its existence, Y Seithawd was led by Roy Morris and consisted of Don Mills, Meriel Mills, Jean Howard, Tal Griffiths, John Griffiths, Albert Davies and Jeanette Hudson.

Roy and his wife, Kay, took us to the home of Don and Meriel Mills. Originally from Llanelli, Don Mills has been a vice-president of the Llanelli Rugby Club, president of the OGGA and was co-chairman with Tal Griffiths of the 1977 Ottawa National. Don is one of four Canadian owners of the Celtic Manor luxury hotel near Newport, Wales. When we were in Ottawa, his mother was visiting from Llanelli and one of his daughters was home from Atlantic College, the prestigious international school at St. Donat's, South Glamorgan.

In 1984, Anne Till of the National Library of Wales, spent six months at the Canadian National Library in Ottawa as part of a libraries exchange program. While in Ottawa, Anne Till compiled a bibliography of Welsh Canadian documents including ephemeral immigrant material, letters, journals, deeds, and so on.

Leaving the home of Idwal and Joyce Richards, our visit to Ontario was over. It was late summer and the fields around the Canadian capital were brimming with beans, broccoli, strawberries and potatoes. We filled our baskets at a pick-your-own farm before crossing the Ottawa River into the officially mono-lingual French province of Quebec.

MONTREAL

In a province where English language schools are closing, there has been pressure on members of the Montreal St. David's Society to move away and find work in other parts of Canada. The Welsh Society is flourishing, however, and was confident enough in 1983 to bid for the National to come to Montreal in 1985.

The St. David's Society of Montreal was founded in 1903. Owen C. Roberts, honorary President of the Society, has been a leader of Montreal Welsh life for many years. Owen was one of the first supporters of *Ninnau* when it started and has written the "News and Views from Montreal" column since 1976.

Since 1983, St. David's Day and other celebrations have been held at the

Officer's Mess of the Black Watch Regiment. Society President Morfydd Gibson's husband is a major in the Black Watch and the Black Watch Pipers often participate in Welsh parties. Mrs. Lillian Dykens, a Welsh Canadian artist in Montreal, decorates the Black Watch Mess with Welsh theme posters, flags and other decorations. The St. David's Day banquet always features a hilarious "eating of the leek" ceremony. Participants are piped in and on eating their leeks are presented with silver tankards brimming with ale. In 1983 Welsh folk dancing was added to the banquet program. St. David's Day services, held at Anglican churches in Montreal, are conducted in three languages—French, English and Welsh.

The other major event of the Montreal St. David's Society is an annual spring cymanfa, held in 1984, at St. James Anglican Church. Conductor of Montreal cymanfaoedd canu is Iwan Edwards of Lachine, formerly of Pontarddulais. Since emigrating to Canada in 1965, Iwan has formed the St. Lawrence Mixed Choir, which has toured Europe several times. Iwan has conducted many regional cymanfaoedd canu in Canada and the United States including several OGGA festivals, the 50th National Cymanfa at Utica and the 1985 National held in Montreal itself.

The majority of the members of the Montreal St. David's Society were born in Wales. Society members go to Wales often and host visitors themselves. Past President, John Williams, and his daughter, Helen, have taken holidays in Wales at Plaid Cymru seminars and Welsh language courses. Other members attended the Brock University Cwrs Cymraeg while Owen Roberts also attended the Cwrs Cymraeg in San Rafael, California. Trelawnyd Male Voice and Port Talbot Male Voice visited Montreal in 1978. When the BBC Welsh Symphony Orchestra played in Montreal in 1983, their third encore was followed, to the orchestra's surprise, by Hen Wlad Fy Nhadau sung to them by members of the Montreal Welsh Male Choir sitting in the audience. The St. David's Society of Montreal hosted the 100 member BBC orchestra and their spouses at a reception afterwards.

Not everyone in the Society is Welsh. Bob Carnier who has no Welsh blood has been one of the Society's most dedicated officers. Bob initiated many of the club's annual activities, such as the Welsh picnic, car rally, corn roast, golf tournament and wine and cheese party, all followed of course by community singing. Other people prominent in the smooth running of the Society have been John Hughes, Terry Pearce, John Truman, Kenneth Male, John Williams, Evelyn Bellis, George Morgan, Arthur Phillips, Ronald Stewart, Constance Kelly, William Kilpatrick and Mrs. Leslie Lavigne.

The Welsh Male Choir of Montreal, led for many years by Tommy Edwards, originally from Cardigan, is still one of the most active Welsh choirs in North America. In addition to singing at Welsh meetings, Scottish ceilidhs and Breton fest noz, the choir appears at charity concerts and ethnic festivals. The choir numbers between thirty and forty voices and has a predominantly Welsh language repertoire. In 1984 Jean Sult was the director of the choir and Wallace Rosser was its president. Soloists with the Montreal Welsh Male

Choir have been Mrs. Evelyn Bellis and Mrs. Undeg Edwards.

Since 1957 the St. David's Society of Montreal has presented the annual Taliesin Jones Scholarship Award. Taliesin Jones was a vice-president of Verdun High School. In 1954 he was killed and his wife, Erna, was severely injured in a traffic accident. The Society spent three years raising $10,000 in Taliesin Jones' memory and has presented annual scholarships to graduates of Verdun High School ever since. Verdun High School closed in May 1984 because of decreased enrollment by English-speaking children. The Taliesin Jones Memorial Fund is now in trust while the St. David's Society decides what direction the scholarship award should take.

Montreal Welsh Canadians have a strong academic representative in John Williams at McGill University. A visit by Welsh teachers from North Wales, investigating French language immersion techniques, was greatly assisted by John Williams. He arranged accommodations for the Welsh party with members of the St. David's Society. The Welsh group was in Canada for thirteen days and visited Montreal and Ottawa. The Welsh also hold occasional chapel services at the University. Tudor P. Jones, the Dean of Caerleon College of Education, was a resident at McGill University for several months in 1984. Mr. Jones won a British Council Travel Grant and while in Montreal was introduced to the St. David's Society by John Williams.

There is a large Breton community in Montreal and Bretons form the largest group in the Montreal Celtic Congress. In January 1976, members of the St. David's Society took part in a Breton language demonstration at the French Consulate. Tommy Edwards led the Montreal Welsh Male Choir in Hen Wlad Fy Nhadau and Ar Brog du Noz. John Williams led the Welsh contribution to the demonstration and protest march. The Montreal Celtic Society was led in the 1970's by members of the Welsh Male Choir and the St. David's Society. John Williams and Ronald and Samantha Stewart of the Welsh Society were particularly active in organizing inter-celtic parties and concerts by visiting musicians. Ronald Stewart became President of the Canadian Celtic Conference, and during his presidency Welsh members were encouraged by the younger Breton constituency, some of whom had been to Wales.

Although the Welsh Society in Montreal is small, its leaders are well organized. The delegation that went to Wilkes-Barre in 1983 consisted of Terry Pearce, Kenneth Male, Iwan Edwards and Owen C. Roberts. The WNGGA, which appoints sites for the National two years in advance, accepted their proposal. At Portland, Oregon in 1984, Columbus, Ohio was designated site of the National Gymanfa for 1986. Margaret Pearce and Jean Male of Montreal were at Portland where they distributed over 1,000 miniature daffodils and brochures to promote their cymanfa in 1985.

In 1984, Terry Pearce said that the Welsh community in Montreal had caught "Welsh fever". As expected, the 1985 National had a great impact on Montreal Welsh life. "Welsh fever" was an expression we had now heard many times from Welsh Canadians and Welsh Americans involved in the enthusiastic preservation of their Welsh heritage.

21

A Tour of New England

The countryside around Quebec was as manicured and pastoral as the fields of central France. Menus of French-Canadian cuisine lured us away from our usual pecuniary reserve. At least our French was good enough to buy fromage and pain at the small epicerie. Our final camping spot in Canada was on the Ile D'Orleans. After a filling lunch of the local specialty of fève au lard (baked beans), we drove via Thetford Mines towards Vermont.

The contrast between Quebec and Vermont was a lot less dramatic than between Washington and British Columbia. People in northern Vermont speak French. Our cousins, John and Kathy, in Brattleboro, Vermont, were French-speaking, having lived in Montreal. The New England sensibility too, was a lot closer to Canadian than the gulf between the lumber camps of Washington and the British atmosphere of Victoria and Vancouver.

VERMONT

Kathy and John live on a large rambling farm just west of Brattleboro. They keep goats, sheep and a few ducks but their main stock is books. Their book shop, housed in an enormous barn, is one of the biggest in Vermont. Among the more famous of their local customers is Saul Bellow, who came in one Saturday morning when we were there.

Over a period of days I was able to study the spine of every volume on the shelves. The number of books on Wales or by Welsh writers surprised me. Dylan Thomas topped the list. Autobiographies included Jean Rhys, Rhys Davies, Gwyn Thomas, Augustus John and Emlyn Williams. Scattered through the A to Z of authors were Gwyn Jones, Tristan Jones, Leslie Thomas, Richard Hughes, Arthur Machen and Alexander Cordell. The British Isles travel section yielded several local histories and one real gem, an account of the great revival in Wales published by Chicago journalist S. B. Shaw in 1905.

Large numbers of Welsh books can be found through American dealers. Even a superficial search can yield rich rewards. In California, Buckabest Bindery has a good selection of Welsh material, from illustrated volumes by David Jones to 19th century editions of the Mabinogion. Religious book dealers have Welsh language bibles and the occasional good quality hymnal. Even a large paperback exchange can yield a surprising handful of Welsh pulp. The Welsh import stores carry contemporary titles while the

Humanities Press in New Jersey prints a regularly updated catalog with over seventy listings from the University of Wales Press.

Philips G. Davies found R. D. Thomas' *Hanes Cymry America* while burrowing in a Midwest bookshop. My greatest find was probably *Rowland's Cambrian Bibliography*. Published in Wales in 1869, this 800 page book is a catalog of all Welsh books written between 1546 and 1800. I found it in a used book store in Atlanta, Georgia.

In Poultney, Vermont there is a Welsh Room in Green Mountain College Library. The Welsh Room dates from a Welsh Ethnic Revival Project which ran from June 1975 to June 1977. This project, from its small and very local beginnings, became one of the most influential episodes in recent North American Welsh history.

News of the quarries in Vermont reached the slate mining area of northwest Wales in the early 1800's. By 1850 several hundred Welsh families were working in the Poultney and Fairhaven slate works. In the words of the Reverend R. D. Thomas, the Vermont quarries were only "small holes" in comparison with those in Merionethshire, but by 1872 when *Hanes Cymry America* was published, he estimated that around 1,350 Welsh people were living in the Poultney area.

In the 1970's twelve original immigrants of the 1900-1920 period were taped for the Welsh Revival Project's oral history department. Margot McKinney Bouchard, the librarian at Green Mountain College, designed a far reaching series of programs "aimed at rebuilding the ethnic consciousness of children and adults in the Poultney area." The project received a $13,000 Ethnic Heritage Grant from the U.S. Department of Health, Education and Welfare. Contributions of books, heirlooms and cash were made by the local Welsh American population. Margot Bouchard wrote two history books for use in local primary and junior high schools. School children were taken to Welsh teas at the homes of Welsh Americans and a series of concerts and quarrymen's suppers were held. Poultney Welsh Presbyterian Church held a small cymanfa ganu and Margot Bouchard, assisted by Gwyneth Wood, taught a small Welsh language class of seven students and two adults.

Margot Bouchard's work was thorough. As a librarian she enlarged the Green Mountain College Welsh collection and arranged to create a permanent Welsh Room. The Welsh Room received a generous cash gift from J. Lloyd Williams of Fair Haven, a descendant of the first Welsh immigrants, and was officially opened with a reception attended by over eighty people on April 27, 1977.

Bethesda, where many of the first immigrants were from, became Poultney's sister village in Wales. Gwyn Williams, a student at Dyffryn Ogwen High School in Bethesda, visited Poultney, and Kathy Mahar was the American student who went to Wales. Gwyn Williams was able to speak Welsh to the older people at a mini-Welsh course held in Poultney in April 1977.

Margot Bouchard compiled a census of Welsh Americans in the Poultney area. She recorded immigrant stories, had Welsh costumes made for loan and school use and publicized the project with a series of slide shows. In 1984, seven years after the project had ended, she was still being asked to speak at historical societies throughout Vermont. The Welsh Room also receives a steady stream of visitors many of whom come from Wales. In 1983, "Welsh Heritage of the Slate Belt" became an official course of the Elderhostel Senior Citizens' College curriculum. Margot Bouchard was the principal lecturer, Gwyneth Wood talked about her personal experience of emigrating from Bethesda and ladies of the Welsh Presbyterian Church in Poultney hosted a Welsh tea for the Elderhostel students.

The Welsh Ethnic Revival Project in Poultney, Vermont took on a much larger dimension when Anne Cowie of Baltimore read about it in *Ninnau*. Anne contacted the Welsh Education Authority with the possibility of arranging a one-week Welsh course to climax the two-year Vermont Welsh revival. The Welsh Language Crash Course, the first held in North America, attracted forty people from around the U.S.A. and Canada. It was covered by a BBC Wales film crew and became the seed that hatched into Cymdeithas Madog.

Although the Welsh revival project ended with the language course, Welsh American interest remained high. Frances Williams from New York City conducted a cymanfa in Bennington in October 1977. Christine Price of Poultney, author of the illustrated book *David and the Mountain*, gave her original sketches to the college library. Mr. and Mrs. Dean Hunter were in Wales in 1978 and brought home a four foot Welsh doll from Caernarfon. They gave the doll to the Welsh Room in memory of their daughter who had been a student at the college.

In 1978 Wayne Jones organized a Welsh Society in Poultney which marks St. David's Day every year with a cymanfa ganu at Peniel Welsh Presbyterian Church. Two hundred people attended the cymanfa in 1984. Idris Jones and Donald Boothman have been singing directors and soloists have been Vernon Ward, Joan Maynard and Sara and Jennifer Riggs.

South of Poultney in South Dorset, Dorothy Jones runs Anglophile Antiques. Dorothy has a Welsh background and sells Welsh prints, small souvenirs and a selection of imported Welsh clothing.

☆

Two of John and Kathy's neighbors, Sat Singh and Satkar Kulsah, were devotees of kundalini yoga. The Kulsahs practised yoga every morning on an outdoor platform at 4:15 a.m. Kathy woke us at 3:45 a.m., and we walked one and a half miles to the Kulsah's property. Wrapped in quilts and blankets our morning practice started with a series of booming chants. These were followed by a series of phenomenally vigorous exercises which combined conventional yoga postures with a rapid breathing technique known as "the breath of fire". Sadharna concluded with Sikh hymns accompanied on a harmonium. These predawn kundalini yoga practices left us feeling unusually energized for the remainder of the day.

Leaving Brattleboro we entered an ecumenical phase. Our next stops were

for meditation at a Zen Buddhist center, followed by a stay with Quaker paci-
fists near Amherst, Massachusetts. We then visited Episcopal junior minister
Earl T. Williams, founder of the Welsh Society of Connecticut. When we left
Earl, we drove to the Integral Yoga Institute near Putnam, Connecticut.

CONNECTICUT

Earl Williams had hung a red dragon flag outside his house in North Haven,
Connecticut. To our surprise there was a letter waiting for us from Arturo
Roberts. The letter was to confirm our "appointment as *Ninnau* corres-
pondents" prior to the Wilkes-Barre National. The approaching National
Cymanfa was now being discussed by almost all the Welsh people that we met.

We spent a pleasant afternoon with Earl hearing about the St. David's
Society of Connecticut Inc. His other major project was running *Ninnau
Dragon Friends*, a flourishing pen friend organization.

Ninnau first started a Welsh Correspondence Club in 1977. As a result of an
article in the *Western Mail*, twenty-eight people wrote to *Ninnau* from Wales,
and Mrs. Lillian Morgan Canaan of Philadelphia became the Welsh Correspondence Club Coordinator. The list of pen friends quickly grew and three
lists with a total of over one hundred correspondents appeared in *Ninnau* in
1978. When Mrs. Canaan was interviewed by Vincent Kane on Good Morning Wales, the Correspondence Club was given another boost, but the club
disappeared from sight in June 1978, and nothing more was heard of it.

Earl Williams' grandfather emigrated to Canada from Corwen, Wales before moving south to settle in Utica. Earl's Welsh enthusiasm dates from his
participation in Welsh Heritage week in 1981 and attending the 1981 National
Cymanfa Ganu in Utica. Earl joined *Ninnau* in February 1982 and *Ninnau
Dragon Friends* was started soon afterwards. Earl has personally written
hundreds of letters promoting *Ninnau Dragon Friends*. On visits to Wales he
distributed posters and flyers at the BBC, the *Western Mail*, the National and
the International Eisteddfod. Earl was interviewed on BBC Wales in March
1983. This broadcast prompted a flood of pen friend applications. *Ninnau
Dragon Friends* has put hundreds of pen pals of all ages in contact with one
another. In 1985 with Pamela Kneller of Syracuse living in Wales, promoting
the pen friend agency, *Ninnau Dragon Friends* grew even more.

Choirs looking for contacts with Welsh American societies wrote to Earl in
1984. As a result he became the representative of Rhos Male Choir, arranging
an East Coast tour for them scheduled for 1985. This led to the re-establishment of the *Ninnau Talent Agency*, an attempt to place visiting Welsh
speakers and musicians with interested Welsh societies. At the end of 1984,
the Talent Agency was trying to arrange dates and venues for mountaineer
Eric Jones, actress Aeronwy Thomas, Mabsant folk group, Rhos Girls Choir,
John Haydn, tenor and harpist Peris Wyn-Alban.

The St. David's Society of Connecticut was started in March 1981 when
about one hundred people held a party on St. David's Day. Earl Williams and

Shirley Keiffer enrolled in the following Welsh Heritage Week and others from the Society attended the Utica National Cymanfa. In October 1981, Owen and Jane Davis and Earl Williams formally launched the St. David's Society. In 1982 over two hundred people attended the Society's second annual St. David's Celtic Nite—a celebration that featured a craft fair and films from Wales in the afternoon, and a dinner and concert in the evening.

The musical ability of the Society is strong. David Katz and Diane Kern have given performances of their own Welsh musical compositions. Rebecca Flannery plays the harp, Lavera Ayers plays piano and Madge Manfred and Shirley Gilmartin have also been harp soloists. The 1984 St. David's Celtic Nite featured hammered dulcimer by Mike Ticard and Breton music by Sonia Malkine. Caernarfon Male Voice Choir was hosted in April 1982, and Ar Log were booked by the Society in August 1982. During 1985 the Society hosted Rhos Male Choir, Rhos Girls Choir and in September the Mabsant folk group.

The Society meets on the second Friday of every month except July and August at St. John's Episcopal Church, North Haven. Typical 1984 programs were: a film night, a reading of works by Dylan Thomas, a Welsh cooking lesson, a Welsh historical figures evening and an evening on the literary works of Wales. One month Hywel and Ruth Thomas visited from Buffalo and conducted a Welsh folk dancing workshop. A large contingent from Connecticut traveled to the New York concert of Côr Meibion De Cymru in November 1983.

The Reverend Jeffrey Rowthorn from Newport, Wales teaches at Yale Divinity School. A member of the Connecticut St. David's Society, Mr. Rowthorn has two hymns in the revised Episcopal Hymnal.

In April 1984 eight students from the West Glamorgan Institute of Higher Education spent two weeks at Hartford State Technical College. The visit was arranged by Marc Clements who had previously visited the U.S.A. as a member of the Dim Byd Eto folk group. The group was presented to both Houses of Government in the Connecticut Legislature and for the first time since colonial days the government of Connecticut was greeted in Welsh.

By 1984, March 1st in North Haven had become "The Festival of The Red Dragon Welsh Day in Connecticut". The event was reported in the local press and Society leaders Jennifer Harvey and Owen Davis were interviewed for over an hour on the radio. The festival featured crafts and imports. Arturo Roberts gave a presentation on Patagonia, and the day ended with a first class concert of music and poetry from Brittany and Wales.

In 1984 the Society had fifty members. Its officers were Owen Davis, President; Jennifer Harvey, Vice-President; David Meade, Treasurer; Earl T. Williams, Jr., Secretary; with Directors Margaret Harvey and Morfydd Glasser. Other prominent officers since the Society was founded have been Diane Kern, Gwyneth Davies, Donald Davis, Eluned Roberts and Shirley Keiffer. Earl told us that the Society has about a dozen members from Wales and requires one officer to be Welsh speaking or born in Wales. He also mentioned that because of the Society's location, members were able to participate in programs by Welsh clubs in New York, eastern Pennsylvania and Massachusetts. In 1985, as a result of choral visits, North Haven became a twin city with Rhos, North Wales. This has additional significance because of nearby Wrexham's close connection with Yale University.

Before leaving North Haven, we visited Yale University, whose major benefactor was Welshman Elihu Yale.

Elihu Yale was born in 1649 and died in 1721. As head of the East India Company and governor of Madras, he amassed a fortune before retiring to the family home in Wrexham, Wales. Saybrook College in Yale University has a Wrexham Tower which is modeled after the tower of St. Giles Parish Church, Wrexham, where Elihu Yale is buried. The relationship between members of the University and St. Giles is close. In 1968 Yale's tomb in Wales was restored at the University's expense, and the Yale class of 1901 paid for the restoration of St. Giles' historic north porch.

The day we were there, Yale University was deserted—abandoned for the summer. We soon found out where all the people were. The Connecticut Turnpike along the coast was packed with traffic. After a year of country roads all to ourselves, the sight of thousands of vacationers crowded on one narrow strip of shore filled us with alarm. Five miles inland, however, the forest parks were deserted. We took a winding inland route on uncluttered roads via State Forest camps to the Integral Yoga Institute at Pomfret Center. After a few days bending and breathing, we continued to Rhode Island.

RHODE ISLAND

Driving through Rhode Island was a relief. It is one of the few American states smaller than Wales, and we were in and out in less than half an hour.

Barrington, Rhode Island, is the home of Llys y Rhosyn Rose Gardens. Llys y Rhosyn is the largest non-commercial rose garden on the East Coast. The Boston Cymrodorion Society has been coming here on summer excursions for many years. Llys y Rhosyn was started in 1948 by Mr. Karl Jones whose grandparents immigrated to Cincinnati from Wales. At its peak the garden had over 7,500 roses as well as hundreds of other plants. Mr. Jones was ninety in 1984 and had reduced the roses to around 3,500. He encourages the Boston Welsh Society to visit the gardens, and he has been a regular correspondent with rosarians in Wales. Mr. Jones has said, "No sober person is ever refused entrance to the gardens. The only thing I insist upon is that if you show up after dark, you bring your own flashlight."

MASSACHUSETTS

Our first stop in Massachusetts was at the site of the first church built by Welsh people in America, the First Baptist Church of Swansea, built in 1663. The founding pastor of the church, the Reverend John Myles, was from Ilston, Swansea, Wales. The church celebrated its 300th anniversary in 1963, and the present building, which dates from 1848, was extensively renovated. At the tricentennial banquet the speaker was Dr. Gwyn Walters. While researching John Myles' original logbook in Brown University Library in Providence, Rhode Island, Dr. Walters discovered the name of John Walters from his own native village in Wales—Felinfoel. He was listed among the members of the Ilston church—to which he would have had to walk over 10 miles to worship. Dr. Walters brought greetings from the mother church in Swansea, Wales and played his recording of a parallel celebration which he attended there. In November 1982 the sanctuary of the church was re-dedicated and the Boston Cymrodorion Welsh Society participated in the celebrations. Members of the Society led by Michele Griffiths presented a one-hour program of singing and recitations with a te bach to follow. The church relates its Welsh background on a fine plaque donated by Edgar Davies of the San Diego Cambrian Society.

The roads on the Massachusetts coast were aggressively crowded. After visiting Plymouth and struggling with the traffic, we headed inland to Massapoag Lake near Brockton. Our cousins Joe and Joan had contacted us— they were staying at a cottage on the lake while attending a candy convention in Boston. Joe had been a candy manufacturer, and he thought we'd get a kick out of going to the convention with them.

The convention was being held in downtown Boston behind the Christian Science Monitor building. On our trip we had eaten almost every kind of food, from Cajun boudin and Indian fried bread to macrobiotic sprouts. In Boston we had our choice of some of the most famous mints, chewing gum, ice cream and chocolates in the United States. Every booth thrust samples of cones, bars and candies at us until we were sick at the sight of sweets. Craving air, we left carrying two bulging bags of samples. Next we had to find a place to camp.

At Wellesley College we had a remote family connection. Suzanne's Aunt Lil, with whom we lived in Wilmington, North Carolina, graduated from Wellesley in the class of 1919. Perhaps we would be able to camp there. The security police assigned us a space in a parking lot and gratefully we unloaded our carrier bags of gums, candies and chocolate bars on them. Wellesley campus became our base for four nights while we explored Boston, Cambridge, Lexington and Concord. We also made contact with members of the Boston Cymrodorion.

The Cymrodorion Society of Boston was founded in March 1892 and is known in its constitution as the Cymrodorion Welsh Associates of Boston and Vicinity. Boston is the home of Edward G. Hartmann, Professor Emeritus in the History Department of Suffolk University and the author of *Americans From Wales*. Professor Hartmann's book was first published in 1967 and was reprinted in 1978. It is a thorough, detailed catalog of Welsh immigration to the United States and has a wealth of information in its lists, footnotes and bibliographies alone. Professor Hartmann has also written histories of the Welsh Congregational Church in New York City, the Welsh Society of

Philadelphia and the Welsh of Wyoming Valley, Pennsylvania. In 1983 Professor Hartmann collaborated with John Nichols on an Atlas of Welsh Churches in America.

Harvard University Library has the only complete collection of *Y Drych* in the country. The University also has an extensive Welsh American collection of pamphlets, newsletters, magazines and other more ephemeral documents.

In more recent years Boston's Welsh connection was probably at its strongest when Meredydd Evans was an assistant professor there during the 1950s. Meredydd Evans lived in the United States for eight years, where he joined the Boston Cymrodorion and appeared on Boston radio singing traditional Welsh folk songs. A record of Welsh songs he made on the Folkways label in 1954 is still available. His American wife, Phyllis Kinney Evans, a graduate of Juilliard and an accomplished musician herself, is a Welsh language activist in Wales and was at the first Cwrs Cymraeg in 1977.

During the 1960s and early 1970s, attendance at the Boston Cymrodorion Society was erratic. Newcomers to the city, like Jean McKeown, a Welsh folk enthusiast from Denver, might take five years to discover that a Welsh Society in the city existed. Jean McKeown regularly visits folk festivals in Wales and she coached the Harvard Glee Club in the Welsh words to Llef.

Officers of the Society have included Earl Alban, Richard Jones, Eirug Davies, Ruth Houlton, Nancy Miller, Eleanor Hutchinson and Anne Roberts. Since 1979 the leading corps has consisted of such people as Dic and Lily Driver, John and Ann Parry, Frances and Alan Davison, Michele and Richard Griffiths, Mair and Richard Lustig, Beverly Rodda, Anne and Alun Jones, John and Dorothy Owen, Pat Johnson and Leslie Evans. The majority of these people were born in Wales and have devoted their time to improving the Society's programs. With the help of other Society members like John Reardon, Bob and Dianne Zwicker, Carolyn Probert, Daniel Griffiths, Ian Davison, Mathew Williams, Gladys Soule and Murray and Barbara Nicolson, they expanded the Cymrodorion's three annual events, the cymanfa, the Christmas party and the March 1st banquet into a calendar of much broader appeal.

The Boston cymanfa is held at such places as Neponset Community Church in Dorchester, the M.I.T. chapel and in Lynn. The Lynn cymanfa organized by Susan Anway and hosted by the Reverend Arvel Steece at the First Church of Christ has since become an annual event in its own right. Boston has a reliable and prominent conductor in Dr. Gwyn Walters, Professor of Divinity at Gordon Conwell Theological Seminary in South Hamilton, Massachusetts. Dr. Walters, originally from Llanelli in Wales, was pastor at the First Welsh Presbyterian Church in Wilkes-Barre before moving to South Hamilton. He has conducted all over North America and has led the Sunday service at many National Cymanfaoedd Canu. Mr. and Mrs. Gwyn Walters' children are also active in Welsh American life. Gwenfair Walters has studied in Aberystwyth and in 1985 Meirwyn Walters, while still an undergraduate at Harvard, was the President of WAY.

T. Gwyn Jones, of Colwyn Bay School, has also conducted the Boston cymanfa several times. While in Boston in 1976, Mr. Gwyn Jones gave a talk to the Harvard Celtic department on the National Eisteddfod and Welsh musical traditions.

Dic Driver, originally from Aberaeron, Wales, attended the Vermont Cwrs Cymraeg in 1977. Immediately afterwards he started Welsh classes in Boston. Anne Lewis Roberts, a graduate of Bangor University, taught the course. In 1979 Welsh language classes were conducted by Dr. Kenneth Nilson, a linguist and Celtic scholar. These Welsh classes attracted more people to the Society who then continued their studies at Cwrs Cymraeg and Welsh Heritage Week. In 1984 Cymrodorion members Beverly Rodda and Leslie Evans attended a Welsh course in Wales and the Cymrodorion co-sponsored Alice Doyle's trip to Cwrs Cymraeg y Cymoedd held in Wilkes-Barre. Boston Welsh language classes have been held at the home of Alun and Anne Jones and as well as a learner's class, there are Welsh conversation groups for beginners, advanced students and native speakers.

In 1978 the Boston Cymrodorion held its first noson lawen on the Saturday evening before the October cymanfa. Alan Davison, originally from Port Talbot, now a professor of chemistry at M.I.T., arranged to hold the noson lawen on the top floor of M.I.T.'s Eastgate Tower. John Parry of the Rhondda Valley was in charge of the program. A lively noson lawen has since become a feature of all Boston Welsh parties.

1978 saw the debut of Brethyn Cartref, a section of the Society that has since diversified into folk singing and dancing, male choral singing, plygain and instrumental music. The organization of Brethyn Cartref by Michele Griffiths has been an important development in the Society. Michele Griffiths was a student of Ray Handy at the Cardiff College of Drama. To everyone's surprise Ray Handy turned up at the 1978 noson lawen taking time out from his "Dylan Thomas Lived Here" American tour.

Beverly Rodda has been the main organizer of the Christmas Revels and St. David's Day entertainment since late 1983. She established the Brethyn Cartref ladies singing group and after taking up the harp in 1984 started accompanying the singing of Frances Davison.

Musicians of the Boston Cymrodorion, including Beverly Rodda, Dorothy Owen and Richard Lustig, have formed a regular ensemble playing at all Brethyn Cartref productions. Other musicians have included Jean McKeown, Lisa Luedtke and Alun Jones. Brethyn Cartref's greatest contribution has been to the annual Christmas party which has become the Boston Cymrodorion Welsh Revels.

We spent an evening with Richard and Mair Lustig at their home in Dedham. Mair is from Aberystwyth and she met Richard while he was studying and she was working in London. Mair became the Society's secretary and folk dance teacher and organized the making of Welsh costumes for Brethyn Cartref members. Beverly Rodda joined us. Beverly had just returned from Welsh Heritage Week and Cwrs Cymraeg and insisted that we speak in

Welsh. Limping through our learners' vocabulary, we tried valiantly to keep up with her.

The Boston Christmas Revels started in December 1980. The Revels feature a Mari Lwyd procession complete with decorated horse's head and responsive singing. Other traditions are passing the gwassael (giant punch bowl), singing plygain carols in the traditional style and folk dancing. While dining at the Christmas Revels, musicians in national costume play Welsh music. After dinner, entertainment features a concert including songs by members of the Boston Welsh Male Chorus dressed in colorful waistcoats and mufflers.

March 1st in Boston is celebrated with a banquet followed by a noson lawen including community singing and folk dancing. The banquet, which is catered by John and Ann Parry and Alun and Frances Davison, attempts as Welsh a menu as possible, featuring Caerphilly cheese, leek soup, faggots and peas, Welsh cakes and other traditional dishes. The banquet attracts over sixty people, and in recent years has been held at the Workshop Women's Club, (although in 1986 there was an unpredictable change of venue.) Every March 1st Dic Driver goes on Boston radio playing Welsh records. One year he was interviewed and played Welsh music on Boston Public Radio.

Regular meetings of the Boston Cymrodorion are held once a month at the Workshop Women's Club in Newton Highlands, at the home of Dianna and Paul Fahey or at the Unitarian Universalist Church in Arlington. Monthly programs have featured a twmpath (barn dance) called by Mair Lustig, a traditional Welsh cooking demonstration by Ann Parry and Frances Davison and dramatic readings of Welsh poets led by Dic Driver and Michele Griffiths.

Other meetings feature performances by some of the many visitors to Boston, among them Dawnswyr Tawerin, Penderyn, Dim Byd Eto and Ar Log. Boston is also one of the most popular destinations for rugby tourists from Wales. Massachussets rivals Florida and California as the state most visited by Welsh rugby teams.

In 1984 the officers of the Boston Cymrodorion were John Parry, President; Alun Jones, Vice-President; Mair Lustig, Secretary; John Owen, Treasurer; Pat Johnson, Social Chairperson; Leslie Evans and Richard Lustig, Publicity; Frances Davison, Librarian; Beverly Rodda, Music Director and Marjorie Owen, Auditor.

NEW HAMPSHIRE

On October 16, 1983 in Keene, the first cymanfa ganu for many years was held at St. James Episcopal Church. The Reverend Arvel Steece, minister of the church organized the cymanfa which was conducted by Gwyn Walters with Jean Travaglini, organist.

Other stirrings of Welsh interest in New Hampshire have been made by Arthur Ketchen of the Institute of Celtic Studies East. In 1982 Arthur

Ketchen broadened the scope of Maine and New Hampshire Celtic festivals by advertising for Welsh and Breton participants. March 1984 was declared Celtic Heritage month and drew attention to Scots, Irish and Welsh contributions to the history of the state.

Before we left, Mair gave us samples of the Boston Cymrodorion newsletters, St. David's menus and cymanfa programs. We filed them away in the roof box of our van. The plastic bags we kept our Welsh American material in were now bursting, but we were glad to be given more. Having seen the enthusiasm of so many Welsh societies, we were starting to think about forming a society ourselves when we returned to Atlanta.

From Boston we drove north via the beaches of New Hampshire to the rocky coves of Maine. We had reserved a campground near Camden and planned to take a week's vacation from the rigors of spending one year on the road.

The whole fourteen months we were traveling we didn't stay in a motel once. Nor did we stop at any of the aurora of fast food chains glittering beside the interstates. In fact, we rarely traveled on the interstate. We had eaten out at the four corners of our route, in New Orleans, Tijuana, Vancouver and Quebec and at a few selected places in between. The van, with its closets, galley and "bedroom", was as compact as a small yacht, and being self-contained we were able to camp where we liked. Our daily schedule, diet and lifestyle had been simplified and our material needs were very few. Away from the rush of weekenders we were experts at finding basic campgrounds. While resting, we spent time exercising, writing letters or mending and cleaning our equipment.

In Rockport, Maine, however, we had actually reserved a space at a commercial, private campground with a laundromat, electric hook-ups, running water, vending machines and expensive cords of firewood. We drove to restaurants and spent whole days doing nothing more useful than shopping and going to the theater at night. A week of stationary indulgence was a welcome break from constantly moving and meeting people.

MAINE

While in Portland, Maine we visited Celtic Designs, an import shop. Celtic Designs has a predominantly Irish and Scottish inventory but does have a fairly good Welsh selection. Anita O'Donnell, the owner, told us that she goes to Britain every other year and makes her contacts at government organized craft fairs over there.

Northport, Maine is the summer home of Welsh American philanthropist, John K. Evans. Mr. Evans emigrated from Wales at the age of seventeen and worked as a waiter in New York City. He later joined Shell Oil, working his way up the corporate ladder until he retired in 1961. He has served as president of the Welsh-American Society of Washington, D.C. and was the first president of the National Welsh American Foundation. John Evans has been a major benefactor of the National Welsh American Foundation which would probably not have been created without his initial and considerable financial support. As President of the Welsh-American Society of Washington, D.C., Mr. Evans helped initiate the Washington Schools Eisteddfod. The Eisteddfod takes the form of a competition between high school choirs who sing a selection of their own and a set piece in Welsh.

In 1983 John K. Evans created the Belfast (Maine) Choral Eisteddfod. The Robert Coller Chorale hosts the Eisteddfod which is held at Belfast High School. John Evans sponsored the first Eisteddfod in 1983; in 1984 it was co-funded by him and the Maine State Commission on the Arts and Humanities. The competitive portion is limited to chorales of sixteen people or less which are judged by a panel of musicians and teachers from Maine schools and colleges. In 1983 and 1984 the Eisteddfod concluded with a party and prize giving at "Cariad", the name of John K. Evans' Northport estate.

TEMENOS

We drove from Rockport, Maine to Shutesbury, Massachusetts in a day—259.3 miles—a long way by our standards. We planned to spend a few days at Temenos, a "primitive woodland retreat", with friends who had once lived and worked at Ittoen, the independent religious community in Japan. We timed our departure from Temenos to arrive in Wilkes-Barre, Pennsylvania in time for the 1983 National Cymanfa Ganu.

Temenos, which is Greek for the enclosure around a temple, is located on top of a mountain surrounded by state forest land. For a while during the 19th century the land where Temenos now stands was a spa attracting people from as far away as Boston and New York. Today, small but persistent mineral springs still seep up through the rocks while the biggest spring feeds an iodine colored bathing pool.

Temenos has no telephone, running water or electricity. We walked two miles through the forest to the lodge, where we were welcomed by Joe and Teresina Havens. Teresina had lived in Ittoen and Ittoen members, after attending The World Conference of Religions in Boston in 1979, had stayed and worked at Temenos. Joe and Teresina are deeply involved in the American alternative community network and Temenos serves as a center for all kinds of groups from Zen Buddhists, forest rangers and country dancers, to pacifists involved in the Nuclear Free Zone campaign.

Inaccessible through much of the winter, Temenos' summer programs have titles like "Dancing to Save the Planet", "Shambala Warriorship", "Forest Learning" and "Strategizing for the Peace and Justice Movement".

Temenos is a crossroads of people attempting radically different approaches to the problems of society today. While there we met Arna Blum, co-founder of the New Era Center in England. We met the secretary of the Hartford anti-cruise missile campaign, a woman who had just returned from the Seneca Women's Peace Camp and Kent Larabi who had just walked from Glasgow to

Leningrad as part of a world-wide walk-for-peace campaign.

Kent told us that while he was in Britain in 1982 all eight of the county councils in Wales had declared themselves nuclear free. This is part of a world-wide effort to make specific areas free of nuclear materials. In America it is an active campaign with a growing number of small towns joining the nuclear-free-zone register.

Wales, too, has an active anti-nuclear movement called CND Cymru. The declaration by the eight Welsh county councils, however, is only a statement of intent which does not reflect reality on the ground. As well as having nuclear power stations at Wylfa and Trawsfynydd, Wales has the largest weapons dump in Europe at Caerwent. There are major British and American bases on Welsh soil and the Royal Ordnance Factory in Llanishen, Cardiff manufactures components for nuclear bombs.

Accommodations at Temenos were distributed through an assortment of tents and cabins. The central lodge where we met and ate was not a sleeping place. The day began with a swim in the Temenos mineral pond. Breakfast was combined with a discussion of dreams. With the number of resident psychologists, dream analysis contributed to a lively and provocative breakfast hour. Work was assigned until lunch and all Temenos visitors were expected to wield a hammer, gather wood, empty the latrines, dig post holes and generally contribute to the serious maintenance of the place. We, like every one else, took our turn to cook, using rain water to boil vegetables, then straining that water to wash the dishes.

Tea at 4 p.m. was followed by meditation and a period of exercise. With eyes closed we moved in response to music, played on a battery operated stereo. This afternoon matinee of "authentic movement" induced feelings of self-discovery that we afterwards tried to articulate in a short discussion.

Teresina often asked for a Welsh blessing at meals or a Welsh prayer at night. I usually complied with a recitation of prayers by Elfed that I'd learned as a child. At morning worship we sang Aberystwyth, Cwm Rhondda and Ton y Botel.

Temenos was an island of remarkable sanity. As stewards of Temenos, Joe and Teresina Havens are frequently consulted by visitors from pacifist and humanitarian groups. The atmosphere at Temenos was trusting and joyful. For every hour of intellectual debate there were two of work, meditation, hymn singing and laughter. When we walked back down the rocky trail we felt deeply refreshed, as though the waters we'd been drinking from had quenched more than our physical thirst.

22

The National

The 52nd National Cymanfa Ganu held in Wilkes-Barre on September 2, 3 and 4, 1983, became the natural conclusion to our trip. The few weeks that followed were a postscript to this climax of our Welsh American tour.

The Sheraton-Crossgates Hotel in Wilkes-Barre Square was the National Cymanfa headquarters. As we drove through Wilkes-Barre, signs above stores and in front of churches welcomed cymanfa-goers. We parked our van in the Sheraton's three-story parking lot and camped there while attending every event we could over the three-day weekend.

We'd seen the welcoming signs, we'd received our WNGGA information packet, but we still couldn't imagine a Welsh festival in the United States. When we stepped into the Sheraton-Crossgates lobby, we realized we had underestimated the dedication of North American Welsh leaders. Women in Welsh costume were there to welcome us. The lobby was crowded with people, decorated with flags and lined with information tables. A group of men were pushing an upright piano through the crowd. They set it up near the hotel registration desk and gathered around to sing hymns. To one side of the lobby was the Welsh Market Place. This was a large room used by import stores like Siani Flewog, Anne Habermehl Imports, Celtic Photos and Crafts and the Celtic Pavilion, among many others. There were fourteen stands in all, including ladies from Wilkes-Barre First Welsh Presbyterian Church selling handmade Welsh dolls. *WAY*, *Ninnau*, and *Y Drych* also had a table each. At the entrance to the Welsh Market Place was a desk where we registered to attend the cymanfa and picked up our convention-style lapel tags.

The National Cymanfa Ganu was on. After two years of planning, Wilkes-Barre was about to host one of the best attended Nationals in the WNGGA's fifty-five year history. Final estimates of attendance varied from as low as 3,000 to over 3,500 people.

The first familiar faces we saw belonged to Alun and Jane Hughes. Jane's Siani Flewog stock was selling fast. Within ten minutes we saw Earl Williams from Connecticut, Cerwyn Davies from Toronto, Pat Viets from Wisconsin and John Nichols from California. Morris and LaVelva Stealey had driven 800 miles from Wales, Wisconsin. Wilkes-Barre was where Morris was born. He grew up speaking Welsh and the theme of the weekend was the Homecoming Cymanfa Ganu. No one remained a stranger long. Handshakes were exchanged as quickly as glances, whether riding on the shuttle bus between cymanfa venues or sitting quietly at the bilingual service. The singing itself was still two days away. Meanwhile, the agenda was filled with meetings and concerts and the opportunity for us to meet Canadian and American Welsh leaders for ourselves.

The *Ninnau* stand was in the forefront of a central row of tables in the Welsh Market Place. We introduced ourselves to Olga and Arturo Roberts who were distributing copies of their paper as liberally as seeds. *Y Drych*'s table was right alongside and we stopped to help Pat Viets give her paper away as fast as it would go.

The opening banquet of the cymanfa was held at the Genetti Motor Inn, about a 300 yard walk from the Sheraton. The Genetti was the main overspill hotel for the weekend and the banquet was followed by a program of singing, a dramatic monolog based on The Corn is Green by Nancy Jones Sanders and an interlude of Welsh jokes by Dr. Islyn Thomas. Dr. Thomas' protagonist was a character named Dai who was everything from a soldier in arms to a Cardigan hill farmer whose hens wouldn't lay. The main speaker was Dr. Robert A. Fowkes. Dr. Fowkes' theme, "Staying Alive" was an antidote to the impression we were beginning to get that the National Gymanfa was a festival attended only by the very old.

The banquet ended with Alun Guy conducting Hen Wlad Fy Nhadau. Mr. Guy introduced us then to the shuddering left hook he delivered on Sunday to demand total vocal commitment.

It had been a long day. Alun Hughes gave us his parking coupon from the Sheraton to get endorsed—our equivalent of a room key. A band of stalwarts started singing around the piano. They would be there until midnight, led by a succession of conductors that included Morris Wrench, Olwen Welk and Ann Davies Thomas.

Very early on the Saturday morning of the National Cymanfa, we visited the restrooms in the hotel lobby and carried back a bowl of cold water for Amiga. The *Ninnau* breakfast began at 7:30, but first we stretched our legs and took Amiga for an early morning walk along the Susquehanna River.

There were about forty people at the *Ninnau* breakfast. Everyone there was connected with the paper one way or another. Jack O. Morgans, contributing editor; Anne Habermehl, editorial assistant; the Reverend John R. Owen, Welsh language editor among many others. We sat with contributors Lee and Nora Morgan and Morris and LaVelva Stealey.

Arturo Roberts opened the meeting by showing us the plaque he'd received the night before. He used this to demonstrate *Ninnau*'s seriousness, portraying *Ninnau* as an institution of the Welsh American establishment. Esther Elias walked in. Oblivious to what was going on she shook the hands of friends she recognized. When Esther sat down, Suzanne brought her coffee and a pastry. I saw Esther later in the Genetti lobby and I asked her opinion of the *Ninnau* meeting. She said she was sorry but she hadn't been able to go. Esther thought she had been served a normal breakfast in the Sheraton cafeteria—being hard of hearing, she hadn't heard a word that any of us had said.

At 9 a.m., the meeting showed no sign of coming to an end. Suzanne stayed while I found a seat in a much larger room next door in time to attend the annual general meeting of the Welsh National Gymanfa Ganu Association of Canada and the United States.

During the 1950's and 1960's, the annual general meeting was very poorly attended. Committee members and trustees almost outnumbered WNGGA delegates. At Wilkes-Barre, however, about 200 WNGGA members were present, and latecomers had to crowd around the door.

After an introduction from WNGGA President Norman Williams, the committee moved through its series of reports. Emmaline Davies read last year's minutes and Gwenfyl Jones brought us up to date on the work of the scholarship committee and the WNGGA's projected folk song book. Dorothy Feeley made the best speech of the morning. Her report on the Welsh Retirement Home and the Women's Welsh Clubs of America left us with a clear idea of what the Women's Federation was all about. The atmosphere at this meeting was formal and concentrated, quite different from the rest of the Cymanfa. During breaks, people studied the agenda and were involved in small conferences among themselves.

Question time was stalled in silence until Douglas C. Jones from Toronto, president of the WNGGA from 1960 to 1962 asked why a transfer of funds had been made from the WNGGA's general fund to the Scholarship Endowment Fund without a constitutional amendment. He also asked why the Endowment Fund had taken over twenty years to issue its first scholarship. The unexpected authority of this question seized the attention of the meeting. Other questions followed. Why had the cymanfa hired a conductor from Wales when there were competent directors in North America? Why weren't there more musicians from Wales on National Cymanfaoedd Canu programs? When was the folk song book going to appear? Shouldn't an annual report be distributed to life members?

Question time was followed by the election of new trustees—two for the eastern United States and two for Canada. Counting the votes created an unscheduled lull in the agenda. This was filled by announcements of approaching regional cymanfaoedd canu. President Norman Williams had to call the meeting to order when the clamor to announce their own cymanfa brought a quarter of the delegates to their feet. The contest was easily resolved by a suggestion that we sing some hymns. That, after all, was the reason we were there.

The introduction of new trustees brought the meeting to an end. We sang Hen Wlad Fy Nhadau for the sixth in what would become at least a dozen times. The main criticisms of the WNGGA appeared to be that sponsoring committees could make the weekend into more of a Welsh festival, a showcase of the Welsh national heritage with the cymanfa as its climax. Watchdogs also felt that each year's minutes should be distributed to voting members.

At noon the Welsh flag was raised in Wilkes-Barre Square. Alun Guy and Norman Williams were made honorary citizens of Wilkes-Barre and entertainment was provided by the Irem Chanters, The St. David's Male Chorus of Scranton and the Youth Choir of the First Welsh Presbyterian Church. Two young girls, Karen Pugh and Amy Lynn Jones sang Hen Wlad Fy Nhadau followed by a large crowd singing the Welsh national anthem together.

Every event at the Wilkes-Barre National was well attended. The WAY luncheon at 12:30 on Saturday afternoon was packed to capacity. We were lucky to get seats. We never could buy a ticket to the Saturday evening concert. At the WAY luncheon, we sat beside Olga and Arturo Roberts and heard President of WAY, Olga and Arturo's daughter, Mair Roberts, present WAY's annual report. Seventeen year old Daryl Williams provided entertainment at the luncheon playing Welsh music on the violin accompanied by his mother on the piano.

Following lunch, we took Amiga for a walk along the river. Afterwards, Suzanne went to Awr y Plant while I went to the WAY meeting held in a room on the hotel's second floor. The first forty-five minutes of the WAY meeting were spent eating cake and potato chips and guzzling cans of Sprite and Coke.

Finally, Meirwyn Walters seeing that something ought to be done, set some chairs in a circle and and suggested we have a question and answer session. Out of over three thousand people at the cymanfa, there were eleven of us at the WAY meeting—Alun Coss, Rod Owen, Mair Roberts, Daryl Williams, Cynthia Jones, Catherine Jones, Megan and John Lloyd, Gwenfair and Meirwyn Walters and myself. Rod, Mair, Megan, Cynthia, Gwenfair and Meirwyn had all been officers of WAY. The pattern appeared to be that involvement in the organization was so discouraging, the majority of past officers were never heard from again.

Apart from their own involvement, no one knew the history of WAY as a whole. Its formation by Gwynn Parri in Milwaukee in 1970 was vaguely recalled, but no one mentioned that since 1978 WAY has been able to vote at WNGGA board meetings. The WAY leadership felt mainly frustration that despite their own support for the National Cymanfa they were still the only young people there. Young people were such an exception, they felt reluctant to be more demonstrative.

Our first resolution was that when we left the meeting, we would confront every person under thirty and tell them what WAY was trying to do. Our second, was to make a plan for the year ahead. Since one of the biggest WAY complaints was that no one kept in touch, we decided at least to write to one another. We were determined to make next year at Portland an example of what WAY could do when it tried. As it turned out, 1984 was a year of genuine progress for WAY. Membership increased and Kevin Bowers made the Portland WAY luncheon into a highlight of the cymanfa weekend.

Challenged to do some work myself, I became *WAY*'s editor. The *WAY* newsletter only appears three times a year and I accepted the position readily. Now I was involved. I took WAY very seriously and ranked its efforts alongside those of Cymdeithas Madog and the National Welsh American

Foundation. If those groups were infinitely better organized, at least WAY had its role to play. Unless the annual National Cymanfa was determined to fossilize, WAY was committed to making the youth contribution as vigorous and significant as possible.

Our meeting ended with a startling burst of applause. Dr. Douglas Jones had come into the back of the room and listened to our debate. He gave us a quick survey of who we could rely on in the WNGGA Committee. In September 1984, this closer contact was confirmed when president Norman Williams moved that a senior trustee be appointed permanent WAY liaison officer.

Now we'd earned our cake and Coke. But we'd missed every minute of Awr y Plant, the one slot of the cymanfa devoted exclusively to younger people. For the rest of the day, we interviewed every younger person we could find. Why were they there? Would they come again? Had they heard of WAY? We more than doubled WAY's rate of enrollment.

An overdose of junk food prevented me from eating any dinner. Suzanne and I left the Sheraton and ate an early evening meal at the Genetti with Pat and John Viets of *Y Drych*. We had a lot to talk about. The cymanfa was fascinating and our meal was a relaxing interlude where we were able to talk the whole thing over and get it in perspective.

By late Saturday afternoon, many new booths had been set up. The Sheraton Lobby was now constantly crowded and more information on the contemporary Welsh American scene had become available. Alun John, conductor of the forthcoming Côr Meibion De Cymru tour, sat autographing records. Maldwyn Pate staffed the Cymdeithas Madog stand which had information on where to learn Welsh practically anywhere in the world. Christine Whittaker was showing a video on the extremely successful choral eisteddfod in Washington, D.C.. Business in the market place was at a peak. By late evening things were a little quieter. The majority of cymanfa-goers were at the grand concert in Irem Temple Mosque. After eating a second dinner with Alun and Jane Hughes, I went to the concert hall to attend the te bach afterwards.

Over the whole weekend, temperatures remained in the upper 80's. The Mosque had no air conditioning. At the entrance to the theater stood a group of men in shirtsleeves waiting for the concert to end. Douglas Jones introduced me to Islyn Thomas who told me how important he too felt WAY was. It was obvious that both men were monitoring the festival and cared deeply about it. It was improving every year they said. Awr y Plant and the Welsh Market Place had totally transformed the daytime atmosphere of the Saturday.

During the crowded te bach, impromptu singing broke out in several parts of the room. About twenty people gathered around a piano and led by Morris Wrench, the singing lasted until midnight. During these spontaneous "rehearsals", the uninhibited joy of men and women singing together gave the festival its main character of harmony and happiness. The Sheraton

Crossgates bar was the quietest place of the weekend. A group of three or more people didn't have time to sit and drink. When someone pulled out a hymn book, a contest would start over which hymn to sing.

The te bach singers were still going strong when I joined a steady crocodile of people returning to the hotel. It was hot. Our airless "room" in the Sheraton parking lot was stifling and Amiga was thoroughly fed up with having to wait for us hours at a time.

SUNDAY

On Sunday morning, the Welsh Market Place was open but the registration desk had been moved to the cymanfa site—the 109th Field Artillery Armory, about a mile away from the hotel. People who had driven to the cymanfa only for the day were in the Market Place early trying to find a souvenir, record, badge or book that hadn't already been sold.

We took Amiga for a walk before attending the bilingual church service at Irem Temple Mosque. The service was memorable for Jack Meadow's announcement of his retirement. He was ill, he had been unable to stand at the WNGGA meeting and he was unable to stand at the Mosque. Nelson Llewellyn became secretary of the WNGGA and Jack Meadows died a year later in August 1984.

Following the bilingual service, we had until 2:30 before the first singing session of the National Cymanfa Ganu. We ate lunch in the van, then I had a meeting with Megan Lloyd, the previous editor of *WAY*. Megan gave me a cardboard box of letterpress, past *WAY* issues, graph paper and glue. She warned me not to expect too much from the job, least of all contributions. By the end of 1984, however, *WAY* had been reviewed in several Celtic newsletters, there had been a *WAY* column in almost every issue of *Ninnau* and *Y Drych* and contact had been made with the Urdd in Wales. The WAY membership had grown, reader participation was up from zero to two or three letters a month, and Claire Tallman, possibly the best contributor and editor that *WAY* has ever had, started sending in her camera-ready articles and art work. In December 1984, WAY contributed to a United Nations International Youth exchange between Boston and Crumlin, Wales. One other important development was a projected young people's page in *Y Drych* giving WAY regular monthly space.

By 1 p.m. on Sunday, there was very little left in the Market Place. Anne Habermehl was loading her harp into her car. The banners had been taken down from the walls. Partly to see how far it was and partly to see the strangely named building where the cymanfa ganu would be held, Amiga and I took a walk to the Field Artillery Armory.

The Armory was a colossal square hangar normally devoted to military drills. The inside had been filled with rows of over 3,000 chairs on the main floor and more on a wide balcony above. The steel brick building was hardly ideal, but Wilkes-Barre organizers were now quoting Alun Guy who, when he saw the Armory, resolved to convert it "into a cathedral".

At the start of the afternoon session, Alun Guy asked us to ignore the bricks and girders and to concentrate on singing the hymns. A murmur of agreement passed through the congregation.

There was no general eagerness to divide into soprano, alto, tenor and bass parts. Men sat in the front center rows, sopranos to the right and altos to the left. This approximate division achieved the desired effect. A puzzled reluctance to separate and sit away from their spouse tugged at the majority of people who preferred to sit together as they would in church.

I found myself between Lee Morgan and Morris Stealey. On the other side of Lee were three brothers from North Wales attending the cymanfa while visiting their sister in Ottawa. Suzanne was hidden among the altos sitting near Olwen Welk and LaVelva Stealey.

Opening with Rachie and closing with Cwm Rhondda, we sang sixteen hymns in the afternoon. We sang the famous hymns with confidence and ease, but an experimental attempt at the lesser known Wilkes-Barre by Daniel Protheroe was less successful. Alun Guy led us through the gears, conducting us in unison, in parts, a verse by men, a verse by women and repeating the chorus with greater and greater force.

Alun Guy conducted dramatically but also with restraint, he did not cajole us or throw his baton on the floor. During powerful moments, his face beamed in a profound and open smile. It wasn't long before his willing choir of voices were on their feet singing joyfully to the uttermost of their ability. Evan Gwyndaf Roberts, the only other figure on the stage, accompanied every hymn with all the keyboard fullness that it was possible to give.

Morris Stealey is well known for his powerful tenor voice. How he could hear my puny contribution above his own was a mystery to me. Was I so much out of key? At the end of one hymn, during the glow of appreciative silence when we all sat down with a murmur and a sigh, he wheeled on me and cried, "You are not singing the tenor part!" I made a greater, red-faced effort to follow the correct line following his lofty and loud rebuke.

There were fewer people at the 7 p.m. evening session than in the afternoon. We found the same seats and were close acquaintances of those around us. The Armory's stark, oblong shape had been forgotten, replaced by the irregular excitement of conversation. This was the final session, with this the cymanfa would be over until Labor Day weekend of next year. Some people had started their journey home, and others had already arranged to meet in Portland in 1984.

Donna Pierce was the soloist for the evening as she had been in the afternoon. Evan Gwyndaf Roberts was the organist. The Reverend Bill Lewis opened the session thanking all those who came on behalf of the Wilkes-Barre Committee. Gwenfyl Jones announced next year's cymanfa and the Reverend Edmund John led a prayer of thanks for the enduring inspiration of the National Cymanfa to all Welsh people in North America.

Wearing a white dinner jacket and red boutonnière, Alun Guy launched the cymanfa ganu into the triumphant choruses of Diadem. Followed by Blaenwern and Ton y Botel, the evening session quickly reached a peak of devout congregational singing.

Singing the great hymns in one national assembly has provided the enduring substance of the North American Welsh community. Whether they are born in Wales or Wilkes-Barre, whether they are Welsh speaking from Ontario or third generation from Nebraska, the National Cymanfa remains their festival. The very passion of the National Cymanfa sometimes startles visitors from Wales.

The final hymn was Sanctus. Anyone who has been to a large cymanfa when unimpeded choral hwyl is bursting from 3,000 hearts and voices, can easily imagine the final echoing clarity of "sanctaidd, sanctaidd, sanctaidd Ior".

Following Hen Wlad Fy Nhadau and a final prayer by the Reverend Edmund John a very gentle and moving ceremony occurred. Everyone joined hands and sang, "God Be With You Till We Meet Again". Then the cymanfa split up into husbands searching for wives, friends looking for friends, hindered by meeting other relatives and friends with the same glowing expression in their eyes. The faces of the people following the National Cymanfa were a radiant expression of joy. There is no doubt that without the profundity of shared experience provided by the National Cymanfa Ganu, the Welsh community in North America would be in serious danger of withering away. It is such a great part of the North American Welsh identity it warrants the importance people attach to it.

The ladies of Wilkes-Barre hosted a grand te bach following the evening session. We had our choice of tea, iced tea, coffee or lemonade with Welsh cakes in abundance. People lingered for hours in the reception rooms, returning slowly on the shuttle bus to Wilkes-Barre Square. We decided to walk back and met Dafydd and Elinor Hughes trying to help a married couple return to their hotel. I don't know how the couple got from the hotel to the Armory, but getting back through the crowd had become a problem. They were both confined to wheelchairs and in the crush found it impossible to board the bus. Dafydd, Elinor, Suzanne and I pushed them back. It was late at night and dark. We had to walk and run over a mile along the road as the sidewalk had too many curbs and obstacles.

At the Sheraton, the piano in the lobby was already being played. As if they hadn't had enough, singers were being led by Ann Davies Thomas and Olwen Welk. Alun Guy was there autographing hymn books. This final gathering was so carefree and informal we brought Amiga in to see how we'd been spending the last three days. That was how people later remembered us. We were the couple who had come to the cymanfa with their dog.

Côr Meibion De Cymru at Niagara Falls, November 1983

Mike Conley, The Standard, St. Catharines, Canada

Dic Jones, Welsh language teacher in
Seattle, Washington

Old Man's Creek Welsh Church, Iowa

Hywel Thomas, organizer of the
Côr Meibion De Cymru tour, 1983

Evan Gwyndaf Roberts, Organist, Utica, New York

Welsh Exhibit, Osterhouse Free Library, February 1982

Flag raising at Luzerne County Courthouse, March 1, 1983

Members of the St. David's Society of Wyoming Valley Inc., November 1984

120th Anniversary, First Welsh Presbyterian Church, Wilkes-Barre, October 1985

WELSH EVENTS IN THE WYOMING VALLEY, PENNSYLVANIA

Ladies from St. David's Welsh Society, Edmonton, Alberta

The Vancouver Cambrian Circle Singers in Cardiff, July 1983

1983 National Cymanfa Ganu Planning Committee, Wilkes-Barre,
Pennsylvania

1981 National Cymanfa Ganu Planning Committee, Utica, New York

Helen F. Richards, Chicago, Illinois

Anne and David Habermehl,
Marion, New York

Earl T. Williams Jr., Connecticut

Joan Phelps, Binghamton, New York

Daisy Heaton, Toronto, Ontario

Margot McKinney Bouchard,
Poultney, Vermont

Suzanne and David Greenslade promoting St. David's Day in Atlanta, Georgia,
February 1984

23

New Jersey & Delaware;
Maryland & Washington, D.C.

I wrote my first issue of *WAY* magazine at Promised Land State Park, half-way between Wilkes-Barre and the New Jersey state line. Here was an opportunity to put into practice some of the ideas we'd been developing during our tour. Leaders of Welsh Societies from Oregon to Ontario had been giving us their views. WAY was a small, undeveloped organization but why shouldn't it try its hardest to fulfill its self-appointed role? Instead of waiting for others to rejuvenate the National Cymanfa, WAY could take the initiative with a youthful magazine.

We had driven west from Wilkes-Barre on our way to Basking Ridge, New Jersey. After giving Olga and Arturo Roberts time to recover, we arrived at their home on September 6, 1983, our 377th day of traveling. They hadn't had much time to rest, however. Olga and Arturo left the cymanfa between the afternoon and evening sessions on Sunday. On Monday evening their guests had been Wilfred Greenway and Mr. and Mrs. Alun Guy at a cookout barbeque.

The Roberts's home was a blend of Wales, America and their native Patagonia. It was a large modern house within commuting distance of New York. Inside, a goucho lariat and guitar sat on the hearth while scenic prints of Wales hung on the walls. Their dog, Castan (Welsh for chestnut), understood her commands in all of the family's three languages: Welsh, English and Spanish.

We met Olga and Arturo's three children, Rees, Mair and Arthur. Mair had enjoyed the cymanfa and was enthusiastic about the part WAY had to play. Rees and Arthur were less keen and had stayed away they said because of the National Cymanfa's "old foginess". Arthur had lived five months in Bala, Wales, and bore no prejudice against Welsh American work. In 1968, Arturo Roberts bought the home of his great-grandfather, M. D. Jones, organizer of the Patagonia colony. While living in a bed-and-breakfast in Bala, Arthur had renovated the house which Arturo had hoped to make into a Welsh American museum. The plan is still being developed, however, and the house is currently leased to a family from Wolverhampton.

Olga was a fabulous cook and when Arturo came home from work at night, we sat down to a splendid meal starting with wine and light hors d'oeuvres and ending with espresso and cookies. Olga cooked with true Argentinian flair and meal times were a long and lingering family occasion.

Arturo was obviously proud of the growth and success of *Ninnau*, a growth cultivated by his administrative and delegational skills. The *Ninnau* office occupied most of the basement of their large house. It was a model of neatness and organization. A small reference library stood at the back and dozens of back issues of *Ninnau* were stacked on wide shelves along one side of the room. Arturo gave me a copy of every issue of *Ninnau* from November 1975, until March 1982, when Suzanne and I discovered it. In the center of the room were columns of file cabinets. Across the front wall was a large desk with typewriters, paste-up boards and the daily tide of incoming mail. On another wall was a large map of North America with colored pins showing the level of circulation and location of *Ninnau* correspondents. It was an impressive operation. Arturo leaves the house at 7 a.m. and gets home at 7 at night. He has a helper with the paper and Olga does a lot of tedious filing, but the majority of work Arturo does himself at night and on weekends.

As publisher and executive editor of *Ninnau*, Arturo Roberts has generated dozens of fruitful ideas in the North American Welsh community. Apart from his specific front page support of new Welsh societies in Georgia, Colorado, Ontario, Connecticut, New Mexico and West Virginia, he also sends the Welsh societies hundreds of promotional copies of *Ninnau*. As guest speaker, he has traveled as far as Ohio, Oklahoma, Pennsylvania and New York. Ideas he has helped develop have led to Welsh Heritage Week, *Ninnau Dragon Friends*, the *Ninnau Talent Agency*, the Côr Meibion De Cymru tour, the (ill-fated) Council of 200 and the more recent Welsh Language Brigade. He has been president of Cymdeithas Madog and a director of the St. David's Society of the State of New York. In May 1984, he became president-elect of the National Welsh American Foundation and in June 1984, was made a vice-president of the London Cymmrodorion.

☆

There are two Welsh societies in New Jersey. Their annual St. David's banquets attract people from New York City and eastern Pennsylvania.

The Welsh Club of Monmouth and Ocean Counties

The Welsh Club of Monmouth and Ocean Counties was started in 1972. The Club has around 100 members and its main annual event is its March 1st covered dish supper. Around eighty people usually attend the supper which is informal and features soloists and community singing. Leaders of the Society have been Tom Bevan, Marilyn Guest, Janet Jones, Tom Kennedy and Barbara Roberts. Marjorie Molleneur has played harp at the supper and soloists have been Fred Guest, Hugh Jones and Bob Jones. Mrs. Vivien Billington of Tŷ Gwyn Imports, Huntington, New York, has provided a Welsh sales boutique at the annual supper. The Society is based in the Long Branch area of New Jersey, and in July 1980, initiated an annual picnic at the home of Mr. and Mrs. Arthur Berry of West Long Branch.

The Welsh Society of Central New Jersey

The Welsh Society of Central New Jersey was founded in 1968. The Society's annual March banquet provides an inexpensive alternative to the formal dinner of the St. David's Society in New York City. The Society's activities are based in the Scotch Plains area with the occasional trip for a picnic at Basking Ridge.

A March banquet is the main annual event, with Welsh imports on sale provided in the past by Tŷ Gwyn Imports, Sian Williams and Margaret Fremont. Over 150 people regularly attend the banquet which features a distinguished guest speaker and good quality entertainment. The Philadelphia Boys Choir led by Carlton Jones Lake sang here in March 1983. Leaders of the Society have been Dr. Phillip Davies, Clem Owens, Edna Reese, Irma Ricka, Walter Jones, Tom Williams, Glyndwr Jones, Jean Haddock, Jenny DuMond, Elizabeth Ijams, Ruth Endicott and Charlotte Martin. In 1984, Sian Williams was the President of the Society; John Ried was Vice-President; Olwen Hollock, Secretary; William Reese, Treasurer and Jenny DuMond, Membership Secretary.

On November 4, 1984, the Welsh Society of Central New Jersey held its first cymanfa ganu. The cymanfa was held at Willow Grove Presbyterian Church, Scotch Plains, and was conducted by the Reverend Cyril Jenkins of Rutgers Presbyterian in New York City. The organist was Karen Miller and the pianist, Fran Pughe. John Pughe organized the cymanfa which was well-attended and very successful. Mike Large, a regular soloist at March banquets, sang at the cymanfa. Other Society soloists have been Marilyn Latzo, Andrea Mathews, Robert Bodycombe, Roberta Keller and "The Singers" of Basking Ridge.

Since 1982, the Welsh Society of Central New Jersey has presented its annual David W. Price Award. David Price was a leader of the Society who died of a heart attack during the 1981 St. David's Day celebration. The first award was made to his widow in 1982. In 1983, certificates were given to Tom Williams, Roland Davies and Thomas Rees who were all instrumental in forming the Society. In 1985, at a March banquet attended by over 100 people, the David W. Price Award was given to Arturo Roberts. This was one of the best managed banquets in the Society's history. Sian Williams designed a twenty-eight page booklet of Welsh history and folk songs which was given to each guest. Mike Large sang and community singing followed. Among the Society's many visitors from Pennsylvania, John L. Hyer has led the singing at many New Jersey celebrations. At the end of an extremely successful year, the December 1984 meeting of the Welsh Society of Central New Jersey featured a well attended public program of carol singing.

DELAWARE

The Welsh Society of Delaware was organized on St. David's Day 1977. The Society was founded by Peter Williams of Flint, Clwyd, head of the English Department of Delaware Technical and Community College, Wilmington. A graduate of the University College of Swansea, Wales, Peter Williams obtained his M.A. and his Ph.D. at the University of Delaware.

Thirty-three people attended the first St. David's dinner at the Ramada Inn, New Castle. A business meeting following concluding with community singing and the formation of a Welsh language class. At a second meeting towards the end of March 1977, Peter Williams was elected President; Secretary, Agnes Holmes; Treasurer, Susan Peden and Lois Sanderson provided a Welsh te bach.

Fifty people attended the Society's third meeting in June, 1977. The guest speaker was John Albert Evans then visiting Anne Cowie prior to the Vermont Cwrs Cymraeg. This meeting was very influential, expanding the membership and making language classes central to the success of the Society. The Society's first Christmas Party in December 1977, was well attended and concluded with Peter Williams conducting Hen Wlad Fy Nhadau.

The evolution of the Welsh Society of Delaware is typical of many recent Welsh American groups. In the pages of *Ninnau* and *Y Drych*, Peter Williams has described his own discoveries of being Welsh. He grew up speaking English in North Wales and while at university majored in English literature. His letters and articles in the Welsh American papers, however, have been among the most spirited defenses of Plaid Cymru, the Welsh language and the Welsh language educational campaign that either paper has printed.

As president of the Welsh Society, Peter Williams has had to teach Welsh lessons, organize St. David's dinners, find and distribute Welsh recipes and even direct the hymn singing at cymanfaoedd canu. His conscientious leadership has introduced other officers and members of the Society to a more contemporary view of Wales. He has also organized excursions to Welsh events in Delta, Philadelphia, Bel Air and Baltimore. In 1980, the Welsh Society of Delaware introduced Welsh language readings to the March 1st Episcopal Church service in New Castle, Delaware, which have now became an annual event.

Since 1980, the Welsh Society has held a cymanfa ganu at Immanuel On The Green in New Castle. In 1984, Eileen Jay designed a phonetic hymnal for the Delaware cymanfa which made a great difference to the singing. Having conducted his first cymanfa at Reading, Pennsylvania, in September 1982, and then another two weeks later at Delta, Peter Williams is now a regular conductor of cymanfaoedd canu in Delaware and in southeastern Pennsylvania, as well as guest soloist at many Welsh events.

The Welsh Society of Delaware meets once every three months at the Parish House of Immanuel On The Green. Members have publicized 18th century Welsh immigration into the state in the 1700's and have drawn attention to the collection of 18th century Welsh furniture at Wilmington's Winterthur Museum.

The Welsh Society of Delaware is one in a series of neighboring east coast cities that includes Delta, Philadelphia, Baltimore, Annapolis and Washington D.C., each within several hours drive. Welsh events at these locations—especially Annapolis—draw larger and larger crowds to increasingly better-organized festivals.

☆

We explored southeastern Pennsylvania, and at Arch Street Presbyterian Church spent an hour with Daniel Williams, secretary of the Welsh Guild. Dan gave us a bulging envelope of Philadelphia Welsh Americana. Delta, Pennsylvania is hidden among a cluster of slate-rich hills, right on the Maryland border. We were now at the Mason-Dixon line, the border between north and south and still a significant boundary to anyone who has grown up in the South.

In Delta, Glenn Grove, the Reverend Richard Baskwill and Bill and Pat St. Clair have created a unique Welsh American environment. Since we were there in 1983, their programs have expanded. For 1985 Delta's scheduled calendar included an elaborate March 1st banquet, a May cymanfa and visits to Delta by harpists Osian Ellis and Caryl Thomas. Under the professional direction of Joseph Ferio, the Delta Welsh Choir is now extremely accomplished and the influence of Welsh activities in this small town have had an effect in Bel Air and in Washington D.C.

MARYLAND AND WASHINGTON D.C.

There are four Welsh American organizations in Maryland. They are the St. David's Society of Baltimore, The Women's Welsh Club of Baltimore, the Welsh Society of Harford County in Bel Air and The Welsh Dragon, an import shop in Annapolis.

The St. David's Society of Baltimore has hosted a St. David's Day dinner every year since 1913. Around 1900 there was a substantial Welsh population in Baltimore. Large numbers of workers from South Wales emigrated there to work in the metal industries. The documentary "Last of the Tough Welshmen" follows the career of Tom Jeffries, a tin plate worker from Llanelli who became foreman of a large plant in Baltimore. Tom Jeffries was the last of a line of Welsh metal workers to be brought from Wales, workers whose expertise quickly led to United States domination of the nickel and tinplate industries at the expense of plants in Wales.

Over 200 people attended the Baltimore St. David's dinner in 1983, the biggest ever in the Society's history. The Reverend Richard Baskwill of Rehoboth Capel Cymraeg, Delta, was the guest speaker and a bus load of visitors drove from Delta for the occasion. The banquet concluded with community singing; soloists included Robert Fox, Marian Myers and Donald Boothman. The Women's Welsh Club of Baltimore, prominent in all Maryland Welsh events, helps arrange the decorations and planning of all Baltimore St. David's Day dinners.

The Women's Welsh Club of Baltimore was founded in 1925. Its latest leaders have been Jane Fox, Winifred Morgan and Barbara Morgan. Winifred Morgan, originally from Swansea, has been one of Baltimore's best correspondents to the Welsh American papers. Jane Fox and Barbara Morgan have both been on the radio promoting Welsh heritage in Maryland. In 1980, the Women's Welsh Club managed to get March 1st proclaimed Welsh Day in Maryland and in the state capital, Annapolis. Baltimore stations played Welsh music including an hour of contemporary music by Grace Williams and Alun Hodinott followed by a recording of the Dafydd Iwan concert in Baltimore, November 1979.

In addition to holding their own monthly meetings, the Women's Welsh Club of Baltimore holds a St. David's dinner of its own, usually about a week after March 1st. Betty Carozza has often been a soloist and Helen Gulden is the accompanist. Other leaders of this very active women's group have been Edna Beall, Cathy Lloyd, Cleo Griffith, Ann Handley, Thelma Evans, Janice Houston, Mary Flinchum, Mary Clawsey, Mrs. Elvet Evans, Thelma Phillips, Catherine Alban, Elizabeth Murphy and Edith Schipferling. Both the Women's Welsh Club and the St. David's Society worked closely with the Civic Center during preparation for Côr Meibion De Cymru's visit to Baltimore in November 1983.

Just north of Baltimore in Bel Air, the Welsh Society of Harford County maintains an active and reliable Welsh calendar of events. Mrs. Winifred Morgan organized the Society in 1979 in time to host Ray Handy who visited Bel Air in April and November 1980.

In 1979, Mrs. Marie Hopkins, a teacher at Harford Community College, organized a March 1st Welsh Festival in Bel Air. Mrs. Hopkins was helped by Winifred Morgan, Mrs. Robert O. Jones, Mrs. Jim Morris and Mrs. Clement Haverly, and the festival lasted from 11 a.m. until 3 p.m. A documentary about the Welsh slate workers in Harford County and southern York County, Pennsylvania, called "A Song For the Welsh" made by Peggy Surgeon of the University of Maryland was screened. A one hour BBC film on the National Eisteddfod was also shown and there were arts, crafts and sales booths. The festival featured a short concert and college staff prepared Welsh dishes for the almost 200 people who attended.

In May 1979, the Bel Air group hosted Parti'r Ffynnon, a thirty voice ladies choir from Flint who were visiting the Washington D.C. area. Marie Hopkins arranged a concert at Fallston Senior High School and Winifred Morgan managed the sale of Parti'r Ffynnon records.

In August 1981, the Harford County Welsh Society organized a week long visit to the Baltimore area by Dawnswyr Tawerin and Penderyn. This major operation involved all three Welsh groups. The Welsh visitors were received at City Hall where they exchanged gifts with the mayor and gave one of several performances. The Dawnswyr Tawerin tour continued in Ohio, Ontario, Virginia, Massachusetts and Pennsylvania.

The Harford County Welsh Society meets on the third Sunday of every month and has forged strong links with the group in Delta, Pennsylvania. When the town of Delta hosted the Pendyrus Choir, Bel Air leaders were involved in planning Delta's ambitious program for 1985.

In Baltimore in the 1970's, Anne Cowie completed a number of projects that had an impact throughout the North American Welsh community. In 1976, Anne visited the "Learners' Tent" at the Welsh National Eisteddfod. Here she met John Albert Evans whose enthusiastic teaching methods immediately caught her attention. John Albert told Anne that he was ready to teach a class in the U.S.A. any time.

While in Baltimore over the Christmas of 1976, Anne Cowie heard of the Poultney Welsh Heritage Project in Vermont. Margot Bouchard welcomed the idea of a Welsh course and the date, venue and teachers were quickly set. Anxious to make the atmosphere at Poultney as exciting as the Eisteddfod Learners' Tent in Wales, Anne Cowie enlisted the help of Maldwyn Pate, Alexander Hamilton and Phyllis Kinney Evans in order to create as Welsh an environment as possible. The success of the Poultney course led to the formation of Cymdeithas Madog, the Welsh Studies Institute. The courses of Cymdeithas Madog have now reached hundreds of students making Welsh classes almost a requirement of any modern Welsh society.

Anne Cowie arrived in the United States in 1964. She grew up in Cardiff and moved to Baltimore when her Welsh husband transferred to Johns Hopkins University Hospital. After being asked many times if Wales "was part of England," in 1970 Anne Cowie made a conscious decision to devote her time to working for Wales.

She wrote a series of articles for the *Baltimore News* including one on Welsh quarrymen and their families along the southeastern Pennsylvania-Maryland state line. She wrote for the *Western Mail* in Wales and made broadcasts for BBC Wales about Welsh affairs in America. In 1976, Anne Cowie did the research for a six-part BBC Wales series on the Welsh in America. In 1978, she researched and arranged American locations for a 90-minute TV documentary commemorating the 25th anniversary of Dylan Thomas' death.

Another aspect of Anne Cowie's work is organizing tours of the U.S.A. for Welsh actors and writers. Through a network of personal friends, she has arranged several visits and campus readings for Ray Handy. In 1978 and 1979, she organized a tour for Welsh actress Elizabeth Morgan. When Ray Handy appeared at Johns Hopkins University, Anne Cowie organized a pre-show reception at her home, bought forty tickets and distributed them to members of the Baltimore St. David's Society. In 1978 Anne hosted Dulais Rhys, Janet Thomas and Selwyn Roderick. Dulais Rhys was then studying at the Peabody Conservatory in Baltimore and he and Janet Thomas played at the 1978 Baltimore St. David's dinner. Also in 1978, Anne Cowie helped organize speaking engagements for Jane Hutt of Welsh Women's Aid.

Having a leader of the caliber of Anne Cowie has been an inspiration to Welsh societies from Wilmington, Delaware to Washington D.C. More recently, an annual focus for Welsh American energies has been provided by Mark Slater, owner of The Welsh Dragon import store in Annapolis.

Born in the Rhondda, Mark Slater came to the United States in 1975 at the age of 27. The Welsh Dragon in Annapolis was launched with a big reception on March 1st, 1981. The Welsh Dragon is located in the historic district of Annapolis and since 1981 its annual March 1st Festival has been a well attended event. In 1984, the Annapolis Welsh Festival made the "best bet" weekend entertainment list of the *Washington Post* and, moreover, attracted over 500 people.

The Annapolis Welsh Festival is organized by Mark Slater with the participation of ladies in Welsh costume from the Women's Welsh Club of Baltimore. The festival is held at The Welsh Dragon store and the Playhouse Circle Theater down the street. The second annual festival in 1982 featured an official twin city proclamation between Annapolis and Newport (Tredaith) in Dyfed, West Wales. The Mayor of Newport, Glyn Rees, and the Mayor of Annapolis, Richard Hillman, exchanged gifts and signed a formal twin city resolution. In 1983, Mayor Hillman and a party from Annapolis were hosted by Glyn Rees in Wales.

On March 1st, Mark Slater hired the Playhouse Theater for the afternoon and showed films from Wales. There was a Welsh ladies costume contest and a te bach with thousands of Welsh cakes and hundreds of cups of tea. More recent festivals have featured entertainment by the Welsh learners class from Washington D.C. and an afternoon of Welsh music played by the Bay Winds Band. Every event at the festival is free.

In 1983, the Welsh Festival in Annapolis featured a performance of The Rainbow Factor—a play by David Price-Gresty of Washington. The Rainbow Factor tells a humorous story of Welsh immigrants to the U.S.A. following World War II and just before their departure from Cardiff.

All three Maryland Welsh societies were involved in the 1984 Welsh Festival in Annapolis. There were guest speakers, hostesses in costume, films, musicians and other forms of entertainment throughout the day. Restaurants in the historic district featured Welsh specialities and when the day was over, neighborhood pubs offered their own form of noson lawen. Visitors to Annapolis for the Welsh Festival came from as far away as Ohio, Virginia, Pennsylvania and New Jersey. It is less than an hour's drive from Annapolis to Washington, D.C. and members of the St. David's Society in Washington are regular customers of the Welsh Dragon with its inventory of over 8,000 items from Wales. In 1985 The Welsh Dragon distributed 120,000 copies of its catalog nationwide, further increasing American awareness of Wales and Welsh products.

WASHINGTON, D.C.

We made the drive from Delta, Pennsylvania to Washington, D.C. in three hours. Elaine John and Janet Owen, two school friends of mine from Mynydd Cynffig were in Gaithersburg, and we spent one night with them. Elaine's husband, Paul, worked for IBM and Janet was visiting while on a world tour of relatives and friends. After corresponding with Janet and missing her in San Francisco and Toronto, our paths finally coincided.

Janet and Elaine had no idea that Welsh people in Canada and the United States were so well organized. My two friends, however, regarded the Welsh American phenomenon and my enthusiasm for it as only mildly interesting. They found my prototype of *WAY* magazine "cute." They had left Wales years before—Elaine to work for the BBC in London, and Janet to join her family in South Africa. Our Welsh American involvement was the least interesting of our experiences to them, neither of whom could ever imagine living in Wales again.

The St. David's Welsh-American Society of Washington, D.C. was founded in 1886. Like the Welsh Society in the Canadian capital, the Society in Washington, D.C. includes among its leaders, teachers, lawyers, journalists, broadcasters, economists, business people, university professors, company executives and members of the diplomatic corps. The Society holds its regular monthly meetings in the Rotunda of the British Embassy. Other meetings such as the language classes are held at a local church.

In 1985-1986, the centennial year of the St. David's Society in Washington, D.C. its officers were Hywel Davies, President; Michael Bowen, Vice-President; Jackie Wintle, Secretary; Gene Owen, Treasurer; Nell Ashley, Historian. Other recent leaders have been David Jones, Glenys Murrel, Emmy Tiffany, Samuel Smith, Alwyn Pritchard, Morley Fox, Sally Bartlet, John Griffith and Christine Whittaker.

After a two month summer break, monthly meetings at the British Embassy start in September. The fall period is the busiest for the Society and programs always feature a cymanfa ganu, a high school eisteddfod fund-raiser and sometimes movies from Wales or a prominent guest speaker. Films shown are of consistent good quality. "Last of the Tough Welshmen" had its American premier in the Rotunda and Tom Jeffries was on hand to answer questions at a reception afterwards. The catalog of films is far superior to those shown by other Welsh American societies. The D.C. club must have access to a film source in Wales that other societies have yet to hear about.

Guests at Welsh meetings in Washington, D.C. have included Islyn Thomas, soprano Beti Mary Owen, broadcaster Angus McDermid, from Bangor, Wales and Douglas Bassett, then director of the National Museum of Wales. In March 1978, Sir Ivor Richard QC was guest speaker at the St. David's banquet. Over 200 people attended this banquet which had been organized by Alice Deisroth, Cyril and Jani Lloyd, Mike Bowen and Nell Ashley, making it one of the most successful in the Society's history.

In 1978 Gareth Ivorian Jones and Ed Terrar Jr. started work on updating and modifying the Society's charter and by 1980, the Society was a registered non-profit organization.

The Welsh-American Society of Washington, D.C. hosted Ray Handy, Olwen Rees, Clive Belman and Christine Pritchard on their "Pryderi and his Pigs" tour in 1974 and 1976. In November, 1979, Dafydd Iwan and Hefin Elis gave a concert in D.C. organized by the Folklore Society of Greater Washington. Over 60 people from the Welsh Society came to see the musicians who were later hosted to a luncheon at the World Bank by Hywel Davies and Frank Owen. Dafydd Iwan and Hefin Elis, while in Washington, were the guests of Evan Parker, a distinguished leader of the Welsh Society and principal organizer of the Welsh classes in Washington D.C. Society members bought over 200 tickets for the Côr Meibion De Cymru Baltimore concert in 1983, and in 1984 hosted the Pendyrus Male Choir on its musical tour.

In November 1980, Hywel Davies started teaching Welsh to a group of 29 students and Welsh language classes have been part of the Society's activities ever since. Teachers have included Nesta Llwyd, Gene Owen and Alwyn Pritchard. The Welsh teacher in 1985-86 was Trevina Newman from Tenby who was in Washington D.C. with her husband, an exchange teacher at the exclusive St. Albans School for Boys.

Originally from Loughor, Hywel Davies has been an officer of the D.C. Welsh Society since 1966 and has been president of the Society four times. He has conducted cymanfaoedd canu in the Greater Washington area and for three years coached the University of Maryland Rugby Club. When the National Welsh American Foundation was launched in March 1980, Hywel Davies was its first treasurer.

St. David's Day in Washington is always celebrated with a banquet which in recent years has been held at Fort McNair Officers Club. Between 100 and 150 people usually attend. First class entertainment at the banquet has included harp music by Caryl Thomas and folk singing and dancing by Maldwyn Pate. In 1982 Donald Boothman sang, accompanied by Sandra Melton on the harp. Guest speakers at the banquet have included: the honourable Richard Hillman, Mayor of Annapolis; the Reverend Elwyn D. Brown; Dr. Arturo Roberts; Dr. Islyn Thomas; Mrs. Rhiani Phillips; and Mr. Jenkin Lloyd Jones, Chairman U.S. Chamber of Commerce and Editor, *Tulsa Tribune*, Oklahoma. Leaders of the Society have been interviewed on local radio and on March 1st Washington radio stations usually broadcast Welsh music and poetry.

Other regular annual events include a cymanfa ganu usually held in November. The Washington Cymanfa attracts around 200 people and has been led by Gwyn Walters of Massachusetts, Carlton Jones Lake of Pennsylvania and John Rees Evans of Fairfax, Virginia. The Gwalia Women's Welsh Club always hosts a reception after the Cymanfa as a fund-raising activity in support of the Welsh Home for the Aged in Rocky River, Ohio. Soloists at the Cymanfa have included Cyril Lloyd, Donald Boothman and John Rees Evans.

Clement Heverly attends regularly as organ accompanist.

Every February, the men of the Washington, D.C. Welsh Society host a St. Valentine's Day program. St. Valentine's Day in 1984 was marked with a very successful evening of Welsh Folk Dancing led by Hywel Thomas of Buffalo. This has now become a regular feature of the Society's calendar.

There are two women's Welsh Clubs in Washington—the Washington Senior Club and the Gwalia Club. In addition to holding their own monthly meetings, both women's clubs play an active part in the work of the St. David's Society. Led by leaders such as Gwen Dunn, Jani Lloyd, Nell Ashley, Dorothy Guerry, Elwynne Williams, Alberta Thomas, Marian Flincham, Alice Deisroth, Rachel Jones Davies and Mrs. Edward Coney, the Women's Welsh Clubs organize many of the receptions following Washington Welsh events. Their own programs feature concerts, movies, Welsh dancing and the occasional noson lawen attended by members of the Welsh community at large.

Every December, the Welsh-American Society of Washington, D.C. holds an eisteddfod fund-raiser at the British Embassy. The sponsoring of the High School Choral Eisteddfod by the Society was the brainchild of Dr. P. Howard Patrick. The idea matured into a reality in the period 1978-81 when the Society was led by a visionary group of officers. Foremost among these was Mr. John K. Evans who was president in 1978 and 1979 and provided generous financial assistance to launch the project.

Bethesda Chevy Chase High School Choir was the host and winner and was awarded a cash prize and an ornate scroll by Welsh calligrapher, Ieuan Rees. Since 1981, Christine Whittaker and Emmy Tiffany have been the main coordinators of the annual Choral Eisteddfod. Eight schools entered in 1982. The competition is open to senior high school choirs of at least thirty voices singing in soprano, alto, tenor and bass parts. Each choir sings for twenty minutes and its selection must include a Welsh language set piece ("Dyddiau Dyn Sydd Fel Glaswelltyn" in 1984). A pronunciation guide and cassette tape is provided by the organizing committee. Prize money awarded in 1984 came to $450 first prize for Woodbridge Senior High, second prize $350 and third prize $300. The Washington High Schools Choral Eisteddfod continues to achieve its principal and original aim, which is to "acquaint the community with a unique aspect of Welsh culture and to perpetuate the Welsh tradition of high standards of musicianship in young people through competition." The 1982 Eisteddfod was recorded on videotape and circulated to schools in the Greater Washington area. In 1985 The Camerata Choir from the University of Maryland took second prize for their singing in Welsh at the Royal National Eisteddfod in Lampeter, Wales.

Although it has received some support from the National Welsh American Foundation and the Cultural Affairs Office of the British Embassy, the main financial support for the Washington Choral Eisteddfod comes from the members of the St. David's Society. In each of the last three years the members have contributed between two and three thousand dollars in support for this event. The fund-raiser itself has become a gala concert. Performers have been Caryl Thomas, harp; Gwen Griffith, soprano; John Rees Evans (a soloist with the Royal Opera Company and member of the Society); readings by Michael Bowen; and a performance by the Eisteddfod's last winner. The event concludes with community carol singing and Hen Wlad Fy Nhadau. More than any other annual event, the Washington Eisteddfod brings the work of the Washington Welsh Society and the sustained traditions of Wales to the attention of the general public. The Washington Schools Eisteddfod is one of the most successful outreach programs managed by any Welsh society in North America.

One result of the Choral Eisteddfod has been the formation of the Welsh Children's Choir of Liberty Grove Methodist Church. Huw W. Jones of Burtonsville, Maryland organized the choir which has a substantial Welsh repertoire. The children's choir performs in Welsh costumes made by the children and by members of the Washington Women's Welsh Clubs.

The St. David's Society in Washington, D.C. is quickly contacted by Welsh visitors to the capital city. It is a regular host to members of BBC Wales, the Wales Tourist Board and visiting Welsh businessmen and academics. The British Embassy gets many queries from all over the U.S.A. regarding Wales and the Welsh language and these are generally passed on to the Society. In 1981, Berlitz School of Languages contacted the Society when it needed a Welsh teacher for its Washington Bureau.

Dewi and Nesta Llwyd joined the Society in 1984. Dewi Llwyd, a BBC Wales TV reporter was studying at American University on a Rotary Foundation Scholarship. Nesta Llwyd, joined the Cymdeithas Madog staff at the Wilkes-Barre Cwrs Cymraeg y Cymoedd in August 1984. The work of the St. David's Welsh-American Society of Washington, D.C. is regularly reported in *Ninnau* and *Y Drych*. Correspondents have included Monte George, Cheryl Mitchel, John Griffith, Peter O. Moyle and the indispensable Barbara Borchadt.

☆

In 1977 and 1978, with the encouragement of John K. Evans, a group of St. David's Society members, all of whom worked at the World Bank or International Monetary Fund, started discussing an ambitious plan for establishing a Graduate School of Business and Management to be located in Wales.

The committee comprising Hywel Davies, Frank Owen, Owen Price, Huw Jones, Ronald Powell, Gareth Ivorian Jones and John K. Evans committed their vision of a Welsh School of Business to paper in the form of a statement of objectives and the broad policies which would govern its operation. They then established contact with Sir Julian Hodge, chairman of the Commercial Bank of Wales and Aubrey Trotman-Dickenson, principal of the University of Wales Institute of Science and Technology (UWIST). Between them, the committee in Wales and the United States developed a more detailed proposal for the projected business center. John K. Evans visited Wales in 1979. He held consultations with Sir Julian Hodge and Sir Goronwy Daniel, vice chancellor of the University of Wales, both of whom encouraged the idea. Dean F. Berry, an American professor at the London School of Economics, worked with the Welsh committee as a consultant. In April and July 1979, Huw Jones, John K. Evans, Ronald Powell and Hywel Davies met on various occasions with their Welsh counterparts at Gregynog Hall, Newtown and in Cardiff to develop the idea. The projected Welsh Business Center was further discussed by leaders of the trade unions, corporations and existing colleges. The proposed plan went as far as to outline the limited company that would finance the school, a design of the school's potential curricula and the slot the school would fill in the University of Wales collegiate system. The initial cost of establishing the school was estimated at around $10 million and a charitable organization managed by the D.C. committee was outlined to raise funds in the United States.

After this promising beginning, the whole project was put on a "back burner" in the spring of 1980 because the Welsh planning committee could not see how the funds could be raised to carry the idea any further. Nor was there great confidence that fund-raising in the U.S.A. would yield a major return. It was also recognized that the federal structure of the University of Wales was not conducive to the integrated concept of the project.

An American mechanism, however, had already been established and the Washington, D.C. committee did not dismantle the tentative fund-raising structure that it had established. Through the initiative of John K. Evans, Hywel Davies and Howard Patrick the idea for a National Welsh American Foundation emerged—a Foundation that would provide funding for Welsh cultural and educational activities in America and Wales.

THE NATIONAL WELSH AMERICAN FOUNDATION

The man largely responsible for honing the embryonic ideas of John K. Evans into the legally incorporated non-profit National Welsh American Foundation was Howard Patrick. Howard spent his childhood in Kenfig Hill and still had relatives living down the street from my parents' home in Wales. While in Washington, I spent an evening with Howard and his wife, Ross, at their apartment in Bethesda, Maryland. While studying music at Princeton in 1968, Howard was offered a four-year fellowship at the University and completed his Ph.D. in 1972. In 1975, he received the Outstanding Educator of the Year Award from American University. Having taken a second degree in legal studies, Howard Patrick now specializes in computer law. When the National Welsh American Foundation (NWAF) was finally established in March 1980, Howard was its first secretary.

In January 1978, under the letterhead of his company, Reciprocal World Traders, Inc., John K. Evans published a full-page letter in *Ninnau* announcing the incorporation of "a formal society and non-profit foundation to function as an action channel ... and a center for the development of mutual, cultural and economic benefits." Postponement of the major project (the Business School in Wales) that gave the emerging foundation its main sense of purpose, however, threw its development into limbo.

Eighteen months later, with an initial donation of $5,000 by J. K. Evans, the fully incorporated National Welsh American Foundation held its first meeting on March 29, 1980. Howard Patrick and Hywel Davies had taken the extremely promising outlines of 1978 and drafted the charter of "a non-profit international organization established to fund, co-ordinate, and advance Welsh American cultural and educational activities." The first meeting was held in Washington, D.C. and the Foundation was launched with a board of directors from both sides of the Atlantic. The first board of NWAF directors consisted of J. K. Evans, President; Sir William Crawshay, Vice-President; Hywel Davies, Treasurer and Howard Patrick, Secretary. Also on the board were Anne Cowie, John Nichols, Islyn Thomas, Emlyn Griffith, Wilfred Greenway, Douglas Bassett, Aneurin Thomas, Arturo Roberts, Edward Hartmann and Donna Lloyd-Kolkin.

Launching a campaign of "New Welsh American Awareness", the first year of the NWAF was spent "unlocking funds" from individuals, corporations, Welsh societies and government departments. One gift of $5,000 was made by Emlyn Griffith and his sister, Jean Barrat, in memory of their parents.

The Foundation was launched with a great deal of enthusiasm. In November 1980, *Ninnau* published a four-page supplement with the articles of the Foundation, an essay on the role it hoped to play and biographies of all its directors. In 1981, the first project to receive NWAF financial support was the Nant Gwrtheyrn residential language center in Wales.

Craig Peters and Glyn Long joined the NWAF board in 1981, and at the second annual meeting grants were made to Côr Gwalia Ohio (Cincinnati), the Washington High School Choral Eisteddfod, and the prize in Wales awarded to the village or town that has done the most in one year to promote the use of the Welsh language.

1981 also saw the establishment of the NWAF's Advisory Council. The Advisory Council consists of celebrities who lend their name to the Foundation's work. Using the board of directors' personal network, the Advisory Council quickly grew to include, among others, Bob Hope, Richard Burton, Lt. General R. H. Groves, General D. C. Jones and Congressmen John Rhodes and Thomas B. Evans. The Welsh Advisory Council has included, among others, Sir Geraint Evans, Sir Emlyn Williams, Earl Lloyd George and Lord Parry.

In 1982 the NWAF presented grants to Cymdeithas Madog; the Celtic Cultural Weekend at Cornell University; Professor Janice Miller at the University of Dallas; and to Medieval and Renaissance Texts and Studies, publishers of Richard Loomis's *Dafydd Ap Gwilym: The Poems*. In 1983, checks were presented to Côr Meibion De Cymru, the Welsh Heritage Fund of Northern California; and the Second Celtic Cultural Weekend at Cornell

University. In 1984, recipients of NWAF assistance were Rehoboth Capel Cymraeg, Delta, Pennsylvania; Cymdeithas Madog; the Welsh Portfolio art exhibit of Western Illinois University; John Bollard at the Consortium of Medieval Studies; and a Welsh student exchange scheme at Campbell University, North Carolina.

Emlyn Griffith became president of the NWAF in 1982, and the Foundation was joined by John Morris, Marian Flinchum and Dr. David Lloyd Mandry. A group of NWAF leaders spent July 4, 1982 in Wales promoting the work of the Foundation and participating in conferences and festivals. Islyn Thomas became president of the NWAF in 1983 and the board was joined by Robert Williams of Canton, New York and Dr. Ellis Roberts of Wilkes-Barre. In May 1984, Wilfred Greenway became President of the Foundation and Sir William Crawshay, Vice-President. Craig Peters was voted Secretary and Jack Pritchard became Treasurer. Arturo Roberts was voted President-Elect to take office in 1985. Directors were Islyn Thomas, Anne Cowie, Evan Parker, John Morris, Douglas Bassett, William Griffiths, Robert Williams, Daniel Williams, Richard Griffiths, Emlyn Griffith, Edward Hartmann, David Lloyd Mandry, Ellis Roberts, Myra Thomas Lawrence and Donna Lloyd-Kolkin.

The National Welsh American Foundation has all the prestige anyone could ask of an award-making charitable organization. The Foundation's directors have succeeded in personally securing donations from some individuals and corporations, but the distribution of 7,500 printed leaflets in 1983 and 1984 brought a poor response from the Welsh American public. By making timely gifts to well chosen Welsh projects, the Foundation is succeeding in its goals. Its outreach policy, however, informing people of those goals, has been less successful. The work of the NWAF is unfamiliar to Welsh society leaders and the almost automatic choices of Welsh societies with a gift to make are still Nant Gwrtheyrn and the Rocky River Welsh Retirement Home. Its leaders realize that the full and exciting potential of the National Welsh American Foundation will remain unrealized without the moral and material support of the Welsh societies themselves. Even so, the NWAF has an inconsistent P.R. program and *Ninnau* and *Y Drych* carry only infrequent articles on the fertility of the Foundation's important work.

24

North Carolina, South Carolina and Tennessee; The St. David's Welsh Society of Georgia

On the 23rd of September, 1983, we made a short, easy drive from Washington, D.C. to Charlottesville, Virginia. Philip Lewis and Sally Gilbert, two close schoolfriends of mine, were living in Charlottesville. Charlottesville was also the home of Suzanne's niece, Darthy. We were looking forward to a grand reunion.

Deeply involved in the Charlottesville country dance and music scene, Darthy took us on tours of the Blue Ridge Mountains, to a blueberry pancake breakfast, country dances and evenings of song and music at a series of welcome home parties.

Philip and I grew up together in Cefn Cribwr, Wales and we'd often talked about opportunities in the United States. When he lost his job during cutbacks at the British Steel Corporation in Port Talbot, Philip bought a plane ticket to Washington, D.C. He got off the Trailways Bus in Charlottesville and Darthy put him up for his first two weeks. Apart from a change of clothes, the only luggage Philip brought was his rugby kit. Within two week he had found a job and was rugby coach for the University of Virginia Rugby Team.

By the time we arrived Philip had been the University of Virginia rugby coach for eighteen months. He was a familiar figure on the Albermarle County Golf Course and had become a juggling teacher. He was even able to show me how to keep three juggling bags in the air. Eggs were more difficult and tennis rackets were impossible.

Sally meanwhile had been selling handmade woollen sweaters in Charlottesville stores. We spent a happy week with our friends and adopted a more carefree attitude to our trip.

One day Philip took us to see Eve Watters who frequently broadcasts Welsh folk songs on University of Virginia radio. On previous visits to Charlottesville we'd spent time with Eve and she'd always insisted on hearing some Welsh singing before we left. Eve and I had a mutual friend, Rod Owen, whom I'd just met for the first time at the Wilkes-Barre National.

Rod Owen was born in Wales and came to the United States when his father, the Reverend John Owen, accepted ministry of the Welsh Church in Detroit. Rod had been a graduate student at William and Mary College in Williamsburg, Virginia before joining the faculty of Mary Baldwin College in Staunton about an hour away from Charlottesville. Rod has been a president of WAY and often returns to Wales where he still has close relatives. In Staunton, Rod and his wife, Linda, organized a children's eisteddfod in March 1981. In June 1981, Rod taught a course at Mary Baldwin College through the Elderhostel system called "Wales: Land of Daffodils and Dragons, Castles and Choristers." The Staunton course ran at the same time as Margot Bouchard's Elderhostel Welsh course in Poultney, Vermont. In April 1984, Rod Owen was interviewed by Eve Watters on University of Virginia radio and Randell Atkinson played a wide selection of Welsh music.

At William and Mary College, Williamsburg, there is a Goronwy Owen Room in Swem Library. The Goronwy Owen room houses a Welsh collection of books and periodicals and has a slate plaque to the poet donated by the Cymmrodorion Society of London. Goronwy Owen, an important Welsh writer, was a teacher connected with William and Mary College from 1758 to 1760. He died while curator of St. Andrews in Brunswick County, Virginia in 1769. Every year on March 1st, a small anniversary is held in the Goronwy Owen Room. Professor David Clay Jenkins, co-ordinator of Welsh activities at William and Mary College, organizes the celebration which has featured readings from the poet's work and harp music by Jane Kilgore of Hampton, Virginia. Tina Jeffreys helps arrange the anniversary which is usually attended by about a dozen people.

Williamsburg is the home of a small non-profit organization called "The American Friends of St. David's Cathedral." Arthur Roach is the president of the Society which raises funds to "assist the ministry of the principal shrine in Wales." The first annual gift of the American Friends of St. David's Cathedral was made at an International Day at the Cathedral on July 5, 1979.

Norfolk, Virginia is the home of Anne Brooke, an educator, whose work has had considerable impact in Wales. Anne Brooke first visited Wales in 1973. She returned in 1975 and enrolled in a Welsh teacher's course at Glamorgan Polytechnic, Pontypridd. When Anne joined Mudiad Ysgolion Meithrin, the Welsh Nursery School Movement, she discovered that well over 75 percent of the parents of children at the Welsh nursery schools spoke no Welsh themselves.

In 1980 Anne Brooke wrote a children's book, *Mi Welais Jac-y-do* (I Saw Jack the Jackdaw), which is a compilation of traditional and contemporary Welsh nursery rhymes. The book was written with vocabulary and pronunciation guides intended for English speaking parents to read to their Welsh speaking children. This timely publication was an instant success and quickly went through several printings. Anne Brooke has since made her home in the Rhondda and has written other best-selling children's books which are used in the schools of Mudiad Ysgolion Meithrin.

In the Hall of Honor in Reston, Virginia, there is a plaque to Welshman, John Lewis (1884-1976). John Lewis was born in Abergynolwyn, Wales, and while living in Kentucky, was a tireless musical and religious teacher along the Ohio Valley. John Lewis has been made a Dean of Kentucky Bandsmen, a "First Citizen" by the Kentucky Daughters of the American Revolution and in 1968, was commissioned as an honorary Kentucky Colonel.

In Alexandria, Virginia, the Reverend Reginald Fuller, head of the Episcopal Seminary served on the faculty of St. David's College in Lampeter for five years. While in Lampeter Reverend Fuller learned to speak Welsh and every year on March 1st leads a bilingual St. David's service at the Seminary.

Our last stop in Virginia was at Richmond where we spent a night with relatives. We made the drive from Richmond to Wilmington, North Carolina along main roads. Having driven this way many times, we took the most direct route. Despite ourselves, we were more interested in our destination than making discoveries along the way.

NORTH CAROLINA

Wilmington, North Carolina, was our first home in the United States. After temple life in Japan and village life in Wales, Atlanta had been overwhelming. Living on the island at Wrightsville Beach while planning our tour, provided the perfect adjustment period.

We'd left Wilmington 418 days before, on August 10, 1982. It was now October 2, 1983. Our tour had been successful. We were neither ragged nor malnourished, and the information we'd collected was enough to convince anyone our trip hadn't been a profitless tour of beauty spots. Suzanne's Aunt Lil gave us a hero's welcome and heroic portions of good food. While at Aunt Lil's we took everything out of the van and cleaned it. We tuned the engine, changed the oil and washed and waxed the van. We spent four days making sure the van was in perfect condition before driving home.

Jayne Pryddarch was now living in Florida. With her departure the Cape Fear Welsh Society had collapsed. We'd seen June Hughes Jones at the National in Wilkes-Barre and spoke to her on the phone. June sometimes saw some members of the Welsh Society, but rarely heard from Jayne. It was an episode that had ended.

At Buies Creek, North Carolina, about 40 miles south of Raleigh, Campbell University has held an exchange relationship with the South Wales Baptist College, Cardiff since 1979. The Reverend Dafydd G. Davies, principal of the South Wales Baptist College, was instrumental in starting the exchange and in 1980, Mr. Davies was awarded an honorary doctorate by the University. The Campbell University Welsh Exchange is coordinated by Dr. Jerry Wallace of the Department of Religion, and in 1984, received financial assistance from the NWAF.

In April 1982, a group of about 30 people from Winston Salem, North Carolina spent two weeks in Cardiff as part of a Friendship Force exchange. Friendship Force is one of the most consistent person-to-person exchanges between non-Welsh Americans and people living in Wales. Friendship Force participants, however, are invariably placed with monolingual English speakers.

Nearer Wilmington at Burgaw, the Hopewell Presbyterian Church

Historical Society led by the Reverend Jack Dail has done some research on the North Carolina-Delaware Welsh Tract. The Welsh migrated to North Carolina from Delaware in the 1730's and the Welsh Tract flourished until around 1880. A historical marker for the tract can be seen on Route 117 north of Burgaw. There is another sign at South Washington, the actual site of the settlement, which is now owned by South Washington Memorial Park.

In Southport, North Carolina, the Curiosity Shop on North Howe Street contains the entire stock of an antique shop that once existed in Llanelli, Wales. The owner, while on a trip to Wales, bought the complete inventory of the Llanelli store and had it crated and shipped to Southport. Visitors to the Curiosity Shop can find Welsh china, cabinets, prints, brasses, furniture, books and records.

SOUTH CAROLINA

The St. David's Society of South Carolina was founded in 1777 and is the second oldest Welsh association in the United States. St. David's Parish, the last parish to be created by the colonial government in South Carolina, was so named because the majority of its settlers were Welsh. The settlement, Welsh Neck, on the Pee Dee River north of Florence, was a well-known colonial outpost in the mid-1700's. Welsh Neck Baptist Church became the mother of 38 baptist churches in South Carolina. The St. David's Society built the first school house in the parish on a hill behind the community and the town that exists there today is known as Society Hill. The St. David's Society which built the school eventually became the St. David's Educational Society in 1883. When the school was absorbed into the county system the Society faded away. Welsh Neck High School became Coler College in 1908.

In 1976 during national bicentennial celebrations, the St. David's Society was reorganized and in 1977, marked its 200th anniversary. Led by Keith Williamson, Lucas Dargon and E. N. Zeigler, the Society has in recent years held an annual March 1st dinner and a picnic/business meeting every May.

TENNESSEE

West of North Carolina in Tennessee, the Welsh Society of Knoxville has, since 1983, made a greater effort to involve more people in its activities.

The Welsh connection in Eastern Tennessee goes back a long way. The Reverend R. D. Thomas, the author of *Hanes Cymry America*, made his final home in Knoxville, living there from 1872 until he died in 1888. North of Knoxville near Oneida, Brynyffynon in Scott County was the last attempted Welsh colony in North America. The Reverend Samuel Roberts of Llanbrynmair led the experiment which lasted from 1856 until 1867. The colony suffered several setbacks but it was the outbreak of the U.S. Civil War which finally broke the commitment of its founders. The whole story of Brynyffynon is described in *A Welsh Colony in Civil War Tennessee* by Wilbur Shepperson.

In 1982, Gwyn Pritchard and Hywel Teifi Edwards visited Brynyffynon, Tennessee; Beulah, Pennsylvania and Cambriol, Newfoundland while filming for a BBC documentary about attempted Welsh colonies in the United States and Canada.

Today the Bradley/Dickey family, descendants of R. D. Thomas and of David Richards (R. D. Thomas' son-in-law), founder of the Knoxville Iron Works, are active members of the Knoxville Welsh Society. There have been Welsh clubs in Knoxville for over 100 years, but the present Society was organized in 1961. There are about 300 people on the membership roster.

About 60 people came to the 1984 St. David's banquet at St. John's Lutheran Church, Knoxville. Community singing was led by Dale Dickey, and Roland Duncan gave a slide lecture on Christianity in Celtic Wales. The Society's other major annual event is a summer picnic. In 1985 a "Festival of Trees" for the benefit of Knoxville's Children's Hospital contained a Welsh Christmas scene sponsored by the Knoxville Welsh Society. The booth was decorated to look like a traditional Welsh parlor at Christmas time.

In June 1984, the Knoxville Welsh Society contributed a booth to the Genealogy for Southeasterners Conference at the University of Tennessee campus. Miss Billie McNamara, one of the most energetic of the Society's new leaders, is a professional genealogist and owns Anglophiles Unlimited, a firm specializing in British research. Over 500 people attended the Genealogy Conference, and the Welsh booth with its battery of Wales Tourist Board flyers, flags and ladies in Welsh costume made quite an impact. The President of the Society, Mrs. Audrey Duncan, who comes from Wales, is completing her anthropology degree at the University of Tennessee, studying the impact of the Welsh population in the eastern part of the state.

In 1985, officers of the Knoxville Welsh Society were Audrey Duncan, President; J. D. Bradley and Sarah Frazer, Vice-Presidents; Margaret Roth, Secretary-Treasurer; Mrs. Mickey Tweed, Social Director; David Davies, Chaplain; Thomas Davies, Music Director and Olive Branch, Historian. Billie McNamara is the Society's Welsh newspaper correspondent.

☆

GEORGIA

From Wilmington, we drove to Savannah. Our hosts were Suzanne's nephew, Richard, and his wife, Debbie. Although our tour of America and Canada was over, as we told Richard and Debbie about our experiences, we realized that the trip had led to the possibility of a wide range of future projects.

Our final day of living in a van came on October 10, 1983. We left Savannah at 8 a.m. and took a deliberately slow, unhurried route along the rural south central roads of Suzanne's home state. After fourteen months of touring the

United States, we savored the impact of Georgia. We stopped repeatedly at country stores, gas stations, roadside stands and local diners. By the time we got to Macon, we were late and picked up Interstate 75, which brought us to Atlanta in an hour and a half.

Our welcome by Suzanne's family in Atlanta was the most loving and considerate. We bought new clothes—our travel gear of strong boots, overalls and thick jackets had served us well, but were out of place in the city. Shopping was followed by visits to the doctor, the dentist and the hairdresser, including a visit to the vet for Amiga. Within a month, we had an apartment. By February we had sold the van, but daily reminders of the trip were the letters that arrived constantly and the heavy files of Welsh American material in our bedroom.

My parents visited for Thanksgiving 1983 and stayed three weeks. They were fascinated by the Welsh American scene and brought us reports of developments at home. Two new village societies had been organized—Y Cefn Gwyrdd (The Cefn Environmental Society) and Dosbarth yr Iaith Gymraeg Cefn Cribwr (The Cefn Welsh Class). Even my father was resurrecting his Welsh. The optimism of Cefn Gwyrdd and Dosbarth yr Iaith had infected him. Welsh was being used in the shops and streets of Cefn Cribwr where it hadn't been spoken for twenty years. In some Cefn Cribwr Sunday Schools, Welsh speaking children outnumbered English speakers. The Welsh-English of the deacons brought stares of amazement from monolingual Welsh speaking infants. The Welsh language energy of Wales was flowing. We'd felt it ourselves and my parents were feeling it at home.

The first meeting of the St. David's Welsh Society of Georgia was held on January 9, 1984. There were nine people present—Jan Sherry, Berwyn Jones, Olwen Xander, Sally Funderburk, the Reverend David Evans, Tom and Alison Edwards and Suzanne and me. Alison was Dorothy Feeley's daughter and Tom Edwards, too, had an Ohio Welsh background. We'd been given the Reverend David Evans' name by Dic Thomas in Ontario and I'd seen Jan Sherry's name on the letters page of the March 1982 issue of *Ninnau*.

Jan Sherry was from Ammanford, Sally Funderburk was from Pontarddulais and Olwen Xander was from Corwen—the Society was launched with these three native speakers. Berwyn Jones was one of the Nebraska Joneses. He'd been to the Jones reunions in Wymore and had sung in the Jones Male Choir.

Eighteen people came to our second meeting in February, 1984, and a story in the *Atlanta Constitution* brought over 80 to the Society's first St. David's Day dinner. In April 1984, Mark Craddock whose interest in Welsh began at the University of Alabama starting teaching Welsh lessons and Sally Funderburk launched *HWYL*, the Society's monthly newsletter.

Membership in the St. David's Welsh Society of Georgia grew from 65 in March to 102 by December 31, 1984. Now that we'd formed a Welsh American Society, what were we going to do with it? We had a large enough group to distill a body of enthusiastic regulars. The Welsh class in particular quickly assisted in the sale of WNGGA hymn books, folk song books and Society T-shirts. Members of the language class comprising Jeannette Scholes, Philip Morgan, Al Williams, Jemille Williams, Sally Stenger, Colin Rogers, Doug Caron and Joy and Jack Floden were the most curious about contemporary happenings in Wales; they were also most willing to participate in the work of a new society.

Despite our fears, the Society did not disappear overnight. Its first year concluded with a prynhawn llawen attended by over 60 people. Entertainment featured singing by Betty Graham and Esther Stroud, a Tom Jones imperso-nation, readings by writer Eileen Faris and an appearance by a champion Welsh corgi. The climax of the concert was a bilingual comedy by Y Dosbarth Cymraeg entitled, "An American Visitor." The afternoon concluded with a potluck dinner organized by Anne Hill and Arlette Davis.

The first fourteen months of the St. David's Welsh Society of Georgia fea-tured the following monthly programs.

1984

January   Nine people attended first meeting at Jan Sherry's house and elected a committee.

February   Second meeting held at David and Suzanne Greenslade's apart-ment—eighteen people present.

March   First St. David's Day dinner in Atlanta, attended by over 80 people. *HWYL* newsletter launched.

April   First meeting held at St. Andrew's Presbyterian Church, Sandy Springs. Weekly Welsh language classes started by Mark Crad-dock.

May   "A Celtic Trilogy" screened. Guest speakers Carolyn Lyons, President of the Tom Jones Fan Club, and Betty Floyd, National Secretary of the Cardigan Welsh Corgi Club.

June   Welsh Society picnic at Murphey Candler Park. Thirty-five people came.

July   First attempted choir practice. Society's constitution and by-laws completed. *HWYL* T-shirts on sale.

August   Summer break. Welsh language seminar held at Sally Funder-burk's house.

September   Mammoth slide show. Extremely successful. Welsh National Cy-manfa Ganu hymn books on sale.

October   Talk on Welsh American genealogical research by Jemille Williams.

November   A program of harp music by Nella Rigell.

December   A concert by Society members and a play, "An American Visitor" produced by the Welsh language class. An extremely successful Christmas meeting.

1985
January   Formed new Welsh language groups—Côr Dewi Sant Atlanta (the Atlanta Welsh Choir) and a Welsh folk dance group.

February   Celtic languages conference. The first inter-Celtic meeting in Atlanta. Membership of the St. David's Welsh Society of Georgia tops 100.

The Society's membership includes about a dozen people from Wales and one family from Patagonia. The majority of members, however, are second and third generation Americans. The primary motivation of those who join is to learn more about the country their parents came from. Typical in their intentions and commitment, members of the Welsh Society in Atlanta have attempted to start a Welsh choir, folk singing and folk dancing. The Society's most successful venture has been its language class. By 1985 Mark Craddock and Janet Francis were teaching two weekly classes and the Society had approved a matching grant for Al Williams to attend the Pella, Iowa Cwrs Cymraeg in August 1985. Apart from Welsh language classes, visiting speakers have presented Society members with other views of their Welsh heritage.

The St. David's Welsh Society of Georgia is one of over 80 Welsh societies in the United States and Canada. Since 1984, Society members have taken subscriptions to the Welsh American newspapers, they have become customers of the Welsh import shops and they have made their own contributions to groups like Cymdeithas Madog, Nant Gwrtheyrn and the National Welsh American Foundation. A few have even made the trip to study Welsh in Wales. They are among thousands of Canadians and Americans with a genuine interest in the immense amount of work being done on behalf of the Welsh language. Fortunately, both in Wales and North America, there are teachers, writers, musicians, suppliers and skillful organizers making more Welsh resources available every year.

During 1985 and 1986, the work of the Welsh societies in North America continued to develop, with every sign of interest in their programs continuing to improve. Networking efforts were begun to create a state-wide Pennsylvania Welsh Association and new Welsh societies were organized in Sarasota, Florida and Indianola, Iowa. In addition, a student exchange program was established between the University of Wales, Aberystwyth and Colgate

University in New York. The level of interest in the National Cymanfa, Cwrs Cymraeg and Welsh Heritage Week showed no sign of entering a decline. The agenda of the Welsh societies themselves, reported in *Ninnau* and *Y Drych* were maintained, if not, in the majority of cases, improved.

There are many ethnic heritage societies in North America. Some are served by grant-assisted magazines, others have their own bureau of information or central bank account. The Welsh have more than their share of active, independent leaders, volunteers who sit down at night and send for language textbooks, who write to choirs and musicians and arrange their concerts with care and imagination.

The Welsh societies provide a substantial travel, business and friendship resource for the people of Wales. In return, the societies satisfy their members with weekly or monthly programs related to the country of their background. The level of activity, however, and a more contemporary view of Wales, supported by personal visits, letters, articles and information, depends, in the end, on the willingness of organizations in Wales to communicate with their Canadian and American friends.

If the information in this book leads to even more fruitful contact between the people of Wales and of the United States and Canada, it will not have been written in vain.

25

Directory of Welsh Contacts in North America

Cymdeithas Madog—The Welsh Studies Institute

Alun Hughes, 329 Queenston Street, St. Catharines, ON L2P 2X8;
  Telephone: (416) 684-5913

Donna Lloyd-Kolkin, 1352 American Way, Menlo Park, CA 94025;
  Telephone: (Home) (415) 327-1340, (Office) (415) 565-3320

Eugene Owen, 4812 College Avenue, College Park, MD 20740;
  Telephone: (301) 864-1183

William Clark, 79 Village Lane, Rochester, NY 14610;
  Telephone: (716) 442-3013

Mary Mergenthal, 2393 Bourne Avenue, St. Paul, MN 55108;
  Telephone: (612) 644-1650

Hank Williams, 91 Angelview Court 24, Fredericton, NB E3B 4X4;
  Telephone: (506) 457-2539

National Welsh American Foundation (NWAF.)

Wilfred Greenway, 216-03 43rd Avenue, Bayside, NY 11361;
  Telephone: (212) 224-9333

Islyn Thomas, 286 Kings Road, Madison, NJ 07940;
  Telephone: (201) 377-0705

Craig Peters, 434 West Academy Street, Wilkes-Barre, PA 18702;
  Telephone: (717) 823-1078

Jack A. Pritchard, 28 Tenth Street, Wyoming, PA 18644;
  Telephone: (Home) (717) 693-2083, (Office) (717) 696-1525

Welsh Associated Youth

Claire Tallman, P.O. Box 3246 Ventura, CA 93006

Meurwyn Walters, 1 Veranda Circle, S. Hamilton, MA 01982

Jay G. Williams, 300 College Hill Rd., Clinton, NY 13323

Welsh Harp Society of America

David R. Watson, 5509 Holmes, Kansas City, MO 66103

Judith Brougham, 4202 Clark, Kansas City, MO 64111;
  Telephone: (816) 561-6066

Welsh Heritage Week

Anne Habermehl, 3925 North Main, Marion, NY 14505;
  Telephone: (315) 926-5318

Welsh National Gymanfa Ganu Association (WNGGA.)

Gwenfyl E. Jones, 334-1844 West 7th Avenue, Vancouver, BC V6J 1SB;
  Telephone: (609) 733-7672

David E. Thomas, 5908 Hansen Road, Edina, MN 55436;
  Telephone: (612) 920-1454

Nelson Llewellyn, 662 Melwood Drive NE, Warren, OH 44483;
  Telephone: (Home) (216) 372-5885, (Office) (216) 652-1292

Catherine Dodd, 3410 Wooster Road 607, Rocky River, OH 44116;
  Telephone: (216) 356-1764

Paul Stevens, 7191 North Lima Road, Poland, OH 44514;
  Telephone: (Home) (216) 757-2157, (Office) (216) 331-0420

Wales Investment Corporation (WINvest)

Richard Deckman, 1725 Washington Road Suite 206, Pittsburgh, PA 15241;
  Telephone: (Home) (412) 831-2275, (Office) (412) 864-4550

Perry Warr, 520 Northwest Highway, Barrington, IL 60010;
  Telephone: (312) 381-8003

Frank N. Lawson, Enterprise Mall Buildings, 34 Maple Street Summit,
  NJ 07901; Telephone: (201) 277-6888

Charles H. Suttcliffe, Mathews & Clark Communications, 410 Cambridge
  Avenue, Palo Alto, CA 94306; Telephone: (415) 327-3721

J. Gwyn Morgan, Inn of the Provinces, Office Tower Suite 1110, 350 Sparks
  Street, Ottawa, ON K1R 7S8; Telephone: (613) 238-6404

Women's Welsh Clubs of America

Welsh Retirement Home, 22199 Center Ridge Road, Rocky River,
  OH 44116; Telephone: (216) 331-0420

Dorothy Feeley, 61 Overhill Road, Youngstown, OH 44512;
Telephone: (216) 331-0420

Y Drych

Pat Viets, P.O. Box 369, De Pere, WI 54115;
Telephone: (Home) (414) 336-9630, (Office) (414) 437-9442

Yr Enfys

T. Elwyn Griffiths, 15 Erw Wen, Caeathro, Caernarfon, Gwynedd, Wales

Ninnau

Arturo Roberts, 11 Post Terrace, Basking Ridge, NJ 07920;
Telephone: (201) 766-6736

ALABAMA

Birmingham: Robert E. Morgan, 1009 Tower Drive, P.O. Box 50063,
Birmingham, AL 35214

ARIZONA

Sun City: Welsh Society meets every third Friday at Menke Funeral Home,
Sun City Room, 12420 North 103 Avenue, Sun City, AZ 85351;
Telephone: (602) 979-6451

Sun City: Eileen Williams, Sun City Welsh Society, 11104 Wilowa Avenue,
Youngtown, AZ 85363; Telephone: (602) 933-1205

Sun City: Hayden Jones, 9608 Shiprock Drive, Sun City, AZ 85851;
Telephone: (602) 977-5376

Sun City: Gilbert Evans, 1561 North Bowling Green Drive, Sun City,
AZ 85351; Telephone: (602) 974-0166

Sun City: Edie Steving, 12834 West Paintbrush Drive, Sun City, AZ 85375;
Telephone: (602) 584-5967

Phoenix: The Bard, Annwn Temple of Gwynfyd, Caer Annwn, 5102 North
16th Drive, Lot 3, Phoenix, AZ 85015

CALIFORNIA

Calistoga: M.I.S. Publications (has Celtic book list with some Welsh
material), P.O. Box 21, Calistoga, CA 94515

Guerneville: Caswell Harps, 14690 Carrier Lane, Guerneville, CA 95446; Telephone: (707) 869-0997

Los Angeles: British Consulate General, 3701 Wilshire, Suite 312, Los Angeles, CA 90010; Telephone: (213) 385-7381

Los Angeles: Samuel Jones, 444 North Windsor Boulevard, Los Angeles, CA 90004; Telephone: (213) 465-1381

Los Angeles: Los Angeles Welsh Presbyterian Church, 1153 Valencia, Los Angeles, CA 90015; Telephone: (213) 383-2141

Los Angeles: Society of Folk harpers (publishes the Folk Harp Journal), P.O. Box 29521, Los Angeles, CA 90029

Los Angeles: Welsh American Society meets at 12 noon on the 2nd Saturday of each month at the Alamitos Bay Sports Club, 1933 Temple Ave. Signal Hill, CA 90804

Sacramento: Ray Herness, Sacramento Welsh Society, 1821 Devonshire Road, Sacramento, CA 95825; Telephone: (916) 489-7218

Sacramento: Roz Corbin, 4112 Galbraith Drive, North Highlands, CA 95660; Telephone: (916) 331-8111

San Diego: Glyn Long (House of Wales, Welsh Choral Society of San Diego) Berlitz School of Languages, 7801 Mission Center Court, San Diego, CA 92108; Telephone: (Home) (619) 748-2714, (Office) (619) 297-8392

San Diego: Mrs. Virginia Reese, San Diego Cambrian Society, 3362 Tulane Court, San Diego, CA 92122; Telephone: (619) 452-8108

San Francisco: British Consulate General, Equitable Building Suite 900, 120 Montgomery Street, San Francisco, CA 94104; Telephone: (415) 981-3030

San Francisco: Buckabest Books & Bindery (has an extensive Welsh books list), M. Simmons, 247 Fulton Street, Palo Alto, CA 94301; Telephone: (415) 325-2965

San Francisco: Celtic Books and Media, 665 Hyde Street, San Francisco, CA 94104,

San Francisco: Welsh Heritage Fund of Northern California, John Nichols, 1777 Valley View Avenue, Belmont, CA 94002; Telephone: (415) 591-1623

San Francisco: Donna Davies, 3727 Fillmore, San Francisco, CA 94123; Telephone: (415) 931-8613

San Francisco: Ladd Griffiths, 852 Gelson Place, El Cerrito, CA 94530; Telephone: (415) (524) 6738

San Francisco: Rees B. Williams, 25 Oak Springs Drive, San Anselmo, CA 94960; Telephone: (415) 457-1036

Sonoma: The Welsh Touch (import store), John and Averil Anderson, 670 Este Madera Court, Sonoma, CA 95476; Telephone: (707) 983-3939

COLORADO

Denver: John Williams, Colorado Welsh Society, 14390 East Marina Drive, Denver, CO 80014; Telephone: (303) 751-6858

Denver: Anne Evans, Colorado Welsh Society, 3310 Braun Court, Golden, CO 80401; Telephone: (303) 278-8228

Denver: Colorado Welsh Society meets at Corona Presbyterian, East 8th Avenue & Downing, Denver, CO 80210; Telephone: (303) 832-2297

Denver: *Viltis*—The Magazine of Folklore and Folk Dance, P.O. Box 1226, Denver, CO 80201

CONNECTICUT

North Haven: Celtic Photos & Crafts (import store), Earl T. Williams, Jr., 10 Hemingway Road, North Haven, CT 06473; Telephone: (203) 239-1410

North Haven: The St. David's Society of Connecticut meets on the second Friday of every month at St. John's Episcopal Church, 3 Trumbull Place, North Haven, CT 06473; Telephone: (203) 239-0156

DELAWARE

New Castle: The Welsh Society of Delaware holds an annual cymanfa at Immanuel Episcopal Church on the Green, 100 Harmony Street, New Castle, DE 19720; Telephone: (302) 328-2413

Newark: Peter Williams, Delaware Welsh Society, 211 Murray Road, Newark, DE 19711; Telephone: (302) 571-2058

FLORIDA

Daytona Beach: Lorraine Kolkin, Space Coast Welsh Society, 399 Glenwood, Satellite Beach, FL 32937; Telephone: (305) 777-1577

Daytona Beach: Glyndwr Williams, Space Coast Welsh Society, 307 Eutau Court, Indian Harbor Beach, FL 32937; Telephone: (305) 777-2095

St. Petersburg: Adlonni Recordings (vintage Welsh records), Margaret C. Brady, 1116-D Oak Court, Dunedin, FL 33528; Telephone: (813) 733-8826

St. Petersburg: Nellie Miller, St. David's Society of St. Petersburg, 10207 Third Street East, Treasure Island, FL 33706; Telephone: (813) 360-8528

St. Petersburg: Doris Pottenger, St. David's Society of St. Petersburg, 230 Regina Drive, North Largo, FL 33540; Telephone: (813) 581-4889

St. Petersburg: The St. David's Society of St. Petersburg meets at Woodlawn Presbyterian Church, 2612 Twelfth Street North, St. Petersburg, FL 33540; Telephone: (813) 822-4477

GEORGIA

Atlanta: British Consulate General, 225 Peachtree Street NE, Suite 912, Atlanta, GA 30303; Telephone: (404) 524-5856

Atlanta: The St. David's Society of Georgia meets every second Sunday at Brookhaven United Methodist Church, 1366 North Druid Hills Road NE, Atlanta, GA 30319; Telephone: (404) 237-7506

Atlanta: Sally Evans Funderburk, 2922 La Vista Way, Decatur, GA 30033; Telephone: (404) 636-9022

Atlanta: Dr. Philip Morgan, 4833 Blyth Court, Dunwoody, GA 30338; Telephone: (404) 396-6573

Atlanta: Olwen Xander, 3512 Southgate Drive, Lilburn, GA 30247; Telephone: (404) 921-7743

ILLINOIS

Chicago: British Consulate General, 33 North Dearborn Street, Chicago, IL 60602; Telephone: (312) 346-1810

Chicago: Hebron Welsh Westminster Presbyterian Church, 800 South Beau Drive, Des Plaines, IL 60016; Telephone: (312) 437-1743

Chicago: Rae Jones, 530 Fair Oaks, Oak Park, IL 60302; Telephone: (312) 848-6513

IOWA

Des Moines: Iowa Welsh Society, Ruth Hall, 408 East Salem, Indianola, IA 50125; Telephone: (515) 961-3201

Iowa City: Iowa City Welsh Congregational Church holds a cymanfa ganu on the first Sunday in July, Stella Thomas, 1529 East College, Iowa City, IA 52240; Telephone: (319) 338-2390

Monticello: Crispin Jones Ltd. (Welsh imports), P.O. Box 83, Monticello, IA; Telephone: (319) 465-5862

Pella: Central College (has a student exchange program with Trinity College, Carmarthen), Office of International Studies, Pella, IA 50219; Telephone: (515) 628-5284, (515) 628-5287

KANSAS

Emporia: Evan W. Roberts, 826 Homewood, Emporia, KS 66801;
Telephone: (316) (342) 4614

Emporia: Margaret Jones, Lyon County Welsh Society, 926 Luther,
Emporia, KS 66801; Telephone: (316) 342-3182

MAINE

Belfast: Belfast Choral Eisteddfod, Belfast High School, Waldo Avenue,
Belfast, ME 04915; Telephone: (207) 338-1790

Portland: Celtic Designs Ltd. (Celtic imports), Anita C. O'Donnell,
17 Wharf Street, Old Port Exchange, Portland, ME 04101;
Telephone: (207) 733-8872

MARYLAND

Annapolis: The Welsh Dragon (Welsh imports), Mark Slater, 211 Main
Street, Annapolis, MD 21401; Telephone: (301) 267-8491

Baltimore: Jane Fox, WWC of Baltimore, 506 Allegheny Avenue, Baltimore,
MD 21204; Telephone: (301) 825-6796

Baltimore: Barbara Morgan, WWC of Baltimore, 4505 Fernhill Avenue,
Baltimore, MD 21215; Telephone: (301) 664-0976

Baltimore: Thelma Evans, WWC of Baltimore, 3843 Monterey Road,
Baltimore, MD 21218; Telephone: (301) 467-6454

Baltimore: Anne Cowie, 12 West Mount Vernon Place, Baltimore,
MD 21201; Telephone: (301) 576-1176

Reverend Richard Price Baskwill: see Delta, PA on page 246

MASSACHUSETTS

Boston: The Boston Cymrodorion meets every third Friday at Workshop
Women's Club, 72 Columbus Avenue, Newton Highlands, MA 02161

Boston: Mair Lustig, Boston Cymrodorion, 28 Trimount Street, Dedham,
MA 02026; Telephone: (617) 326-8660.

Boston: John Parry, Boston Cymrodorion, 11 Scotland Road, Lexington,
MA 02173; Telephone: (617) 862-3587

Boston: Alun Jones, Boston Cymrodorion, 50 Manemet Road, Newton,
MA 02159; Telephone: (614) 964-4598

Boston: British Consulate General, Prudential Tower Suite 4740, Prudential
Center, Boston, MA 02199; Telephone: (617) 437-7160

Boston: Roundup Records (carries contemporary folk and Celtic material),
P.O. Box 147, East Cambridge, MA 02141

Pepperell: Rampant Lion (Celtic imports), c/o Scotch Pine Farms, Pepperell, MA 01463

MICHIGAN

Detroit: Bobby Jones Open Committee, c/o Robert A. Jones, Computer Dynamics Inc., 29792 Telegraph Road, Southfield, MI 48032; Telephone: (313) 357-4200

Detroit: The Welsh Society of Detroit meets and holds an annual cymanfa ganu at Redford Presbyterian Church, 22122 West McNichols Street, Detroit, MI 48219; Telephone: (313) 531-0347

Detroit: Florence Rutherford, 14266 Winston Road, Detroit, MI 48239; Telephone: (313) 534-7622

Detroit: The World of Wales (Welsh imports), 5455 Forest Way, Bloomfield Hills, MI 48013; Telephone: (313) 855-9408

Grand Rapids: The Celtic Corner (Celtic imports specializing in Cornish material), 361 Ann Street NE, Grand Rapids, MI 49505; Telephone: (616) 361-1156

MINNESOTA

Lake Crystal: Edythe Peterson, 221 North Main, Lake Crystal, MN 56055; Telephone: (507) 726-2977

Lake Crystal: Margaret and Irwin Williams, Welsh Historic Farm Site, Route 2, Lake Crystal, MN 56055; Telephone: (507) 947-3369

Minneapolis: Voices of the Red Dragon Welsh Choir rehearses at Bread of Life Lutheran Church, 2901 38th Avenue South, Minneapolis, MN 55406; Telephone: (612) 721-4292

Minneapolis: Cymanfaoedd canu and Christmas teas are held at Park Avenue United Methodist Church, 3400 Park Avenue, Minneapolis, MN 55407; Telephone: (612) 825-6836

Minneapolis: The St. David's Society of Minnesota holds spring and fall cymanfaoedd canu at Plymouth Congregational Church, 1900 Nicollet Avenue, Minneapolis, MN 55403; Telephone: (612) 871-7400

Minneapolis: A cymanfa is held on the Sunday closest to March 1st at St. David's Episcopal Church, 13000 St. David's Road, Minnetonka, MN 55343; Telephone: (612) 935-3336

Minneapolis: Mae Anderson, 1918 Johnson Street NE, Minneapolis: MN 55418; Telephone: (612) 789-8923

Minneapolis: Dorothy Jones, Minnesota St. David's Society and Editor of Society Newsletter, 5301 Harriet Avenue, Minneapolis, MN 55419; Telephone: (612) 824-1784

Mankato: Marion T. Carr, Tours of Wales, 108 Clover Lane, Mankato, MN 56001; Telephone: (507) 338-4580

St. Peter: Professor Ellis Jones, Gustavus Adolphus College, St. Peter, MN 56082; Telephone: (507) 931-4184

MISSISSIPPI

Hernando: American Daffodil Society, *Daffodil Journal*, Leslie Anderson, Route 3, 2302 Byhalia Road, Hernando, MS 38632

MISSOURI

Kansas City: The St. David's Society of Kansas City meets at Second Presbyterian Church, 55th & Oak, Kansas City, MO 64112; Telephone: (816) 363-1300

Kansas City: Kansas City St. David's Society, David Isaac, 631 West 59th Terrace, Kansas City, MO 64113; Telephone: (816) 361-1913

St. Louis: Dressel's Pub (has many visitors from Trinity College, Carmarthen), 419 North Euclid, St. Louis, MO 63108; Telephone: (314) 361-1060

St. Louis: Mrs. Max Arnold, 3563 Lost Meadow, St. Louis, MO 63129; Telephone: (314) 487-3565

St. Louis: Mrs. Stanley Jones, 27 Anawood Drive, Arnold, MO 63010; Telephone: (314) 296-3747

NEBRASKA

Lincoln: Mrs. Leonard Egan, Welsh Society of Nebraska, 2101 Bradfield Drive, Lincoln, 68502; Telephone: (402) 435-0342

Lincoln: Marjorie Roderick, Welsh Society of Nebraska, 2411 South 35th Street, Lincoln, 68506; Telephone: (402) 489-8751

NEW HAMPSHIRE

Keene: Rev. Arvel Steece, 156 George Street, Keene, NH 03431; Telephone: 603-352-2657

Keene: A cymanfa ganu is held every October at St. James Episcopal Church, 44 West Street, Keene, NH 03431; Telephone: (603) 352-1019

Nashua: Institute of Celtic Studies East, c/o Arthur Ketchen, 4 Greenlay Street, Nashua, NH 03063; Telephone: (603) 880-3706

NEW JERSEY

Atlantic Highlands: Humanities Press, (University of Wales Press representative in America and source of other Celtic books), 171 First Avenue, Atlantic Highlands, NJ 07716, (201) 872-1441

Jersey City: British and Commonwealth Institute, c/o Charles Sweeting, 129 Magnolia Avenue 205, Jersey City, NJ 07306

North Plainfield: Olwen Hollock, 1 Linda Lane, North Plainfield, NJ 07060; Telephone: 201-757-6182

Scotch Plains: The Welsh Society of Central New Jersey holds a cymanfa ganu every November at Willow Grove Presbyterian Church, 1961 Raritan Road, Scotch Plains, NJ 07076; Telephone: (201) 232-5678

Scotch Plains: Elizabeth Ijams, 240 Marian Avenue, Fanwood, NJ 07023; Telephone: (201) 889-1648

Scotch Plains: Dr. Phillip Davies, Welsh Society of Central New Jersey, 24 Essex Road, Scotch Plains, NJ 07076; Telephone: (201) 889-4942

NEW MEXICO

Albuquerque: Edwin Lewis, New Mexico Welsh Society, 301 Solano NE, Albuquerque, NM 87108; Telephone: (505) 265-0021

Albuquerque: Rhianwen Gerard, 513 Barlane NW, Albuquerque, NM 87107; Telephone: (505) 344-6539

Albuquerque: Ceridwen Roberts, 1625 Fornax Road SE, Rio Rancho, Albuquerque, NM 87108; Telephone: (505) 265-0021

NEW YORK

Albany: Evan Pritchard, 715 Lake Avenue South, Albany, NY 12208; Telephone: (518) 465-6569

Binghamton: An annual March 1st cymanfa ganu is held at Boulevard United Methodist Church, 113 Grand Boulevard, Binghamton, NY 13905; Telephone: (607) 797-5675

Binghamton: R. Bruce McGregor, 14 Hillside Dr., Binghamton, NY 13905

Binghamton: Medieval & Renaissance Texts & Studies (published R. M. Loomis'—*Dafydd ap Gwilym: The Poems*), State University of New York at Binghamton, Binghamton, NY 13901

Binghamton: Joan Phelps, Nantglyn, RD 1, Box 516, Greene, NY 13778; Telephone: (607) 656-4402

Binghamton: Diane Dunham, 1030 Taft Avenue, Endicott, NY 13760; Telephone: (607) 754-5302

Buffalo: Buffalo St. David's Society meets at The International Institute, 864 Delaware Avenue, Buffalo, NY 14209; Telephone: (716) 883-1900

Buffalo: Buffalo St. David's Society holds an annual March 1st service at St. Paul's Episcopal Cathedral, 128 Pearl, Buffalo, NY 14202; Telephone: (716) 853-6668

Buffalo: Jim and Terri Winston, 1337 Greenbriar Lane, North Tonawanda, NY 14120; Telephone: (716) 693-7786

Huntingdon: Ty Gwyn Imports, P.O. Box 403, Huntingdon, NY 11743; Telephone: (516) 271-6570

New York: British Consulate General, 845 Third Avenue, New York, NY 10022; Telephone: (212) 752-8400

New York: British Information Services (Welsh tourist information), 845 Third Avenue, New York, NY 10022; Telephone: (212) 752-8400

New York: Rivendell Bookshop (Celtic material), 45 East Seventh Street, New York, NY 10003; Telephone: (212) 533-2501

New York: A cymanfa ganu is held every April at Rutgers Presbyterian Church, 236 West 73rd Street, New York, NY 10023; Telephone: (212) 877-8227

New York: St. David's Society of the State of New York (permanent office), 71 West 23rd Street, New York, NY 10010; Telephone: (212) 924-8415

New York: Welsh Congregational Church, Rutgers Presbyterian Church, 236 West 73rd Street, NY 10023; Telephone: (212) 877-8227

New York: Women's Welsh Club of New York, 23-29 28th Street, Astoria, NY 11105

Remson: Burton & Margaret Jones, Box 16 Jones Road RD1, Remson, NY 13438; Telephone: (315) 831-5913

Remson: First Baptist Church, Remson, NY 13438

Remson: A cymanfu ganu is held the last week in September in Remson Main Street, Capel Cerrig, Remson, NY 13438

Richville: Helen Reed, Box J, Richville, NY 13681

Schenectady: Mair Jarvis, 957 State Street, Schenectady, NY 12307; Telephone: (518) 346-1874

Syracuse: Council Films (has a movie on the results of the Welsh Revival), 716 James Street, Syracuse, NY 13203; Telephone: (315) 422-0363

Utica: Some Utica Welsh events are held at First Presbyterian Church, 105 Genessee Street, New Hartford, NY 13413; Telephone: (315) 732-5111

Utica: The St. David's Society of Utica holds its Welsh Heritage Days Festival every September at Moriah Presbyterian Church, 1116 Park Avenue, Utica, NY 13501; Telephone: (315) 704-8604

Utica: Irene Jones, Utica St. David's Society, 203 Oxford Road, New Hartford, NY 13413; Telephone: (315) 737-5853

Utica: Mr. & Mrs. Robert A. Jones, 63 Root Street, New Hartford, NY 13413; Telephone: (315) 733-8493

Utica: Norman E. Williams, 2804 Brighton Place, Utica, NY 13501; Telephone: (315) 735-5037

NORTH CAROLINA

Buies Creek: An annual student exchange with the South Wales Baptist College is organized by Campbell University, Buies Creek, NC 27506; Telephone: (919) 893-4111

Southport: Old Curiosity Shop (Welsh antiques), Eleanor P. Smith, 113 North Howe Street, Southport, NC 28461; Telephone: (919) 457-6118

OHIO

Cincinnati: John F. Griffith, Welsh Society of Cincinnati, 3060 Observatory Avenue, Cincinnati, OH 45208; Telephone: (513) 321-1034

Cincinnati: Mary Lewis, Welsh Society of Cincinnati, 2747 Cypress Way, Cincinnati, OH 45212; Telephone: (513) 531-7654

Cincinnati: William Hinds, Welsh Society of Cincinnati, 117 Strathmore, Fort Thomas, KY 40175; Telephone: (606) 261-8482

Cleveland: The Welsh Home, 22199 Center Ridge Road, Rocky River, OH 44116; Telephone: (216) 331-0420

Cleveland: Women's Welsh Clubs of America, c/o The Welsh Home, 22199 Center Ridge Road, Rocky River, OH 44116; Telephone: (216) 331-0420

Cleveland: British Consulate General, 1650 Illuminating Building, 55 Public Square, Cleveland, OH 44113; Telephone: (216) 621-7674

Columbus: A cymanfa ganu is held every October at Brookwood Presbyterian Church, 2685 East Livingston Avenue, Columbus, OH 43209; Telephone: (614) 235-3451

Columbus: Merryum Crafts (Welsh imports), Marian Davis, 1542 Elmwood Avenue, P.O. Box 12023, Columbus, OH 43212

Columbus: David E. Morgan, (Tours to Wales), 1963 Wickford Road, Columbus, OH 43221; Telephone: (614)(221) 3318

Columbus: Welsh Society of Central Ohio, P.O. Box 12023, Columbus, OH 43212; Telephone: (614) 486-2627

Gomer: Martha Evans, Box 27, Gomer, OH 45808

Gomer: Alpha Advertising (Welsh imports), Wanda Hoffman, Box 26, 7370 Gomer Road, Gomer, OH 45809; Telephone: (419) 642-3521

Gomer: The Welsh group in Gomer can be contacted through Allen County Museum, 620 West Market Street, Lima, OH 45801; Telephone: (419) 222-9426

Granville: Palmer Jones, 17 Spring Hill Road, Granville, OH 43023; Telephone: (614) 587-1322

Granville: Jane L. Jones, Welsh Society in Granville, 3086 London Street, Granville, OH 43023; Telephone: (614) 587-2926

Jackson: Jackson Schools Eisteddfod, Jackson High School, Jackson, OH 45640; Telephone: (614) 286-2202

Niles: Gordon Brooks, 1381 Salt Springs Youngstown Road, Niles, OH 44446; Telephone: (216) 544-6441

Oak Hill: Welsh Heritage Museum, East Main Street, Oak Hill, OH 45656

Oak Hill: Mildred Bangert, 415 East Main Street, Oak Hill, OH 45656; Telephone: (614) 682-7057

Springfield: Arthur Machen Society, Wittenberg University, Springfield, OH 45501

Springfield: The Hymn Society of America National Headquarters, Wittenberg University, North Wittenberg Avenue, Springfield, OH 45501; Telephone: (513) 327-7511

Warren: Nelson Llewellyn, WNGGA, 622 Melwood Avenue NE, Warren, OH 44483; Telephone: (216) 372-5885, (216) 652-1292

Youngstown: Dorothy Feeley, 61 Overhill Road, Youngstown, OH 44512; Telephone: (216) 331-0420

Youngstown: Morris Wrench, 2023 Kirk Road, Youngstown, OH 44511; Telephone: (216) 799-4182

OKLAHOMA

Tulsa: The Owain Glendower Society, c/o Stafford G. Davis, 2144 Elmwood, Tulsa, OK 74106; Telephone: (918) 584-0794

Tulsa: D. L. Edwards, 3844 South Atlanta, Tulsa, OK 74105; Telephone: (918) 743-1805

OREGON

Aloha: Doreen Purdy, 4020 SW 196th St., Aloha, OR 97007; Telephone: (503) 649-5405

Beavercreek: An annual cymanfa ganu is held every June at Bryn Seion Welsh Church, Beavercreek, OR 97004

Portland: Emmaline Davies, 2902 Southeast 92nd Street, Portland, OR 97226; Telephone: (503) 771-6442

Portland: Betty Pierce, 19591 South Henrici Road, Oregon City, OR 97226; Telephone: (503) 631-2418

Portland: The Cambrian Society meets every first Saturday every month at Waverly Heights Congregational Church, 3300 Southeast Woodward Street, Portland, OR 97202; Telephone: (503) 238-1337

PENNSYLVANIA

Allentown: The Welsh American Society of Lehigh County meets at St. Michael's Evangelical Lutheran Church, Ninth & Turner Streets, Allentown, PA 18102; Telephone: (215) 432-4051

Delta: Rehoboth Capel Cymraeg, Main Street, Delta, PA 17314

Delta: Glenn Grove, Box 258, 305 Main Street, Delta, PA 17314; Telephone: (717) 456-7379

Delta: Bill and Pat St. Clair, Main Street, Delta, PA 17314; Telephone: (717) 456-7394

Delta: Reverend Richard Price Baskwill, 809 Kellog Road, Lutherville, MD 21093; Telephone: (301) 823-1814

Edwardsville: The Cynonfardd Eisteddfod is held every April at Dr. Edwards Memorial Congregational Church, Main & Church, Edwardsville, PA 18704; Telephone: (717) 287-4581

Edwardsville: Mrs. Jan Whittaker, Annual Cynonfardd Eisteddfod, 23 Church Street, Edwardsville, PA 18704; Telephone: (717) 288-2085

Edwardsville: First Welsh Baptist Church, 25 Green Street, Edwardsville, PA 18704; Telephone: (717) 287-4652

Hazleton: Welsh Congregational Church, Hazle Village, Hazleton, PA 18201; Telephone: (717) 454-9065

Johnstown: An annual cymanfa ganu is held the first Sunday in May at Memorial Baptist Church, 201 Vine Street, Johnstown, PA 15901; Telephone: (814) 535-1859

Lahaska: The Celtic Pavilion (Welsh and Breton imports), Ruth & John Brown, 5812 Route 202, Lahaska, PA 18931; Telephone: (215) 794-3396

Lansford: A cymanfa ganu is held every September at First Baptist Church, Lansford, PA 18232; Telephone: (717) 645-2212

Lansford: Linda Murphy, 547 Arlington St., Tamaqua, PA 18252

Moscow: Welsh Congregational Church U.C.C. of Springbrook, R. D. Galeville Road, Moscow, PA 18444; Telephone: (717) 872-9058

Nanticoke: Nebo Welsh Baptist Church, 17 Prospect Street, Nanticoke, PA 18634

Olyphant: Welsh Baptist Church of Olyphant, 148 Rebecca Avenue, Olyphant, PA 18447

Pen Argyl: Holliehobbers (Welsh imports), Gary Williams, Department N16, 223 ½ South Robinson Avenue, Pen Argyl, PA 18072; Telephone: (Home) (215) 863-7641, (Office) (215) 863-5824

Philadelphia: The Welsh Guild, Arch Street Presbyterian Church, 1724 Arch Street, Philadelphia, PA 19103; Telephone: (215) LO3-3763

Philadelphia: Cambrian Society of Delaware Valley holds its March 1st banquet at Addisville Reformed Church Hall, 945 Second St. Pike, Richboro, PA 18954; Telephone: (215) 357-4277

Philadelphia: Devon Welsh Baptist Church, 945 North Valley Forge Road, Devon, PA 19333

Philadelphia: Women's Welsh Club of Philadelphia meets at St. Stephen's Episcopal Church, 19 South Tenth, Philadelphia, PA 19147; Telephone: (215) 922-3807

Pittsburgh: Pittsburgh St. David's Society holds an annual cymanfa on the second Sunday in October at Shadyside Presbyterian Church, 5121 Westminster Place, Pittsburgh, PA 15232; Telephone: (412) 682-4300

Pittsburgh: Dave Renshaw, Pittsburgh St. David's Society, 1329 Rockland, Pittsburgh, PA 15216; Telephone: (412) 561-5521

Pittsburgh: J. C. Williams, Pittsburgh St. David's Society, 5006 William Flynn Highway, Gibsonia, PA 15044; Telephone: (412) 443-6470

Pittsburgh: Jane Snyder, Pittsburgh St. David's Society, 2010 Lacross Street, Pittsburgh, PA 15218

Plymouth: Welsh Presbyterian Church, 121 Gaylord Avenue, Plymouth, PA 18651

Plymouth: First Welsh Baptist Church, West Shawne Avenue & Girard Avenue, Plymouth, PA 18651; Telephone: (717) 779-9102

Pottsville: Karen Saylor, Pottsville Welsh Society, 504 Union Street, Schuylkill Haven, PA 17962; Telephone: (717) 385-0132

Pottsville: Welsh Baptist Church, Ashland, 601 Edwards Avenue, Pottsville, PA 17901

Reading: William Griffiths, RD 1, Wernersville, PA 19565;
Telephone: (717) 693-3489

Reading: Faith King, 612 F. Lake Drive, Douglasville, PA 19518;
Telephone: (717) 929-3772

Reading: A cymanfa ganu is held every September and the Welsh Society of Berks County meets at Trinity Lutheran Church, 527 Washington, Reading, PA 19601; Telephone: (215) 374-4861

Scranton: The St. David's Male Chorus of Scranton rehearses at Hyde Park Presbyterian Church, South Hyde Park Avenue & Washburn, Scranton, PA 18504; Telephone: (717) 343-5329

Scranton: An annual cymanfa ganu is held every March at Jackson Street Baptist Church, 1206 Jackson, Scranton, PA 18504;
Telephone: (717) 347-3151

Scranton: Lackawanna County St. David's Society meets at First Welsh Baptist Church, 213 South Main Avenue, Scranton, PA 18504;
Telephone: (717) 347-3151

Scranton: Scranton Anthracite Museum Complex HQ, R.D. 1, Bald Mountain Road, Scranton, PA 18504; Telephone: (717) 963-4804

Shamokin: An annual St. David's Day cymanfa ganu is held at Mount Zion Welsh Congregational Church, Grant & Church Streets, Shamokin, PA 17872; Telephone: (717) 648-4111

Shenandoah: Welsh Baptist Church, 27 South West Street, Shenandoah, PA 17976

Slatington: Cymanfa Ganu of Slatington, Box 124, Slatington, PA 18080

Slatington: An annual November cymanfa ganu is held at United Presbyterian Church, R.D. 3, Route 873, Slatington, PA 18080;
Telephone: (215) 767-8113

Warrior Run: Welsh Presbyterian Church, Chestnut Street, Warrior Run, PA 18706

West Pittston: Cambrian Club of West Pittston, c/o Mrs. D. Carpenter, 131 Elm Street, West Pittston, PA 18634; Telephone: (717) 654-7070

Wilkes-Barre: The Celtic World (Welsh imports), John Sheehan, R.D. 2, Box 132, Dallas, PA 18612; Telephone: (717) 675-0675

Wilkes-Barre: Craig Peters, NWAF, 434 West Academy Street, Wilkes-Barre, PA 18702; Telephone: (717) 823-1078

Wilkes-Barre: First Welsh Presbyterian Church of Wilkes-Barre, 52 South Meade Street, Wilkes-Barre, PA 18702; Telephone: (717) 829-9409

Wilkes-Barre: Second Welsh Congregational Church, Hazle & Parrish, Wilkes-Barre, PA 18702; Telephone: (717) 829-3790

Wilkes-Barre: Welsh Bethel Baptist Church, Parrish & Loomis, Wilkes-Barre, PA 18702; Telephone: (717) 822-3372

Wilkes-Barre: Parsons Welsh Baptist Church: 187 Austin Avenue, Wilkes-Barre, PA 18705

Wilkes-Barre: Jack A. Pritchard, see *NWAF* on page 233

Wilkes-Barre: Donna Morgan, 428 North Maple Avenue, Kingston, PA 18704; Telephone: (717) 287-7245

Wilkes-Barre: John W. Simmons, 84 Miner, Wilkes-Barre, PA 18702; Telephone: (717) 823-5484

RHODE ISLAND

Barrington: Llys-y-Rhosyn Rose Gardens, 93 Rumstick Road, Barrington, RI 02806; Telephone: (401) 245-6379

SOUTH CAROLINA

Florence: St. David's Society of South Carolina, P.O. Drawer 150, Florence, SC 29503

Florence: Eugene N. Zeigler, St. David's Society of South Carolina, 246 West Evans Street, Florence, SC 29503; Telephone: (803) 662-3281

SOUTH DAKOTA

Ipswich: Parti Ceredigion gave a sell-out performance in this old Welsh community, City Office, 120 Ninth Street, Ipswich, SD 57451; Telephone: (605) 426-6961

TENNESSEE

Knoxville: Ms. Billie R. McNamara, 5012 O'Barr Drive, Knoxville, TN 37914; Telephone: (615) 637-6711

TEXAS

Dallas: Tom Cross, 4209 Walnut 207, Garland, TX 75042; Telephone: (214) 494-0201

Dallas: Nathan Hughes, 403 Shadow Bend, Richardson, TX 75081; Telephone: (214) 235-3208

Dallas: John A. Williams, 5836 Preston Haven Drive, Dallas, TX 75230; Telephone: (214) 368-6816

Houston: British Consulate General, 601 Jefferson, Suite 2250, Houston, TX 77002; Telephone: (713) 659-6276

UTAH

Midvale: Welsh Heritage Research Foundation (Genealogy), 461 Ivy Drive, Midvale, UT 84047; Telephone: (801) 561-8307

Provo: An annual Welsh American Eisteddfod is held on the weekend nearest March 1st at College of Humanities, Brigham Young University, Provo, UT 84602; Telephone: (801) 378-2775

Salt Lake City: Ann Davies Thomas, 1474 Beacon Drive, Salt Lake City, UT 84108; Telephone: (801) 582-9700

VERMONT

Poultney: Welsh Presbyterian Church, Poultney, VT 05764

Poultney: The Welsh Room, Green Mountain College Library, Green Mountain College, Poultney, VT 05764; Telephone: (802) 287-9313 Margot McKinney Bouchard; Telephone: (802) 287-9051

South Dorset: Anglophile Antiques (some Welsh items), Dorothy Jones, Old Schoolhouse, South Dorset, VT 05263; Telephone: (802) 362-1621

VIRGINIA

Williamsburg: American Friends of St. David's Cathedral, P.O. Box 786, Williamsburg, VA 23185

Williamsburg: Goronwy Owen Room, Swem Library, William and Mary College, Williamsburg, VA 23186; Telephone: (804) 253-4408, (804) 253-4550

Staunton: Rod Owen, 816 Monroe Street, Staunton, VA 24401; Telephone: (703) 885-1840

WASHINGTON

Seattle: Pethau Cymreig/Austral Enterprises, David Morgan, P.O. Box 70190, Seattle, WA 98107; Telephone: (206) 282-3300

Seattle: Puget Sound Welsh Association meets every Friday at North Minster Presbyterian Church, 7706 25th Street NW, Seattle, WA 98117; Telephone: (206) 783-3402, (206) 782-5495

Seattle: Northwest Welsh Choir, Benton Williams, 8253 Southeast Bay Street, Port Orchard, WA 98366; Telephone: (206) 871-2120

Seattle: Jennifer Ducey, 507 North 68th, Seattle, WA 98103; Telephone: (206) 783-7364

Seattle: Joel Ware, 816 North 59th, Seattle, WA 98103; Telephone: (206) 783-9880

Seattle: Lona Yates, Seattle Women's Welsh Club, 2225 Fourth Avenue Apt. 703, Seattle, WA 98121; Telephone: (206) 624-5449

Spokane: Mrs. Robert Valentine, St. David's Society of the Inland Empire, 3503 North Calispel, Spokane, WA 99215; Telephone: (509) 327-9384

Spokane: Haydn Morgan, East 1604 Pinecrest Road, Spokane, WA 99203; Telephone: (509) 624-7746

WASHINGTON D.C.

Bethesda: Hywel Davies, Welsh American Society of Washington, D.C., 6106 Randall Lane, Bethesda, MD 20816; Telephone: (301) 320-5832

Washington D.C.: The Welsh American Society of Washington, D.C. holds its monthly meetings at The British Embassy, 3100 Massachusetts Avenue, NW, Washington D.C. 20008; Telephone: (202) 462-1340

Washington D.C.: Christine Whittaker, Washington Schools Eisteddfod, 1901 Columbia Road, Washington D.C. 20009; Telephone: (Home) (202) 265-6923, (Office) (202) 347-7774

University Park: Jackie Wintle, 6806 Fortieth Avenue, University Park, MD 20782

Potomac: Evan J. Parker, 9520 Accord Drive, Potomac, MD 20854; Telephone: (301) 983-0922

WEST VIRGINIA

Bruceton Mills: Unicorn Limited Inc. (Welsh and Celtic Books), P.O. Box 397, Bruceton Mills, WV 26925

Huntington: The Welsh Society of West Virginia meets at Johnson Memorial Methodist Church, 513 Tenth Street, Huntington, WV 25701; Telephone: (304) 525-8116

Huntington: Darlene Parry, 127 Kings Highway, Huntington, WV 25705; Telephone: (304) 525-5075

Huntington: W. Vincent Lewis, Welsh Society of West Virginia, 1916 Twelfth Avenue, Huntington, WV 25701; Telephone: (304) 522-1533

Ravenswood: Dr. David L. Mandry, 606 Professional Circle, Ravenswood, WV 26164; Telephone: (304) 273-2641

WISCONSIN

Cambria: An annual cymanfa ganu is held at First Presbyterian Church, 121 West Florence, Cambria, WI 53923; Telephone: (414) 348-5859

Cambria: Catherine Mays, 215 West Commerce Street, Cambria, WI 53923; Telephone: (414) 348-5640

Fond Du Lac: A Christmas cymanfa ganu is held at Salem United Methodist Church, 120 Cheboygan, Fond Du Lac, WI 54935; Telephone: (414) 921-6805

Madison: Thomas Buckhauser, Cambrian Heritage Society, 5724 Monticello Way, Madison, WI 53719; Telephone: (608) 273-0209

Madison: Roy Schubert, Cambrian Heritage Society, 5002 Sheboygan Avenue, Madison, WI 53705; Telephone: (608) 727-3355

Madison: Mr. Wynn Davies, 537 Caromar Drive, Madison, WI 53711; Telephone: (608) 238-1817

Milwaukee: Dr. Lincoln Hartford teaches Welsh at Kenwood United Methodist Church, 2319 East Kenwood Boulevard, Milwaukee, WI 53211; Telephone: (414) 332-5935

Milwaukee: Arline Barsamian, 501 Drexel Boulevard South, Milwaukee, WI 53172; Telephone: (414) 762-3624

Milwaukee: Ruth Williams, 4900 North Hollywood, Milwaukee, WI 53217; Telephone: (414) 964-3092

Milwaukee: Wales Wool Shop (imported Welsh clothing), 2634 North Downer Avenue, Milwaukee, WI 53211; Telephone: (414) 332-9665

Oshkosh: Lucille M. Bean, 1005 Devonshire Drive, Oshkosh, WI 54901; Telephone: (414) 233-0253

Oshkosh: Dorothy Kutz, 1820 Alaska Street, Oshkosh, WI 54901; Telephone: (414) 231-9828

Racine: T. Glynn Roberts, Racine Welsh Society, 1225 Monroe Avenue, Racine, WI 53405; Telephone: (414) 633-8584

Ripon: Olwen Welk, Welsh Gymanfa Ganu Association of Wisconsin, 321 East Sullivan St., Ripon, WI 54971; Telephone: (414) 748-6237

Wales: Morris Stealey, Drws Coch, Box 92, Wales, WI 53183;
Telephone: (414) 968-3356

Canada

ALBERTA

Calgary: Ken Mason, Calgary Welsh Society, P.O. Box 158 Station M,
Calgary, AB T2P 2H6; Telephone: (403) 281-4847

Calgary: Roland Thomas, 240 Templeton Circle NE, Calgary, AB T1Y 5T6

Edmonton: British Consulate General, 1404-10025 Jasper Avenue,
Edmonton, AB T5J 1S6; Telephone: (403) 428-0375

Edmonton: Hugh Dawe, St. David's Male Choir of Edmonton, 8726 116
Street, Edmonton, AB T6G 1P7; Telephone: (403) 467-5754

Edmonton: Gerry Stone, St. David's Welsh Society of Edmonton,
331 Southridge, Edmonton, AB T6H 4M9; Telephone: (403) 434-8050

Edmonton: Susan Mayse, 11126 73rd Avenue, Edmonton, AB T6G 0E4;
Telephone: (403) 436-3284

Lethbridge: Southern Alberta Welsh Society, Ross Hughes, 2-1410-43
South, Lethbridge, AB T1K 3S5; Telephone: (403) 328-0651

Medicine Hat: Mrs. Celia Griffiths, Medicine Hat Welsh Society,
20 Rossland Green SE, Medicine Hat, AB T1B 2BH;
Telephone: (403) 526-9238

Ponoka: Glyn Owen, Ponoka Dewi Sant Society, RR 1, Ponoka,
AB T0C 2H0; Telephone: (403) 783-2423

Ponoka: Hughie Roberts, Box 298, Ponoka, AB T0C 2H0

BRITISH COLUMBIA

Vancouver: British Consulate General, 602 West Hastings, Vancouver,
BC V6B 1P6; Telephone: (604) 683-4421

All Vancouver Welsh groups can be contacted at Cambrian Hall, 215 East
17th Avenue, Vancouver, BC V5V 1A6; Telephone: (604) 876-2815

Vancouver: Vancouver Welsh Society, Alan T. Jones, 5195 Hoy Street,
Vancouver, BC V5R 4N9; Telephone: (604) 437-0304

Victoria: Dr. David Lintern, Victoria Welsh Society, 2778 Penelope Place,
Victoria, BC V9B 3K2;
Telephone: (Home) (604) 478-9607, (Office) (604) 478-1796

NEW BRUNSWICK

New Brunswick: Hank Williams, 91 Angelview Court 24, Fredericton, NB E3B 4X4; Telephone: (506) 457-2539

ONTARIO

Brantford: Graham Morgan, RR6, Brantford, ON N3T 5L8

Brantford: George Jones, RR 6, Brantford, ON N3T 5L8; Telephone: (519) 647-2234

Hamilton: Lyn Harry, Hamilton Academy of Music, 20 King St. East, Suite 301, Hamilton, ON L8N 1A3; Telephone: (416) 529-4051

Kingston: The Celtic House (Celtic imports), 68 Brook Street, Kingston, ON K7L 1R9; Telephone: (613) 542-2533

Kingston: Lyn Jones, 50 Bonnycastle Court, Kingston, ON K7M 2S3;- Telephone: (613) 542-9724

London: London Welsh Society meets at All Saints Church, 289 Hamilton Road, London, ON N5Z 1R4; Telephone: (519) 439-4611

London: Christine Scott, 73 Highview Avenue West, London, ON N6J 1A3

Oshawa: Oshawa & District Welsh Society, P.O. Box 804, Oshawa, ON L1H 7H1

Oshawa: Barbara Parry, Oshawa & District Welsh Society, 56 Hawley Crescent, Whitby, ON L1N 6V9; Telephone: (416) 579-7266

Oshawa: Oshawa & District Welsh Society Newsletter, c/o 652 Buchan Avenue, Oshawa, ON L1J 3A3

Oshawa: David Pugh, Oshawa & District Welsh Society; Telephone: (416) 576-1405

Ottawa: British High Commission, 80 Elgin Street, Ottawa, ON K1P 5K7; Telephone: (613) 237-1530

Ottawa: Tal Griffiths, 52 Amberwood Crescent, Ottawa, ON K2E 7B9; Telephone: (613) 825-4687

Ottawa: Don Mills, 30 Portland Crescent, Kanata, ON K2H 1Z3; Telephone: (613) 592-1374

Ottawa: Roy Morris, Ottawa Welsh Choral Society, 305 Salter Crescent, Kanata, ON K2H 1Z3; Telephone: (613) 592-1222

Niagara Falls, Lewis Edwards, 4802 Drummond Road, Niagara Falls, ON L2E 6CG

Niagara Falls, Mair Monkhouse, 16 Madison Street, Fort Erie, ON L2A 3Z8; Telephone: (416) 871-4075

Peterborough: Gwaenydd Jones, 21 Leanne Avenue, RR 7, Peterborough, ON K9J 6T8

St. Catharines: Siani Flewog (Welsh imports), Jane Hughes, 329 Queenston Street, St. Catharines, ON L2P 2X8; Telephone: (416) 684-5913

Toronto: All Toronto Welsh groups can be contacted at Dewi Sant Church, 33 Melrose Avenue, Toronto ON M5M 1Y6; Telephone: (416) 485 7583

Toronto: British Consulate General, 8th Floor, 200 University Avenue, Toronto, ON M5H 3E3; Telephone: (416) 593-1290

Toronto: Mrs. Lowrie Taylor, 1234 Canborough Crescent, Pickering, ON L1V 3K9

Toronto: Daisy Heaton, 72 Hillside Drive, Toronto, ON M4K 2M6

Toronto: Gerwyn Thomas, Toronto Welsh Rugby Club, 40 Araman Drive, Agincourt, ON M1T 2P6; Telephone: (416) 291-6155

QUEBEC

Montreal: Owen Roberts, 51-47 East Avenue, Lachine, PQ H8T 2P4; Telephone: (514) 637-4977

Montreal: Iwan Edwards, 840 38th Avenue, Lachine, PQ H8T 2C3; Telephone: (514) 634-5962

Montreal: An annual Montreal cymanfa ganu is held every May at St. James the Apostle, St. Catherines & Bishop, Montreal, PQ H4G 1P5

Montreal: British Consulate General, Room 901, 635 Dorchester Boulevard West, Montreal, PQ H3B 1R6; Telephone: (514) 866-5863

SASKATCHEWAN

Atwater: Johnnie Thomas, Box 9, Atwater, SK S0A 0C0

Rouleau: Mrs. Llywela Argue, P.O. Box 162, Rouleau, SK 50G 4H0

Celtic

Breton: (International Committee for the Defense of the Breton Language (ICDBL), c/o Lois Kuter, 143 Plymouth Road, Plymouth Meeting, PA 19462; Telephone: (215) 828-4115

Breton: ICDBL Canada, c/o Yann Plunier, 932 Pierre Viger, Boucherville, PQ J4B 3W2

Celtic Colloquium: c/o Associated Students, University of California, Berkeley, CA 94720; Telephone: (415) 642-0256

Eastern States Celtic Association, c/o John M. Jones, 2011 Ferry Avenue T-9, Camden, NJ 08104

Celtic Studies Association of North America, c/o Catherine McKenna, English Department, Queens College, Flushing, NY 11367; Telephone: (212) 520-7149

Hunter Celtic Festival, Exposition Planners, Bridge Street, Hunter, NY 12442

Keltica, Society of Inter-Celtic Arts and Culture, 96 Marguerite Avenue, Waltham, MA 01254; Telephone: (617) 899-2204

Cornish: Lodeneck Press (Cornish material); 14/16 Market Street, Padstow, Cornwall, Great Britain

Cornish: Newodhow Kernewek Canadegyon, David Short, Box 1946, Gibsons, BC VON 1Vo, Canada

Cornish: Cornish Nationalist Party, Trelispen, Gorran, St. Austell, Cornwall, Great Britain

Gaelic Books Council, Department of Gaelic, University of Glasgow, Glasgow G12 8QQ, Scotland

Ireland: Irish Embassy, 2234 Massachusetts Avenue NW, Washington D.C. 20008; Telephone: (202) 462-3939

Manx: North American Manx Association, c/o Elizabeth Clucas, K605, 1541 East 191 Street, Euclid, OH 44117; Telephone: (216) 486-2246

Manx: Sheerwater Press (Manx books), Welch House, Church Road, Onchan, Isle of Man, Great Britain

Manx: Yn Cheshagt Ghailckach (Manx learning material), Bnr. Audrey Ainsworth, 3 Bayr Glion y Chruitcheree, Dodish, Isle of Man, Great Britain

Miscellaneous

Cardigan Welsh Corgi Club of America, Betty Floyd, 1388 Sheridan Road, Atlanta, GA 30324; Telephone: (404) 634-8260

Pembroke Welsh Corgi Club of America, Deborah Harper, RR 2, Box 218, Black Brook Road, Pound Ridge, NY 10576; Telephone: (914) 234-3447

Rugby: Eastern Rugby Union, Michael Machado, 90 Caryl Avenue, Yonkers, NY 10705; Telephone: (914) 968-4346

Rugby: Mid West Rugby Union, Bradley Sharp, c/o Clayton Brokerage, 1 Riverfront Plaza, Louisville, KY 90202

Rugby: Pacific Rugby Union, John Seggar, 172 East 1964 Street, Oren, UT 84057

Rugby: Western Rugby Union, Vernon Davis, P.O. Box 1100, Pasadena, TX 77501

The Friendship Force, 575 South Omni International, Atlanta, GA 30303; Telephone: (404) 522-9490

Tom Jones National Headquarters, 10100 Santa Monica Boulevard, Suite 205, Los Angeles, CA 90067

Welsh Black Cattle Association, Sue Case, Route 1, Box 76B, Shelburn, IN 47879; Telephone: (812) 383-9233

Welsh Pony Society of America, Valerie Lapicola, 5051 Townline Road, East Troy, WI 53120; Telephone: (414) 642-5051

Welsh Terrier Club of America, Mrs. Bardi McLennan, 66 Lord Highway, Weston, Ct 06883

Wales

Association of Male Voice Choirs, Organising Secretary, D. G. Evans, 28 Crown Street, Port Talbot, West Glamorgan Telephone: (0639) 892045

Barn, Rhydwen Williams, 30 Stryd Llewellyn, Trecynon, Aberdare, Mid Glamorgan; Telephone: (0685) 881034

BBC Wales, Broadcasting House, Llandaf, Cardiff, South Glamorgan, CF5 2YR; Telephone: (0222) 564888

Canolfan Iaith Nant Gwrtheyrn, Llithfaen, Pwllheli, Gwynedd LL53 6PA; Telephone: (075 855) 334

Cymdeithas Yr Iaith Gymraeg, 5 Maes Albert, Aberystwyth, Dyfed; Telephone: (0970) 4501

Honourable Society of the Cymmrodorion, 118 Newgate Street, London, EC1A 7AE

Llangollen International Musical Eisteddfod, Eisteddfod Office, Llangollen, Clwyd, LL20 8NG; Telephone: (0978) 860236

London Welsh Association, 157-163 Grays Inn Road, London WC1; Telephone: 01-837-3722

Mudiad Ysgolion Meithrin, 10 Park Grove, Cardiff, South Glamorgan, CF1 3BN; Telephone: (0222) 36205

National Library of Wales, Penglais, Aberystwyth, Dyfed, SY23 3BU; Telephone: (0970) 3816

Royal National Eisteddfod of Wales, 10 Park Grove, Cardiff, South Glamorgan, CF1 3BN; Telephone: (0222) 398399

Royal Welsh Agricultural Society, Llanelwedd Hall, Builth Wells, Powys, LD2 3SY; Telephone: (0982) 553683

Sain (Recordiau) Cyf., Llandwrog, Caernarfon, Gwynedd, LL54 5TG; Telephone: (0286) 831111

Sianel Pedwar Cymru (S4C), Sophia Close, Cardiff, South Glamorgan, CF1 9XY; Telephone: (0222) 43421

Urdd Gobaith Cymru, Swyddfa'r Urdd, Aberystwyth, Dyfed, SY23 1EN; Telephone: (0970) 3744

Wales Tourist Board, Brunel House, 2 Fitzalan Road, Cardiff, South Glamorgan, CF2 1UY; Telephone: (0222) 464120

Welsh Arts Council, 9, Museum Place, Cardiff, South Glamorgan, CF1 3NX; Telephone: (0222) 394711

Welsh Books Council (Cyngor Llyfrau Cymraeg), Castell Brychan, Aberystwyth, Dyfed, SY23 2JB; Telephone: (0970) 4151

Welsh Development Agency, Treforest Industrial Estate, Pontypridd, Mid Glamorgan CF37 5UT; Telephone: (9385) 2666

Welsh Folk Dance Society, Dolawenydd, Betws, Ammanford, Dyfed, SA18 2HE; Telephone: (0269) 2837

Welsh Joint Education Committee, Fourth Floor, Arlbee House, Greyfriars Road, Cardiff, South Glamorgan, CF1 3AE; Telephone: (0222) 32326

Welsh Music Information Centre, Music Department, University College, P.O. Box 78, Cardiff, South Glamorgan, CF1 1XL; Telephone: (0222) 874000 (Ext. 5126)

Welsh Nation (Plaid Cymru), 51 Cathedral Road, Cardiff, South Glamorgan, CF1 9HD; Telephone: (0222) 31944

Welsh Rugby Union, P.O. Box 22, Cardiff, South Glamorgan, CF1 2PP; Telephone: (0222) 390111

Western Mail, Thompson House, Havelock Street, Cardiff, South Glamorgan, CF1 1WR; Telephone: (0222) 33022

Y Cymro, Gwasg Caxton, Croesoswallt (Oswestry), England, SY11 1RD; Telephone: (0691) 655321

Y Faner, Gwasg y Sir, Bala, Gwynedd, LL23 7PG; Telephone: (0678) 520262

Yr Academi Gymreig (Welsh Academy of Writers), Mount Stuart House, Mount Stuart Square, Cardiff, South Glamorgan, CF1 6DQ; Telephone: (0222) 492025. Welsh Section; Telephone: (0222) 492025

Index

Index

Bollard, John, 223
Book of Tofu, 39
Boone, Daniel, 140
Booth, Rev. Sidney, 83
Boothe, Raymond Lynn, 115
Boothman, Donald, 190,214,218
Borchadt, Barbara, 220
Boston Cymrodorion, 192,193,194,195,197,
198
Boston, MA, 42,47,80,151,194,195,196,198,
199,206
Boston Public Radio, 197
Boston Welsh Male Chorus, 197
Boswell, David, 178
Bouchard, Margot McKinney, 167,189,190,
215,225
Boulder, CO, 23,24
Boulding, Chris, 46
Boulding, Pam, 46
Boulevard United Methodist Church,
Binghamton, NY, 158
Bove, Marie, 162
Bowen, Euros, 36
Bowen, Dr. Geraint (Archdruid), 177,182
Bowen, Michael, Wa.DC, 217,220
Bowen, Viva, 79
Bowers, Craig, 54
Bowers, Dale, 52
Bowers, Kevin, 52,91,204
Bowers, Richard, 143
Bowie, Jim, 21
boxing, 35
Boyce, Max, 174,177
Boyfriend, the, 177
Boys, Llinos Owen, 105
Bradley family, 228
Bradley, J.D., 228
Brady, Margaret C., 19
'brain drain', the, 177
Braithwaite, Elizabeth, 147
Brake, Helen, 9
Brake, Olen, 9
Brampton, ON, 180
Branch, Olive, 228
Brant Men of Song, 172
Brantford Harlequins, 170
Brantford, ON, 169,170,172
Braswell, Allan, 35
Brattleboro, VT, 188,190
Brazell, David, 19
Brazier, Gwyneth, 58
Bread of Life Lutheran Church, Minneapolis,
83
Brecon Cathedral Choir, 107
Brecon, Wales, 107

Brethyn Cartref, 196
Breton, 47,103-104,150,186,187,192,198,246
Bridgend RFC, 170,171
Bridgend Sports Club, 170,171
Bridgend, Wales, 12,166,180,181
Brigham Young University, 68,69
Brigham Young University A Cappella Choir,
108
Brimelow, Lois, 111
Brinkley, Sally, 58
Britannia Associates, NY, 147
Britannia, SS, 87
British Amateur Golf Tournament, 107
British and Commonwealth Institute of NY,
162
British Columbia, 38,56,173,174,188
British Council, 149,169; travel grant, 187
British Embassy, Wa.DC, 217,219,220
British Fair, Denver, 25
British Fair, Philadelphia, 129
British Government the, 103,145
British High Commission, ON, 177
British Isles, 188
British Observer, the, 42
British Open Golf Tournament, 107
British Steel Corporation, 224
Briton Ferry, 118,182
Britt, David, 118
Brittany, (also see Breton), 46,139,192
Broadview, Chicago, 100
Broadway, NYC, 30
Brock University, ON, 90,100,159,166,186
Brockton, MA, 194
Brockville, ON, 165,176
Brooke, Anne, 225
Brookfield, MO, 5
Brooklyn, NY, 160
Brooks, Gordon, 124
Broome Cty., NY, 159
Brougham, Judith, 6,47
Brown, Anne, 59
Brown, Arthur, 132
Brown, Rev. Elwyn D., Wa.DC, 218
Brown, Evelyn, 184
Brown, John, 139
Brown, Margaret, NY, 158
Brown, Peggy, CO, 25
Brown, Ruth, 139
Brown University, RI, 194
Brownfield, Lilian, 116
Brownfield, Thomas, 116
Brunswick County, VA, 225
Brussels, Belgium, 104
Bryce Canyon National Park, UT, 28
Brycheiniog, ON, 165

263

D

E

Eden, 64
Eden United Church of Christ, Chicago, 100
Edina, MN, 83
Edinburgh, Scotland, 19,112
Edmonton, AB, 60
Edmonton St. David's Welsh Male Choir, 60
Educational Trust Fund of Wales, 154
Edwards Plateau, TX, 21
Edwards, Alison, GA, 229
Edwards, D.L., OK, 8
Edwards, Dafydd, Wales, 8,116,117
Edwards, Dorothy, NY, 161
Edwards, Elizabeth, MN, 81,82,105
Edwards, Hywel Teifi, Wales, 228
Edwards, Iwan, PQ, 154,165,186,187
Edwards, John G., WI, 89
Edwards, Jonathan, entertainer, 82
Edwards, Ken, BC, 58
Edwards, Lewis, ON, 123,164,165,166
Edwards, Rt. Hon. Nicholas, 145,166
Edwards, Owen, NY, 153
Edwards, Rev. T.C. (Cynonfardd), 135,136
Edwards, T.D., hymnist, 128
Edwards, Thomas, BC, 56
Edwards, Tom, GA, 229
Edwards, Tommy, PQ, 186,187
Edwards, Trebor, singer, 43
Edwards, Undeg, 187
Edwardsville, PA, 131,134,135-136
Efrog Newydd (see New York)
Egan, Mrs. Leonard, 9
Eglwys y Cymry Efrog Newydd, (see Welsh
  Congregational Church of New York)
Ehrhardt, Marian, 30
Eiguren, Joe, 65,66,67
Eirie County, NY, 147
Eisteddfod (in N. America): Belfast ME 199;
  Buffalo NY 147; Cymdeithas Madog 167;
  Cynonfardd 135,136; Dressel's Pub 4;
  Emporia KS 7; Jackson Schools OH 115;
  National Association of America 124;
  Pittsburgh 135; Richville NY 156; San
  Francisco 32,41,95; Toronto 178,181;
  Trumbull Cty. Association 124; Utah 68,69;
  Utica 152,155; Vancouver 56; Virginia 225;
  Washington Schools 199,205,219,220,222;
  —fund-raiser 217,219,220
eisteddfod, Breton, 103
Eisteddfod, Llangollen International, 9,37,59,
  60,73,107,108,109,184,191
eisteddfod, Urdd, 106,181
Eisteddfod, Welsh National, 2,4,11,16,18,33,
  39,45,46,51,57,59,92,100,103,106,109,110,
  125,148,151,153,154,158,159,160,168,178,
  181,191,214,215,219

El Paso, TX, 10,20,22
El Salvador, 28
Elderhostel, 190,225
Elfed (see Lewis, Howell Elvet,)
Elias, Esther, 103,105,142,144,167,202
Elis, Hefin, 153,173,218
Elk Creek, MO, 12
Elko, NV, 66
Elliot, Scott, 179
Ellis, Dan, 141
Ellis, David, 175
Ellis, David Maldwyn, 153,157
Ellis, Ernest, 141
Ellis, Osian, 17,47,162,213
Elorriaga, Ambrosio, 64
Elwah River, WA, 52
Ely, NV, 66
Emmanuel College Cambridge, 107
Emporia, KS, 7,68
Endicott, NY, 158
Endicott, Ruth, 211
endowment fund, WNGGA, 122
Engler, Scott, 48
English, 143
English Congregational Church, Lansford,
  PA, 137
Enid, OK, 8,117
Episcopalian Cathedral, Albuquerque, NM,
  22
Episcopal Seminary, VA, 226
Eskimo, 126
Eslisk, Wendell, 2
ethnic, 9,19,21,111,126,136,143,232
Ethnic Festivals & Fairs (Welsh
  participation); NY 157; ON 179; PA 142;
  PQ 186; WA 53;
Ethnic Heritage Grant, 189
ethnic mosaic, 182
European Center for Folk Studies, 90
European Village, WI, 89
Evangeline Parish, LA, 13
Evans, Al, NE, 9
Evans, Alun, dart player, 35
Evans, Anne, CO, 25
Evans, Arthur, ON, 166
Evans, Betty, ON, 176
Evans, Cyril, ON, 180
Evans, Rev. D.J.Wynne, Toronto, 181,182
Evans, Rev. David, GA, 229
Evans, Delyth, Wales, 8,116
Evans, Dorothy, ON, 184
Evans, Mrs. Elvet, MD, 214
Evans, Edith, harpist, 38
Evans, Edithe, NY, 155
Evans, Edwin, NY, 152

Index

H

Index

275

I

J

Index

Melrose, LA, 13
Melville, SK, 59
Memorial Baptist Church, Johnstown, PA, 141
Memphis, TN, 10
Menke Funeral Parlor, Sun City, AZ, 30
Menominie, WI, 90
Mentra Gwen WWC, OH, 121
Mercer, Ken, 184
Merched y Ddraig Goch, 58
Merched y Wawr, 39
Merche's Meatmarket, Opelousas, LA, 13,21
Meredith, Nancy, 111
Mergenthal, Mary, 82-83,169
Merionethshire, Wales, 153,189
Merthyr Tydfil, Wales, 35,52,68,69,100,126
Metoyers, Augustine, 13
Metz, Clem, 131
Mexico, 21,27,35,36
Mi Welais Jac-y-do, 225
Miami, FL, 63,66
Michigan, 30,87,104,105,106,107,108
Mid-Glamorgan, 1,12
Mid-Glamorgan County Council, 167
Mid-Wales Development Board, 61
Middlepoint, OH, 135
Midvale, UT, 69
Midwestern Rugby Union, USA, 172
Mikesell, Janet, 52
Miles, Wendy, 161
Miller, David, WI, 94
Miller, Janice, 222
Miller, Karen, NJ, 211
Miller, Nancy, MA, 123,195
Miller, Nellie Wilson, FL, 18
Miller, Sara, PA, 138
Miller, Stan, ON, 179
Miller, William, OH, 116
Milligan, Mary, 157
Million Dollar Highway,CO, 23
Million pounds appeal, (Welsh National Eisteddfod), 153,159
Mills, Don, 164,184,185
Mills, Merriel, 184,185
Milwaukee Folk Choir, 90
Milwaukee International Inst., 89
Milwaukee Journal, 97
Milwaukee Public Museum, 90
Milwaukee, WI, 87,88,89-90,93,96,97,105, 117,131
Mineral Ridge, OH, 136
Minneapolis, MN, 2,49,80,81,82,83,89,108, 117
Minnesota, 11,30,46,49,77,78-85,87,88,117, 119,123,165,166,168,169

Minnesota-Iowa Cymanfa Ganu, 11,79
Minnesota-Iowa Cymanfa Ganu Association 78
Minnesota Valley, MN, 78
Minnesota Welsh Society, 81,82,83,84
Miranda, Michael, 163
Mississippi River, 16,84,123
Missouri, 3-6
Missouri River, 77
Mitchel, Maxine, 7
Mitchel, Cheryl, 220
Mobile, AL, 17
Modern Languages Association 49
Moel Cwm Cerwyn, Wales, 12
Moencopi, AZ, 28
Molleneur, Marjorie, 210
Monkhouse, Mair, 147
Monmouth County, NJ, 210,211
Monmouth Schools, 171
Montana, 76
Montgomery City, PA, 103
Montgomery Kennel Club, PA, 103
Montgomeryshire, (also see Powys), 101
Montreal, PQ, 19,27,87,105,122,154,165, 167,183,185-187,188
Montreal Celtic Congress, 187
Montreal Celtic Society, 187
Montreal St. David's Society, 49,185,186,187
Montreal Welsh Male Choir, 49,186,187
Moore, Richard, 156
Moran, WY,70
Morgan, Barbara, MD, 214
Morgan, Celia, 58
Morgan, Ceri, darts, 35
Morgan, David, NY, 159,161,163
Morgan, David, PA, 131
Morgan, David, (Pethau Cymreig), WA, 52
Morgan, David E., OH, 115,116
Morgan, Donna, PA, 135
Morgan, Dora, OH, 126
Morgan, Edward, PA, 140
Morgan, Elizabeth, actress, 215
Morgan, Elizabeth, PA, 140
Morgan, Gareth, TX, 20
Morgan, George, PQ, 186
Morgan, George, WHW, 150
Morgan, Graham, ON, 172,173
Morgan, Gwilym J., PA, 132
Morgan, Haydn, 53,63
Morgan, Ilah, WI, 88,94
Morgan, John, PA, 129
Morgan, Kay, WI, 88
Morgan, Lee, WI, 88,94,95,202,207
Morgan, Leslie, DBRW, 146
Morgan Log House, PA, 140

283

N

O

X

ACKNOWLEDGEMENTS

No register of this type would be possible without the help of a large number of people. The author would like to thank everyone who contributed to the actual production of the book—in particular the following individuals:

☆

Alun Hughes, Palmer Jones, Margot Bouchard, Mildred Bangert, W. Craig Peters, Anne Habermehl, Nelson Llewellyn, Dorothy Feeley, Donna Morgan, Benton Williams, Douglas Jones (Toronto), Daisy Heaton, Olwen Welk, Hywel M. Davies.

Edythe Peterson, J. C. Williams, George Jones (Brantford), Graham Morgan (Brantford), Earl T. Williams Jnr., Mary Mergenthal, Mair Lustig, Ellis Jones, Donna Davies, Gwynn Parri, Idwal Parri, Anne Cowie, Helen F. Richards, Esther Elias, Joan Phelps, Dan E. Williams, Doris Pottenger, Samuel L. Jones (Los Angeles), Catherine Mays, Betty Pierce, Stanley W. Williams, Llywela Argue, Lyn Harry, Billie R. McNamara, John F. Griffith, Glyn Long, Virginia Reese, Robert A. Jones (Utica), Dorothy Walters, Dave Renshaw, Bill & Pat St. Clair, Glenn Grove, Marjorie Tayloe, W. Vincent Lewis, Glyndwr Williams (FL), Eileen Williams (AZ), Edie Steving, Ceridwen Roberts, Rhianwen Gerard, Peter Williams (DE), Dr. Gwyn Walters, Mark Slater, Judith Brougham, Evan Pritchard (Albany), John C. Williams (Denver), D. L. Edwards (OK), Hywel Thomas (Buffalo), Evan Roberts (KS), Martha Evans, Mae Anderson, Margaret Egan, Jack A. Pritchard, Mr. P. James (Alberta), Stella Maye Thomas, Margaret Jones (Remson), David E. Morgan (Columbus), Mair Jarvis, Ronald Dennis, Susan Mayse, Mrs. Robert Valentine, Daniel Reese, William Griffiths (PA), Winifred Morgan (MD), Thomas R. Barber, Stafford G. Davis, Marian Davis (Columbus), Jennifer Ducey, Joel Ware, Barbara Parry (Oshawa), Rae Jones (IL), Anne Evans (CO), Harold Evans (Utica), Doug Powell (Vancouver), Hughie Roberts (Ponoka), Johnnie Thomas (Saskatchewan), Dr. David Lintern, Fred Jones (Macomb IL), Ellen E. Roberts (Utica), Tony Lewis (Kenfig Hill), Viv Fisher, Dr. Robert E. Morgan.

Also—Lois Kuter (ICDBL), Michael Machado (Eastern States Rugby Union), Roslyn Raney, Joe Eiguren, Bill Means, Wilmington Star News, The Atlanta Constitution, The Standard (St. Catharines), M. D. Evans (Black Mountain Press), Sain (Recordiau) Cyf., The Folk Harp Journal, Office of International Studies, Central College, Pella, Iowa, The Council for the Development of French in Louisiana and, *Americans from Wales* by Edward G. Hartmann.

With a special thank you to—my mother Mrs. Eirlys Greenslade, my wife Suzanne, Liane Jenkins, David Lewis Watkins, Vicki Sanders and Gwin Lawler.

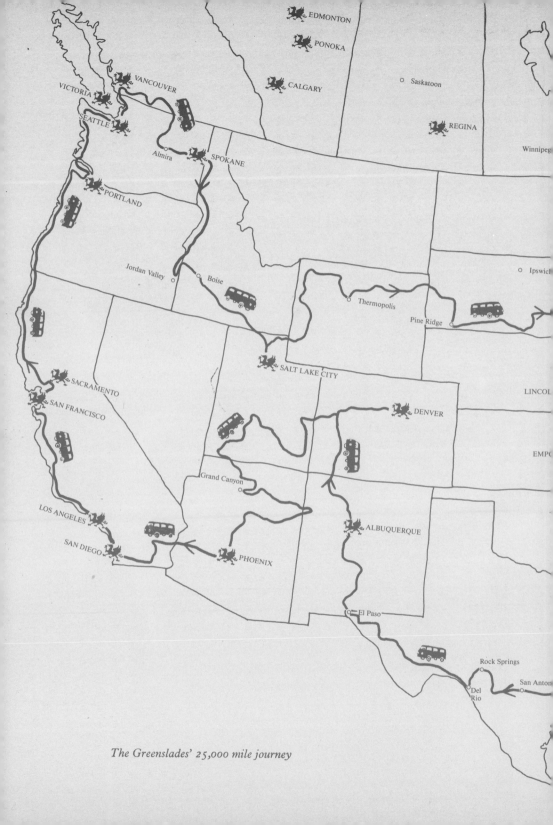

The Greenslades' 25,000 mile journey